Sisters in the Struggle

Sisters in the Struggle

*African American Women in the
Civil Rights–Black Power Movement*

*Bettye Collier-Thomas
and V. P. Franklin*

New York University Press

NEW YORK AND LONDON

NEW YORK UNIVERSITY PRESS
New York and London

Library of Congress Cataloging-in-Publication Data
Sisters in the struggle : African American women in the
civil rights–black power movement / edited by
Bettye Collier-Thomas and V. P. Franklin.
p. cm.
Includes bibliographical references and index.
ISBN 0-8147-1602-4 (acid-free paper) —
ISBN 0-8147-1603-2 (pbk. : acid-free paper)
1. African American women civil rights workers—History—
20th century. 2. African American women civil rights workers—
Biography. 3. African American women political activists—
History—20th century. 4. African American women political
activists—Biography. 5. African Americans—Civil rights—
History—20th century. 6. Black power—United States—
History—20th century. 7. Civil rights movements—United
States—History—20th century. 8. African American leadership—
History—20th century. 9. United States—Race relations.
I. Collier-Thomas, Bettye. II. Franklin, V. P. (Vincent P.), 1947–
E185.61 .S615 2001
323.1'196073'0922—dc21   2001001550

New York University Press books are printed on acid-free paper,
and their binding materials are chosen for strength and durability.

Manufactured in the United States of America
10 9 8 7 6 5 4 3

in memory of

Gwendolyn Brooks
Gladys Collier Oden
Gail Lynetta Franklin

Contents

All illustrations appear as a group following page 148.

Acknowledgments

In 1987, the Ford Foundation awarded Bettye Collier-Thomas, the founder and Executive Director of the Bethune Museum and Archives (BMA), a grant for research and sponsorship of a conference on black women in the Civil Rights Movement. Collier-Thomas was involved in surveying the important role that Mary McLeod Bethune, the National Council of Negro Women, the National Association of Colored Women, the Alpha Kappa Alpha Non-Partisan Council, and other women's organizations had played in the Civil Rights Movement. She was also involved in reviewing the emerging scholarship, which rarely mentioned the women or organizations.

Without the support of Lynn Walker and Sheila Biddle, program directors at the Ford Foundation, the project would not have been launched. In 1989, the project moved to Temple University when Collier-Thomas joined the History Department and became Director of the Center for African American History and Culture (CAAHC). In 1995, V. P. Franklin became co-director of the project to develop a national conference on "African American Women in the Civil Rights–Black Power Movement" which was held at Temple University on November 20–21, 1997. Special thanks are due to the Bethune Museum and Archives for administration of the grant.

We also thank James Turner and Sharon Harley, who served as members of the conference planning committee, as well as Julian Bond, Diane Bevel Nash, Rosalyn Terborg-Penn, Dorothy Cotton, Clayborne Carson, Kathleen Cleaver, Aldon Morris, Gloria Harper Dickinson and others who participated in a roundtable discussion and suggested approaches and ideas for the project. Researchers Marya McQuirter, Michael Collins, Jerry Bjelopra, Danielle Smallcomb, Richard Woodland, and Fatima Aliu followed up research leads and identified sources for the bibliography. The work of CAAHC administrative assistant Joanne Hawes Speakes was indispensable to organizing the conference.

We also thank Charlotte Sheedy and Neeti Madan, our agents, and Stephen Magro, our editor at NYU Press.

We are especially thankful for our families, in particular Charles J. Thomas, Thelma and Joseph Collier, Vincent F. Franklin, Jack Franklin and Garland Franklin, who continue to help us endure the stresses that accompany our efforts to balance professional and family lives, and help to anchor us in the realities of daily life. We appreciate the personal perspectives and scholarly insights of friends and colleagues Ed Collins, Bernice Johnson Reagan, Lillian S. Williams, Sandra Bowen Motz, Linda M. Perkins, June Patton, Charles Payne, Elsa Barkley Brown, Bernice McNair Barnett, Francile Rusan Wilson, John Hope Franklin, C. Eric Lincoln, Paul Coates, Sylvia Jacobs, Janet Sims-Woods, Alexa B. Henderson, Tony Montiero, Cheryl Townsend Gilkes, Mary Frances Berry, Kenneth Kusmer, Wilbert Jenkins, Olga Dugan, Thomas Battle, Diane Jacox, Gloria Richardson, and Margaret Coleman.

In the Whip of the Whirlwind
African American Women in the
Civil Rights–Black Power Movement

The time
cracks into furious flower. Lifts its face
all unashamed. And sways in wicked grace.
Whose half-black hands assemble oranges
is tom-tom hearted
(goes in bearing oranges and boom).
And there are bells for orphans—
and red and shriek and sheen.
A garbage man is dignified
as any diplomat.
Big Bessie's feet hurt like nobody's business,
but she stands—bigly—under the unruly scrutiny,
stands in the wild seed.
In the wild weed
she is a citizen,
and, in a moment of highest quality, admirable.
It is lonesome, yes. For we are the last of the loud.
Nevertheless, live.
Conduct your blooming in the noise and whip of the
whirlwind.

                    —Gwendolyn Brooks, from "The Second
                              Sermon on the Warpland"[1]

From the time that African women arrived on the shores of what came to be known as the "New World," they have been caught up in a whirlwind of forces oftentimes beyond their control. Having survived the horrors of the Middle Passage was not enough; these mothers, grandmothers, and daughters were shackled and hurled into makeshift vehicles that carried them to dank dungeons and desolate shacks. The women were forced to do back-breaking labor, the same as the men, but had to endure the added burden of unwanted sexual intimacies of the slavers. These women lived, and sometimes died, for their children, and created families that helped to sustain them when the howling winds of oppression swirled and threatened to engulf the few things that came to matter most. Strengthened by an unshakable faith in God's justice, from slavery to freedom they managed to "conduct their blooming in the noise and the whip of the whirlwind."[2]

Over the last two decades historians and other scholars have begun to document and interpret the unique experiences of African women in the New World in general, and in the United States in particular. Through narrative histories, encyclopedias, anthologies, monographs, biographies, articles, and reviews, we have a better understanding of the conditions for African American women during slavery, the social and economic changes that came with Reconstruction, the role that African American women played in progressive social reform movements, the origins and activities of the black women's club movement, black women's contributions to American war efforts, and the great advancements they made in the first half of the twentieth century in the fields of education, business, sports, and entertainment.[3]

Historians of U.S. history are beginning to define the years from 1954 to 1965 as the "Civil Rights Era." From the U.S. Supreme Court's *Brown v. Board of Education* decision in 1954 declaring segregation in public education unconstitutional to the famous Selma to Montgomery, Alabama March in 1965, the demand for an end to legal segregation and discrimination in voting, housing, education, employment, and public accommodations was the dominant social and political issue facing the American population. Civil rights protests and demonstrations were organized in all sections of the United States, not just in the South; and the civil rights legislation passed during these years changed the social and political status of the majority of American citizens, not just African Americans. With the emergence of the student rights, antiwar, women's liberation, and Black Power movements after 1965, a new era of social protest and activism was launched in American society.[4]

For African Americans, the roots of the Black Power movement can be traced to the 1920s and Marcus Garvey's Universal Negro Improvement Association. Black Power was nourished in the 1930s by the National Negro Congress and in the 1940s by A. Philip Randolph's March on Washington Movement, and it came to fruition in the 1950s and 1960s with the Nation of Islam and the black nationalist ideologies of Malcolm X. Throughout the first half of the twentieth century, African Americans demanded equal treatment and first-class citizenship rights to lay the groundwork for the development of black political and economic power. And African American women made significant contributions to all these campaigns as well as to the Civil Rights–Black Power Movement.[5]

There are several book-length studies of African American women and the Civil Rights Movement. *Women in the Civil Rights Movement: Trailblazers and Torchbearers, 1941–1965,* edited by Vicki L. Crawford, Jacqueline A. Rouse, and Barbara Woods, focused on both black and white women, and provided the first assessment and overview of the wide range of activities that women pursued to bring about an end to legal segregation and discrimination in the southern states. More recently, Lynne Olson in *Freedom's Daughters: The Unsung Heroines of the Civil Rights Movement from 1830 to 1970* discussed black and white women's contributions to civil rights activities and the modern feminist movement in the 1960s. Presenting portraits of well-known figures as well as "unsung heroines," Olson describes how participation in civil rights campaigns helped to raise the political consciousness of black and white women and laid the groundwork for the Women's Liberation Movement. Olson ends her story in 1970, however, and presents no information on the impact of the Black Power Movement on the development of feminist consciousness among African American women in the 1970s and 1980s.

Belinda Robnett's *How Long? How Long? African-American Women in the Struggle for Civil Rights* is a sociological analysis of black women's leadership in the various civil rights campaigns. Robnett argued that African American women in leadership positions often served as the "bridge" between local civil rights struggles and national protest organizations. Charismatic figures, such as Martin Luther King, Jr. and James Farmer, set the national civil rights agenda and moved from coast to coast generating moral and financial support for the civil rights campaigns. Many African American women leaders operated at the local level, establishing the links and connections with grassroots organizations that provided the mass support for civil rights goals and objectives.[6] Peter J. Ling and Sharon Monteith's *Gender in the Civil Rights Movement* contains essays that examine the nature of women's and men's leadership roles within the Civil Rights Movement, and presents a "gendered analysis" of black literature and cultural politics in the post–Civil Rights Era.[7] While all four volumes provide important information on black women and the Civil Rights Movement, none explores in any detail the issues and organizations associated with Black Power and their impact on the social and political consciousness of African American women.[8]

Sisters in the Struggle presents autobiographical, biographical, and sociopolitical analyses of African American women in the Civil Rights–Black Power Movement. The personal testimonies of black women activists are an important source of documentary evidence and analysis of black women's contributions to social protest movements. Although biographical studies often depend on autobiographical materials for the portraits presented, eyewitness accounts by highly educated professionals provide a form of analysis often superior to that of scholars attempting to reconstruct an individual's past circumstances. We are fortunate to be able to make these eyewitness accounts available to our readers.[9]

Biographical analyses have been important in documenting the contributions to U.S. history of women in general, and African American women in particular. Through the critical examination of primary sources, such as autobiographies, letters, and interviews, as well as secondary sources, such as magazine articles and institutional histories, the biographers provide their personal assessments of the words and deeds of the individual under analysis. While considered more "objective" than autobiographical accounts, biographical studies are the personal and professional reflections of the individual researcher on the lives and activities of their subject.[10]

Rather than focusing on the actions of one individual, sociopolitical analyses examine collectivities and their place in the social environment and political context of their times. Utilizing autobiographical, biographical, statistical, and other types of documentary evidence, these studies attempt to reconstruct historical moments to reveal and assess social, political, and economic changes and continuities. Sociopolitical analyses are extremely important for understanding the contributions of African American women in the Civil Rights–Black Power Movement, the social changes that took place in American society for African American women, and the dramatic shifts in political consciousness among African American women and men that became the legacy of future generations.

Part I, Laying the Groundwork: African American Women and Civil Rights Before 1954, explores the civil rights activities of African American women prior to the launching of the modern phase of the Civil Rights Movement. The speech by Mary McLeod Bethune titled "Closed Doors" is an important personal statement by a nationally recognized black leader on civil rights goals and objectives. Ella Baker's early career as a community organizer is the subject of a biographical portrait based on new primary and secondary sources. The civil rights activities of the National Association of Colored Women, the National Council of Negro Women, and other black women's organizations before 1950 are also the subject of analysis in Part I.

Part II presents excerpts from the life stories of Rosa Parks, Charlayne Hunter Gault, and Dorothy I. Height. Each of these women wrote about important events in the Civil Rights Movement in which they were intimately involved. As eyewitnesses, they chronicle their own motivations and involvement and the impact that these events had on their lives, the larger society, and the course of American history.

Part III, Women, Leadership, and Civil Rights, includes biographical studies of the leadership provided by Septima Poinsette Clark and Fannie Lou Hamer to civil rights campaigns. The third essay examines the roles and contributions made by African American women in the Mississippi Freedom Democratic Party in the 1960s.

Part IV, From Civil Rights to Black Power: African American Women and Nationalism, describes the conditions and circumstances for African American women in the transition from civil rights to Black Power in the black freedom struggle. There are two biographical studies in this section. One essay examines the leadership provided by Gloria Richardson for the civil rights campaigns in Cambridge, Maryland in the early 1960s, and the other focuses on Ruby Doris Smith Robinson's activities as a leader of the Student Nonviolent Coordinating Committee. African American women's responses to Malcolm X's "promise of protection" is the subject of analysis in this section as well as gender ideologies and the multifaceted roles of women in the Black Panther Party.

Part V, Law, Feminism, and Politics, includes an essay that examines the impact of the "Free Joan Little" Movement on the development of a black feminist consciousness in the mid-1970s. Another essay compares black feminist consciousness exhibited by the black women appointed to President John F. Kennedy's Commission on the Status of Women in 1960 to that of the members of the National Black Feminist Organization and the Combahee River Collective in the 1970s. The final essay provides a comprehensive overview of African American women in elective office at the local, state, and national levels.

In many ways this volume demonstrates the coming of age of African American women's history and presents new information and theoretical approaches, and suggests future areas of research. These powerful and important studies make it all too clear that although in the whip of the whirlwind, African American women conducted their blooming admirably.

NOTES

1. Gwendolyn Brooks, "The Second Sermon on the Warpland," in *Blacks* (Chicago: The David Company, 1987), 453.

2. See, for example, Deborah Gray White, *Arn't I A Woman: Black Women in the Plantation South*, 2d ed. (New York: Norton, 1998); Darlene Clark Hine and David Barry Gaspar, eds., *More Than Chattel: Black Women and Slavery in the Americas* (Indianapolis: Indiana University Press, 1996).

3. Jacqueline Jones, *Labor of Love, Labor of Sorrow: Black Women, Work, and the Family from Slavery to the Present* (New York: Basic Books, 1985); Sharon Harley and Rosalyn Terborg-Penn, eds., *The Afro-American Woman: Struggles and Images* (Port Washington, NY: Kennikat Press, 1978); Tera Hunter, *To 'Joy My Freedom: Southern Black Women's Lives and Labors After the Civil War* (Boston: Harvard University Press, 1997); Cynthia Neverdon Morton, *Afro-American Women of the South and the Advancement of the Race, 1895–1925* (Knoxville: University of Tennessee Press, 1989); Dorothy Salem, *To Better Our World: Black Women and Organized Reform, 1890–1920* (Brooklyn, NY: Carlson Publishing, 1990); Anne Meis Knupfer, *Toward a Tendered Humanity and a Nobler Womanhood: African American Women's Clubs in Turn of the Century Chicago* (New York: New York University Press, 1996); Rosalyn Terborg-Penn, *African-American Women and the Struggle for the Vote, 1880–1920* (Bloomington: Indiana University Press, 1998); Evelyn Brooks Higginbotham, *Righteous Discontent: The Women's Movement in the Black Baptist Church, 1880–1920* (Cambridge: Harvard University Press, 1993); Stephanie J. Shaw, *What a Woman Ought to Be and to Do: Black Professional Women Workers During the Jim Crow Era* (Chicago: University of Chicago Press, 1996); Elizabeth Clark Lewis, *Liv-*

ing In Living Out: African American Domestics in Washington, D.C., 1910–1940 (Washington, DC: Smithsonian Institution, 1994); Bettye Collier-Thomas, *Daughters of Thunder: Black Women Preachers and their Sermons, 1850–1979* (San Francisco: Jossey Bass Publishers, 1998); Darlene Clark Hine, Elsa Barkley Brown, and Rosalyn Terborg-Penn, eds., *Black Women in America: An Historical Encyclopedia* (Brooklyn, NY: Carlson Publishing, 1993).

4. Bettye Collier-Thomas and V. P. Franklin, *My Soul Is a Witness: A Chronology of the Civil Rights Era, 1954–1965* (New York: Henry Holt & Co., 2000), 243–46.

5. V. P. Franklin, *Black Self-Determination: A Cultural History of African-American Resistance* (Brooklyn, NY: Lawrence Hill Books, 1992); Tony Martin, *Race First: Marcus Garvey and the Universal Negro Improvement Association* (Westport, CT: Greenwood Press, 1976); Paula Pfeiffer, *A. Philip Randolph: Pioneer of the Civil Rights Movement* (Baton Rouge: Louisiana State University Press, 1990); William E. Van Deburg, ed., *Black Nationalism in the Modern Era* (New York: New York University Press, 1997).

6. Vicki L. Crawford, Jacqueline A. Rouse, and Barbara Woods, eds., *Women in the Civil Rights Movement: Trailblazers and Torchbearers, 1941–1965* (Brooklyn, NY: Carlson Publishing, 1990); Lynne Olson, *Freedom's Daughters: The Unsung Heroines of the Civil Rights Movement from 1830 to 1970* (New York: Scribner, 2001). Belinda Robnett, *How Long, How Long? African American Women in the Struggle for Civil Rights* (New York: Oxford University Press, 1997). See also Peter J. Ling, "A Question of Leadership," *Reviews in American History* 27 (1999): 289–97.

7. Peter J. Ling and Sharon Monteith, eds., *Gender and the Civil Rights Movement* (New York: Garland Publishing, 1999).

8. There are several works that include discussions of the Civil Rights–Black Power Movement as part of broader discussions of African American women's history. See Paula Giddings, *When and Where I Enter: The Impact of Black Women on Race and Sex in America* (New York: William Morrow, 1984), 311–14, 347–50, 277–92; Deborah Gray White, *Too Heavy a Load: Black Women in Defense of Themselves, 1894–1994* (New York: Norton, 1999), 176–211; Darlene Clark Hine and Kathleen Thompson, *A Shining Thread of Hope: The History of Black Women in America* (New York: Broadway Books, 1998), 266–94; Joy James, *Shadowboxing: Representations of Black Feminist Politics* (New York: St. Martin's Press, 1999), 73–122.

9. For an examination of the significance of autobiographies in African American history, see V. P. Franklin, *Living Our Stories, Telling Our Truths: Autobiography and the Making of the African American Intellectual Tradition* (New York: Oxford University Press, 1996).

10. See, for example, Jacqueline A. Rouse, *Lugenia Burns Hope: Black Southern Reformer* (Athens: University of Georgia Press, 1989); and Adrienne Lasch

Jones, *Jane Edna Hunter: A Case Study of Black Leadership* (Brooklyn, NY: Carlson Publishing, 1990). An excellent source of biographical information on African American women is Jessie Carney Smith, ed., *Notable Black American Women* (Detroit: Gale Research, 1991) and *Notable Black American Women, Book II* (Detroit: Gale Research, 1996).

Laying the Groundwork
African American Women and Civil Rights
Before 1950

The essays in Part I focus on the period before 1950 and examine the civil rights activities and concerns of African American women and their organizations. In many ways, the activities of these women laid the groundwork for the modern phase of the Civil Rights Movement that began in the 1950s. Elaine M. Smith in her introduction to the speech "Closed Doors" points out that during her lifetime, Mary McLeod Bethune was sometimes referred to as the "First Lady of the Race." Widely known as an educator, institution builder, and civil rights activist, Bethune was one of several black women leaders who often worked in a variety of mixed-gender and feminist organizations to eliminate legal segregation and discrimination from American life. In "Closed Doors," Bethune described the conditions under which African Americans were forced to live and work, and the barriers they confronted in their effort to achieve first-class citizenship. Using her own personal experiences as a black woman, Bethune dramatically expressed the frustrations and hindrances African Americans faced in an American society supposedly committed to "liberty and justice for all."

V. P. Franklin and Bettye Collier-Thomas's essay, "For the Race in General and Black Women in Particular: The Civil Rights Activities of African American Women's Organizations, 1915–1950," describes how black women's organizations attempted to pry open the "closed doors" confronting African Americans. We point out that contrary to the arguments presented in some of the emerging scholarship on black feminism, African American women did not define an exclusively feminist agenda for advancing the race. The women's groups had as part of their overall mission a commitment to engage in activities for the advancement of the African people at the local, national, and even the international levels. Through an analysis of the activities of the New Jersey State Federation of Colored Women, a division of the National Association of Colored Women (NACW), the National Council of Negro Women (NCNW), and the Alpha Kappa Alpha Sorority's Non-Partisan Council, we explain how African American women systematically organized social welfare services in black communities and worked for the passage of legislation to eliminate segregation and discrimination in education, voting rights, the military, employment, and other areas. Civil rights activism became part of these women's group identity, and the social and political agenda they pursued was meant to benefit African Americans in general and black women in particular.

Unlike Mary McLeod Bethune, who received great acclaim and formal recognition for her contributions to black advancement, Ella Baker for many years was an unsung hero of the Civil Rights Movement. Several recent publications have begun to document Baker's influence within the Southern Christian Leadership Conference (SCLC) and the Student Nonviolent Coordinating Committee (SNCC); however, Barbara Ransby's essay, "Behind-the-Scenes View of a Behind-the-Scenes Organizer: The Roots of Ella Baker's Political Passions," presents an intimate portrait of Baker's early years in North Carolina, her relations with her mother, and her circle of friends in the 1930s and 1940s who helped develop and sustain her radical democratic humanism. Baker's experiences in the 1930s with the Worker's Education Project of the Works Progress Administration (WPA), the Young Negroes Cooperative League, and other leftist groups introduced her to economic alternatives to the capitalist system, while her travels throughout the South in the 1940s as field secretary for the NAACP provided her with the personal knowledge needed for organizing the black working classes. Ella Baker's passionate attachment to her political and economic principles inspired a new generation of men and women to look beyond what is, and to work selflessly to bring about what ought to be.

Chapter 1

"Closed Doors"
Mary McLeod Bethune on Civil Rights

INTRODUCTION
Elaine M. Smith

Mary McLeod Bethune (1875–1955) stands as an eminent American and one of the country's most distinguished women. Like about a half dozen other African Americans, she transcended a field to make "an essential contribution to the development of Black America." Especially in relation to black women, her contributions to major historical developments warranted often-repeated encomiums as "First Lady of Race." She achieved this status despite an unpromising beginning, including an extremely dark complexion. Her farming parents were slaves, as were most of her sixteen siblings. She attended two missionary-supported black schools: one five miles from her home outside rural Mayesville, South Carolina; the other, Barber Scotia, a residential girls' seminary, in Concord, North Carolina. Afterward, she spent a year at the integrated Moody Bible Institute in Chicago. Returning to the South, she launched a teaching career. Inspired in part by educational role models Emma J. Wilson and Lucy Laney, this career choice blossomed into much more. Along the way, she experienced marriage and motherhood, but they proved minor hindrances to a public life, even though initially, the public frowned on black or white women in that arena. Bethune, however, would not be deterred because of her passionate belief in the leadership ability of black women and their need to fulfill their essential functions in advancing the race.

In the decades before the U.S. Supreme Court repudiated the "separate but equal" doctrine (1954) and virulent, legalized, and pervasive racial subordination sometimes made black militancy a matter of "you walked down the street with your head up," Bethune understood the centrality of the civil rights struggle to American democracy and to the world. Bethune also helped to blaze the way to the Civil Rights Era (1954–1965) by providing encouragement to people of African descent, using the political system to her advantage, and participating in freedom-fighting organizations. With highly acclaimed accomplishments, oratory, and courage, she inspired her racial kin to hold on and fight for the time when color was irrelevant to opportunity. With regard to achievements, this formidable woman worked wonders. She founded and developed an initially small, nondescript elementary school into Bethune-Cookman College, a baccalaureate institution which thrives today. She engineered new military and public service opportunities for black women both nationally and internationally. While a bureaucrat in the nation's capital during the desperation and anxiety of depression and war, like the "Mother of the Race," she succored youth with social services, educational grants, vocational training, and government-facilitated jobs. Also, she became an at-large leader of Black America, as indicated by her organizing and sustaining the mostly male Federal Council on Negro Affairs, better known as the "Black Cabinet." This involved bringing "together for unified thought and action all the Negroes high in government authority" in service to the race.

In addition to her triumphs, African Americans took heart from this remarkable woman through her magnificent oratory. Speaking in choice diction, free of regional flavor, she used her "organ-chimed voice" to fire up occasions in ways most listeners found memorable. Consequently, she was much sought-after. Bethune's raw courage, another attribute inspiring the masses, caused the *Washington Post* to editorialize that it was "equal to any crisis." Certainly the white-robed Ku Klux Klan could not intimidate her, even while marching twice in front of her school in Daytona Beach, Florida: once to retaliate for her sitting in a railway car for whites only; the other, to prevent her and other black women from registering to vote.

Besides dispensing greatly needed encouragement to people of color, Bethune advanced civil rights through the political system, first as a Republican, and after the 1932 presidential election, as a Democrat. Aubrey Williams, the director of the Depression-spawned National Youth Administration in which Bethune reigned over "Negro Affairs," attested, "She was a damn good politician. She knew how to use other people for ends she wanted to achieve . . . She had good goals . . . She used any means at hand to achieve them."[1] Bethune put her celebrity to work in the political campaigns of several liberal Democratic politicians, including presidents Franklin D. Roosevelt and Harry Truman, U.S. Senator Herbert Lehman from New York, and California Congresswoman Helen Gahagan Douglas. She campaigned nonstop, however, for the effective enfranchisement of African Americans and their use of the ballot to advance an agenda that embraced antilynching, employment, education, health care, and housing.

Bethune pressed for an end to discriminatory policies and practices through organizations. She worked in and with many, including the National Association for the Advancement of Colored People, the National Urban League, Commission on Interracial Cooperation, Southern Conference for Human Welfare, Southern Conference Educational Fund, National Committee to Abolish the Poll Tax, and National Committee for Justice in Colombia, Tennessee (1946). Her earliest and dearest freedom-fighting organizations, such as the National Association of Colored Women and the International Council of Women of the Darker Races, were "womanist," so named because these black sister groups addressed gender and race issues simultaneously without necessarily criticizing black men. Although these activist black women eagerly endeavored to work with white women's groups, sometimes racism sparked friction, as in 1925 when the International Council of Women sponsored an entertainment in Washington, DC, with segregated seating. Bethune, president of the National Association of Colored Women, worked with others in reversing the practice. This experience proved valuable in mounting larger assaults against legal segregation, especially during her tenure as president of the National Council of Negro Women, which she founded in 1935.

While helping to blaze the path to civil rights by inspiring a race, using the political process, and participating in numerous progressive organizations, at intervals Mary McLeod Bethune addressed predominantly white audiences. "Closed Doors," the speech that follows, targets such northeastern groups in the latter half of 1936. She declares therein that white racism has produced the greatest handicap known: to be black, and then to be a black woman. Moreover, she intimates that if most whites had their way, they would even consign people of color to a segregated eternity. This titan engages her audience diplomatically, however, using the metaphor "door" for civil rights. Even though African Americans confront "Closed Doors," they want to enter "every door." She understands that in her era some "doors" were shut so tightly that they could not be opened; but "with tact, skill, and persistence," others would. Additional doors would give way because African Americans would batter them down. Bethune attributes President Franklin D. Roosevelt with an inclination "to open doors to the Negro." Scholars would later emphasize that in the 1930s, Roosevelt's administration did not exclude African Americans from the New Deal programs. Knowing what the federal government needed to do, what African Americans were doing and would do, Bethune challenged white America to open these doors. Otherwise, this places blacks in a position analogous to the patriots who fought in the American Revolution. From a fount of democratic ideology, Christian principle, and human decency, Bethune joins a long black continuum of freedom-seeking voices—male and female—speaking to the conscience of America.

"CLOSED DOORS"

Mary McLeod Bethune

Frequently from some fair-minded speaker who wishes his platform utterances to fall on pleased ears, comes this expression: "Do not continually emphasize the fact that you are a Negro, forget that," and quite as frequently there is always the desire to hurl back this challenge, "You be a Negro for just one short twenty-four hours and see what your reaction will be." A thousand times during that twenty-four hours, without a single word being said, he would be reminded and would realize unmistakably that he is a Negro.[2]

These are some of the experiences he would have that would be exactly as mine often are: One morning I started to catch a train. There was plenty of time to make the train with ease. Although several taxicabs passed as I stood on the corner trying to hail one, several minutes passed before one would stop to serve me, and so caused me to be three minutes late in catching that train.

On another occasion with time to spare, with sufficient money in my pocket to have every comfort that was necessary, I found that I was compelled to take a "jim crow" car in order to reach my destination in Mississippi. As a passenger on that "jim crow" car there was no service that I could receive in securing a meal, although from every other coach accommodations could be had.

When last winter a number of Negro women were discussing where their respective children should attend school, they were [limited to the consideration] of Negro schools exclusively, since they were all members of a southern community. Then as they thought of further education for their children they were again limited to those institutions which will accept a limited number of Negro students. Some little while ago one of the best lecturers in this country was giving a lecture at the close of the Mid-week religious service, and there again, although the services and the lecturer appealed to me, there was no way that I could, with any sense of self-respect, enter when I realized the segregation and separation that awaited me on that occasion.

Not only the cultural avenues, but the economic fields are closed also. My boy belonged to a labor union, but when there came the chance for the distribution of jobs, it was not until all white applicants had been supplied, and then even though he is a skilled laborer, nothing was offered him in his own field, but he was forced to accept a job as a common laborer.

The white-collar jobs are largely closed to the majority of Negroes, although they have given themselves to the making of this country. The very forests that the Negroes have turned into fertile fields are often not open to them.

As I walked down the street, passing restaurants, cafes, hotels, not necessarily with blazing, glaring signs, but with a subtle determination there is the expression "no admittance."

Whether it be my religion, my aesthetic taste, my economic opportunity, my educational desire, whatever the craving is, I find a limitation because I suffer the greatest known handicap, a Negro—a Negro woman.

As the director—mother of the next generation guiding the Negro youth of this land, the citizenry who must share the responsibility of this country, whatever it is, I find that the Negro youth cannot have, and enjoy, the highest places of citizenship, but must measure up to that standard, nevertheless. As a part of the citizenry of this country, the greatest country in all the world, he is expected to be a superior being despite the ever-increasing limitations. The outstanding Negro has proportionately more than met this requirement in the fields of letters, music, economics, and research education, in fact, in every line of endeavor.

The doors in almost every field—political, educational, economical, and social—are closed, barred against him, but they must be opened. Shall it be a question whether or not the Negro, himself, will batter down the doors; whether or not the government will open some of them for him; whether or not the fair-mindedness of the country shall force them to open is a question. But they must be opened if the Negro is to live up to, and attain, unto his best.

Theoretically, to be an American citizen implies that every American citizen shall have life, liberty, and pursuit of happiness without anyone else's let [permission] or hindrance. Yet, these rules do not apply equally to the Negro as [they do] to the white man. There are very many doors that are shut against the Negro, but all of these are not barred. They may be opened with tact, skill, and persistence.

The first privilege of a citizen is to be well-born. The day of the midwife is largely passed, and the expectant mother should have the best care of physician and hospital. Many children are handicapped for life by not having had the proper medical attention preceding birth, at birth, and immediately following birth. Even then there is general medical assistance along these lines for white people, [t]he door is generally shut to the Negro. In many places, if he is taken into the hospital at all, he is taken into the cellar or some isolated corner and given scarce attention by unwilling hands. The necessary food for mother and child is often beyond the reach of such persons, not only because of color only. These handicaps follow child and adult in the Southland and are often present in the Northland, where equality, on the surface, is pretended.

Next to birth and life itself come housing and sanitary conditions. The Negro sections of most southern towns are just across the railroad where there are neither paved streets, under drainage, nor sufficient lighting. Nor are there rules of health that compel those who occupy these sections to observe the most common rules of sanitation. The Federal Housing and Community Bills have not gone far enough to penetrate across the railroad where the people who most need them may be accommodated. And even in the North and more liberal communities the Negro often finds himself in the old, and often abandoned part of the community, where the better class of white people have left to move into up-to-date, better ventilated, better heated, and better constructed homes.

The child handicapped at birth for want of proper medical and home surroundings most often finds that his school facilities are both very limited and very poor. The school houses, if such they may be called, are poorly constructed and lighted, and have straight-back benches with seats often too high for small children, or too small for older pupils, neither properly lighted nor properly heated. When the parents are too poor to buy suitable books, no provisions are made for buying them. In many places there is an attempt to segregate colored taxation to colored schools, which means the white child gets ten months of schooling under favorable conditions while the colored child gets four or five months with very poor facilities, and poorly educated and equally poorly paid teachers. These conditions make it very easy for the Negro in later years to "knock and not be heard." The Negro is expected to be a citizen and obey all laws which he often has no facilities for knowing and certainly no opportunity for making.

It is notorious that the Negro is deprived of his civil rights in public places. He has no opportunity to contact the white community in those things which make for right living, worthwhile accomplishments, and high citizenship. The cultural advantages of the concert, lectures, and public discussions are closed to him. He is further handicapped by not being able to work at the ordinary trades controlled by labor unions. It matters not what a Negro's qualifications are, it is difficult for him to become a member of a united labor organization, and to function as a member of the AFL [American Federation of Labor]. These labor organizations control most of the worthwhile employment and scrupulously exclude the Negro from membership and even where the Negro is permitted to join he is given the most menial work, and the least paying jobs.

In railroad travel the Negro is segregated in the South and made to ride in filthy, dingy, unsanitary cars. At the railroad station there is some kind of a toilet facility marked "colored." But even these facilities are denied those who by virtue of their economic conditions are forced to ride in buses. These bus lines often have only one set of toilet accommodations for men and for women which means white men and women. The colored passenger who often has to shift for himself, has to go to a nearby house or go to the woods and bushes in order to get an opportunity for the proper evacuations. Then too, when he enters the buses, he is assigned to the seats over the wheels where he is both cramped and jolted.

A colored man may be a fireman on a southern train, and may know all about how to run the engine, but if the engineer gets sick or dies, a white man must be sent for to move the train off the tracks into the barn. The labor union forbids him to join the union or place his hand on the throttle.

In states in which the State Board controls the sale of liquor, such as Pennsylvania, a colored man is not permitted to be a salesman, but [permitted to be] a janitor or truck driver. And although the government will furnish him money by way of relief to buy the liquor, the government will not see that he has a chance to earn a living for his wife and family through dispensing the liquor.

In the armed branch of the government the Negro can be little more than common fodder. In the Navy it matters not what his qualifications may be, he can rise no higher than a mess boy; and the same thing is generally true of the Army. The once vaulted 9th and 10th Calvaries and the 24th and 25th Infantries have virtually been abolished to the colored man and he can only be a cleaner in that branch of the government. But in case of actual war, he is conscripted and sent to the front as shock troops. This prejudiced viewpoint on behalf of the government not only deprives colored men of the privilege of playing soldier, but also prevents them and their families from getting what could come to them through wages.

Beginning as the Negro did with the founding of the colonies, contributing as he has to every phase of American life, he should have the same rights, privileges, immunities, and emoluments that have been and are accorded to any American citizen, and the government standing *in loco parentis* should neither make nor allow any discriminations or differences in any of her citizens, and should go a step further and see that no citizen, group of citizens, municipal or state government treat the Negro differently from all other citizens. That means that in the positions of responsibility, honor and trust, without ... the right to earn a living at any trade or occupation for which he is qualified, the government should see to it that the Negro is not barred therefrom.

The Negro wants a fair chance to work out his own destiny and to continue to contribute to the honor and glory of the nation. But this is impossible if he is to be handicapped, circumscribed, separated, and segregated.

The Negro wants equality of opportunity. He asks the privilege of entering every door and avenue that he may be able to prove his value. The Negro asks: "Can America, the land of the free, continue to refuse to answer this knock at these now closed doors; to refuse to grant him these quested opportunities of equality whereby he will make a finer, higher and more acceptable citizen?" The Negro must go to a separate church even though he claims to be of the same denomination [as some whites]. He is not allowed to sing, in unison with the white man, the grand old hymns of Calvin, the Wesleys—the triumphant songs of Christ and eternal glory.

When at last he is called to his final resting place on earth, even his ashes are not allowed to mingle with those of his white brother, but are borne away to some remote place where the white man is not even reminded that this Negro ever lived.

Judging from all that has preceded the Negro in death, it looks as if he has been prepared for a heaven, separate from the one to which the white man feels he alone is fit to inhabit.

Thus in death and for eternity, as in life, the white man would see the Negro segregated.

The rankest injustice is meted out to the Negro when he has helped in every way the development of the country, and yet finds that he is not permitted to share fully and freely in that development.

The principle of justice is fundamental and must be exercised if the peoples of this country are to rise to the highest and best, for there can be neither freedom, peace, true democracy, or real development without justice. The closed door of economic inequalities, of educational limitation, of social restrictions comprise the greatest injustice possible. None need fear the change for which we plead. The door of opportunity with all its ramifications, leading into every avenue, can be opened without this evolution causing revolution. This is a high challenge to America—to the church—and to the state. Just now there seems to be an effort on the part of our great leader [Franklin D. Roosevelt], the President of the United States, to open for the Negro some of the doors that have been closed. Too, there is a determination on the part of the Negro to open, or batter down, some of these closed doors. But more, there must be an equal plan or cooperation on the part of the American public to join in the effort. How will this challenge be met?

It seems to me that here is his challenge to America. Can it—will it? If it further closes the door of opportunity to a part of its own citizenry, it will be guilty of the very outrage that led to its own founding.

Awake America! Accept the challenge! Give the Negro a chance!

NOTES

1. Aubrey Williams quoted in Earl Devine Martin, "Mary McLeod Bethune: A Prototype of the Rising Consciousness of the Negro" (M.A. thesis, Northwestern University, 1956), 84.

2. "Closed Doors," speech delivered by Mary McLeod Bethune, ca. 1936, typescript, Bethune Cookman College.

Chapter 2

For the Race in General and Black Women in Particular

The Civil Rights Activities of African American Women's Organizations, 1915–50 [1]

V. P. Franklin and Bettye Collier-Thomas

> To work and serve the hour in helping to solve the many problems confronting the race; to study the conditions in the cities and counties; and in the spirit of Christ, by personal contact and sympathy, to lift as we climb.
>
> —Motto, National Association of Colored Women (1896) [1]

When Jennie L. Moton, president of the National Association of Colored Women (NACW), issued the call for the twenty-first biennial convention to be held in Boston in July 1939, she pointed out that the group was returning to the city where African American women first came together to address their pressing concerns, and made it clear that the goals of the organization remained the same since Josephine St. Pierre Ruffin's call in 1896. "Mrs. Ruffin sent forth a call to the colored women of the country and asked them to meet her in Boston as guests of the New Era Club." Jennie Moton declared that "for 43 years the organization that grew out of this call has been working for the uplift of the Race generally and for the advancement of Race women in particular." [2]

At the NACW's 1939 convention, the delegates participated in a roundtable on "How the Negro May Obtain His Rights by Legislation," as well as symposia on "Family Relations" and "Healthy Relationships Between Mother and Child."[3] Among the convention's resolutions was one endorsing the Gavagan-Wagner-Van Nuys federal antilynching bill then pending in the U.S. Congress, and another expressing their appreciation to New York Mayor Fiorello La Guardia for his recent appointment of Jane M. Bolin to a ten-year term as judge in the city's Domestic Relations Court. Bolin became the first African American woman judge in the United States.[4]

The NACW activities at the 1939 convention were not a reflection of the concerns and objectives of its members merely in that year, but throughout the organization's history. Moreover, these activities and objectives were shared with many other national, state, and local black women's organizations throughout the first half of the twentieth century. Although the term "civil rights" did not come into widespread usage until the 1940s, black women's organizations were active in campaigns before and after that decade to protest racial discrimination in education, voting, public accommodations, armed services, and housing. Indeed, some black women's groups took the lead in developing strategies at the national level to advance the civil rights of the African American population.

Several historians have suggested that the "metalanguage of race" served as a "global sign" that overshadowed and obscured class and gender conflicts internal to the black community. Evelyn Brooks Higginbotham, Kenneth Goings, Deborah Gray White, and others have argued that the preoccupation with "race work," "racial uplift," and essentialist notions of "black womanhood" have tended to obscure the significant tensions and conflicts among African Americans of different class or regional backgrounds.[5] According to Evelyn Higginbotham, "race not only tends to subsume other sets of social relations, namely gender and class, but it blurs and disguises, suppresses and negates its own complex interplay with the very social relations it envelopes."

This has meant that "black women of different economic and regional backgrounds, of different skin tones and sexual orientations, have found themselves in conflict over the interpretation of symbols and norms, public behavior, coping strategies, and a variety of micro political acts of resistance to structures of domination."[6]

Although there may have been conflict among African American women at the "micro political" level over "strategies of resistance," when we examine the civil rights activism carried out by black women's organizations, we find broad solidarity on a wide range of issues across class, regional, and color lines. Poor and working-class African American women joined and sometimes led these organizations and participated fully in campaigns aimed at ending racial discrimination and the destruction of the structures of domination that oppressed African Americans in general and African American women in particular. Through a detailed examination of the civil rights activities of the New Jersey Federation of Colored Women's Clubs, the Alpha Kappa Alpha Sorority's Non-Partisan Council on Human Rights, the National Association of Colored Women, and the National Council of Negro Women between 1915 and 1950, we are able to document black women's commitment to the advancement of the race in general and black women in particular.

The New Jersey State Federation of Colored Women's Clubs

In October 1915, the Reverend Florence Spearing Randolph, temperance and suffrage activist and AME Zion minister, called together thirty women's clubs to meet in Trenton, New Jersey to improve the coordination of black women's programs and activities throughout the state. This meeting resulted in the founding of the New Jersey Federation of Colored Women's Clubs. Initially composed of women's temperance organizations, by 1917 the federation had expanded to 56 clubs, including many church missionary societies, with over 2,600 members. In 1924, the membership had expanded to 3,500 and included 85 women's clubs "doing work for human betterment, church, civic, literary, business or political."[7]

While many of the club representatives were teachers and business women and the wives of lawyers, physicians, and other professionals, there were also many representatives who were domestic servants, day laborers, and other service workers. And from the earliest years, the federation was active in civil rights as well as issues important to black women. At the first annual meeting held in July 1916 in Englewood, New Jersey, among the speakers were NAACP executive secretary Roy Nash, who sought support for the antilynching crusade, and NACW vice president Mary B. Talbert, who spoke about the needs of black women migrants to northern cities and towns.[8] At each of the federation meetings between 1916 and 1922, the federation members not only passed resolutions denouncing lynching and antiblack violence, such as the Tulsa Race Riot in 1921, but raised funds to support the groups leading the antilynching crusade. At the 1921 annual meeting held in Summit, New Jersey, the federation resolved

> that we denounce lynch law and that we urge that the value of human life be emphasized by press and pulpit . . . that this Federation desires to go on record as standing solidly back of the NAACP in its appeal to all clubs, organizations and individuals to watch the Dyer Bill, which makes lynching a federal crime and to send telegrams to our representatives urging passage of that bill.

In 1923, the federation raised over $1,500 to support New Jersey's Anti-Lynching Crusade.[9]

During World War I, the New Jersey Federation worked with the Women's Council on National Defense on its program of training young women for employment in war industries, and raised funds for the house opened by the YWCA to entertain black troops stationed at Fort Dix, New Jersey.[10] During and after the war, the federation sponsored forums and educational programs on women's suffrage and legislative issues, and participated in the activities organized by the Tri-State Legislative Conference of Women from New Jersey, New York, and Connecticut. The other major activities of the federation in the 1920s included the sponsoring of programs on "Race History," the provision of scholarships for black students, and the funding of housing and training programs for black women migrants to the cities and towns of New Jersey.[11] One of the major reasons why the federation was committed to improving the conditions for urban and rural black masses in New Jersey was because many of the club leaders were members of the black working class. Violet Johnson served as vice president of the New Jersey Federation and the New Jersey branch of the National Negro Business League during the 1920s.[12] Johnson was born in Wilmington, North Carolina, but spent most of her life in Summit, New Jersey, where she worked as a domestic servant for the John Eggers family. One summer while visiting North Carolina the Eggers met and employed Johnson as their servant. Johnson relocated to Brooklyn, New York with the family, where she was one of eight servants, who were mostly of Irish background, and were employed in the Eggers home. In 1896, Johnson accompanied the family to Summit, New Jersey, where John Eggers moved his printing business.[13] In Summit, Violet Johnson became active in club work and in 1915 and 1916 served as president of the Young Women's Uplift Club and the Girls Patriotic League. With the formation of the New Jersey Federation of Colored Women's Clubs in 1915, Johnson became active in that group, serving as vice president between 1926 and 1931.[14]

Violet Johnson worked for the Eggers until the late 1920s, when she established the Girls Industrial Home. Similar to the National Training School for Girls in Washington, DC, founded by Nannie Helen Burroughs and the Woman's Convention, auxiliary to the National Baptist Convention, Johnson's school trained young black girls and women to be domestics and secured employment for them. As the national director for Women's Work for the National Baptist Convention, Johnson was in fact replicating in New Jersey a successful Baptist training program.[15]

With the coming of the Great Depression, many of the women's clubs belonging to the New Jersey federation became involved in providing food, clothes, and other forms of relief to unemployed workers.[16] The New Deal federal relief programs began operation in the state in 1934, and the federation sponsored forums and panel discussions on the questions, "How Can the Negroes Take Advantage of the Recovery Program?" and "How Adequate Are the Social Welfare Programs for Negroes in New Jersey?" The group also lobbied the governor and other state officials to gain the appointment of African Americans to state relief agencies and programs. At the 1936 annual convention held in Bordentown, New Jersey, the federation formed a commission to meet with New Jersey Governor Henry T. Moore about "the matter of placing a Negro representative on state bodies, especially relief bodies, in which much of the money spent goes to Negro residents."[17] As a result of these efforts, when the New Jersey legislature in July 1938 formed the State Commission for the Study of Negro Population in Urban Centers, Evelyn V. Brock, vice president of the New Jersey Federation, was immediately appointed to the commission by State Assembly Speaker Herbert J. Pascoe.[18] Through the end of the decade the federation remained vigilant and addressed the issue, "How Clubs May Meet the Acute Needs in their Community." Through educational forums, lobbying, scholarship programs, and fundraising for social welfare activities, the federation addressed the important civil rights issues facing the African American community.[19]

At the New Jersey Federation's annual meeting in July 1942, after the United States had entered World War II, the theme was "How Can Club Women Make Democracy Real in America?" At that meeting the club representatives committed their membership to working with the American Red Cross to provide clothes, supplies, and other materials for U.S. soldiers. Throughout the war years, the club women were active in supplying books and other reading material and recreational programs for the black troops stationed at Fort Dix and in other military installations throughout the state. The practice of racial discrimination in restaurants, hotels, and other public facilities in New Jersey limited the recreational opportunities for black military personnel. The black women's clubs viewed their important contribution to American democracy as meeting the social and recreational needs for blacks in uniform.[20]

Even before the end of the war, the New Jersey Federation began lobbying state officials for the integration of adult education programs in local communities. In April 1945, the federation adopted and sent a resolution to state commissioner of education John W. Bosshart requesting that the postwar adult education programs in New Jersey, similar to those provided for returning veterans in other northern states, not be organized on a segregated basis in "separate schools." Dr. Everett C. Preston, state director of adult education, had announced the plan for adult training, but did not specify that it would be open to all residents, regardless of race, creed, color, or national origin.[21] Even more importantly, the New Jersey Federation added its support to the NAACP and other organizations lobbying for the passage of legislation creating the State Commission Against Discrimination. In 1945, New Jersey became the second state to form a governmental agency to investigate complaints of employment discrimination by employers with state contracts.[22]

The New Jersey Federation's efforts to obtain fair employment legislation was the beginning of sustained group activities in the name of "civil rights" in the postwar period. Under the leadership of Margaret Caution, the federation, along with the state NAACP branches, and the African Methodist Episcopal Zion's Church's New Jersey Conference, became an active participant in the Joint Council on Civil Rights. By 1941, the New Jersey Federation had become one of the most influential organizations in New Jersey. Its power was related to the prominence of its members and the organization's activism on issues of equality for women and racial justice. In 1947 in a resolution to the New Jersey Constitutional Convention, the New Jersey Federation emphasized its long history of working for "equal opportunity for all people and the full enjoyment of the rights, privileges and benefits of the State of New Jersey." The resolution targeted the use of restrictive covenants by real estate agents to exclude African Americans and Jews from certain housing areas, segregation and discrimination in public education, and the denial of business and industrial employment opportunities to African Americans. The Federation acknowledged that education and legislation were insufficient remedies for addressing the prejudices of "the average man," and recommended adding a paragraph to the proposed new state constitution under section five "Rights and Privileges" stating that "Property taken for public use shall be enjoyed without discrimination because of race, color, religion, or national origin."[23]

At the New Jersey Federation's 1948 convention, held in Bordentown, New Jersey, where the theme was "The Challenge of Civil Rights," the delegates representing fifty-one black women's organizations voted to send a petition to Governor Alfred E. Driscoll urging him "to take the lead . . . in the appointment of qualified colored persons to State commissions and boards" and to "broaden the field of colored employment in state educational institutions."[24] Later that year, Governor Driscoll named the members of the newly created Women's Advisory Council to the State Department Against Discrimination. Three federation members, Elizabeth Thomas, Jersey City; Delia Martin, East Orange; and Omega V. Mason, Salem, were appointed to the council.[25]

At the New Jersey Federation's 1949 convention, also held in Bordentown, the representatives again demonstrated their ongoing commitment to the advancement of the race in general, and to black women in particular. The over one hundred delegates passed resolutions calling for the passage of the fair employment practices, antipoll tax, and other civil rights bills then pending in the U.S. Congress. The delegates also sent a telegram to President Truman commending him for his support for the National Housing Act, which provided federal funds for the construction of low- and middle-income housing. The telegram also commended Truman for his appointment of qualified black women to key positions in his new administration.[26]

Alpha Kappa Alpha's Non-Partisan Council on Human Rights

Alpha Kappa Alpha (AKA), founded in 1908, was the first Greek-letter sorority established by African American college women. From the beginning the members agreed that they should be working to find solutions to "the problems of girls and women," but the group also committed its membership to "action related to the needs, interests, and potentialities of the community in which the group is situated."[27] With the Summer School for Rural Negro Teachers, first organized in 1934, AKA sponsored classes in child development, social sciences, music, art, and a wide variety of subjects for teachers who were working in one of the poorest areas in the country. The AKA's Mississippi Health Project, which began the following year, provided a Traveling Clinic that in 1935 covered hundreds of miles providing smallpox, diphtheria, and other immunizations and health services to thousands of impoverished children and adults.[28]

In 1938, the AKAs moved into the arena of civil rights activism with the establishment of the Non-Partisan Lobby for Economic and Democratic Rights and later the AKA Non-Partisan Council on Public Affairs. Under the leadership of Norma Boyd, AKA became the first African American organization to hire a full-time representative to monitor and lobby for legislation and other governmental actions that reflected the collective interests of the African American community.[29] Boyd believed that "we can ask for and support such measures as will assure for our people decent living conditions, permanent jobs, and voice in determining the conditions under which they will live and work. We can reach these objectives only by making our power felt in the halls and on the floors of Congress."[30]

Although the Non-Partisan Council was founded by Alpha Kappa Alpha sorority, whose members were college-educated, professional women, throughout its ten years the council was engaged in lobbying and various educational activities aimed at the advancement of African American masses in general, and working-class black women in particular. William P. Robinson, a young law student, became the council's first representative; the group participated in protests against police brutality in Washington, DC, and lobbied the U.S. Congress for the expansion of the federal public works program and the extension of the minimum wage to women employed in the laundry industry. In 1940, the council lobbied for the elimination of discrimination in public accommodations, federal housing projects, and medical hospitalization programs, and protested lynchings and the disfranchisement of the southern black population.[31] With regard to National Defense Programs, at a conference held in Washington, DC in December 1940, the council recommended that "all Negroes avail themselves of the opportunities offered in vocational training and apprenticeships in the arsenals and shipyards which are being used in the Defense Program." The council itself would concentrate on "the welfare of Negro troops in the cantonments and the employment of Negro nurses and librarians at training centers."[32]

In 1941, the council worked toward the passage of legislation for the erection of the George Washington Carver Monument in Missouri as well as an antidiscrimination amendment to the National Nurse's Training Act, and worked with Mary McLeod Bethune and the Washington Committee for the Negro Woman in the National Defense to secure increased participation by black women in the National Defense Program.[33]

Following the U.S. entrance into World War II, the council was extremely active in protesting individual and institutionalized practices of racial discrimination in the Armed Forces and in defense industries. In July 1942, the Non-Partisan Council sponsored a five-day institute at Howard University on "Negro Americans and Defense Planning." Topics discussed were: "Employment, Including Training, Recruitment and Placement"; "Trends in the Improvement of National Income and Consumption"; "Functional Development Programs for Urban and Rural People"; "Planning for the Improvement and Development of Special Skills"; and "Consumer Reaction to Prices and Rationing."[34] Dr. Malcolm S. McLean, co-chairman of the newly formed Fair Employment Practices Commission (FEPC), discussed "Present Strategies in the Employment of Minority Groups"; Mrs. Chase Going Woodhouse, director of the Institute of Women's Professional Relations, described the "Progress in Training and Placement of Women in War Industries"; Oveta Culp Hobby, director of the Women's Auxiliary Army Corps, spoke on "Training and Placement of Women in the Army"; and representatives from the U.S. Department of Agriculture, Federal Housing Authority, and Farm Security Administration also gave presentations.[35]

In the case of the Women's Army Corps (WACS), successor to the Women's Auxiliary Army Corps, and other branches of the armed services, the council also lobbied extensively for the inclusion and promotion of African American women at all levels in the chain of command. The AKA Non-Partisan Council was most active in securing nondiscriminatory policies in the WAVES, SPARS, and Women Marines.[36] In October 1942, the Navy's Director of Officer Procurement Kenneth Castleman rejected the application of AKA member and Indiana University graduate Doris Eloise Hill of Trenton, New Jersey, on the grounds that "she did not appear to qualify for any other division of the Women's Reserve." Thomasina Johnson, the council's legislative representative, declared, "Are we Americans out to win a war for all people who want democracy, or are we not? If we aren't, let us know it. If we are, it's about time we were about it." Johnson went on to point out that racially discriminatory policies and practices were contributing to the low morale and "critical attitude of darker people toward this war."[37]

It was the Non-Partisan Council that released information to the public about Secretary of Navy Frank Knox's decision in July 1943 to recruit African American women for a separate training program to be installed at a black college. The council mobilized the Congress of Industrial Organization's (CIO) Women's Auxiliaries, the NAACP, the National Urban League, and other groups to make official protests to President Franklin Roosevelt.[38] As a result of these protests, Knox did not move to implement the change. In April 1944, Illinois Congressman William A. Rowen introduced into Congress House Resolution 522, which sought "to direct the Committee on Naval Affairs to conduct an investigation with respect to the status of Negro women in relation to the women's uniformed services of the Navy, Marine Corps, and Coast Guard."

The Committee was asked to determine

(1) whether discrimination on account of race or color is practiced in (A) the initial acceptance for service of Negro women, (B) the exclusion of Negro women from any specific type of duty after initial acceptance for service and (C) the selection of officers' training of Negro women and the appointment to, advancement in, commissioned rank of Negro women; and (2) to what extent consideration of race or color are impeding the full utilization and development of professional and technical skills of Negro members of the women's uniformed services.[39]

The resolution was referred to the House Committee on Rules, where it remained. However, the AKA Non-Partisan Council launched a nationwide campaign and urged the membership of over twenty national organizations and

> Negroes throughout the country to send letters to the [new] Secretary of the Navy James V. Forrestal, President Roosevelt, the northern members of the House Rules Committee, stating that House Resolution 522 must be passed and that the Navy must admit Negro women into the WAVES, SPARS, and Marines on an integrated basis.[40]

Finally, the AKA Council efforts were rewarded, and in October 1944, Secretary Forrestal announced that black women would be accepted as enlisted personnel and officers in the navy on an integrated basis.[41] The council then urged that "Negro women take advantage to forge ahead to greater opportunity for themselves and to help bring about the ultimate defeat of the enemy."[42]

Even before the end of the war, the Non-Partisan Council took up the cause of black war veterans in general, and black women veterans in particular. In a resolution passed in October 1944 and forwarded to President Roosevelt, the Council expressed concern about "the right of Negro veterans to receive impartial treatment in matters pertaining to hospitalization, vocational rehabilitation, insurance, pensions and compensation, and the right of Negro citizens to employment and integration in all branches and levels of the United States Veterans Administration." The resolution condemned the practice of sending black veterans only to the separate black hospital in Tuskegee, Alabama, and called for the employment of black personnel, particularly black nurses, at all veterans' hospitals and other facilities, in other than "menial and routine jobs."[43] In 1945, the Non-Partisan Council led successful campaigns to oppose the establishment of a separate black veterans hospital in Mississippi and to include antidiscrimination provisions in the National Hospital Construction Act, which required that state hospital facilities should be provided to residents "without discrimination on account of race, creed, or color."[44]

In the immediate postwar period, as a result of its participation in meetings and conferences at the U.S. State Department, the Non-Partisan Council submitted memoranda to federal officials making specific "Recommendations for Peace" and urging them to develop a "mass educational program" to improve international, intergroup, and interracial understanding. The council was concerned that international exchanges fostered by the State Department be open to all students and not discriminate on the basis of racial, religious, or ethnic background.

When deliberations began among State Department officials for the launching of the United Nations (UN) in 1945, the AKA's Non-Partisan Council's activities moved from the area of civil rights to human rights. Even before it became the first sorority or fraternity accredited as an Observer in 1947 at the deliberations of the UN General Assembly, the council made efforts to disseminate to representatives from Latin America and other countries information on the need to protect and guarantee the rights of minority groups. The council participated in the State Department's conferences in October 1947 and in February 1948 called to examine the proposed "International Bill of Human Rights" and subsequently the proposed UN "Covenant and Declaration of Human Rights."[45]

In May 1946, Thomasina Johnson Norford announced she would step down as director of the Non-Partisan Council to become Chief of the Division on Minority Affairs for the U.S. Employment Service, one of the highest positions held by a black woman in the federal government. At that point the AKA leadership decided to open up the lobby to participation by other fraternal groups. After a series of meetings in 1947 and 1948, the American Council on Human Rights (ACHR) was organized by Alpha Kappa Alpha, Alpha Phi Alpha, Delta Sigma Theta, Phi Beta Sigma, Sigma Gamma Rho, Zeta Phi Beta, and later Kappa Alpha Psi. Under the leadership of Elmer Henderson and Patricia Roberts (Harris), the council's objectives were to engage in "social action" and "the promotion of legislation" to achieve "broader opportunities in employment, adequate housing for the underprivileged on a nondiscriminatory basis." Throughout the 1950s and 1960s, the American Council on Human Rights played an active role in promoting civil rights legislation in the areas of education, transportation, employment, public accommodations, housing, and the armed services.[46]

The final report of the National Non-Partisan Council was presented to the AKA annual meeting held in Detroit in 1948. While the leaders expressed mixed emotions about the council's dissolution, the report provided a long list of civil rights and human rights accomplishments in the national and international arenas.[47]

Civil Rights and Black Women's Organizations
in the Postwar Era

Black women's organizations became even more involved in civil rights campaigns for the advancement of African Americans and other minority groups at the end of World War II. One area where these groups were most active was in the campaigns for the establishment of fair employment practices commissions (FEPCs) at the local, state, and national levels. Following A. Philip Randolph's call in December 1940 for a "March on Washington" to protest racially discriminatory hiring practices by defense contractors and government agencies, President Roosevelt issued Executive Order 8802 on June 25, 1941, just days before the proposed march. It stated that

> there shall be no discrimination in the employment of workers in defense industries or Government because of race, creed, color or national origin . . . And it is the duty of all employers and of labor organizations . . . to provide full and equitable participation of all workers in defense industries, without discrimination because of race, creed, color or national origin.

The Fair Employment Practices Committee was set up to investigate complaints of discrimination in violation of the order. Although the Committee had no power to punish employers or defense contractors, the hearings focused attention on discriminatory practices that could lead to the loss of future government contracts.[48]

Once the war was over, the Committee went out of existence on April 29, 1946. However, as early as 1944 numerous groups, including the National Committee for a Permanent FEPC, the NAACP, CIO, National Urban League, and the AKA Non-Partisan Council, were mobilized to gain the passage of permanent FEPC legislation. Although legislation was introduced into each session of Congress between 1945 and 1955 calling for a permanent FEPC, it was never passed because of opposition from powerful southern Democratic politicians. Meanwhile, these same groups became involved in campaigns to have FEPC statutes passed by municipal and state governments. In 1945 and 1946, fair employment practice commissions were established through legislation in New York, New Jersey, and Massachusetts.[49]

As part of the celebration of the Golden Jubilee of the National Association of Colored Women (NACW), held in Washington, DC in

July 1946, the AKA's former legislative representative Thomasina Johnson Norford chaired a forum devoted to "The Role of Club Women in the Field of Legislation." The participants discussed the statements sent to the convention by Carroll Reese, chairman of the Republican National Committee, and Democratic Senator James M. Meade of New York declaring their full support for anti–poll tax, anti-lynching, and permanent FEPC legislation.[50] As part of their activities

> more than 200 women silently marched to both the White House and the Senate Building bearing placards denouncing the recent Georgia lynchings of four colored citizens. They picketed the White House and converged on the Senate Building where representatives of each state sought their Senators and demanded that they support the anti-lynching bill and vote for "cloture."[51]

The issue of civil rights for African Americans and other racial and ethnic minorities in the United States became a dominant political issue beginning in December 1946, when Harry S. Truman announced the appointment of the President's Committee on Civil Rights. The committee, which included Philadelphia attorney Sadie T. M. Alexander and other distinguished black and white leaders, was to make recommendations for future executive and legislative action. The committee's report *To Secure These Rights* was issued on October 29, 1947, just ten days before the 12th Annual Convention of the National Council of Negro Women (NCNW) was to be held in Washington, DC. The presidential committee concluded that "the national government of the United States must take the lead in safeguarding the civil rights of all Americans. We believe that this is one of the most important observations that can be made about the civil rights problem today." The committee recommended the passage of federal anti-lynching and antipoll tax legislation, stricter enforcement of existing statutes to uphold minority rights, the elimination of racial segregation, and the establishment of a permanent FEPC.[52] On November 6, 1947, in a press release issued by the NCNW, Mary McLeod Bethune declared that

> it is my firm belief that the recent issuance of the Civil Rights report by the President's Committee has stimulated [black] women all over the country to take an increased interest in present-day issues. They are coming to Washington in such great numbers because they are conscious of their new responsibility and because they know we propose to study the

more pressing issues in workshops during the convention: (1) health, education and child welfare, (2) employment, and (3) housing.[53]

The NCNW had been active in the civil rights arena from its organization by Mary McLeod Bethune in 1935. The group worked closely with the NAACP in lobbying for the passage of the antilynching legislation, and in 1938 was instrumental in organizing the Conference on Governmental Cooperation in the Approach to the Problems of Negro Women and Children. In 1940 and 1941, the NCNW was one of the major supporters of A. Philip Randolph's March on Washington Movement and mobilized and sent out letters and information to hundreds of women's groups to obtain their participation. During the war, the NCNW organized the Washington Committee for the Negro Woman in the National Defense to secure increased participation by black women in the National Defense Program. The NCNW was also an active participant in the Committee for Racial Democracy in the Nation's Capital, which was formed in 1943 to bring about the desegregation of governmental facilities for black workers. And along with the AKA's Non-Partisan Council, the NCNW worked to recruit and integrate African American women into the WAVES, WACS, SPARS, and Marines.[54]

Over 660 delegates attended the NCNW convention in November 1947 and endorsed a "Ten-Point Program" which emphasized many of the recommendations made in the report of the President's Committee on Civil Rights. The areas targeted for specific action included the lobbying of members of Congress for the passage of legislation (1) to remove all restrictions on voting in elections and primaries, (2) to end restrictive covenants and similar devices to maintain segregation in housing, (3) to make lynching a federal crime, (4) to provide increased federal funding for education on a nondiscriminatory basis, and (5) to outlaw discrimination in employment on the basis of race, creed, color, or national origin. The Ten-Point Program also called for the NCNW (6) to support the efforts of the United Nations to maintain world order and peace, and (7) to participate in food distribution programs to peoples and countries in need. The NCNW called for (8) an amendment to the Social Security Act which would extend its benefits to domestic and agricultural workers, and (9) increased federal aid for local public health services. The NCNW also committed its membership (10) to the establishment of programs to prevent and control juvenile delinquency. The NCNW "Ten-Point Program" was publicized widely in the black press.[55]

In 1948, when civil rights became one of the dominant issues in national politics, black women's clubs and organizations worked at the grassroots levels to support the policies and positions taken by President Harry Truman. In June 1948, the delegates to the Democratic Convention voted to adopt a strong civil rights platform which called upon the Congress to support President Truman in guaranteeing "the basic and fundamental American principles: (1) the right of full and equal political participation; (2) the right to equal opportunity of employment; (3) the right to security of person; (4) and the right of equal treatment in the service and defense industries." The platform was vehemently opposed by many southern delegates who walked out of the convention and subsequently formed the States' Rights or "Dixiecrat" Party, then ran South Carolina Governor Strom Thurmond for president.[56]

Many black women's groups mobilized to support voter registration campaigns. Mary McLeod Bethune in September 1948 pointed out that the NCNW was a "nonpartisan organization"; however, "some people have not learned how important the franchise is. In all my talks throughout the nation I have urged women to set up block organizations to instruct women on how to register and vote." The *Washington Afro-American* accurately predicted that "if a large number of women are enlisted through this action, the NCNW could indirectly contribute to a Truman victory." ACHR director Norma Boyd made these same points in an Alpha Kappa Alpha "Civil Rights Forum" held in Newark, New Jersey in October 1948.[57]

The NCNW held its thirteenth annual meeting in Washington, DC in October 1948, and similar to the "Ten-Point Program" issued in 1947, the over 1,000 delegates pledged to work "for the writing of the principle of Fair Practice in employment in national law, the abolition of lynching, the abolition of segregation and discrimination in the armed forces, and the elimination of the poll tax and other similar devices as a prerequisite for voting."[58] In addition, the group passed a "Seven-Point Program for Full Citizenship" and resolved that "in order to attain the civic, social, and economic goals which we have set for ourselves, it is essential that we assume full citizenship responsibility. The National Council of Negro Women has as one of its basic program activities training for citizenship and the exercise of the franchise." The group would emphasize in its citizenship training "the importance of the ballot in choosing representatives in government who are in sympathy with the program for the furtherance of Civil and Human Rights."[59] The NCNW's registration drive among black voters in the northern and midwestern states contributed to Harry Truman's come-from-behind victory in the extremely close 1948 presidential election.

In January and February 1948, A. Philip Randolph, president of the Brotherhood of Sleeping Car Porters, and other leaders organized the National Association Against Discrimination in the armed forces. American Council on Human Rights president Norma Boyd was among the black leaders who met with President Truman in February 1948, and threatened the launch of a "civil disobedience movement" against the military draft unless segregation and discrimination was ended in the armed services. In February 1948 Truman issued Executive Order 9981 which banned racial segregation in the Armed Forces and created the President's Committee on Equality of Treatment and Opportunity in the Armed Services. The Committee issued its report *Freedom to Serve* in 1949, which provided a blueprint for the complete desegregation of the U.S. military.[60]

Unfortunately, that same year the antilynching and anti–poll tax legislation, as well as the bill calling for the creation of a permanent Fair Employment Practices Commission, were blocked in the U.S. Congress by southern Democrats.[61] As a result, in November 1949 the NAACP spearheaded the formation of the National Emergency Civil Rights Mobilization, whose purpose was "to break down opposition to the passage of the civil rights bills." Over sixty organizations supported the Civil Rights Mobilization, including the NACW, NCNW, and Alpha Kappa Alpha and Delta Sigma Theta sororities. In December 1949, the Women's Division of the National Emergency Civil Rights Mobilization was formed, headed by Aretha McKinley, an officer in the New York City NAACP. The purpose of the Women's Division was to make black women aware that

> they have a three-fold stake in the fight for civil rights legislation. They have the right to speak up against unfair employment practices since these effect both themselves and their husbands, they are also concerned with discrimination and segregation as these questions apply to housing problems and so directly effect their homes. In addition women have the right to speak up for the future of their children.[62]

Hundreds of black women representing numerous clubs, sororities, and other organizations attended the three-day Civil Rights Conference in Washington, DC, January 15–17, 1950.[63]

In the early 1950s, the NCNW and NACW continued their active roles in the area of civil rights through their participation in programs and activities organized by the NAACP and the National Emergency Civil Rights Mobilization at the local, regional, and national levels. Alpha Kappa Alpha, Delta Sigma Theta, and other black sororities maintained their support for civil rights causes through their affiliation with and financial support of the American Council for Human Rights. By mid-decade, with the launching of the Montgomery Bus Boycott and the huge increase in nonviolent direct action protests to obtain civil rights objectives, the NCNW, NACW, and Alpha Kappa Alpha and Delta Sigma Theta sororities were thrust into the emerging Civil Rights Movement.[64]

In the period from 1915 to 1950, conflicts undoubtedly were generated within and between black women's organizations over skin color, social class background, or even regional differences. At the same time, this survey of the civil rights activities of black women's organizations demonstrates that social activism, as well as feminist ideology, were important aspects of the club women's group identity. These organizations were formed to advance the social, economic, and political conditions for African American women, while at the same time improving the circumstances for African Americans in general. Unlike the situation in the late 1960s and 1970s, there was no conflict between their feminist objectives and civil rights activism. Indeed, for many black women leaders, such as Ida Wells Barnett, Mary Church Terrell, Mary McLeod Bethune, and others, civil rights activism became part of their personal identity.

NOTES

1. Elizabeth Lindsay Davis, *Lifting As They Climb* (Washington, DC: National Association of Colored Women's Clubs, 1933), 21; Charles Harris Wesley, *The History of the National Association of Colored Women's Clubs: A Legacy of Service* (Washington, DC: National Association of Colored Women's Clubs, 1984), v.

2. *Chicago Defender*, July 8, 1939; See also *Indianapolis Recorder*, July 1, 1939.

3. *Chicago Defender*, August 5, 1939; August 19, 1939.

4. *Baltimore Afro-American*, August 12, 1939. See also Jessie Carney Smith, "Jane M. Bolin," in Jessie Carney Smith, ed., *Notable Black American Women*, Vol. I (Detroit: Gale Research, 1992), 94–95.

5. See, for example, Kenneth Goings, *Uplifting the Race: Black Leadership, Politics, and Culture in the Twentieth Century* (Chapel Hill: University of North Carolina Press, 1996); Evelyn Brooks Higginbotham, *Righteous Discontent: The Women's Movement in the Black Baptist Church, 1880–1990* (1993); and Deborah Gray White, *Too Heavy a Load: Black Women in Defense of Themselves, 1894–1994* (New York: Norton Press, 1999).

6. Evelyn Brooks Higginbotham, "African American Women's History and the Metalanguage of Race," in Darlene Clark Hine, Linda Reed, and Wilma King, eds., *"We Specialize in the Wholly Impossible": A Reader in Black Women's History* (Brooklyn, NY: Carlson Publishing, 1995), 18.

7. For information regarding Randolph and the New Jersey Federation, see Bettye Collier-Thomas, *Daughters of Thunder: Black Women Preachers and Their Sermons, 1850–1979* (San Francisco: Jossey-Bass-Publishers, 1998), 101–6; and Bettye Collier-Thomas, "Minister and Feminist Reformer: The Life of Florence Spearing Randolph," in Judith Weisenfeld and Richard Newman, eds., *This Far By Faith: Readings in African American Women's Religious Biography* (New York: Routledge, 1996), 181–83; *Proceedings of the New Jersey Federation of Colored Women's Clubs Conference and First, Second, and Third Annual Meetings, Trenton, Englewood, Plainfield, Bordentown, July 1915–1918* (n.p., Charles Harmon Printer, 1918), 7–8.

8. Ibid., *Proceedings of the New Jersey Federation*, 9–10.

9. Ibid., 20–21; see also *New York Age*, July 13, 1918; September 6, 1919; August 13, 1921; October 28, 1922.

10. *New York Age*, August 10, 1918; October 19, 1919.

11. Ibid., April 10, 1926; *NACW National Notes*, July 1924, 9.

12. *Pittsburgh Courier*, April 4, 1931.

13. Betty Adams, Historian at Fountain Baptist Church, Summit, NJ, telephone interview with Bettye Collier-Thomas, December 21, 1999.

14. *Pittsburgh Courier*, April 4, 1931.

15. Adams interview; *Pittsburgh Courier*, April 4, 1931.

16. *New York Age*, March 21 and October 10, 1931; October 14, 1933.

17. Quote from *New York Age*, July 11, 1936; see also July 6, 1935 and July 18, 1936.

18. Ibid., July 30, 1938.

19. *New York Age*, July 30, 1938.

20. *New Jersey Afro-American*, July 28, 1942.

21. *Newark Herald*, April 28, 1945.

22. Ibid.

23. Clement Alexander Price, *Freedom Not Far Distant: A Documentary*

History of Afro-Americans in New Jersey (Newark: New Jersey Historical Society, 1980), 260–62.

24. *Washington Afro-American*, May 1 and July 31, 1948.

25. Ibid., January 29, 1949.

26. Ibid., July 16, 31, 1949.

27. Marjorie H. Parker, *Alpha Kappa Alpha: In the Eye of the Beholder* (Washington, DC: Alpha Kappa Alpha, 1978), 8; See also Earnestine Green McNealey, "Alpha Kappa Alpha Sorority," in Darlene Clark Hine, Elsa Barkley Brown, and Rosalyn Terborg-Penn, eds., *Black Women in America: An Historical Encyclopedia* (Brooklyn, NY: Carlson Publishing, 1993), 23–25.

28. Ibid., Parker, *Alpha Kappa Alpha,* 77–92.

29. "The National Non-Partisan Council on Public Affairs," Alpha Kappa Alpha, *Ivy Leaf* 18 (March 1940): 5; see *"The IVY LEAF" 1921–1998*, University Publications of America, Research Collections, Bethesda, Maryland, 1999.

30. Ibid., Parker, *Alpha Kappa Alpha,* 93.

31. Ibid., 94–95. See also *New York Age*, December 14, 1940.

32. *New York Age*, December 14, 1940.

33. Parker, *Alpha Kappa Alpha,* 95–96; *Washington Afro-American*, April 19, May 17, and June 7, 1941.

34. *Chicago Defender*, July 25, 1942.

35. Ibid., July 25, 1942.

36. Bettye Collier-Thomas, "Recovering the Military History of Black Women," *Minerva's Musings*, 1, no. 1 (Spring 1983): 76–80; Lorraine Underwood, "Minority Women and the Military," *LEGACY*, 4, no. 3 (Spring 1991): 5–7; Brenda L. Moore, "African American Women in the U.S. Military," *Armed Forces and Society: An Interdisciplinary Journal*, 17, no. 3 (Spring 1991): 363–84.

37. *New York Age*, October 24, 1942. See also Parker, *Alpha Kappa Alpha*, 95–97.

38. *New York Age*, July 24, 31, 1943.

39. "House Resolution 522," April 28, 1944, copy in Series 18, Box 1, "Alpha Kappa Alpha, 1930s, 1943–49," National Council of Negro Women Papers, Bethune Council House National Historic Site (hereafter cited as BCH-NHS).

40. *Chicago Defender*, June 10, 1944.

41. Ibid., November 4, 1944.

42. Ibid., November 11, 1944.

43. Norma A. Boyd to Franklin D. Roosevelt, October 21, 1944, in Series 18, Box 1, AKA, 1930s, 1943–49, BCH-NHS.

44. *New York Age*, December 1, 29, 1945.

45. Parker, *Alpha Kappa Alpha,* 97–99; See also Hanes Walton, Jr., *Black Women at the United Nations: The Politics, a Theoretical Model, and the Documents* (San Bernardino, CA: The Borgo Press, 1995).

46. Parker, *Alpha Kappa Alpha,* 101–6.

47. Ibid.

48. For information on the FEPC, see Herbert Garfinkel, *When Negroes March: The March on Washington Movement in the Organizational Politics for FEPC* (Glencoe, IL: Free Press, 1959).

49. *Chicago Defender*, February 23, 1946; *Washington Afro-American*, April 5, 1947.

50. *Baltimore Afro-American*, August 10, 1946; *Chicago Defender*, August 10, 1946. The participants in the forum were Thomasina Johnson Norford, Anna Arnold Hedgeman, Venice Spraggs, Elsie Austin, Georgia Ellis Jones, and Jennetta Welch Brown.

51. *Chicago Defender*, August 10, 1946.

52. President's Committee on Civil Rights, *To Secure These Rights* (Washington, DC: Government Printing Office, 1947), 3.

53. NCNW Press Release, November 6, 1947, in Series 2, Box 3, folder 35, NCNW Papers, BCH-NHS.

54. Bettye Collier-Thomas, *National Council of Negro Women, 1935–1980* (Washington, DC: NCNW, 1981), 2–7; Collier-Thomas, "Recovering the Military History of Black Women," 76–80.

55. Press Release, November 6, 1947; November 15, 1947, Series 2, Box 3, folder 35, NCNW Papers, BCH-NHS. See also *Baltimore Afro-American*, November 8, 15, 22, 1947.

56. Peter M. Bergman and Mort M. Bergman, *The Chronological History of the Negro in America* (New York: New American Library, 1969), 517–18.

57. *Washington Afro-American*, September 18, 1948; October 30, 1948.

58. *Baltimore Afro-American*, October 23, 1948.

59. "Findings and Recommendations of the Thirteenth Annual Convention, NCNW, October 10–13, 1948," 7–8, in Series 2, Box 3, Folder 41, NCNW Papers, BCH-NHS.

60. *Washington Afro-American*, January 1, 1949. See also Sherie Mershon and Steven Schlossman, *Foxholes and Color Lines: Desegregating the U.S. Armed Services* (Baltimore: Johns Hopkins University Press, 1998); and Paula Pfeiffer, *A. Phillip Randolph and the Struggle for Civil Rights* (Louisiana: Louisiana State University Press, 1995).

61. For detailed information on each of the civil rights bills pending in the U.S. Congress in 1949, see *Congress and Equality: The Bulletin of the American Council on Human Rights* 1 (Summer 1949): 3–5.

62. *New York Age*, January 7, 1950.

63. *Washington Afro-American*, January 28, 1950.

64. McNealey, "Alpha Kappa Alpha," 24; Paula Giddings, "Delta Sigma Theta Sorority," in Hine, Barkley Brown, and Terborg-Penn, eds., *Black Women in America*, 320.

Chapter 3

Behind-the-Scenes View
of a Behind-the-Scenes Organizer
The Roots of Ella Baker's Political Passions

Barbara Ransby

Ella Baker is perhaps best known for her role as a supporting actor in the Civil Rights Movement drama of the 1950s and 1960s. But the breadth and depth of her role in the Black Freedom Movement is often underrated. From the 1930s until her death in 1986, Ella Baker participated in over thirty organizations and campaigns ranging from the Negro cooperative movement during the Depression to the Free Angela Davis campaign in the 1970s. Her best documented role in the modern Civil Rights Movement was first as national director of the Southern Christian Leadership Conference (SCLC), and more importantly as founder and advisor to the Student Nonviolent Coordinating Committee (SNCC) for its first six years of existence. Although many people can claim credit for the political impact SNCC had on the larger Civil Rights Movement and the nation, Ella Baker was probably the single most influential individual within the organization. James Forman, the executive secretary of SNCC, once observed that there were many people who knew the light that was SNCC without ever knowing the spark that was Ella Baker.[1] Kwame Ture (Stokley Carmichael), who succeeded John Lewis as chairman of SNCC in 1966, described Baker as "one of the most powerful individuals, if not the most powerful, in SNCC—no question."[2] Activist, historian, cultural performer, and former SNCC member Bernice Johnson Reagon recognizes Ella Baker as her "political mother."[3]

Ella Baker was a physical and psychological anchor for the Student Nonviolent Coordinating Committee, even though she was not a student, and only partly subscribed to its professed commitment to non-violence.[4] A veteran organizer, and fifty-seven years old when the student-led sit-ins began in February 1960, Baker became a key source of support, guidance, and stability for the youthful leaders, who would come together to officially found SNCC the following October. Baker helped to convene the founding meeting, garnered space and resources, drafted many of the group's early documents, and advised its leaders on strategy, structure, and life. But she did more than that. She provided intellectual and political leadership to SNCC, even as she cast herself as a mere facilitator. The young SNCC leaders would model themselves after Ella Baker, follow her example, and, in practice, build upon her political philosophy: a philosophy based on militant antiracism, grassroots popular democracy, a subversion of traditional class and gender hierarchies, and a long-term vision for fundamental social and economic change.

In addition to the lessons Ella Baker conveyed and the example she set, she also provided SNCC activists with a strong connection to history. A common myth about the Civil Rights Movement, especially the Black Power phase of the movement, is that these periods of intense political protest simply erupted on the national scene with little connection to early periods of struggle. But while the intensity and widely publicized character of the protests may have represented a departure from the past, the spirit of determined resistance did not. Ella Baker often railed against the stereotype that black southerners were passive and complacent before 1955. And if any single life or political career belied this myth, it was hers.

Ella Baker fought on the front lines of the Black Freedom Movement in the United States for over a half century. After her arrival in Harlem in the late 1920s, she immersed herself in the radical political activities there. She condemned Italy's invasion of Ethiopia. She protested the unfair treatment of black domestic workers during the Depression. And she helped launch the Young Negroes Cooperative League to ameliorate the suffering of the poor and explore socialist alternatives to capitalism. During World War II she joined forces with the National Association for the Advancement of Colored People, and traveled throughout the South recruiting new members. She raised funds for the Montgomery Bus Boycott and left her home in New York City to move to Atlanta, where she served as the first staff person of the coalition that emerged out of it, the Southern Christian

Leadership Conference. Most notably, in 1960 Ella Baker was instrumental in the formation of the Student Nonviolent Coordinating
Committee, an organization that would become a pivotal and cat-
alytic force within the growing liberation movement.

Ella Baker was an advisor, a teacher, and a confidante to many young
people who came of age politically in the 1960s. But she knew much
more about their lives than they knew about hers. In the words of SNCC
leader and Baker protege Robert Moses, "We didn't know much about
Ella's life before SNCC . . . (but) she brought (that) history with her."[5]
Ella Baker is often referred to as a behind-the-scenes leader; in this essay
I will provide a behind-the-scenes view of Baker herself. I will focus on
the ways in which gender, class, and her own history helped to shape
the political views and personal style that the young SNCC activists
came to know in the 1960s. In particular, I will grapple with the ways in
which Ella Baker's family politics, the kindling of her own political passions, and her relationships with other activists—especially women—
influenced her development as a radical political activist and intellectual. What and who motivated her to do the work she did and to do it
the way she did it? What sustained her during her more difficult times?
And what were the private negotiations and trade-offs that allowed her
to be the public figure she was?

Early Intellectual Influences

One of the chief sources of inspiration for Ella Baker's early political
awakening, and one that helped to inform her personal and political
sensibilities, was her early involvement, through her mother, in the
black Baptist women's missionary movement of the early 1900s. Although many of her recollections about her childhood single out her
maternal grandfather as an influential force in her life, it was probably Ella's mother, Georgianna Ross Baker, who had the greatest impact on her thinking and development.[6] Georgianna Baker was a
stern and pious woman, an avid reader, an articulate social activist
with a strong and proud personality.[7] Ella Baker admired her mother
greatly and credited her with her early politicization. In her words: "I
was young when I became active in things and I became active in
things largely because my mother was very active in the field of religion."[8] Ella and her siblings often accompanied their mother to local

and regional missionary meetings, sometimes as participants and sometimes as quiet observers.[9]

Georgianna's strong belief in God and her conviction that such faith must be translated into deeds was the guiding philosophical force in her life. In the minutes of one of her missionary meetings she admonished others to "let Christ take the first place in your vocation and life. Inquire of the Lord what he would have us do. Let us stay on the job for Christ."[10] For her, staying on the job meant making a difference in the here and now. According to Ella Baker, her mother and her female colleagues formed smaller groups within the Black Baptist Church in order for the women "to be able to have some identity of their own."[11] At their meetings Ella observed not simply the ritualistic expressions of faith, but the actual business of applying religious principles, particularly the principles of Christian charity and service, in the real world. The Missionary Association sponsored an orphanage, aided the sick and elderly, funded scholarships for black college students, and provided aid to local church-affiliated grammar schools.[12] Moreover, Ella witnessed this important work being organized and carried out by confident, competent, and committed African American women. These women ran their own meetings, managed their own funds, and maintained a certain margin of autonomy within the church. Their collective example of strength and activism had a distinct effect on Ella's evolving consciousness and self-image.

Georgianna Baker and her religious co-workers preached and practiced an activist woman-centered faith, which was an extension of the Social Gospel doctrine being espoused by white and black Protestant denominations at the same time. Theirs was a religious practice that urged women to act as positive agents for change in the world. In her study of black Baptist women, Evelyn Brooks Higginbotham describes this tradition as a type of black feminist theology. "Black Baptist women encouraged an aggressive womanhood that felt personal responsibility to labor no less than men, for the salvation of the world (and) . . . their evangelical zeal fervently rejected a fragile, passive womanhood or the type preoccupied with fashion, novels, and self-indulgence."[13] This description fit Georgianna Baker perfectly.

Ella Baker respected her mother's fortitude, compassion, and social engagement. And years later, in the mostly secular context of the political and civil rights organizations with which she worked, Ella would, to a large extent, emulate her mother's examples of zealous

and selfless service on behalf of those victimized by injustice and social inequity, albeit armed with a different language and with expanded political objectives. She would also find the courage and self-
confidence to challenge not only dominant political and economic interests, but male dominance and class elitism within the Civil Rights
Movement as well. Ella Baker defied the dominant society's proscrip-
tion about "What a Woman Ought to Be and Do."[14] The foundation
for this defiance had been laid during her girlhood in North Carolina.

Ella Baker built upon a secularized and expanded version of her
mother's social and religious activism, but she also made her own
choices and forged her own path. That path was sometimes a lonely
one. Baker graduated from Shaw University in 1927 and migrated to
New York City, where her political career as an organizer began in
earnest. But she was always, as she put it, committed more to a cause
than an organization. Therefore, at least from a distance, her community appears fragmented. She did not live her political life inside a
single organization. And within each of the organizations with which
she was associated, her outspokenness and unwillingness to compromise on matters of principle, or to concede to the voices of the powerful and well positioned, earned her enemies as well as friends. Since
each of her organizational affiliations was short-lived, her career was
somewhat nomadic. So, then, what sustained her? What kept her optimistic and gave her confidence that her work mattered? The answer,
in part, is that she enjoyed a network of relationships that nurtured
her emotionally and intellectually over the years, particularly her relationships with other women activists, many of which transcended
political affiliations and endured over many years.

Ironically, Ella Baker's most visible political affiliations were with
prominent men. She once commented, "I was in lots of situations
where I was the only black or the only woman."[15] She worked closely
with some of the best known black male political leaders of the twentieth century, including Thurgood Marshall, W. E. B. Du Bois, Walter
White, A. Philip Randolph, and Dr. Martin Luther King, Jr. But while
many of the men she worked with were well known, it was the
women with whom she worked that she knew well and who knew
her the best. During the 1930s, she maintained an eclectic circle of
friends, drawn from her co-workers on the Worker's Education Project of the Works Progress Administration (WPA). The program was
run by a woman, and staffed primarily by women teachers. Its pur-

pose was to offer courses and workshops for adult workers, many of whom were active in the burgeoning trade union movement. It was a gathering place for leftists of all types. "We had a lovely time," Baker recalled, "we talked politics and revolution all day."[16]

Baker's area of expertise was consumer affairs. She ran workshops and classes all over Harlem advocating buying co-ops and consumer clubs to offset the ravages of the depression and to explore alternatives to capitalist social relations.[17] She targeted women's groups in Harlem such as the Harlem Nurses Association and the Harlem Housewives League. After work Baker would go out for a beer with her friend Emma Lance, a WPA worker, where they discussed "affairs of the heart," in Emma's words.[18] These personal relations with strong activist women kept Ella Baker going.

The Harlem branch of the YWCA was another source of emotional and intellectual sustenance for Ella Baker during the bleak years of the Depression. The Harlem Y was a focus of activity, staffed by strong, bright, and determined black women, such as Dorothy Height, Anna Arnold Hedgeman, Viola Lewis Waiters, and Margaret Douglass.[19] Black feminist poet, lawyer, and activist Pauli Murray, who was also a dear friend of Ella Baker's for many years, described the group as follows:

> None of these women would have called themselves feminists in the 1930s, but they were strong independent personalities who, because of their concerted efforts to rise above the limitations of race and sex, and to help younger women do the same, shared a sisterhood that foreshadowed the revival of the feminist movement in the 1960s.[20]

This was one of the places where Ella Baker found the inspiration and intellectual challenges that aided her in defining her own identity as a political activist, a woman, and an intellectual. She spent many hours at the Y forging ties with this thriving black women's community.

Ella Baker and Pauli Murray, both native North Carolinians, enjoyed a lifelong friendship and comradeship, which began when they worked together on the same WPA project. Murray later supported Baker's leadership initiatives in the NAACP in the 1940s; both women were candidates for office on the Liberal Party ticket in the early 1950s; and Murray again applauded and encouraged Baker's work with SNCC in the 1960s.[21]

Marvel Cooke, who was a Communist Party organizer and Ella

Baker's co-author of a 1935 article on black domestic workers, described Baker as a "new kind of Negro woman. She was tough, smart and out to make a difference. . . ."[22] These words could have also described Cooke. A writer, former aide to W. E. B. Du Bois, and close friend to Paul and Eslanda Robeson, Marvel Cooke was as much of a radical activist as Ella Baker. These women friends and associates helped to mold the political activist that Ella Baker was becoming. Although one of the main political activities that Baker was involved in during this period was the Young Negroes Cooperative League, working closely with George Schuyler and a core of mainly male leaders, she still maintained an intimate circle of close female friends in whom she confided and who provided a much-needed support system.

During the 1940s, when Ella Baker found herself working first as a field secretary and then as a national director of branches of the NAACP, she again developed and maintained some strong friendships. Perhaps her closest relationship there was with membership secretary Lucille Black, who was one of the anchors of the NAACP National Office for over thirty years. One male colleague and former suitor described Lucille as a "tall, voluptuous brown-skinned woman with a hearty laugh" who worked hard and enjoyed a stiff shot of bourbon now and then. Lucille read Kafka, loved jazz, hated cooking, and never married. She was Ella Baker's friend and confidante long after Baker had parted ways with the NAACP. Theirs was typical of the kind of enduring relationships Ella maintained throughout her adult life.[23]

Baker's job with the Association was not an easy one. For one thing, it called for her to travel several months out of the year. While on the road she worked almost to the point of exhaustion and often doubted whether the time and energy she invested was actually paying off in results. Travel was difficult, office space and supplies were limited, and the hectic pace was taxing on her health and spirits. Traveling mostly by train, Baker would typically leave one town on Sunday morning after a week-long visit, only to have another series of meetings with local officials upon her arrival in the next town, followed by speeches at up to five churches on a given Sunday afternoon, while suffering the indignities of Jim Crow segregation along the way.[24]

In the course of her work-related travels, Baker maintained an active correspondence with Lucille Black, expressing not only her political analyses of the situations she encountered, but her emotional reactions as well. In one letter Ella complained to Lucille: "Today, I am worn to a frazzle. Train connection[s] are not so good . . . [and the situation] leaves me quite frayed."[25] In another letter she confesses quite candidly:

> The outlook for this trip does not appear rosy. I am constantly challenged to "pass a miracle," which will demonstrate how small, isolated, and rural communities can initiate active branches in the absence of some major tragedy . . . The best I can do is try to jolt or scare them into action, and make an effort to maintain it through correspondence long enough to bring the branch membership up to at least fifty members. But such are the trials of those who must act as Mother Confessor to the Little Folk. So let it be.[26]

These letters seemed to have been an important outlet through which Baker could vent her frustrations and disappointments as she undertook the difficult and dangerous work of grassroots organizing in the Jim Crow South of the 1940s.

Another person to whom Baker grew particularly close during her years at the NAACP national office was a young woman named Charlotte Crump. Crump worked as the association's coordinator of publicity and promotions. She and Ella often went out to lunch or to dinner after work together, where they would relax and, as Charlotte put it, "gripe about this or that."[27] Although some of their correspondence was business-related, there was always a very personal tone to their exchanges. Crump signed her letters "affectionately" or "faithfully" and jokingly chastised Ella to "get a little rest because we don't want to have to carry you into [the offices] on a stretcher when you return."[28] Ella Baker was apparently known for overworking and pushing herself to the limit. Friends like Crump had to constantly remind her to take it easy. These were just some of the personal relationships that nurtured Ella Baker psychologically and emotionally.

Baker had a community of friends and comrades, some men, but mostly women, who provided her with a sounding board for her problems, reassurance of the importance of her work, and a sense that she was not alone. Ella Baker had all this—but *Miss* Baker also had a husband—one whom many of her colleagues never knew existed. While in this essay I have primarily focused on Ella Baker's relationships with other women, I also want to look at how she negotiated her marital relations as a way to gain insights on her gender identity from yet another angle. One of the most complex and difficult areas of Baker's life I have explored is in the area of romance and sexuality. Probably the most mysterious chapter in Ella Baker's private life was her marriage of over ten years to fellow North Carolinian, and Shaw classmate, T. J. Roberts.

Roberts was an eccentric character and the marriage itself was anything but conventional. He was a quiet and unassuming man who did not interfere with Ella's principal passion, which was politics. In fact, Roberts kept such a low profile that when the FBI was spying on Ella Baker in the 1940s, they assumed he was a female relative living with her and apparently had no idea she was married.[29] Many close friends were also unaware of what Baker later referred to as her "domestic arrangement."[30] The marriage was wholly unorthodox. First of all, Ella never assumed her husband's last name, an unusual act of independence in the 1930s. She also did not always confine herself to the same house, or even the same city, to perform whatever wifely duties might have been expected of other women of her generation. She traveled extensively for the NAACP, several months out of the year, leaving Roberts behind.[31] In interviews about her life over the years she repeatedly minimized the importance of her married life upon her political work and bluntly declined to answer probing questions that attempted to unravel her marital mystery. This may have been largely a matter of privacy to Ella Baker, but it had a more tangible political impact as well.

Ella Baker was a role model for younger women in the way that she carried herself in movement circles. One young woman activist recalled that Baker's refusal to talk about her marriage was "the first time I had met a woman who did not tolerate a discussion of her marital status."[32] Whatever the motive for Baker's circumspection, the net effect was to give other women, especially younger ones, a greater sense of autonomy as political actors regardless of their connections or lack of connections to men in the movement. This was an important dynamic since in other social change organizations women were frequently defined, respected, or dismissed based on with whom they were romantically involved. Bernice Reagon described the impact of Ella Baker's actions on her as follows: "This came to mean that I could be on the same board with my father, or women dating men could be on the same committee, and those intimate relationships were not brought into the organization's discussion."[33]

Most of Ella Baker's young proteges in SNCC were not only unaware of her marital status, they knew little or nothing about her personal life at all. It was only after she had been working with the group several years that she confided in a few of them that she had, at one time, been married. It was around 1963, three years after SNCC was founded under Baker's leadership, that the organizational minutes began to occasionally refer to Ella Baker as Mrs. rather than Miss Baker.[34] Interestingly, many of the SNCC activists remember Baker being quite open and frank about almost everything else except her former marriage. "It was one of the few things she just wouldn't talk about," recalled Bernice Johnson Reagon.[35] "When I asked her about her husband she would say 'oh no, it's not important,'" remembers Joyce Ladner.[36]

Whatever her reasons for marrying, it was clear that Baker maintained some ambivalence and trepidation about the confines of traditional married life, especially as it related to women. She remembered quite vividly and with great regret her mother's own eclipsed ambitions. In Ella Baker's eyes, her mother—a strong, capable, talented woman—had been forced to abandon many of her dreams because of her domestic responsibilities, sexism in the larger society, and restrictive gender roles within the black community. In describing her mother, Ella Baker observed, "she was a very bright girl . . . and at the time, of course, that she came along, there were only certain things that women, especially black women, could do . . . and so she taught (for awhile, but) . . . she never worked after she married. And then of course children started coming."[37] Like most women of Georgianna Baker's generation, the experiences of pregnancy and childbirth were painful and dangerous. Georgianna was pregnant a total of eight times, suffering four miscarriages or still births, and one death. Only three births resulted in the children surviving until adulthood.[38]

Ella Baker recalled, "had [mother] not been female, she probably would have gone on into something else. But the time was not yet right for being female and not married and so she married."[39] Baker was intent on not following the same path. But perhaps the time still was not right for being female and not married. Ella Baker did marry. However, she declined to have children of her own, and opted for a rather open and unrestricted marital arrangement that was far from traditional. Even though Ella Baker accepted guardianship of her nine-year-old niece Jackie in 1946, she still acknowledged that if she had any more family responsibilities than that, she would not have been able to do much of the work she did over the years. When asked some years later why she never had children of her own, Ella confessed, "I wasn't interested, really, in having children, per se."[40] Perhaps Baker's lack of interest in giving birth had to do also, in part, with her mother's painful experience in that regard. Interestingly, in conversations and interviews, Baker often downplayed gender issues, yet in her personal and political behavior, she consciously violated most of the social conventions that dictated proper female behavior. She especially rebelled against her socialization as a middle-class black woman.

Another area in which politics were deeply implicated in Ella Baker's personal choices was her analysis of race and class in American society and her own class identification and status. When she was a child, Baker's family was not wealthy but they were better off than most of their black counterparts in the South in the late nineteenth and early twentieth centuries. They were literate landowners in an era when property and education were key measures of class status. Ella Baker graduated as valedictorian of Shaw University in 1927, a feat which placed her among an elite minority of college-educated African Americans.[41] There were certain class privileges that she could have claimed as a result of her background and education, but she never did. She turned down secure teaching jobs—vowing never to teach because that was what was expected of Negro women—to work at low-paying, insecure jobs in civil and human rights organizations instead. As she put it, she literally "eked" out an existence during her entire life. However, this was a choice Baker made consciously and she seemingly had no regrets. In fact, she held the strong conviction that class privilege and material comforts stood in the way of black political leaders effectively leading mass protest struggles.

She observed once while organizing for the NAACP that she was able to bond more readily with local people because she didn't have any mink coats or fancy jewelry to alienate her from those people who had none of these luxuries.[42] She criticized people who bought into the elitist politics of respectability, arguing that the movement had to be as concerned about the civil rights of the town drunk as of the more respectable citizens.

At the same time that Ella Baker criticized some of the more bourgeois and self-possessed tendencies among some sectors of the black middle class, her own middle-class upbringing was steeped in the values of racial uplift and a strong sense of social obligation to those less fortunate.[43] She recognized that the conceptualization and use of privilege could go in many directions. Ultimately, however, she went beyond her family's sense of obligation to the poor and forged a political solidarity with the poor by committing, or at least attempting to commit, the kind of "class suicide" that Guinean revolutionary Amilcar Cabral often referred to in terms of the role of the middle class in the struggle against colonialism. Baker was born into an ascendant black middle class family. She died, eighty-three years later, with virtually no material wealth. As she put it, "I've been identified over a long period of time with people, a lot of whom had nothing."[44] That conscious class allegiance was her choice. Ella Baker was a radical egalitarian and a humanist in her personal life as well as her public pronouncements.

So, what is Ella Baker's lasting political legacy? One of the traits most often cited to describe Baker is her deep and abiding concern for the individuals with whom she worked. SNCC leader Robert Moses recalled "what struck me was that he (Martin Luther King, Jr.) wasn't as interested in me as a person as Ella was."[45] Former student activist Diane Nash echoed a similar sentiment: "Ella would pick me up and dust me off emotionally," after a particularly difficult period.[46] For Ella Baker, politics were not impersonal, academic, or abstract. Politics were immediate and measured in flesh and blood realities. She followed up with local people after the smoke of battle had cleared. Her view was that you have to love the people around you, and those struggling right next to you, as much as the anonymous and amorphous mass of humanity. She was concerned about others, not as faceless victims, but as members of her extended family. In her travels throughout the South on behalf of the NAACP, Baker met hundreds of ordinary black people and she established some enduring relationships. She slept in these people's homes, ate at their tables, spoke in their churches, and earned their trust. And she was never too busy, despite her grueling schedule, to send off a batch of cards expressing gratitude, sympathy, or wishing an ailing branch member a speedy recovery.[47]

A friend who knew Ella Baker for over fifty years recalled how she would meet you on the street and argue one day and then hug you and have you over for a meal the next. She didn't hold grudges and "she exuded a kind of warmth" that I would suggest was as much a by-product of her political views and convictions as it was her personality.[48]

Ella Baker also insisted upon democratic practice, and declined to eclipse such practices for the sake of expediency. Inclusion, debate, and collective decision making were important. Process was important. The means never justified the end, because Baker felt the end was determined in large part by how a movement and a people fought to realize that end. According to Baker, we cannot get a little power and then "ape the insiders" in the way that we treat one another, lest we replicate the same kind of injustices that we set out initially to defeat.

For Ella Baker the ultimate triumph of a leader was his or her ability to suppress ego and ambition and to embrace humility and a spirit of collectivism. This principle coexisted with a militant spirit and a vocal engagement in struggles, internal and external to the movement. Whether Baker was forceful and outspoken versus quiet and unassuming had much to do with the environment she found herself in. When she was being marginalized or excluded by colleagues with inflated egos, she did not hesitate to be assertive. When she was in a position to exercise power and authority, she relented and submitted to a more collective process. The most important task of a radical democrat was to empower others, not oneself. And it was only by distancing the struggle from one's own personal ambitions that any leader could be truly effective. Ella Baker immersed herself in a community of strong and committed activists, many of them, in order to keep herself true to those values. Just as there are no "self-made men," there are no "self-made women." Ella Baker was as much a product of her family, her era, and a vast web of personal and political relationships, as well as her own agency. But Ella Baker was no saint. She made mistakes, doubted herself, and sometimes succumbed to the pressures and frustrations embedded in her life's work. Her friend and colleague, the historian, Vincent Harding, observed that Ella Baker often fantasized that one day she would write her own autobiography, something she never got around to doing.

But she wanted the text to be titled "Making a Life, Not Making a Living." This embodies many aspects of who Baker was and what she represented in the movement—unconcerned with material gains, committed to politics as a passion and not a professional career, and wedded to the humanistic notion that the vision of a different kind of society has to be rooted in a vision of different kinds of human beings. We have to refashion our lives and personal relationships as we attempt to refashion the world. There are no short cuts. It is the richness and complexity of Ella Baker's story that offers us the gift of renewed optimism—that even as the imperfect souls that we are, we have within us, and most importantly together, the ability to not only better understand and chronicle history, but to create our own.

NOTES

1. James Forman, *The Making of Black Revolutionaries* (Seattle, WA: Open Hand Publishing, 1985).

2. Kwame Ture, interview with the author, February 18, 1998, Chicago, IL.

3. Bernice Johnson Reagon, telephone interview with the author, May 5, 1991.

4. As Clayborne Carson points out in his book, *In Struggle: SNCC and the Black Awakening of the 1960s*, the leaders of SNCC had collectively outgrown their name by 1962 when most of the organizers were no longer students, and many of them had begun to talk about nonviolence as a tactic rather than a philosophy.

5. Robert Moses, interview with the author, September 7–9, 1996, Cambridge, MA.

6. Ella Baker recalled her grandfather fondly in several interviews between 1968 and 1988. However, Mitchell Ross died when Ella Baker was six or seven years old and they never lived in the same state. The person with whom she had the most contact and who she describes most vividly was her mother.

7. Jenny Newell, interview with the author, June 10, 1991, typescript, Littleton, NC.

8. Lenore Bredson Hogan, interview with Ella Baker, March 4, 1979, typescript, Highlander Folk School, Monteagle, Tennessee, 15.

9. Ibid., 14.

10. Minutes of the Thirteenth Annual Session of the Women's Auxiliary Progressive Baptist Convention of North Carolina (WAPB), Elizabeth City, NC, Oct. 29–Nov. 1, 1931, 7.

11. Hogan, interview with Ella Baker, 15.

12. WAPB Minutes, Oct. 29–Nov. 1, 1931.

13. Evelyn Brooks Higginbotham, *Righteous Discontent: The Women's Movement in the Black Baptist Church, 1880–1920* (Cambridge: Harvard University Press, 1993), 139.

14. Stephanie J. Shaw, *What a Woman Ought to Be and to Do: Black Professional Women Workers During the Jim Crow Era* (Chicago: University of Chicago Press, 1996).

15. Hogan, interview with Ella Baker, 22.

16. Aldon Morris, Interview with Ella Baker, August 28, 1978, New York City.

17. Works Progress Administration, Workers Services Division, NYC reports,1938–39, Box 19, WPA Papers, National Archives, Washington, DC.

18. Emma Lance, Letter to Ella Baker, circa 1930s, Ella Baker Papers I, document #79, Schomburg Center for Research in Black Culture, New York.

19. Pauli Murray, *Song in a Weary Throat: The Autobiography of a Black Activist, Feminist, Lawyer, Priest and Poet* (Knoxville: University of Tennessee Press, 1989), 74–75.

20. Ibid., 75.

21. Ibid.

22. Marvel Cook, interview with the author, April 14, 1996, Harlem, NY.

23. Herbert Hill, interview with the author, May 24, 1996, Madison, WI.

24. NAACP Papers, Series II, Box C307, General Branch Files, Library of Congress (hereafter cited as LOC). The letters throughout the file illustrate this pattern.

25. Ella Baker, Letter to Lucille Black, May 4, 1942, NAACP Papers, II, Box A572, folder: "Staff, Ella Baker, 1940–1942," LOC.

26. Ibid., May 25, 1942.

27. Charlotte Crump, Letter to Ella Baker, Oct. 9, 1941, NAACP Papers, Series II, Box A572, folder: "Staff, Ella Baker, 1940–1942," LOC.

28. Charlotte Crump, Letter to Ella Baker, March 2, 1942, Baker to Wilkins, April 1, 1942, and Walter White, Memo to Ella Baker, Oct. 18, 1941, NAACP Papers, Series II, Box A-572, folder: "Staff, Ella Baker, 1940–1959," LOC.

29. FBI Files on Ella Baker, NY 100-136886-6, misc. report, Sept. 10, 1941.

30. Casey Hayden and Sue Thrasher, interview with Ella Baker, April 19, 1977, New York, Southern Oral History Project: University of North Carolina, Chapel Hill, 58. See also Conrad Lynn and Herbert Hill interviews.

31. Although the exact dates of her marriage are not verifiable (no record in NC, NY, or NJ), her niece, Jackie Brockington, and her close friend, Lenore Taitt Magubane, both recall she was still married in the mid-1950s.

32. Bernice Johnson Reagon, telephone interview with the author, May 5, 1991.

33. Ibid.

34. Student Nonviolent Coordinating Committee Papers, 1959–1972, microfilm version, "Chairman's Files, 1960–63."

35. Bernice Johnson Reagon, telephone interview with the author, April 9, 1991. Jackie Brockington declined to discuss Roberts in much detail because, in her words, "Aunt Ella never wanted to talk about it (the marriage)."

36. Joyce Ladner, interview with the author, March 12, 1991, Washington, DC.

37. Hogan, interview with Ella Baker, 86.

38. Hayden and Thrasher, 8.

39. Morris, Interview with Ella Baker.

40. Ellen Cantarow, Susan Gushee O'Malley, and Sharon H. Strom, *Moving the Mountain: Women Working for Social Change* (Old Westbury, NY: Feminist Press, 1980), 73.

41. Catalogues and Bulletins, 1927, Shaw University Archives, Raleigh, NC.

42. Morris, interview with Ella Baker.

43. Ibid. See Hayden and Thrasher interview for descriptions of Baker's family's class identification. For further discussion of social activism and the black middle class, see Darlene Clark Hine, *Speak Truth to Power: Black Professional Class in United States History* (Brooklyn, NY: Carlson Publishing, 1996); Shaw, *What a Woman Ought to Be and Do*.

44. Hogan, interview with Ella Baker, 79–80.

45. Robert Moses, interview with the author.

46. Diane Nash, interview with the author, March 4, 1993, Chicago, IL.

47. Ella Baker, Memo to Walter White, May 3, 1946, NAACP Papers, Series II, Box C307, General Branch Files.

48. John Henrik Clark, interview with the author, April 5, 1996, Harlem, NY.

Part II

Personal Narratives

Part II draws on the recollections of three important women in the Civil Rights Movement—Rosa Parks, Charlayne Hunter Gault, and Dorothy I. Height—and allows them to convey, in their own words, the momentous events in which each of them participated. These personal testimonies hold particular importance because the voices of black women have seldom been given recognition outside or even within the Civil Rights Movement.

This section begins with Rosa Parks' dramatic retelling of the incidents surrounding her arrest on December 1, 1955 and the launching of the Montgomery Bus Boycott. Parks emphasizes that at the time she never considered that she might provide the NAACP with a test case to challenge legal segregation practiced by the local transit company. Parks engaged in this extremely important act of resistance because she was "tired of giving in." Given her reputation in the community, Parks became the perfect person to rally around. Most blacks in Montgomery agreed with the young woman who announced at Parks' trial, "They've messed with the wrong one now." Parks also describes the planning and execution of the Montgomery Bus Boycott, and makes it clear that despite the loss of their jobs, she and her husband remained active in the boycott, dispatching cars, attending meetings, and raising money for the cause.

In the essay, "'Heirs to a Legacy of Struggle': Charlayne Hunter Integrates the University of Georgia," Charlayne Hunter Gault describes the legal maneuvering that took place to allow her and fellow classmate Hamilton Earl Holmes in 1961 to become the first African Americans to enroll at the University of Georgia. The self-esteem instilled in Hunter Gault by her grandmother while growing up in Atlanta allowed her to deflect much of the abuse she received when she was finally admitted to the school. Hunter Gault makes the connection between the events at the university and the subsequent desegregation of public elementary and high schools in Georgia.

In the early 1960s, Dorothy I. Height, as president of the National Council of Negro Women (NCNW), was also a member of the Council of United Civil Rights Leadership, the informal organization that included civil rights leaders Martin Luther King, Jr., A. Philip Randolph, Whitney M. Young, James Farmer, and John Lewis. Height points out that black women had demonstrated their commitment to the Civil Rights Movement in many ways, including the formation of vital organizations, such as the NCNW's Educational Foundation which provided college scholarships for civil rights activists. Despite the important role played by black women in the movement, Height reveals that the male leaders often refused to grant them public recognition. In the essay "'We Wanted the Voice of a Woman to Be Heard': Black Women and the 1963 March on Washington," Height describes how black women were prohibited from addressing the crowd of over 200,000 people. Attorney and civil rights activist Pauli Murray delivered a speech in the Fall of 1963 which dramatically expressed black women's disaffection and frustrations over their treatment by male civil rights leaders. Height points out that their treatment and Pauli Murray's statement raised the feminist consciousness of many African American women who decided that they would no longer continue to suffer sexism silently in the struggle to end racism and discrimination in American society.

Chapter 4

"Tired of Giving In"
The Launching of the Montgomery Bus Boycott

Rosa Parks

People always say that I didn't give up my seat because I was tired, but that isn't true. I was not tired physically, or no more tired than I usually was at the end of a working day. I was not old, although some people have an image of me as being old then. I was forty-two. No, the only tired I was, was tired of giving in.

The driver of the bus saw me still sitting there, and he asked was I going to stand up. I said, "No." He said, "Well, I'm going to have you arrested." Then I said, "You may do that." These were the only words we said to each other. I didn't even know his name, which was James Blake, until we were in court together. He got out of the bus and stayed outside for a few minutes, waiting for the police.

As I sat there, I tried not to think about what might happen. I knew that anything was possible. I could be manhandled or beaten. I could be arrested. People have asked me if it occurred to me then that I could be the test case the NAACP had been looking for. I did not think about that at all. In fact if I had let myself think too deeply about what might happen to me, I might have gotten off the bus. But I chose to remain.

Meanwhile there were people getting off the bus and asking for transfers, so that began to loosen up the crowd, especially in the back of the bus. Not everyone got off, but everybody was very quiet. What conversation there was, was in low tones; no one was talking out loud. It would have been quite interesting to have seen the whole bus empty out. Or if the other three had stayed where they were, because if they'd had to arrest four of us instead of one, then that would have given me a little support. But it didn't matter. I never thought hard of them at all and never even bothered to criticize them.

Eventually two policemen came. They got on the bus, and one of them asked me why I didn't stand up. I asked him, "Why do you all push us around?" He said to me, and I quote him exactly, "I don't know, but the law is the law and you're under arrest." One policeman picked up my purse, and the second one picked up my shopping bag and escorted me to the squad car. In the squad car they returned my personal belongings to me. They did not put their hands on me or force me into the car. After I was seated in the car, they went back to the driver and asked him if he wanted to swear out a warrant. He answered that he would finish his route and then come straight back to swear out the warrant. I was only in custody, not legally arrested, until the warrant was signed.

As they were driving me to the city desk, at City Hall, near Court Street, one of them asked me again, "Why didn't you stand up when the driver spoke to you?" I did not answer. I remained silent all the way to City Hall.

As we entered the building, I asked if I could have a drink of water, because my throat was real dry. There was a fountain, and I was standing right next to it. One of the policemen said yes, but by the time I bent down to drink, another policeman said, "No, you can't drink no water. You have to wait until you get to the jail." So I was denied the chance to drink a sip of water. I was not going to do anything but wet my throat. I wasn't going to drink a whole lot of water, even though I was quite thirsty. That made me angry, but I did not respond.

At the city desk they filled out the necessary forms as I answered questions such as what my name was and where I lived. I asked if I could make a telephone call and they said, "No." Since that was my first arrest, I didn't know if that was more discrimination because I was black or if it was standard practice. But it seemed to me to be more discrimination. Then they escorted me back to the squad car, and we went to the city jail on North Ripley Street.

I wasn't frightened at the jail. I was more resigned than anything else. I don't recall being real angry, not enough to have an argument. I was just prepared to accept whatever I had to face. I asked again if I could make a telephone call. I was ignored.

They told me to put my purse on the counter and to empty my

pockets of personal items. The only thing I had in my pocket was a tissue. I took that out. They didn't search me or handcuff me.

I was then taken to an area where I was fingerprinted and where mug shots were taken. A white matron came to escort me to my jail cell, and I asked again if I might use the telephone. She told me that she would find out.

The matron returned and told me to come out of the cell. I did not know where I was going until we reached the telephone booth. She gave me a card and told me to write down who I was calling and the telephone number. She placed a dime in the slot, dialed the number, and stayed close by to hear what I was saying.

I called home. My husband and mother were both there. She answered the telephone. I said, "I'm in jail. See if Parks will come down here and get me out."

She wanted to know, "Did they beat you?"

I said, "No, I wasn't beaten, but I am in jail."

She handed him the telephone, and I said, "Parks, will you come get me out of jail?"

He said, "I'll be there in a few minutes." He didn't have a car, so I knew it would be longer. But while we were still on the phone, a friend came by in his car. He'd heard about my being in jail and had driven to our place on Cleveland Court to see if he could help. He said he'd drive Parks to the jail.

The matron then took me back to the cell.

As Parks' friend had indicated, the word was already out about my arrest. Mr. Nixon had been notified by his wife, who was told by a neighbor, Bertha Butler, who had seen me escorted off the bus. Mr. Nixon called the jail to find out what the charge was, but they wouldn't tell him. Then he had tried to reach Fred Gray, one of the two black lawyers in Montgomery, but he wasn't home. So finally Mr. Nixon called Clifford Durr, the white lawyer who was Mrs. Virginia Durr's husband. Mr. Durr called the jail and found out that I'd been arrested under the segregation laws. He also found out what the bail was.

Meanwhile Parks had called a white man he knew who could raise the bail. His friend took him over to the man's house to pick him up. I don't remember how much the bail was.

Just then the matron came to let me know that I was being released. Mrs. Durr was the first person I saw as I came through the iron mesh door with matrons on either side of me. There were tears in her eyes, and she seemed shaken, probably wondering what they had done to me. As soon as they released me, she put her arms around me, and hugged and kissed me as if we were sisters.

I was real glad to see Mr. Nixon and Attorney Durr too. We went to the desk, where I picked up my personal belongings and was given a trial date. Mr. Nixon asked that the date be the following Monday, December 5, 1955, explaining that he was a Pullman porter and would be out of Montgomery until then. We left without very much conversation, but it was an emotional moment. I didn't realize how much being in jail had upset me until I got out.

As we were going down the stairs, Parks and his friends were driving up, so I got in the car with them, and Mr. Nixon followed us home.

By the time I got home, it was about nine-thirty or ten at night. My mother was glad to have me home and wanted to know what she could do to make me comfortable. I told her I was hungry (for some reason I had missed lunch that day), and she prepared some food for me. Mrs. Durr and my friend Bertha Butler were there, and they helped my mother. I was thinking about having to go to work the next day, but I knew I would not get to bed anytime soon.

Everyone was angry about what had happened to me and talking about how it should never happen again. I knew that I would never, never ride another segregated bus, even if I had to walk to work. But it still had not occurred to me that mine could be a test case against the segregated buses.

Then Mr. Nixon asked if I would be willing to make my case a test case against segregation. I told him I'd have to talk with my mother and husband. Parks was pretty angry. He thought it would be as difficult to get people to support me as a test case as it had been to develop a test case out of Claudette Colvin's experience. We discussed and debated the question for a while. In the end Parks and my mother supported the idea. They were against segregation and were willing to fight it. And I had worked on enough cases to know that a ruling could not be made without a plaintiff. So I agreed to be the plaintiff.

Mr. Nixon was happy as could be when I told him yes. I don't recall exactly what he said, but according to him, he said, "My God, look what segregation has put in my hands." What he meant by that was that I was a perfect plaintiff. "Rosa Parks worked with me for twelve years prior to this," he would tell reporters later.

> She was secretary for everything I had going—the Brotherhood of Sleeping Car Porters, NAACP, Alabama Voters' League, all of those things. I knew she'd stand on her feet. She was honest, she was clean, she had integrity. The press couldn't go out and dig up something she did last year, or last month, or five years ago. They couldn't hang nothing like that on Rosa Parks.

I had no police record, I'd worked all my life, I wasn't pregnant with an illegitimate child. The white people couldn't point to me and say that there was anything I had done to deserve such treatment except to be born black.

Meanwhile Fred Gray, the black attorney, had called Jo Ann Robinson and told her about my arrest. She got in touch with other leaders of the Women's Political Council, and they agreed to call for a boycott of the buses starting Monday, December 5, the day of my trial. So on the Thursday night I was arrested, they met at midnight at Alabama State, cut a mimeograph stencil, and ran off 35,000 handbills. The next morning she and some of her students loaded the handbills into her car, and she drove to all the local black elementary and junior high and high schools to drop them off so the students could take them home to their parents.

This is what the handbill said:

> This is for Monday, December 5, 1955.

> Another Negro woman has been arrested and thrown into jail because she refused to get up out of her seat on the bus and give it to a white person.

> It is the second time since the Claudette Colvin case that a Negro woman has been arrested for the same thing. This has to be stopped.

> Negroes have rights, too, for if Negroes did not ride the buses, they could not operate. Three-fourths of the riders are Negroes, yet we are arrested, or have to stand over empty seats. If we do not do something to stop these arrests, they will continue. The next time it may be you, or your daughter, or mother.

> This woman's case will come up on Monday. We are, therefore, asking every Negro to stay off the buses Monday in protest of the arrest and

trial. Don't ride the buses to work, to town, to school, or anywhere on Monday.

You can afford to stay out of school for one day. If you work, take a cab, or walk. But please, children and grown-ups, don't ride the bus at all on Monday. Please stay off all buses Monday.

Early that Friday morning, Mr. Nixon called the Reverend Ralph David Abernathy, minister of the First Baptist Church. Mr. Nixon had decided that black ministers could do more to mobilize support in the community than anyone else. He also called eighteen other ministers and arranged a meeting for that evening. Mr. Nixon had to work as a porter on the Montgomery–Atlanta–New York route, so he would be unable to attend, but he talked to them all about what he wanted them to do.

On the morning of Friday, December 2, after I made that call I promised to make, I called Felix Thomas, who operated a cab company, and took a cab to work. I was not going to ride the bus anymore. Mr. John Ball, who was in charge of men's alterations at Montgomery Fair, was surprised to see me. He said, "I didn't think you would be here. I thought you would be a nervous wreck." I said, "Why should going to jail make a nervous wreck out of me?" And then as soon as I got off for lunch, I went to Fred Gray's office.

Ever since Fred had opened his law practice in Montgomery, I had often done that. I'd pick up something from the store for my lunch. He usually brought his lunch. We would eat lunch together, and then sometimes I would answer the telephone while he ran out and did an errand or something, and then it was time for me to go back to work. Fred didn't have a secretary, and I often helped him out. The day after I was arrested, Fred Gray's office was like a beehive. People were calling and dropping by to ask about the boycott and the meeting the ministers had called for that night.

After work, I went to that meeting at the Dexter Avenue Baptist Church. I explained how I had been arrested, and then there were long discussions about what to do. Some of the ministers wanted to talk about how to support the protest, but others wanted to talk about whether or not to have a protest. Many of them left the meeting before any decisions were made. But most of those who stayed agreed to talk about the protest in their Sunday sermons and to hold another meeting on Monday evening to decide if the protest should continue.

A group of ministers at that meeting formed a committee to draft a shorter leaflet that was basically a condensation of the leaflet that Jo Ann Robinson and the others of the Women's Political Council had written. It said:

> Don't ride the bus to work, to town, to school, or any place on Monday, December 5. Another Negro Woman has been arrested and put in jail because she refused to give up her bus seat. Don't ride the buses to work, to town, to school, or anywhere on Monday. If you work, take a cab, or share a ride, or walk. Come to a mass meeting Monday at 7:00 P.M., at the Holt Street Baptist Church for further instruction.

On Sunday the *Montgomery Advertiser* ran a copy of Jo Ann Robinson's handbill on the front page, and that helped spread the word to people who might have missed the leaflets or didn't go to church. But no one could be sure if the protest would be successful. Just because they read a leaflet or heard about it in church, it didn't mean that people would stay away from the buses. All eighteen black-owned cab companies in Montgomery had agreed to make stops at all the bus stops and charge only ten cents, the same fare as on the buses. But people would have to wait for a cab that had room for them. To make matters worse, it looked like rain for Monday.

The sky was dark on Monday morning, but that didn't make any difference. Most black people had finally had enough of segregation on the buses. They stayed off those buses. They waited at the bus stops for the black-owned cabs to come along. Or they walked or got a ride. As a result, the Montgomery city buses were practically empty. Oh, a few black people took the buses, but they were mostly people who had not heard about the protest. Some of them were scared away from the buses. The city police had vowed to protect anyone who wanted to ride, and each bus had two motorcycle escorts. But some of the people who didn't know what was going on thought the police were there to arrest them for riding the buses, not to protect them. And then there were those few who didn't want to be inconvenienced. When the bus they were on passed a bus stop full of black people waiting for cabs, they ducked down low so nobody would see them.

That day I had no idea what the result was going to be, but I think everybody, I think as Mr. Nixon said, "We surprised ourselves." Never before had black people demonstrated so clearly how much those city buses depended on their business. More important, never before had the black community of Montgomery united in protest against segregation on the buses.

I didn't go to work that Monday. Instead that morning I went down to the courthouse for my trial. Parks went with me. I did not spend a lot of time planning what to wear, but I remember very clearly that I wore a straight, long-sleeved black dress with a white collar and cuffs, a small black velvet hat with pearls across the top, and a charcoal-gray coat. I carried a black purse and wore white gloves. I was not especially nervous. I knew what I had to do.

A lot of folks were down at the courthouse. Some people couldn't get in. Parks was almost prohibited from entering the courthouse. But when he said he was my husband, he was permitted to enter. You could hardly see the street for the crowds. Many members of the NAACP Youth Council were there, and they were all shouting their support.

There was a girl in the crowd named Mary Frances. She had a high-pitched voice, and it just came through the air: "Oh, she's so sweet. They've messed with the wrong one now." She said it like a little chant, "They've messed with the wrong one now."

It wasn't a long trial. The bus driver was the main prosecution witness. Only then did I learn what his name was, James F. Blake from Semen, Alabama in Elmore County.

The prosecution also called as a witness a white woman who testified that there had been a vacant seat in the back of the bus and that I had refused to take it. This was not true. Later I learned that Professor J. E. Pierce, who had served with me on the NAACP defense committee . . . , was very upset about the woman's statement. He told Mr. Nixon, "You can always find some damn white woman to lie."

I was not called to testify in my own behalf. Although my lawyers, Charles Langford and Fred Gray, entered a plea of "Not Guilty" for me, they did not intend to try to defend me against the charges. The point of making mine a test case was to allow me to be found guilty and then to appeal the conviction to a higher court. Only in higher courts could the segregation laws actually be changed, because the judges in the local courts were not going to do anything to change the way things were. So I was found guilty of violating the segregation laws and given a suspended sentence. I was fined $10.00, plus $4.00 in court costs. The crowd reacted angrily, but there was no organized protest.

Earlier that day Reverend Abernathy, who was about twenty-nine years old at the time, and some other ministers had met and decided to form the Montgomery Improvement Association (MIA). Mr. Nixon was there, and so was Fred Gray. The reason they wanted to form a brand-new organization was that they thought it would be better than just leaving the organizing to an established group like the NAACP. The NAACP was a relatively weak organization in Alabama, it was not a mass organization. Membership was kind of small, and you could hardly get people to join. They also wanted to rule out the NAACP so that the powers that be could not charge that this demonstration, this show of strength, was being led by outside agitators. That's what the whites liked to do, say that any trouble was caused by outside agitators. They refused to believe that black people in Montgomery had the courage to stand up for their rights.

So they met that afternoon, and then they decided they should elect a president, and they elected the Reverend Martin Luther King, Jr., pastor of the Dexter Avenue Baptist Church.

At the time I didn't know Dr. King. I had met him in August 1955 when he was guest speaker at an NAACP meeting, but I didn't often attend the Dexter Avenue Baptist Church, which was right across the street from the big white state capitol building with its Confederate flag. I found out later that I knew his wife, Coretta. I did not know her well, but I had been to concerts where she sang. I didn't even know she was married to a minister.

Dr. King was new to Montgomery, and Dr. Abernathy had been trying to get him active in civil rights work. Rufus Lewis attended Dexter Avenue Baptist Church and had a very good opinion of what registered voters could do there. It was Rufus Lewis who nominated Dr. King to be president of the MIA.

The advantage of having Dr. King as president was that he was so new to Montgomery and to civil rights work that he hadn't been there long enough to make any strong friends or enemies. Mr. Nixon thought he was a good choice. That night they had the meeting at the Holt Street Baptist Church, which was right in the black community so people wouldn't be afraid to attend. They didn't know how many people to expect, and they were not prepared for how many showed up. People filled that church, and hundreds more stood outside, so they set up a loudspeaker system so those people outside could hear what was going on inside. The meeting was already on when I got there, and I had a hard time getting into the church because there were so many people, inside and outside. I made it to the platform, and they gave me a seat.

The main thing they wanted to decide at that meeting was whether to continue the boycott. Some people thought we should quit while we were still ahead. And hardly anybody thought the boycott could go longer than the end of the week, which was four more days. If it did, it could be very dangerous, because everyone knew the whites wouldn't stand for it.

Mr. Nixon spoke first, as I recall. He was probably worried that people wouldn't really support a long boycott. He remembered all those years when it had been impossible to get black people to stand together. He said,

> You who are afraid, you better get your hat and coat and go home. This is going to be a long-drawn-out affair. I want to tell you something: For years and years I've been talking about how I didn't want the children who came along behind me to have to suffer the indignities that I've suffered all these years. Well, I've changed my mind—I want to enjoy some of that freedom myself.

Dr. King was introduced to the audience as the president of the new Montgomery Improvement Association. He was a fine speaker, and he gave a speech that really got the crowd excited. He received loud cheers and applause and Amens. Then I was introduced. I had asked did they want me to say anything. They said, "You have had enough and you have said enough and you don't have to speak." So I didn't speak. The other people spoke. I didn't feel any particular need to speak. I enjoyed listening to the others and seeing the enthusiasm of the audience.

After that the Reverend Ralph Abernathy read the list of demands that the Montgomery Improvement Association was going to present to the bus company and the city's white leaders. There were three demands: (1) courteous treatment on the buses; (2) first-come, first-served seating, with whites in front and blacks in back; (3) hiring of black drivers for the black bus routes. Then he asked the audience to vote on these demands by standing if they wanted to continue the boycott and make the demands. People started getting up, one or two at a time at first, and then more and more, until every single person in that church was standing, and outside the crowd was cheering "Yes!"

The boycott lasted through that week, and then through the next. No one had any idea how long it would last. Some people said it couldn't last, but it seemed like those who said that were the white people and not us. The whites did everything they could do to stop it.

The police started getting after the groups of blacks who were waiting at the bus stops for the black-owned cabs to pick them up. Then they threatened to arrest the cab drivers if they did not charge their regular fare, which I think was forty-five cents, to go downtown instead of ten cents like the buses charged. White private citizens resisted the boycott too.

A lot of people lost their jobs because they supported the boycott. Both Parks and I lost our jobs, but neither of us was fired. He resigned. Mr. Armstrong, the white owner of the private barbering concession at Maxwell Field Air Force Base, issued an order that there was to be no discussion of "the bus protest or Rosa Parks in his establishment." Parks said he would not work anywhere his wife's name could not be mentioned.

I was discharged from Montgomery Fair department store in January of 1956, but I was not told by the personnel officer that it was because of the boycott. I do not like to form in my mind an idea that I don't have any proof of. The young man who ran the tailor shop at Montgomery Fair had opened his own shop down the street, and he stayed at the store through Christmas only because he wanted to get his bonus money. Then the first week of January he was just going to work full-time in his own shop. So the explanation they gave me about not keeping me on was that they didn't have a tailor. Of course, I could do the stitching work, the work of the shop, but I had never been required to do any fitting of men's clothing in the store. The young man who was working as a helper didn't have any experience in fitting at all. They closed the shop. They gave me two weeks' pay and my bonus money, and I went home.

This was a blessing in a way, I guess, because then I didn't have to worry about how I was going to get to and from work without riding the buses. After that I worked at home, taking in sewing. I started traveling quite a bit, making appearances because of my arrest and the boycott. And then I did work for the MIA.

I was on the executive board of directors of the MIA and I did whatever was needed. I dispensed clothing and shoes to people who needed them. We had an abundance of clothing and shoes sent to us from all parts of the country. Many people needed those things because they were out of work and unable to buy clothing. Those who had jobs wore out many pairs of shoes walking to and from work. I also worked for a short while as a dispatcher for the MIA Transportation Committee.

When the police started arresting cab drivers for not charging full fare, the MIA asked for volunteer drivers. Jo Ann Robinson was one. The churches collected money and bought several station wagons. Ordinary black people contributed, and so did some important white people in Montgomery, like the Durrs. As a dispatcher, I was responsible for taking calls from people who needed rides and then making calls to the drivers of private cars and the church station wagons to see that the people were picked up wherever they were.

After a while quite a sophisticated system was developed. There were twenty private cars and fourteen station wagons. There were thirty-two pickup and transfer sites, and scheduled service from five-thirty in the morning until twelve-thirty at night. About 30,000 people were transported to and from work every day.

Around the middle of February a group of white attorneys came up with an old law that prohibited boycotts, and on February 21, a grand jury handed down eighty-nine indictments against Dr. King, more than twenty other ministers, leaders of the MIA, and other citizens. I was re-indicted.

We were all fingerprinted. News photographers had heard about the indictments and were there to photograph us being fingerprinted. The picture of me being fingerprinted was carried on the front page of the *New York Times*. In later years people would use that picture, thinking it was from my first arrest. The MIA paid everybody's bail, and we were released and went home until the trials started.

The trials began in March, and Dr. King was the first to be tried. It was March 19 and I went down to the courthouse. People crowded around and tried to get inside, but they weren't letting in anyone unless they had a seat. They wouldn't let anyone sit on the floor or stand in the aisle. There were a lot of witnesses in his defense, testifying about conditions on the buses. Our neighbor, the woman whose husband was shot, was asked if she rode the buses, and she said No. They wanted to know why she stopped riding, and she said she never rode the buses anymore after her husband was shot to death by a policeman on the bus. All of them had personal reasons. One woman got up there and talked real long. She got insulted because they wouldn't let her keep talking. She said, "I could tell you some more." People were not reluctant to speak out.

They found Dr. King guilty. He was sentenced to pay a $500 fine or serve a year at hard labor. He never did either, because the conviction was appealed successfully. He was the only one they actually tried. But of course he was more determined than ever to continue the boycott, because of the way the city of Montgomery had treated us. The people were willing. All through the spring we walked and car pooled.

There was a lot of interest in the boycott from outside Montgomery now, because of all the attention from the press. I was invited to tell about what had happened to me at various churches, schools, and organizations. I did whatever I could—accepting expense money but no speaking fees—and this helped raise money for station wagons and other expenses. I spent most of the spring making appearances and speeches. Parks was concerned for my safety, but I had no unpleasant experiences.

In June a special three-judge federal District Court ruled two-to-one in favor of our suit against segregation on the buses. But the city commissioners appealed the decision to the U.S. Supreme Court. We knew it would take several months for the Supreme Court to decide.

Summer came and I was back in Montgomery. We still stayed off the buses. The white people tried to break the boycott by not giving the church cars any insurance. All the churches operated the station wagons, and had their names on the sides. Without insurance, the cars could not operate legally. Every time they got insurance from a new company, the policy would suddenly be canceled. But Dr. King got in touch with a black insurance agent in Atlanta named T. M. Alexander, and T. M. Alexander got Lloyd's of London, the big insurance company in England, to write a policy for the church-operated cars.

Next, Mayor Gayle went to court to try to get an order preventing black people from gathering on street corners while waiting for the church cars. Mayor Gayle said they were a "public nuisance" because they sang loudly and bothered other people. He got a court to issue such an order, but that order came on the very same day that the U.S. Supreme Court ruled in our favor, that segregation on the Montgomery buses was unconstitutional.

That was on November 13, 1956. Dr. King called a mass meeting to tell us the news, and everybody was overjoyed. But the MIA did not tell the people to go back on the buses. The written order from the Supreme Court would not arrive for another month or so. We stayed off the buses until it was official.

Back in Montgomery, the written order from the U.S. Supreme Court arrived on December 20, and the following day we returned to the buses. The boycott had lasted more than a year. Dr. King, the Reverend Abernathy, Mr. Nixon, and Glen Smiley, one of the few white people in Montgomery who had supported the boycott, made a great show of riding the first integrated bus in Montgomery. Some of the books say I was with them, but I was not. I had planned to stay home and not ride the bus, because my mother wasn't feeling well. Somebody must have told three reporters from *Look* magazine where I lived, because they came out to the house and waited until I had finished doing whatever I was doing for my mother—fixing her breakfast or something. Then I got dressed and got into the car with them, and they drove downtown and had me get on and off buses so they could take pictures.

Integrating the Montgomery buses did not go smoothly. Snipers fired at buses, and the city imposed curfews on the buses, not letting them run after 5 P.M., which meant that people who worked from nine to five couldn't ride the buses home. A group of whites tried to form a whites-only bus line, but that didn't work. The homes and churches of some ministers were bombed, as I mentioned. But eventually most of the violence died down. Black people were not going to be scared off the buses any more than they were going to be scared onto them when they refused to ride.

African Americans in other cities, like Birmingham, Alabama, and Tallahassee, Florida, started their own boycotts of the segregated buses. The direct-action civil rights movement had begun.

Chapter 5

"Heirs to a Legacy of Struggle"
Charlayne Hunter Integrates the University of Georgia

Charlayne Hunter Gault

> On January 9, 1961, I walked onto the campus at the
> University of Georgia to begin registering for classes.
> Ordinarily, there would not have been anything un-
> usual about such a routine exercise, except, in this in-
> stance, the officials at the university had been fight-
> ing for a year and a half to keep me out. I was not so-
> cially, intellectually, or morally undesirable. I was
> Black. And no Black student had ever been admitted
> to the University of Georgia in its 176-year history.
> —Charlayne Hunter Gault, 1993[1]

And so it began, a new history for the University, the state, and for
my classmate Hamilton Earl Holmes and me. I was nineteen and he
was twenty and neither one of us had given much thought to making
history. What we wanted, in a real sense, was to fulfill our dreams—
dreams that we had nurtured for as long as we could remember.
Hamilton wanted to be a medical doctor, to follow in the footsteps of
his doctor grandfather, who had a medical practice in Atlanta, on
"Sweet Auburn Avenue," a dynamic hub of black business and professional activity that was a source of pride not only in Atlanta, but all
over the country. Blacks, of course, had no choice but to locate in their
own communities because this was what the law demanded. This
was the Deep South and laws dating back to 1896 when the ruling in

Plessy v. Ferguson dictated "separate but equal." And while separate was always the case, it was never equal, except inside our communities, in places that laws could not touch. Where black parents like the Hunters and the Holmes and the people in the communities where they lived—in the neighborhoods, the schools, and the churches— could not give us first-class citizenship, they labored instead to give us a first-class sense of ourselves. "Sweet Auburn" was one of the places where that sense was nurtured. There were black druggists, newspaper owners, restaurateurs, entertainers, barbers, beauticians and preachers, to name a few, who stood, like Hamilton's grandfather, as role models for little black boys like him and little black girls like me.

My dream did not emanate from "Sweet Auburn," although the *Atlanta Daily World*, [one of] the oldest black [dailies] in the country, was published there. My dream was of becoming a journalist, my role model—the comic strip character Brenda Starr. My grandmother, Frances Wilson Layson Brown Jones, may have been my first role model. Her mother, who had become pregnant by the young son of the white family she worked for and was then fired when it became obvious, had taken her out of school in the third grade to help earn their living. But even three years of education was enough to whet a lifelong appetite for and love of learning. Every day, in the little town of Covington, Georgia, where we lived, she read three newspapers and I sat at her knee reading what we called the "funny papers." I was an only child for eight years, and given to sustained flights of fantasy, fueled in part by the comic strip adventures of Brenda Starr, girl reporter. Her life was glamorous, challenging, mysterious, and fun. It never occurred to me that such fun was not intended for Black girls in the Deep South. And no one in my family ever told me not to dream. In fact, I remember the first time I told my mother that I wanted to be a journalist when I grew up. Considering the times, her response was extraordinary: "If that's what you want to do, [do it]," she said simply.

Somehow, perhaps instinctively, she knew that it was dreams that propelled ambition. And propelled we were—both "Hamp," as he was widely known, and me—through our five years at the Henry MacNeal Turner High School. Hamp and I pursued our classwork and extracurricular activities with equal passion. By senior year, he had reached the pinnacle of success for the scholar/athlete: quarterback of the team and class valedictorian. And so had I: Editor of the school newspaper and Homecoming Queen. Hamp and co-captain James Bolton presented me with the coveted pigskin at the victorious Homecoming game.

Indeed, we were having fun and doing well at the same time. Hamp was soon to be on the way to Morehouse College, the prestigious men's school located in the heart of the Atlanta University Center, a complex of black institutions of higher learning that for generations had turned out some of the great minds of black America. I was on my way to Wayne State University in Detroit, having found out from an older classmate who went there to study engineering that they had a good journalism program.

In those days, any black student who wanted to study in a field that was offered only by white schools in the state was entitled to "out of state aid," a device constructed by the white authorities to insure that no blacks ever even thought of applying to one of their institutions. I would be entitled to state aid, since no black institution had a journalism school.

But one day, a small delegation of some of Atlanta's most respected younger adult leaders visited Turner. They were part of a group of progressive Atlanta professionals who called themselves ACCA, the Atlanta Committee for Cooperative Action. They were interested in talking to a couple of Turner's best students, in the hope of interesting them in attending Georgia State College, an all-white institution located in Atlanta. Their aim was to develop a test case that would challenge the state of Georgia to start implementing the Supreme Court's landmark *Brown v. the Board of Education* decision that in 1954 had ordered an end to segregated, separate, and unequal public education.

Hamp's father, Tup, who had earlier been involved in attempts to desegregate Atlanta's golf courses, had spoken with some of them [the members of ACCA] earlier and when he learned that they were looking for a couple of students with high moral character and good grades, he "volunteered" his son, Hamp, easily, he believed, the smartest student in Georgia. He was probably right.

Unsure of exactly what the institution had to offer, Hamp and I agreed at least to go and have a look. We were aroused by the prospect of superior facilities for premed study and a course of study for journalism more than with the prospect of making history, as became clear shortly after we arrived at the place and routinely asked to see the catalogue of courses. The people in the registrar's office obliged, as if a request of this nature was nothing out of the ordinary.

What surprised me was that the catalogue was so thin. And within minutes it was clear that Hamp, too, was not only surprised, but disappointed. I could tell by looking at his face, normally serious, but this time somber. Within minutes, we were out the door, leaving behind the smiling staff of the registrar's office.

"They don't have anything I'm interested in," I said, matter-of-factly. "Me either," Hamp added. But even as the faces of the adults who had accompanied us began to sag, Hamp spoke again.

"I think I would like to try over there," he said, his forefinger jabbing the air and pointing north. I knew immediately, and so did the adults, that he meant the jewel in the system's crown, the University of Georgia. Once before, some years back, Horace Ward, a young black man from Atlanta, had made an attempt to enter the law school and had not been successful. He had gone to law school elsewhere. But while there was some confidence in ACCA's ability to protect us in Atlanta if we were admitted to the smaller and closer Georgia State, ACCA had no resources in Athens. But that proved only a fleeting thought at the time, in the face of our determination to go for the jewel.

We had been accompanied to Georgia State by M. Carl Holman, a tall, lanky bespectacled English professor who was teaching at Clark College, and Jesse Hill, Jr., an actuary at the all-black Atlanta Life Insurance Company, also located on "Sweet Auburn."

Other members of this team included Whitney M. Young, Jr., then Dean of the Atlanta University School of Social Work, and, of course, the legal staff that was the local legal arm of the NAACP. It was headed by Donald L. Hollowell, the Atlanta-based lawyer who would have been a multimillionaire if he had been paid for all the [Jim Crow] cases he had taken. When, in the months ahead, the Atlanta Student Movement would take to the streets against segregated public facilities, one of their rallying cries was "(Martin Luther) King is our leader, Hollowell is our lawyer, and we shall not be moved."

Meanwhile, we "routinely" sent for the applications to the university through the mail. But the small army of ACCA and the legal group went over every aspect of the procedure, down to insuring that every "I" was dotted, every "t" crossed.

On July 11, 1959, the story hit the Atlanta papers: "Two Negroes

Try Doors at Athens." It also contained the resistance strategy of the University—to argue that they were denying our admission not because we were black, but because the dormitories were full and the only freshmen who could be admitted had to be bona fide residents of Athens.

From then on, there would be occasional headlines as our legal team pursued first one, then another of the administrative remedies necessary to demonstrate that the state was lying in order to avoid compliance with the *Brown* decision. Finally, with every lie exhausted by our efforts, the move to take the case into courts was made and accepted.

It was in December 1960, just before the Christmas holidays, that I was summoned home to Atlanta from Detroit, where I was now a sophomore at Wayne State. Hamp was attending Morehouse. The trial was held in Athens, before Federal District Judge William Bootle.

Our lawyers knew what they needed to knock down the state's case, and Vernon Jordan and Morehouse College Registrar Gerald Taylor had the crucial pieces of evidence in their pockets: a case identical to mine in which a white female student had been admitted.

Constance Baker Motley had come down from the NAACP Legal Defense and Educational Fund, Inc.'s headquarters in New York to be a part of the team. Skillfully, she set the traps that would cause the University's officials to ensnare themselves in their own words. In the world of deception they lived in, they could not publicly acknowledge that they or their admissions policies were racist. So Mrs. Motley asked if they would favor the admission of a qualified Negro to the University, if all other things, like dormitory space, were available. Registrar Walter N. Danner answered yes. The news story in the *Atlanta Journal and Constitution* the following day revealed her strategy. It read: "The University . . . registrar has testified in Federal Court here that he favors admission of qualified Negroes to the University."

On January 6, 1961, Federal Judge Bootle ordered Hamilton and me admitted to the University of Georgia, forthwith.

> Two, four, six, eight
> We don't wanna integrate.
> Niggah go home!

These were some of the words that greeted us when we arrived to a boisterous crowd of students and media. But none of it was particularly menacing.

Halfway through our registration procedures, however, Judge Bootle inexplicably granted the state a stay of his desegregation order. We retired to the home of a prominent black couple in Athens and waited while Attorneys Motley and Hollowell appealed the stay before Appeals Court Judge Elbert Tuttle.

Several hours later, Vernon Jordan received the call that resulted in the next day's headline: "Tuttle Boots Bootle." My mother's reaction was "God is good, isn't he?"

But the worst was yet to come.

We finished registering that day and began classes the following day. Tuesday night, a crowd gathered outside my dormitory. It grew increasingly agitated, especially when swelled by fans disappointed in the last-minute defeat of the Georgia basketball team at the hands of their arch-rival from hell, Georgia Tech. The boisterousness gave way to a mean-spiritedness that resulted in bricks being thrown through my window, the only one with a light on in the dormitory, thanks to the word that had gone out to the other residents throughout the day to turn off their lights when it got dark. My room was also the only residential room on the first floor. The University, resisting the desegregation order at every turn, had turned the Women's Student Government Office on the first floor into my "suite," next to the lobby, while all other rooms were on the second floor. This made it very convenient for the girls upstairs to take turns pounding on the floor above my head.

Eventually, despite their late arrival, the police broke up the mob. The tear gas that was used was floating into the dormitory as the dean came in and informed me that Hamp and I were being suspended "for our safety." I began to cry, not from the gas, as was the case with some of the girls upstairs, but because I was seized with a feeling of failure. I packed quickly, ignoring the shards of glass that now lay on my clothes from the first brick that came sailing through my window. As the dean escorted me out, the girls from upstairs had formed a semicircle in the lobby, in front of which I had to pass. As I walked past, one threw out a quarter that landed in front of me.

"Here nigger," the voice called out, "change my sheets."

I was angry, but not afraid, for deeply imbedded in my soul were the words my father's mother taught me when I was a little girl. I resisted then, but she persisted, teaching me her favorite, the 23rd Psalm, which came back to me as I walked away: "Yea, though I walk through the valley of the shadow of death, I will fear no evil. Thy rod and thy staff they comfort me, all the days of my life." It was a long way from those steamy hot Florida sessions of my childhood, but my grandmother, like all of my nurturers, clothed me in values that served as a suit of armor, all the days of my life, including this cold night in Georgia.

Hamp was living with a black family a few minutes away and by the time I arrived there, he had been apprised of all that had transpired. He didn't want to leave without his car, but fearful of what could happen to him riding between police cars on that route of small-town bigots from Athens to Atlanta, I threw a fit and insisted that he ride with me in the state trooper's car. Embarrassed by my public display, even in the face of unfriendliness, he quickly relented.

We arrived safely in Atlanta in the wee hours of the Thursday morning. Before the day was over, our attorneys had once again prevailed in court and we were ordered back to the University. But we decided to take a day off and return the following Monday.

Under heavy guard, we walked back onto the campus that Monday. Georgia's entry in the Civil Rights Revolution had begun.

Two sometimes lonely, sometimes frustrating, but sometimes fun years from then, Hamp and I would graduate—he, Phi Beta Kappa and ready for medical school; I, ready to enter the world that I had so long dreamed of, as a graduate of the Henry W. Grady School of Journalism. And by this time, Jim Crow was on the run throughout the state, high schools and elementary schools had started being desegregated the fall after our admission to the University, and the students of the Atlanta University System—Morehouse, Spelman, Clark, Morris Brown had started the Student Movement. They had marched, demonstrated, and had gone to "jail without bail" for "Freedom Now." The struggle was not over, but, something had now changed in Atlanta (and in Georgia), and something had changed in us. We had been protected and privileged within the confines of our segregated communities. But now that we students had removed the protective covering, we could see in a new light both our past and our future.

We could see that past—the slavery, the segregation, the deprivation and denial—for what it was; a system designed to keep us in our place and convince us, somehow, that it was our fault, as well as our destiny. Now, without either ambivalence or shame, we saw ourselves as the heirs to a legacy of struggle, but struggle that was ennobling; struggle that was enabling us to take control of our destiny. And, as a result, we did not see ourselves or the other young people demonstrating in one way or another throughout the South as heroes to be praised, celebrated, or fretted over. We were simply doing what we were born and raised to do. While not everybody in the adult black community was on board, the Atlanta Student Movement had spoken in terms that became the watchwords for all of us: "Ain't gonna let nobody turn me 'roun'."

NOTES

1. Charlayne Hunter Gault, *In My Place* (New York: Vintage Books, 1993). Reprinted with permission of the author.

Chapter 6

"We Wanted the Voice of a Woman to Be Heard"

Black Women and the 1963 March on Washington

Dorothy I. Height

I had been active in the Civil Rights Movement long before the 1963 March on Washington. One of the significant turning points came in 1962 when Stephen Currier called together a group of black leaders because he felt that the Taconic Foundation, which he headed, and which had been very supportive of black causes, could take a lead in trying to get other philanthropic sources to give more support. And so, he called together Dr. Martin Luther King, Jr., President of SCLC; Whitney Young, Executive Director of the National Urban League; A. Philip Randolph, President of the Brotherhood of Sleeping Car Porters; Roy Wilkins, Executive Director of the NAACP; James Farmer, National Director of CORE; C. Eric Lincoln, a scholar who was doing a study on the Black Muslims; Jack Greenberg, Executive Director of the NAACP Legal Defense Fund; and myself.

The point of the gathering was to begin to see how American philanthropy could be more supportive of black organizations. At the outset, the Student Nonviolent Coordinating Committee (SNCC) was not there, but later, SNCC was added, with James Forman coming into the picture. The plan was that each leader would assume responsibility for chairing a group to study some area of philanthropy as it related to African Americans. Each took a field. I chose private voluntary organizations to assess their policies, governing boards, and what kind of support they gave, as well as the racial composition of the decision makers.

For a stipend, each of us was required to make an agreement with the Taconic Foundation to attend a meeting at least every six weeks. The agreement stipulated that no substitute organizational representatives would attend the meetings. We would make this a serious study.

One thing to bear in mind is that the group did not start out to become the "United Civil Rights Leadership." All of the organizations had a civil rights agenda. It was as if it was part of a divine design that, for over a year before the assassination of Medgar Evers on June 23, 1963, we had been meeting together steadily, discussing our differences, and considering our different tactics.

For example, we recognized that the NAACP had gone into the courts many times to get certain things done. At times, it was feared that the advances made by the NAACP would be lost if SNCC caused a disruption, or was involved in direct confrontation. But we had worked through these issues together. There was also a lessening of the tension that had existed in the beginning. Dr. King once said, "Well, you know, one thing I did with the marches was to make the NAACP look respectable." Before that, many had asked, "Why do they (the NAACP) go into the courts?" And he said, "We have never found a way of dealing with our problems that was acceptable to the majority of the country." No matter what we did, we were criticized. Now we were marching, and the cry was that we shouldn't have the children marching.

It was not until Medgar Evers was assassinated that the group really began to concentrate on specific civil rights issues. It happened that on June 24, 1963, just after Evers was assassinated, Stephen Currier, along with Roy Wilkins and Whitney Young, sent a plea and called the group to the Carlyle Hotel in New York, where we had often met. Currier wanted to alert the whole community to the significance of what was happening. So he hosted a breakfast, attended by major philanthropic interests, where he made a strong plea for support for the movement. The very first real money given to the civil rights organization, some $900,000, was pledged on that morning.

I'll never forget that breakfast. Roy Wilkins was on his way to Arlington, Virginia to Medgar Evers' burial. Each of us was asked to make some statement. I spoke from the angle of what was happening to our young women in the hands of law enforcement officers, in the makeshift jails, and in the whole struggle for equality. Whitney Young made a passionate plea, and said, "We all know more about what needs to be done than we have the resources to do." Out of that meeting, there developed a plan to form what was to be called the Council of United Civil Rights Leadership (CUCRL). We had to organize in order to sustain the relationships, and to utilize the financial support, which was partly taxable and partly tax exempt.

I think it was very significant that the fourteen months prior to Evers' death, by holding the regular meetings, we had grown beyond separate organizational identities, and had much more of a sense of common concern about civil rights. There was no longer the subtle competitive spirit with which we had to deal at the outset. There was not that self-consciousness about "my organization."

We were driven by critical issues. The only time that someone did not attend the meeting was when Dr. King was in the Birmingham jail, or when James Farmer was in jail in Louisiana. At those times, Andrew Young and Floyd McKissick came and substituted for King and Farmer, respectively. We had experienced a real bonding. It was as if the hand of God had brought us together.

The national civil rights crisis emanating from the assassination of Medgar Evers, and from other atrocities, became the force behind making the Council of United Civil Rights Leadership a formal organization. Within that group, the National Council of Negro Women (NCNW) had the NCNW Educational Foundation, headed by Daisy Lampkin, which became a mechanism in the distribution of some of the tax-exempt funds. Thus, the NCNW provided college scholarships for some 114 students, including Marion Barry, Ivanhoe Donaldson, Bernard LaFayette, Stokley Carmichael, and other activists, whose education had been interrupted by their civil rights activities.

The NCNW also became the repository for funds donated for the education of the children of Medgar Evers, which NCNW held until their mother called for them. The NCNW redoubled all its efforts and focused on the civil rights rallies and marches, and supported all of the essential human rights issues.

As a result of my involvement with the Council of United Civil Rights Leadership, when the 1963 March on Washington was being planned, people quite naturally asked me, "What's going to happen?" Many prominent women were concerned about the visible participation and representation of women leaders in the program. Most of these women thought that the CUCRL was organizing the March and making decisions about the platform. When the question was raised, we were always referred to Bayard Rustin, the Executive Director of the March, appointed by A. Philip Randolph, who first issued the call.

I went along with Anna Arnold Hedgeman, a woman with a long history of working for freedom and equality, to meet with Bayard Rustin. We discussed the women's participation in the March. We were amazed to hear the response, "Women are included." Rustin asserted that, "Every group has women in it, labor, church," and so on. When we asked Rustin who was doing the planning, he referred to the heads of the National Council of Churches, NAACP, National Urban League, several Jewish groups, and other organizations. When the question was raised in the CUCRL meetings, it was always referred back to Bayard Rustin. There was an all-consuming focus on race. We women were expected to put all our energies into it. Clearly, there was a low tolerance level for anyone raising the questions about the women's participation, per se.

The men seemed to feel that women were digressing and pulling the discussion off the main track. But it wasn't just a male attitude. There were black women who felt that we needed to stick with the "real" issue of race. It was thought that we were making a lot of fuss about an insignificant issue, that we did not recognize that the March was about racism, not sexism. We knew all that. But, we made it clear that we wanted to hear at least one woman in the March dealing with jobs and freedom. We knew, first hand, that most of the Civil Rights Movement audiences were largely comprised of women, children, and youth.

Prior to the 1963 March on Washington, whenever there was a civil rights rally, the platform was filled predominantly by males. When we said that we wanted the voice of a woman to be heard, and gave the names of women to be considered, such as Deborah Partridge Wolfe, and Anna Arnold Hedgeman, and mentioned that there were a number of possibilities, Rustin and others would say that they did not know who to choose. The women were quick to say that they were ready to make a selection or nomination, but we could never get to that point. We knew that other groups had not had the question raised on who they would choose. But it came up around the concerns of women.

It was unnerving to be given the argument that women were members of the National Urban League and all of the other organizations, and so, they were represented. As the time approached, there was no agreement on having the students speak either. SNCC was carrying on direct action protest activities. Roy Wilkins said that at times the SNCC students were upsetting all the good work that the NAACP had done. He emphasized that the NAACP worked through the courts. There was real tension in the meetings of the Council of Civil Rights Leadership at the beginning of the discussions about the March. But, as a woman, I just kept saying that I did not see how we could leave our young people out. We needed them around the table.

Unlike the women, SNCC more aggressively pursued the issue of having a student speaker at the March. When John Lewis demanded to speak, the students were prepared to demonstrate. The organizers of the March held out, right up to the end. The students made threats. Their prepared remarks were questioned. Although it was announced that Lewis would speak, actually it was right on the grounds of the Lincoln Monument that the decision was made to let him speak. Among the established black male leadership, there was concern about what he would say. This was widely reported in all the newspapers.

Nothing that women said or did broke the impasse blocking their participation. I've never seen a more immovable force. We could not get women's participation taken seriously. The March organizers proffered many excuses. They said, "We have too many speakers as it is. The program is too long. You are already represented." They said, "We have Mahalia Jackson." Oh yes, we said, "But she is not speaking. She's not speaking on behalf of women, or on behalf of civil rights. She's singing."

To address the issue, the organizers gave a number of us prominent seats on the platform. We were seated. In all the March on Washington pictures, we're right there on the platform. There were several women who just refused to do anything. Some were so angry that they didn't really want to take part. The women represented a cross section of organizations, including labor, religion, and social welfare groups. What actually happened was so disappointing, because actually women were an active part of the whole effort. Indeed, women were the backbone of the movement. A look at the pictures gives the impression that we were intimately involved.

Within the CUCRL, I think that Whitney Young, Martin Luther King, Jr., and James Farmer showed the greatest concern. But even they did not take an active stand. They passed the question on. They said, "We'll check with Mr. Randolph, and check with Bayard." The women came to feel that they were getting a kind of runaround.

Our white sisters find it hard to understand the positions we often take. It is characteristic of black women to put the race issue ahead of everything else, so that when we confront sexism, we are not an angry caucus. We fully supported the 1963 March on Washington because we felt it would strike a major blow against racism. However, it did not go down easily that the young people were only reluctantly admitted. I think the women began to say that "this March has to speak up for jobs and freedom," ironic as that may seem.

Essentially, the race issue, and not the gender issue, had won out again. In the end, like everyone else, we were thrilled by the success of the March.

Despite the fact that the March organizers and many of the male leaders asked groups not to call any meetings, and not to organize gatherings with the people who came to Washington, NCNW had set up a meeting called "After the March, What?" This proved especially important because women were able, once again, to get some perspective. Over and above the planned agenda, women talked freely of their concern about women's participation. We could hardly believe that after all we were doing in the Civil Rights Movement, the men leaders could conclude, "You have a place in all of the participating national organizations, so you are represented." Those who supported the demand for direct representation showed no sensitivity to the need to move on the issue. What was most discouraging was that there was no sign of remorse among the male leadership, no feeling that there was any injustice. They believed that this was the right thing to do. After all, there were speakers from a diversity of national bodies, Protestants, Catholics, Jews, the NAACP, the Urban League, Labor, and the Southern Christian Leadership Conference. The organizers had stressed that in all of these organizations, women carried vital roles. As we worked through the meeting, again and again, the point was made that women were fully supportive of the March. Once we saw we were not going to prevail, we did so with our eyes open, and the experience itself helped open our eyes.

It did not go unnoticed that some of the male leaders wanted to act as though Bayard Rustin had made a unilateral decision. There was no easy way to find out who made the decision. It simply had been decided. That was one thing, but it also put us on guard that if we didn't speak up, nobody would. And we began to realize that if we did not address issues such as this, if we did not demand our rights, we were not going to get them. The women became much more aware and much more aggressive in facing up to sexism in our dealings with the male leadership in the movement.

Following this meeting to assess the status of the movement, and to chart the next steps, the NCNW held a Leadership Conference on November 14, 1963. One invited speaker was Pauli Murray, a noted legal scholar, educator, and well-known activist in a number of civil rights groups. As a consultant to the President's Commission on the Status of Women, Murray had written a memorandum proposing to examine state laws and practices that discriminate on the basis of sex in the context of the 14th Amendment to the Constitution. This was considered a new approach to the issue of discrimination and was accepted by the committee in its final report. The NCNW invited Murray to speak about black women's struggle for equality.

In her speech, "The Negro Woman in the Quest for Equality," Pauli Murray captured the feeling of black women about their exclusion from direct participation in the March on Washington, as well as their feelings about their treatment in the overall movement. Her speech was well received, and elicited a great deal of discussion. Murray traced the history of black women and their struggle for equality from slavery to freedom, noting the similarities and differences in their status from that of white women, race being the main distinction. She noted that in their quest for equality, black women had been willing to overlook gender discrimination in order to gain racial equality. However, she stated clearly:

> The civil rights revolt, like many social upheavals, has released powerful pent-up emotions, cross currents, rivalries, and hostilities. In emerging from an essentially middle class movement and taking on a mass character, it has become a vehicle to power and prestige, and contains many of the elements of in-fighting that have characterized labor's emergence, or the pre-independence African societies. . . . What emerges most clearly from events of the past several months is the tendency to assign women to a secondary, ornamental, or "honoree" role instead of the partnership role in the civil rights movement which they have earned by their courage, intelligence, and dedication. It was bitterly humiliating for Negro Women on August 28, to see themselves accorded little more than token recognition in the historic March on

Washington. Not a single woman was invited to make one of the major speeches or to be part of the delegation of leaders who went to the White House. The omission was deliberate.[1]

Pauli Murray's speech really captured the feelings of the moment and it galvanized the women. Although Pauli's speech was widely reported in the black press, I don't think it made much of an impression on the men. The speech influenced and resonated among black women in particular, and we began to do several things. We frequently quoted Mary Church Terrell's statement, "We labor under the double handicap of race and sex." We began to popularize that statement to awaken other women. Out of this came a great debate. I'll never forget it.

Looking back on the March on Washington, most people remember Dr. King's great "I Have a Dream" speech. However, for many black women who were actively involved in the Civil Rights Movement, especially those in leadership positions, the blatantly insensitive treatment of black women leaders was a new awakening. We began to reflect upon the importance of black women in our community. They are the backbone of the churches. The evidence of their work can be seen everywhere. It made some of us sit up and think in new and different ways. We were forced to recognize that, traditionally, black women, through their unstinting support of race movements and their willingness to play frequently unquestioned subordinate roles, and to put the men out front, made it seem that this was acceptable. Little or no thought had been given to ourselves as women.

It was invaluable that Pauli Murray had lifted the situation to the context of equality. That was an important contribution. Her paper was used widely. It forced us to take a hard look at the actual treatment we received at the March on Washington and the public reaction. I don't think the male/female relationships, in connection with the Civil Rights Movement, had ever been dealt with or even viewed quite as they were on the occasion of the 1963 March on Washington.

Without a doubt, the March on Washington was a vital and critical point in the whole Civil Rights Movement. I think the righteous indignation that was expressed throughout the whole country about the situation, the atrocities, somehow is gone now. But it was there! There was a time when the whole nation seemed to have felt this injustice. And, while there were many who didn't agree with it, there was an overall favorable mood. That mood is not here now.

I guess that some of the progress that's been made is misleading to many of our young people. They are now going through open doors and they don't know how they got opened. They don't understand that the struggle has just begun. It's not over!

Likewise, the March on Washington experience, as proud as everybody was of Mahalia Jackson, brought into bold relief the different perspectives of men and women on the whole issue of gender. Though every statistic showed us that a number of our families were headed by women, we were still dominated by the view that if men were given enough, the women would be better off. There was not that sense of equal partnership. For many of us, the March opened that sense of equal partnership. For many of us, the March opened up the dialogue. It made it necessary. We had to talk about it.

NOTES

1. Pauli Murray, "The Negro Woman in the Quest for Equality," typescript, speech delivered at the National Council of Negro Women's Leadership Conference, held at the Statler Hilton Hotel, November 14, 1963, National Council of Negro Women Papers, Bethune Council House, National Historical Site, Washington, DC.

Part III

Women, Leadership, and Civil Rights

The three essays in Part III focus on black women leaders who operated primarily at the grassroots level. Septima Clark, Fannie Lou Hamer, Annie Devine, Victoria Gray, and other women activists made significant contributions to civil rights campaigns by utilizing local organizations and institutional networks to mobilize working-class black southerners. These women also maintained the important linkages between local movement organizations and the national civil rights leadership. To a very great extent their success as civil rights activists was closely related to their family background and personal experiences that prepared them well to assume responsible leadership positions.

Jacqueline Rouse's essay, "'We Seek to Know . . . in Order to Speak the Truth': Nurturing the Seeds of Discontent—Septima P. Clark and Participatory Leadership," examines the significant contributions of Septima Clark to voting rights campaigns in the South during the Civil Rights Movement. For many years Clark was a teacher in Charleston, South Carolina and participated in the legal campaigns to equalize salaries for black and white teachers. Clark also taught in separate black schools on the Sea Islands in South Carolina, and after attending workshops at the Highlander Folk School in Monteagle, Tennessee, an integrated retreat and planning center for community activists, she began to develop adult education programs to achieve "Literacy and Liberation." The "Citizenship Schools" that Clark established provided literacy training for black southerners to prepare them to register to vote. In the early 1960s, after Tennessee officials closed the Highlander Folk School, the Citizenship School program was taken over by the Southern Christian Leadership Conference (SCLC) and Clark became the director. SCLC's citizenship training program formed the basis for the "Voter Education Project" which was responsible for the registration of thousands of southern black voters. Rouse presents a detailed examination of Clark's educational and political vision and the significant impact the Citizenship Schools had on the southern Civil Rights Movement.

Fannie Lou Hamer, Annie Devine, and Victoria Gray were among the founders of the Mississippi Freedom Democratic Party (MFDP), which was organized in 1964 to challenge the all-white Democratic party in the state. Hamer, Devine, and Gray carried out grassroots organizing for the Party among the black working classes in numerous cities and towns. Vicki Crawford's "African American Women in the Mississippi Freedom Democratic Party" presents a detailed account of these women's political organizing and argues that it was black women's spirituality and formal church networks that supported their successful civil rights activism.

Fannie Lou Hamer achieved a high degree of visibility during her lifetime, and there has been a tendency among those who knew her to discuss her leadership in terms of the impact she had on their personal lives—"This is what Fannie Lou Hamer meant to me." But what did the things Fannie Lou Hamer experienced in her life mean to her? In her essay, "Anger, Memory, and Personal Power: Fannie Lou Hamer and Civil Rights Leadership," Chana Kai Lee describes how Hamer's subjective experience informed her political activism. Lee examines specific events in Hamer's life—her decision to register to vote, her eviction from her home, the beating in the Winona, Mississippi jail—and suggests how they defined who she was and helped to explain the kind of leadership she provided.

Chapter 7

"We Seek to Know . . . in Order to Speak the Truth"

Nurturing the Seeds of Discontent—Septima P. Clark and Participatory Leadership[1]

Jacqueline A. Rouse

> I believe "Social Justice" is not a matter of *money* but of *will*, not a problem for the economist but a task for the patriot, requiring leadership and community action rather than investment.[2]
>
> —Septima P. Clark

In a eulogy presented at the funeral of Septima Poinsette Clark, the Reverend Joseph E. Lowery, president of the Southern Christian Leadership Conference (SCLC), described the importance of Clark's work and her relationship to the SCLC. Reverend Lowery asserted that "her courageous and pioneering efforts in the area of citizenship education and interracial cooperation won her SCLC's highest award, the Drum Major for Justice award." In a similar vein, the Reverend C. T. Vivian, a former SCLC leader who had worked with Clark and Reverend Martin Luther King, Jr., remarked that "she understood that if we could break through the illiteracy, we could break into mainstream America."[3]

For sixty years, Septima Poinsette Clark dedicated her life to the cause of universal literacy, voter registration, women's rights, and civil rights. Without formal title or formally recognized leadership, Clark fought on many different fronts at the same time, and successfully

fulfilled many daunting challenges for the modern Civil Rights Movement. In *Parting the Waters: America in the King Years 1954–1963*, Taylor
Branch accurately describes Clark as having "one of the most powerful
impacts on the whole scene."[4] Fellow worker Andrew Young credited
her work in developing the Citizenship Schools program as forming
"the base on which the whole civil rights movement was built."[5]

The Citizenship program formed the foundation for the highly
successful Voter Education Project launched in 1962 by the Southern
Christian Leadership Conference (SCLC), the Congress of Racial
Equality (CORE), the NAACP, the Urban League, and the Student
Nonviolent Coordinating Committee (SNCC). Though Clark excelled
as a master teacher, her true gift was demonstrated in her success in
teaching illiterate rural adults to read and write, and training barely
literate southerners to become teachers in the Citizenship Schools.
She possessed a special ability to recognize natural leaders among
poor uneducated farmers, midwives, and draymen; and the grandmothers who had nurtured and educated their children and grandchildren by working as washerwomen and domestics. Plain and un-
pretentious, bright and confident, possessing age-old "mother-wit"
or common sense, Septima Clark moved among the unlettered and
uncelebrated and became a legend in her time.[6]

With a "quiet dignity," and a group-centered ideology, Clark
forged her way into the hearts of the people to become what sociologist Belinda Robnett calls a "professional bridge leader," a grassroots
leader who moved from one rural community to another teaching literacy and citizenship, a leader with the ability to connect the needs of
the people with the goals and objectives of a movement. Robnett
coined the term "bridge leaders" to describe the pivotal positions of
grassroots leaders in the Civil Rights Movement. Although a bridge
leader could be male or female, Robnett perceives this type of leadership as primarily female. Women, who were capable of being formal
leaders, were frequently excluded and tended to concentrate their
work in areas perceived as support work. Septima Clark, Ella Baker,
and Daisy Bates were prominent bridge leaders whose contributions,
until recently, have been obscured in the emerging historical scholarship. Analyzing leadership patterns in the Civil Rights Movement,
Robnett concludes in *How Long? How Long? African-American Women
in the Struggle for Civil Rights*, that "central to the success of a social
movement is an intermediate layer of leadership, whose task includes

bridging potential constituents and adherents, as well as potential formal leaders, to the movement."[7]

Clark was responsible for the development of the Citizenship Schools program, which included adult literacy classes designed to help functional illiterates acquire political literacy and to identify and train a grassroots leadership. She provided SCLC and other civil rights organizations with a basic program through which they could achieve the critical goal of building a southern African American electorate, which not only would vote, but also would provide the critical margin for the election of African Americans to political office. But who was this remarkable woman, and where does she fit in the long history of African American leadership in the United States?[8]

Growing Up in Charleston

Septima Poinsette Clark was born on May 3, 1898 in Charleston, South Carolina, the daughter of Peter and Victoria Poinsette. Septima's father, Peter Porcher Poinsette, was born a slave; and her mother, Victoria Warren Anderson Poinsette, the daughter of a native American and a Haitian immigrant, was born in Charleston but spent her early years in Haiti. Raised by her older brothers, cigar dealers in Haiti, Victoria frequently boasted that her Haitian upbringing prepared her to deal with racism in the United States. Victoria's experience as a free person in Haiti, an independent black-controlled country, as well as her social position among the Haitian elite, gave her a strong sense of confidence and determination, and contributed to her willingness to challenge aggressively all forms of racial oppression.[9]

Unlike Victoria, Peter Poinsette believed that his enslaved condition was ordained by God and hence he rejected ideas of rebellion and resistance. Peter was born and raised on the Wando Plantation in North Charleston, South Carolina, owned by Joel Poinsette, a botanist and a former U.S. diplomat to Mexico, who was known for his benevolent treatment of his slaves.[10] Although Peter disagreed with the rebellion and resistance practiced by slaves who sometimes stole or destroyed their master's property, he maintained solidarity with other enslaved Africans and did not betray their goals. During the Civil War, Peter Poinsette worked as a laborer for the Confederate regiment stationed in Charleston. At the end of the war, he emerged as a free man who was a devout Christian, devoid of any animosity; and willing to work to educate his children. Peter's recognition of the importance of education developed as a result of his experience as a trusted slave who was responsible for accompanying Joel Poinsette's children to school each day. It was his responsibility to go with the plantation owner's children, and remain outside the building until the end of the day, and escort the children back to the plantation. Illiterate for most of his life, Peter Poinsette was adamant about the education of his children, and would administer corporal punishment if they were unwilling to attend school.[11]

Clark viewed herself as the embodiment of her parents' experiences. The balanced perspectives of her parents were apparent in Septima's personality and in her commitments. Like her father, she could be compassionate and generous, and similar to her mother she could be tough, determined, and fearless. Septima also displayed attributes of simplicity and humility, traits reminiscent of her father. These served her well in her work with rural working-class African Americans, a group essential to the success of SCLC and the Voter Education Project. Septima also exhibited her mother's arrogance, aggressiveness, courage, and determined spirit. Later in life, as she reflected upon her willingness to challenge southern white patterns of dominance, Clark asserted that fear actually escaped her. She was not afraid of the White Citizens Councils, the Ku Klux Klan, the white mobs guarding the southern courthouses, or even the harrowing ride down the narrow mountain roads of Monteagle, Tennessee, following her arrest at the Highlander Folk School. In situations such as these, Septima remembered her mother challenging a policeman who had approached their house to apprehend their pet dog, which apparently had injured a neighbor's child. As the policeman entered the family's property without notice, Victoria warned the officer "don't you come in here." Just in case the officer underestimated her because she was a small woman, Victoria assured him that she was prepared to protect her property. The policeman retreated without accomplishing his objective. This incident, reflecting her mother's courage, made an indelible impression on the young Septima.[12]

Of equal importance to Septima's development of her personality and her ability to serve as a professional bridge leader was her inheritance of her father's caring nature—his concern for people in varied stations of life. Peter Poinsette taught her that the measure of her worth as an individual would come from her service to the least of humankind. Slavery had taught Peter Poinsette tolerance for the weaknesses of others. Christianity had taught him that in one's weakness, God is made great. Thus, Septima learned that three things were important—a strong belief in God, an education, and a willingness to serve those who were less fortunate. She credited her father for providing her with the skills to become a significant and influential worker among the indigenous people of Johns Island and in the civil rights campaigns in the South.[13]

In 1916, following her graduation from the Avery Institute, a private school in Charleston sponsored by the American Missionary Association, Clark passed the state examination for teachers and received a license allowing her to teach in rural public schools. Although African Americans taught in segregated black schools throughout South Carolina, they were not allowed to teach in the public schools of Charleston. Beginning her teaching career on Johns Island in 1916, Clark was confronted with the most abject living conditions she had ever seen, and witnessed first hand the impact that poverty, racism, and intragroup gender discrimination could have on the lives of black people. Clark quickly learned that education on the Island was determined by the agricultural contract between the black sharecroppers and the landowners. The children of sharecropping families could only attend school during the months of December, January, and February, known as the "lay by" season. Clark observed that the inability of the masses of blacks to read and write condemned them to a lifetime of sharecropping and poverty in a system akin to antebellum slavery. As more and more young people expressed a desire to attend school and flee the impoverished life they knew, Clark's classes expanded. Not limiting her work to teaching, Clark nursed the sick, sewed clothing for the children, and gave of her time helping people in need. In this manner, a bond of trust was established between Clark and the local community. Soon the adult residents began to come to her home at night to learn the basics of reading and how to write their names.[14]

Launching a Career of Political Activism

Clark spent three years on Johns Island. During that time she crusaded for the equalization of teachers' salaries and was active in the movement to have African American teachers employed to teach in the public schools in Charleston and to be public school principals. In 1919, Clark returned to Charleston to teach sixth grade at the Avery Institute, the private school for African Americans from which she had graduated. One night, while attending an NAACP meeting, she met Edwin Harleston, a prominent black artist and civil rights activist, and Thomas E. Miller, former Reconstruction congressman from South Carolina and former president of South Carolina State College. Harleston and Miller had organized the Charleston branch of the NAACP, and at the first meeting discussed its role in securing civil and political rights for African Americans.[15] Clark joined the NAACP in protesting the arrest of a local black delivery boy, who was accused of stealing a watch from a white female customer. The woman later found the jewelry in a garment she had sent to the laundry. Local blacks asked the woman to retract her story to secure the release and clear the name of the young boy. The woman's compliance was viewed as a victory for the NAACP and helped to unite and solidify the Charleston branch.[16]

Following the success of its first protest, the NAACP took up the issue of black teachers in the city's public school system. School board members declared that the black community did not wish to have black teachers, and that this was an initiative sponsored by the "mulattoes." Clark, assisted by Avery Institute students, went door-to-door, collecting signatures to refute the board's charges. Clark joined with Harleston and Miller in their drive to collect 20,000 signatures, from all social classes and occupations, to demonstrate that the black community supported the right of black teachers to teach in Charleston's public schools. The statute was passed in 1920, and in 1921, Charleston hired its first black teachers. Clark was employed to teach at a local elementary school.[17]

Clark had been introduced to political activism and soon sought to improve the plight of black children throughout Charleston. Having gained a reputation as an advocate for equal rights, she began work with Charleston's Young Women's Christian Association (YWCA). The city maintained a segregated black YWCA, which included recreational facilities for young females, but no similar institution existed for black boys. To address this issue, Clark and sympathetic white YWCA workers met with Mayor Wehman to discuss the need for additional recreational facilities for African Americans in the city. Although he was willing to receive the white women, the mayor turned his back when Clark began to speak. Undaunted, Clark made her point about the lack of structured recreation for the city's young black males. Shortly thereafter, municipal facilities were made available for black male youngsters. Remembering this incident some years later, she told a friend, "I know that there is educational value in action." This experience tested Clark's leadership, endurance, creativity, and commitment.[18]

In 1920, Septima Poinsette married Nerie Clark, a sailor. Sadly, Nerie Clark died of kidney failure in December 1925. Two children were born of this union, but only one survived. Following her husband's death, Clark taught for a year in the mountains of western North Carolina, near her husband's family, before returning to Johns Island to teach for three years. In 1929, in search of better economic and employment opportunities, Septima Clark moved to Columbia, South Carolina, where she resided until 1947. During the summers in the 1930s and 1940s, Clark enrolled in courses at Columbia University in New York City and at Atlanta University, where she studied with W. E. B. Du Bois. She received a Bachelor of Arts degree from Benedict College in 1942 and a Master of Arts degree from Hampton Institute in 1945. Du Bois's lectures on the debilitating effects of racism and segregation made the connection between protest and education and reinforced for Clark the importance of dedicating her life to campaigns for social justice.[19]

In Columbia, Clark taught in the elementary department of Booker T. Washington High School. This was the most prominent public school for African Americans in South Carolina. Also employed at Booker T. Washington were several noted civil rights activists, including Modjeska Simkins, a mathematics teacher; and J. Andrew Simmons, the principal of Booker T. Washington. Clark, Simkins, and Simmons collaborated with South Carolina NAACP attorney Harold Boulware and NAACP counsel Thurgood Marshall in the development of a lawsuit to obtain the equalization of teachers' salaries. In South Carolina, as in most southern states, black teachers' salaries were about half that of whites. Arguing that teachers with equal qualifications should receive equal pay, the NAACP, represented by Thurgood Marshall, took Viola Duvall's class action suit on behalf of Charleston's black teachers to federal court, and in 1945, Federal District Judge J. Waties Waring ruled that there could be no difference in the salary scales for black and white teachers.[20] Reflecting upon this experience, Clark declared that:

> My participating in [the] fight to force equalization of white and Negro teachers' salaries on the basis of equal certification, of course, is what might be described by some, no doubt, as my first "radical job." I would call it my first effort in social action challenging the status quo, the first time I had worked against people directing a system for which I was working.

In actuality, Clark had worked against the system, indirectly challenging the white authorities on many earlier occasions.[21]

Clark was very pleased with her teaching in Columbia, her affiliation with the local branch of the NAACP, and her acceptance and fellowship within Columbia's black community. In 1947, she returned to Charleston to care for her ailing mother, where she was again employed as a teacher in the public school system. She renewed her affiliation with the YWCA, which was a hotbed for civil rights activism, and supported a number of political causes. Work with the YWCA also brought Clark into closer relationship with Judge and Mrs. J. Waites Waring. Judge Waring, a ninth-generation white Charlestonian, had become a voice of social justice for black Charleston. In 1947, he ruled the all-white Democratic primary unconstitutional in South Carolina, and subsequently blacks began to vote in local, state, and national elections. This action alienated Waring from white Charleston. He became further estranged when he divorced his southern wife to marry an outspoken northern liberal. Snubbed by most white Charlestonians, the Warings developed social and political relations with black activists. Following a keynote speech made by Mrs. Waring at a YWCA function, in which she lambasted white Charlestonians and called for an end to discrimination and full desegregation of public facilities, Clark and other black activists friendly with the Warings were snubbed by some blacks and placed under surveillance by the white authorities.[22]

Septima Clark and the Highlander Folk School

Colleagues at the YWCA introduced Clark to the work of the Highlander Folk School. Located fifty miles northeast of Chattanooga,

Tennessee, the school was known as a retreat and planning center for community activists. Labeled by white southerners as a "Communist school," Highlander training programs during the 1930s and 1940s focused on the need for labor unions, especially in the textile industries. Advocating equality of the races, Highlander flagrantly violated segregation laws and customs, and provided integrated housing and other accommodations. Highlander sponsored workshops which concentrated on the elimination of racial stereotypes, the breaking down of social barriers, and the development of leaders. The school was attended by many black and white activists, including Rosa Parks and Martin Luther King, Jr. During the summer of 1954, following the Supreme Court's *Brown v. Board of Education* decision, Clark attended the Highlander School's summer workshop.[23]

At Highlander, Clark met many whites and blacks working for an end to legal racial segregation. Workshop sessions addressed how the Supreme Court's decision could be implemented. She returned to Charleston to organize the black public school teachers. She invited Myles and Zilpha Horton, Highlander's organizers and founders, to Charleston to share their views on interracial work. Charleston's black teachers were experiencing difficulty securing bank loans to continue their graduate programs in education. So they established a credit union. The Hortons demonstrated how the teachers' collective work could secure group solidarity, while laying the foundation for a credit union.[24]

In the summer of 1955, Clark carried several carloads of black Charlestonians to Highlander. Most were amazed to learn of whites who were truly interested in the plight of African Americans. They were even more dumbfounded to discover that blacks and whites actually ate, slept, and worked together at Highlander. Some of the participants from Charleston were uncertain about the full extent of the integration practiced at the school, and chose to eat from the baskets of fried chicken they brought with them, just in case. Clark, frustrated by their stance, was assured by Horton: "Give them a few days, after the food runs out and they will [come] down [to the dining hall]." By the middle of their first week, the participants had joined the others. However, such racial harmony amazed even those participants who came with organizing experience. For example, one particular session included NAACP officer Rosa Parks and the well-known white activist, Virginia Durr, from Montgomery, Alabama. Durr was a frequent visitor to

Highlander and a member of the school's board of directors. It was at Durr's insistence and because of her support that Rosa Parks attended the 1955 workshop.[25]

Rosa Parks developed a friendship with Clark and Parks began to discuss her work as the advisor to the NAACP's Youth Council in Montgomery. Parks was reluctant to talk openly about her work, fearing that someone from her hometown would learn of her attendance at Highlander. However, Clark succeeded in getting Parks to share with the workshop participants information about the Women's Political Council, a group of black women in Montgomery whose political activism from the late 1940s and later during the Montgomery bus boycott formed the backbone for the civil rights campaigns in that city. The Women's Political Council stressed the need to work with youth to encourage them to seek elective office, learn about politics, and prepare for leadership. Rosa Parks's shyness and fears of possible reactions from whites in Montgomery convinced Clark to accompany Parks to Atlanta, where she took the bus back to Montgomery. Virginia Durr had done the same thing for Parks's trip to Highlander. Then in December 1955, Clark was totally stunned when she read a newspaper account about Parks's refusal to give up her seat on a public bus to a white person and her subsequent arrest. Clark stated that no one would have guessed that within a few short weeks, shy Rosa Parks would make such a dramatic statement. Clark often credited Parks with being the catalyst for her own determination to assist her people in acquiring full freedom.[26]

During the latter part of 1955, Myles Horton asked Clark to direct a Highlander workshop for black middle-class residents, mainly from Chattanooga and Nashville, Tennessee. These participants had been recruited through churches, social groups, and the YWCA; and their expenses had been paid by Highlander. Although they were literate and their higher economic status partially shielded them from some of the everyday abuses experienced by poor blacks, they still endured the blatant discrimination imposed by legal segregation—they could not vote and were either excluded or discriminated against in housing and public accommodations. Clark experienced little success with this group. Unlike the middle-class black teachers in Charleston and other parts of the South who worked regularly with poor children and adults, she was unable to get these wealthier residents to work with the poor blacks in their community. Clark stated:

I don't know whether they were afraid to try to teach others, or if they had some highfalutin idea that poor people were so far beneath them that they wouldn't fool with them. Many middle-class blacks were extremely hostile and prejudiced one to the other. That's the way they were. And so going to Highlander with them, we had a hard time. We got them to see what conditions they were living under, but we couldn't get them to do any of the work in their community to help others to change. Couldn't get them to do that. That's the one big reason why, when we started the Citizenship Schools, I felt it would be best not to try to use middle-class blacks as teachers. It would be better to use people from the community in which they lived who could just read well aloud and write legibly, rather than trying to use the others. That's why we got Bernice Robinson to run the first school that we set up on Johns Island in 1957. She was the first teacher we had for the whole South and after we had a success with Bernice in that school, then we could get others.[27]

The white South's violent response to the *Brown v. Board of Education* decision, particularly the escalation of militant activities among the White Citizen Councils and the Ku Klux Klan, led to physical and economic reprisals against politically active blacks. Blacks in Charleston realized that their civil rights would only be protected by their ability to exercise the franchise. Southern Democrats allowed some blacks to vote in the general elections if they possessed receipts indicating payment of their poll taxes. With the elimination of the white primary in 1944, white public officials continued to use literacy tests to restrict black voting. The literacy qualification meant that residents must be able to read and interpret a portion of the state's constitution to the registrar's satisfaction, to be added to the voting rolls. However, many registrars required black applicants to pass lengthy examinations, and to correctly answer absurd and unrelated questions, such as "How many bubbles are there in a bar of soap?" Clark related a story about a black professor from Tuskegee Institute who read perfectly the Alabama state constitution. The registrar, not to be outdone, then asked the professor to read a document written in Chinese. Incensed, the professor departed.[28]

Esau Jenkins, one of Septima Clark's former students on Johns Island, had an old school bus he used to carry workers from the island to downtown Charleston. One rider, Annie Wine, told Jenkins that she would register to vote if he would teach her how to pass the literacy test. Jenkins then used the forty-minute round trip ride to establish a classroom on wheels. Workers were taught basic information about local and national governments, but mainly they were taught to memorize the section of the state constitution that voters were required to read. Indeed, Mrs. Wine memorized the section so well that as the person in line before her misread the constitution, she openly corrected the reader. To which the registrar replied, "No coaching, please."[29] When Wine's turn came, she merely had to show her property tax receipt in order to receive her certification. Jenkins knew that it would be only a matter of time before the white officials would catch on to this plan. Blacks needed to know how to read and write. In fact Bernice Robinson recalled that, as the number of blacks registering increased, "the whites realized what was happening and started switching the sections you had to read, but they didn't catch on until the late fifties, and by that time we were really teaching people how to read, not just memorize."[30]

During the summer of 1956, Clark invited her cousin Bernice Robinson, a beautician, and Esau Jenkins to accompany her to Highlander. The workshop centered on discussions of world citizenship using the United Nations as a theme. Participants were asked to develop plans for implementing the summer's work in their respective communities. Jenkins stated that he was not familiar with the United Nations, but his people needed to know how to read and write and he wished Highlander could help him establish a school on Johns Island for that purpose. Sensing the urgency and the desperation in his voice, for the next two weeks the workshop concentrated on creating a workable plan for Jenkins.[31]

Septima Clark and the Launching of the Citizenship Schools

The year 1956 ushered in two significant events for Clark—the beginning of the Citizenship School on Johns Island, which laid the foundation for mass organizing in the modern Civil Rights Movement; and the termination of Clark's employment with the public school system of Charleston. As part of the southern response to the *Brown* decision, in an attempt to control the political activism of African Americans, a number of southern state legislatures passed laws designating the NAACP a subversive organization, suggesting that the association was linked to the Communist Party. State officials declared that African

Americans were pawns in the Communists' plan to take over the United States. In South Carolina, all public employees were required to state whether or not they were members of the NAACP, and to acknowledge all other organizational affiliations. Membership in the NAACP was grounds for termination of employment by the state.[32] In response to this intimidation, Clark organized a letter-writing campaign directed to the 726 black teachers. Clark recalled,

> I said to myself, "The KKK is an organization, and the White Citizens' Council is an organization, and they can belong to those. Why can't I belong to the NAACP?" Then I thought, "If we just admit it, surely they can't throw out all of us. There are too many [of us]. I got in touch with all [the black teachers], but only forty-two would admit to being members—eleven met to plan to see the superintendent, and when the day came to go see him, eleven showed up, and when it was the hour to go, only five of us went. All forty-two who admitted being members were dismissed, and I've never been able to teach in South Carolina since."[33]

The firing in 1956 of Clark and other black teachers in Charleston who admitted to being members of the NAACP was representative of the struggle occurring in a number of cities throughout the South. At the end of the 1955–56 school year, many black teachers who had voted, were members of the NAACP, or who openly acknowledged support for school integration, faced dismissal from their teaching positions. For example, in Greenville, Mississippi, White Citizens Council members demanded that local school boards dismiss black teachers whose names appeared on the voting rolls. In Georgia, the state board of education adopted a resolution that forbade teachers from joining the NAACP, and that threatened the revocation of the teaching licenses of those who refused to quit the organization. In Missouri and Oklahoma, black teachers who lost their positions due to desegregation plans filed breach of contract suits against school officials.[34]

The firing of Clark and other African American teachers was part of a larger effort to repress all efforts to integrate public schools in South Carolina and throughout the South, and to undermine the efforts of the NAACP and other civil rights organizations seeking an end to the southern system of segregation and discrimination. Although most persons, including Clark, acknowledged that her termination was related to her membership in the NAACP, they understood that many whites in Charleston wanted to silence and destroy

Clark and her leadership. Clark's firing was a symbolic act, and was about much more than a black woman who happened to be vocal about her NAACP membership. Though membership violated the South Carolina statute, membership in the NAACP did not automatically produce activism. Clark had established a highly visible, militant public persona in Charleston and at Highlander, and such overt militancy had to be cut off at its economic roots. Following her dismissal, Clark accepted a full-time position at Highlander as the Director of Workshops. Clark was required to organize and conduct the workshops held primarily in the summer, recruit participants, and raise funds to support the Highlander program.

During the fall of 1956, Clark collaborated with Esau Jenkins and Myles Horton in the development of the first black Citizenship School, which opened under the auspices of the Highlander Folk School in January 1957 on Johns Island. The school became the prototype for others that were opened on the South Carolina Sea Islands and later throughout the South. Although the initial purpose of the schools was to enable blacks to meet the literacy requirements for voting in South Carolina, the primary goal was education for empowerment. Clark fervently believed that there was a relationship between "Literacy and Liberation." She developed what Brazilian educator Paulo Freire later referred to as a "pedagogy of the oppressed," that utilized material culture and the daily experiences of individuals who were functional illiterates, to teach reading and writing skills, and to generate an understanding of the relationship of education to freedom and the acquisition of one's civil rights.[35]

The first citizenship school, held in rooms in the back of a local cooperative operated by black farmers to sell their produce, had no textbooks or other formal reading materials, only the things adults wished to read. Windows were covered so that whites and/or their spies would not know what was going on. Clark, remembering the problems she encountered earlier working with middle-class blacks at Highlander, asked her cousin Bernice Robinson to serve as the school's first teacher. Bernice Robinson, a beautician, protested that she did not have the education. But Clark and Jenkins told her that

> We don't want a certified teacher because they are accustomed to working by a straitlaced curriculum. They wouldn't be able to bend, to give. We need a community worker to do it who cares for the people, who

understands the people, who can communicate with the people, and someone who has been to Highlander who knows Highlander's philosophy, so there's nobody to do it but you. Either you do it or we don't have the school.

Robinson, who was familiar with the Charleston area because of her work with the NAACP, accepted the challenge.[36]

Scheduling classes around the agricultural calendar of the islanders, the citizenship school was conducted during the "lay by" months of December, January, and February. On the first night, Robinson arrived ready to use basic materials borrowed from elementary school teachers. She quickly realized that her plan must be altered. Robinson announced to the students that she was not a teacher, and that her job was primarily to facilitate the learning process. In turn, the students informed her of their desire to understand and master basic information, useful for daily living. Robinson utilized items from the day-to-day lives of the students, who expressed a need to master the fundamentals of writing a money order, filling out a department store catalog order form, signing their names to official documents, and being able to read well enough to register to vote. Robinson began by asking the students to recite their activities for the day. These became stories for the students to write about and to read aloud. They used bank checks, money orders, and catalog forms as practice writing materials; newspaper advertisements from local grocery stores for arithmetic. Men were asked to determine how many gallons of gas were required to drive from the island into Charleston. Farmers had to work out the mathematical calculations necessary for putting up a fence.[37]

Some of the adult students were members of churches and lodges where they were required to make oral presentations. Conscious of their impediments, students asked Robinson to assist them with public speaking. The young people laughed at the adults as they tried to read aloud, mispronouncing words. Robinson then decided to have the young and old prepare for classroom debates by using contemporary materials. Following much coaching on language skills and presentation, many of the students performed very well.[38] At the end of the first session of the Citizenship School, all fourteen of the original students received certificates. Clark recalled that "They could read and write their own names, and they could do arithmetic."

The numbers of black registered voters on Johns Island increased, and word of the school's success spread rapidly. This triggered an excitement and an interest in attending the Citizenship School among the residents on the other islands. By 1958 classes were established on Wadmalaw Island, Edisto Island, and in North Charleston. Bernice Robinson's responsibilities grew as new schools were developed on other islands. She recruited and drove the teachers to Highlander's summer workshops, opened new schools, and supervised existing ones. Classrooms varied from kitchens, to beauty parlors, to neighboring yards under trees. Whites soon realized that there had been a groundswell of activity among the black islanders. Newspaper stories noted this activism, in an attempt to intimidate blacks into abandoning their political involvement. Clark feared that blacks would revert to the earlier position of fear and complacency, but as she traveled around the islands, she found they were determined to continue to register and vote.[39]

During her three-year tenure (1957–1960) as Director of Workshops and chief fundraiser for Highlander, Clark traveled throughout the United States speaking to friends, sponsors, and benefactors of the Highlander Folk School, seeking financial support for the school's program of social reform. The high visibility of the school, and its interracial character, made it a target for Tennessee officials, who argued that the school violated state segregation laws and should be closed down. During the 1950s and 1960s, activities and gatherings that had an interracial composition were frequently characterized as "Communist inspired forums" for the dissemination of "propaganda." In July 1959, state troopers descended on Highlander as Clark was conducting a workshop. They began searching the institution's buildings, including the private residence of Myles Horton. Unaware of their presence, the workshop participants continued to view a film, "The Face of the South." The police officers entered and demanded that the film be cut off. Clark and the participants refused and the equipment was disabled by the troopers. Faced with a threatening confrontation, the group began to sing freedom songs, including "We Shall Overcome," adding a new verse, "I am not afraid." Having allegedly found a beer can in Horton's home, the troopers arrested Clark and several others on trumped up charges of selling liquor in a dry state. Bail, set at $500, was paid by May Justus, a longtime Highlander supporter. The charges against Clark were later dropped, but the newspaper headlines read: "Septima Clark Arrested for Possession of Whiskey."[40]

Following the raid on Highlander, Myles Horton and Martin Luther King, Jr. met to discuss the possibility of the Citizenship School Program being transferred to SCLC. The idea of moving the program to SCLC was introduced in 1959 by Ella Baker, who was then SCLC's acting executive secretary. Clark and the Highlander program would remain in Monteagle, Tennessee until 1961. By that time King had come to realize how much SCLC needed Septima Clark and the citizenship training program, to help raise funds and revitalize its defunct Crusade for Citizenship program.

Septima Clark and the Southern Christian Leadership Conference

The SCLC's founding in 1957 had coincided with the passage of the 1957 Civil Rights Act, which among other things made interference with an individual's voting rights a federal offense. Then King and SCLC officials decided to concentrate on black voter registration in the South. In February 1958, SCLC launched the "Crusade for Citizenship," an unsuccessful attempt to increase the number of southern black voters. Like Clark, SCLC leaders recognized that political disfranchisement was an important aspect of southern black oppression and identified the achievement of voting rights as the next goal for collective action. Unfortunately, SCLC's Crusade for Citizenship program failed to obtain its goal in the late 1950s because of white resistance and its inability to increase the number of eligible residents who could pass the literacy tests used by most southern states. Voting, unlike bus boycotts and mass protests, required that one be able to read and write. The question was how to train the masses of illiterate and semiliterate black people to read and write in a short period of time.

Beginning in late 1959 and continuing through 1960, Clark traveled to Atlanta on weekends for sessions planning with SCLC. On Monday mornings Clark would be driven to a designated town in the South, where she would spend a week or two trying to convince the local black residents to establish Citizenship Schools or help with SCLC's organized protests and marches. Clark developed a good working relationship with Ella Baker, SCLC's Associate Director, who went to Highlander during the summer of 1960 and worked with Clark in training young people to assume leadership roles in the Civil Rights Movement. At Highlander, Baker became convinced that the Citizenship School program was exactly what SCLC needed, but it took Baker two years to convince King to attend Highlander workshops and see what they were doing.[41]

In 1961, when the Highlander Folk School was finally closed by white state officials and after continuous prodding from Ella Baker and Myles Horton, King recruited Clark to work with SCLC in Atlanta. The Highlander leadership training program had served its purpose, but given the steady advance of the Civil Rights Movement between the years 1954 and 1960, Clark and other leaders recognized the need for a program that stressed both leadership training and citizenship education and provided rural blacks with the basic skills necessary for achieving literacy and ultimately the right to vote. In an article published in *Freedomways*, entitled "Literacy and Liberation," Clark reflected on the importance of Highlander, and how she and other school officials had come to the realization that literacy and liberation went hand in hand. "The basic purpose of citizenship schools is discovering and developing local community leaders." For Clark, leadership was not necessarily synonymous with having a college education or middle-class status. Clark felt that for the Civil Rights Movement to succeed, grassroots leadership had to be developed, and she believed that the Citizenship Schools were essential to achieving that goal.

> In 1954 in the South, segregation was the main barrier in the way of the realization of democracy and brotherhood. Highlander was an important place because Negroes and whites met on an equal basis and discussed their problems together.
>
> There was a series of workshops on Community Services and Segregation, Registration and Voting, and Community Development. Then it became evident that the [South] had a great number of functional illiterates who needed additional help to carry out their plans for coping with the problems confronting them.[42]

Clark's definition and use of the term literacy was very broad. Although reading, writing, and arithmetic were important, being literate also meant that one understood the meaning of citizenship and how to acquire citizenship rights. As an example of the relationship of literacy to liberation, Clark cited the case of black maids and custodians in the Atlanta public schools asking the Atlanta Board of Education for a raise in pay. Clark recalled that "it was such an audacious step for them to take" that the superintendent of schools wrote an article for the *Atlanta Constitution* entitled "Maids Ask City Schools for a Raise." The maids and custodians complained that they had only three days release time during the Christmas season, whereas other employees had two weeks. They also asked for salary increases that would meet the basic living standards. The maids and custodians sent copies of the letter to the mayor and two members of the board of education, and concluded, *"Literacy means liberation."*[43]

The Citizenship School program developed at the Highlander Folk School was funded by grants from the Emil Schwarzhaupt Foundation, the Marshall Field Foundation, and the Ford Foundation, and in 1961 the entire program was moved to SCLC. In Atlanta, Clark focused on citizenship training, voting, and literacy, literally replicating the Highlander program, with Andrew Young and Dorothy Cotton as staff members. A center in Liberty County, Georgia owned by the American Missionary Association became the home for the program. Although Andrew Young was the director of citizenship education, which was merged with the voter registration program, Clark was in charge of the overall project.[44]

Like Clark, Young was transferred to SCLC with the Highlander Citizenship Program, becoming its director. Dorothy Cotton had worked with Wyatt T. Walker in the Petersburg Improvement Association. When Walker accepted a position with SCLC, Cotton joined him. Cotton's role was to serve as a cultural emissary for SCLC, who utilized music and folklore as vehicles for generating interest and support among rural blacks. This technique had also been used at Highlander.[45] The Citizenship School staff reported to SCLC's Atlanta office and worked with Wyatt T. Walker in establishing the program and in creating the center in Liberty County, Georgia. They did not bring people in south Georgia to the center during the first month. Instead, the staff traveled throughout Georgia, Florida, Alabama, Mississippi, and Louisiana recruiting students.[46]

The SCLC Citizenship Schools were highly successful. Between 1961 and 1970, 897 were established in southern states where there were large concentrations of African Americans. The schools were held in many places, including private homes, beauty parlors and barber shops, and when necessary, in outdoor venues frequented by ordinary black people. Clark endorsed the statement made by Andrew Young that "the Citizenship Schools were the base on which the whole Civil Rights Movement was built," and she added that:

> It's true because the Citizenship Schools made people aware of the political situation in their area. We recruited the wise leaders of their communities, like Fannie Lou Hamer in Mississippi. Hosea Williams started out as a Citizenship School Supervisor. The Citizenship School classes formed the grassroots basis of new statewide political organizations in South Carolina, Georgia, and Mississippi. From one end of the South to the other, if you look at the black elected officials and the political leaders, you find people who had their first involvement in the training program of the Citizenship School.[47]
>
> It was 1962 before the major civil rights groups were ready to do something about voter registration. But we had developed the ideas of the Citizenship Schools between 1957 and 1961. So all the civil rights groups could use our kind of approach, because by then we knew it worked.[48]

One of the first projects launched by the SCLC Citizenship School program was centered in south Georgia. Clark went to Savannah to canvass and to organize because of the work of activist Hosea Williams. According to Clark, Williams was trying to get people to register to vote but he "didn't know that he had to teach them to read and write so they could answer the thirty questions that the Georgia [literacy test] had for them to answer." Following the success of the Savannah Citizenship School, Hosea Williams established schools in eighteen other counties in the southeastern part of Georgia.[49]

Potential grassroots leaders and teachers in locales throughout the state of Georgia were identified and brought to the SCLC Citizenship School headquarters established in Liberty County. The SCLC underwrote the expenses of all persons who participated in its weeklong training workshops. Utilizing the carefully honed and developed techniques that had proven successful in South Carolina, Septima Clark supervised the workshops which included many persons who could barely read or write, and demonstrated how they could instruct others. Participants were shown the relationship between voter registration, voting, and the achievement of personal and community goals.[50]

At the end of the Citizenship School's training workshops, participants returned to their home towns where they received $75 per month to teach others the skills they learned. For many participants, this was more money than they had ever received from employers. Citizenship School teachers frequently became grassroots leaders, who gradually replaced the local clergy as leaders. Many black ministers were more dependent on white people's approval and were often afraid to openly join or support the Civil Rights Movement. Assessing the position of the local black ministers, Clark said:

> Of course I understand those preachers . . . Often they weren't against the Movement; they were just afraid to join it openly. It's simply a contradiction: so many preachers supported the Movement that we can say it was based in churches, yet many preachers couldn't take sides with it because they thought they had too much to lose.[51]

Black ministers have received the greatest scholarly and public recognition as the leaders of the Civil Rights Movement. However, black women through their community activism were often the grassroots leaders. Black women actively organized through their network of missionary and other church-based associations, as well as in the National Association of Colored Women and the National Council of Negro Women. They used these networks to raise money and to disseminate information about meetings, conferences, protests, and marches. Many church women who worked with the Citizenship Schools were also members of the NAACP and various civic associations. Through their extensive networks they were able to perform bridging functions between local and national civil rights organizations.[52]

In analyzing Clark and the female leadership of her generation, one can identify some of the connections between the activism of early twentieth-century club women with the women of the modern Civil Rights–Black Power Movement, and in many cases recognize their work as "bridge leaders." Such women came of age during the post–Reconstruction era and inherited a long history of racial consciousness and gender networking, bonding, and organizing.[53] Women like Ella Baker, Modjeska Simkins, and Septima Clark had been influenced and molded by older women who worked in cooperative efforts for the passage of antilynching, suffrage, employment, education, housing, and other legislation designed to improve the lot of black women and men. These women worked in traditional race protest organizations or affiliated groups in their quest to improve the quality of life for African Americans. Though they sometimes collaborated with white women, as was the case in the antilynching and suffrage campaigns, their primary objective was black social and political advancement.[54]

Clark and other activist women, such as Ella Baker, Gloria Richardson, and many lesser known figures, demonstrated another definition of leadership based on the experiences and perspectives of female activists. As a result of their presence, work, and acceptance by the masses as leaders, male activism ceased to be the only acceptable model of leadership. Leadership at the grassroots level reflected the ability of individuals—regardless of sex—to influence and organize people for social change. Working at the grassroots level, with the rural and unlettered black masses, Clark communicated the message that the local residents could be entrusted with the power to make decisions that impacted *their* lives and likewise could train their brothers and sisters in the struggle.

Charismatic, hierarchical leadership came under attack in the 1950s, especially from Septima Clark and Ella Baker, whose work with indigenous communities, leading by example and establishing new models of viable leadership, opened up new opportunities for the growth and development of future leaders. When they began their work with Martin Luther King and SCLC, Clark and Baker recognized that the civil rights campaigns could be hampered by a rigid leadership structure. At the same time, women in positions where they demonstrated important leadership skills often were not given the formal titles, nor the respect, their work deserved. Women in SCLC were denied recognition as leaders, or even as influential facilitators. Clark's ability to nurture, support, and develop grassroots black leaders who would carry out SCLC's program at the local level was not given any formal recognition. Essentially, Clark was not viewed as a "leader" because women's activities did not fit the traditional definition of "leadership." Clark, Baker, and Cotton's roles were considered "supportive" of the leadership that was provided by the men.

Clark is remembered by many for her courage and willingness to stand up to any man, black or white. Clark frequently confronted sexism in the black male groups she worked with, but she did not challenge the male's right to be the central voice for "the race." She believed in SCLC, shortcomings and all, and accepted King's concept of the beloved community, and his total commitment to nonviolent social change.

Septima Poinsette Clark's contributions to the Civil Rights Movement were many, yet it is impossible to provide a serious evaluation of her work without first understanding her strong commitment to "Literacy and Liberation." Clark's development of the Citizenship Schools, which became essential for civil rights mobilization, was the key to SCLC's successful voter registration campaign in 1961 and 1962 and the programs later launched by the Council of Federated Organizations (COFO).[55] Septima Poinsette Clark and her citizenship training crusade was a vital factor in launching the southern black liberation movement.

NOTES

1. Quote from Septima P. Clark, "The Vocation of Black Scholarship—Identifying the Enemy," unpublished essay, Septima Clark Collection, Robert Scott Small Library, College of Charleston, Charleston, SC (hereafter cited as SPC-RSS).

2. Letters from Septima P. Clark to Elizabeth Waring, May 19 and August 18, 1961, Howard University, Moorland Spingarn Research Center, Judge Julius Waites Waring Papers, box 110-9, folder 263 (hereafter cited as JWWP-MSRC).

3. "Mourners recall 'extraordinary life' of Septima Clark," by Barney Blakeney, Charleston, SC, *The Evening Post/The News and Courier*, December 20, 1987.

4. Taylor Branch, *Parting the Waters: America in the King Years 1954–1963* (New York: Simon and Schuster, 1988), 575–79.

5. Cynthia Stokes Brown, *Ready From Within: Septima Clark and the Civil Rights Movement* (Navarro, CA: Wild Trees Press, 1986), 70.

6. Cynthia Stokes Brown, "Septima Clark (1898–1987)," in Jessie Carney Smith, ed., *Notable Black American Women* (Detroit: Gale Research Inc., 1992), 70, 189–93.

7. Belinda Robnett, *How Long? How Long? African-American Women in the Struggle for Civil Rights* (New York: Oxford University Press, 1997), 22, 90–91, 191.

8. Septima Clark's Citizenship Schools program was also adopted by the Congress of Racial Equality (CORE), the National Association of Colored People (NAACP), the Urban League, and the Student Nonviolent Coordinating Committee (SNCC).

9. Grace Jordan McFadden, "Septima P. Clark and the Struggle for Human Rights," in Vicki L. Crawford, Jacqueline A. Rouse, and Barbara Woods, eds. *Women in the Civil Rights Movement: Trailblazers and Torchbearers, 1941–1965* (Brooklyn, NY: Carlson Publishing, 1990), 85; Septima Poinsette Clark, interview by Judy Barton, November 9, 1971, typescript, Charleston, SC, Oral History Project, Septima P. Clark Collection, Robert Scott Small Library, Special Collections, College of Charleston, Charleston, SC, 7 (hereafter cited as Barton Interview, RSS-SPC); Brown, *Ready From Within*, 89.

10. Septima Poinsette Clark, interview by Jacquelyn Dowd Hall, July 25, 1976, typescript, Charleston, SC, Southern Oral History Program, University of North Carolina at Chapel Hill (hereafter cited as Hall Interview, SOHP-UNC); Barton Interview, RSS-SPC, 5–7.

11. Brown, *Ready From Within*, 87–88; Septima P. Clark, *Echo in My Soul* (New York: E. P. Dutton and Company, 1962), 13–15.

12. LaVerne Gyant and Deborah F. Atwater, "Septima Clark's Rhetorical and Ethnic Legacy: Her Message of Citizenship in the Civil Rights Movement," *Journal of Black Studies*, 26, no. 5 (May 1996): 583; Clark, *Echo in My Soul*, chap. 2; Brown, *Ready From Within*, 96.

13. Barton Interview, RSS-SPC, 8–10.

14. Barton Interview, RSS-SPC, 6–7; McFadden, "Septima P. Clark and the Struggle for Human Rights," 86; Clark, *Echo in My Soul*, 52.

15. McFadden, "Septima P. Clark and the Struggle for Human Rights," 86–87.

16. Barton Interview, RSS-SPC, 15–16; Grace Jordan McFadden, "Clark, Septima Poinsette (1898–1987)," in Darlene Clark Hine, Elsa Barkley Brown, Rosalyn Terborg-Penn, eds., *Black Women in America: An Historical Encyclopedia* (Brooklyn, NY: Carlson Publishing, 1993), 249.

17. McFadden, "Septima P. Clark and the Struggle for Human Rights," 86–88; Brown, *Ready From Within*, 110; McFadden, "Clark, Septima Poinsette," 249.

18. Eliot Wigginton, ed., *Refuse to Stand Silently By: An Oral History of Grass Roots Social Activism in America, 1921–1964* (New York: Doubleday, 1992), 238–39; Clark, *Echo in My Soul*, 91–93; letter from Septima Clark to Elizabeth Waring, August 28, 1961, box 110-9, folder 232, JWWP-MSRC.

19. McFadden, "Clark, Septima Poinsette," 249–50; Brown, *Ready From Within*, 113–14.

20. McFadden, "Septima P. Clark and the Struggle for Human Rights," 89. For a discussion of the impact of salary discrimination on black teachers, and Clark's involvement, see Stephanie J. Shaw, *What a Woman Ought to Be and to Do: Black Professional Women Workers During the Jim Crow Era* (Chicago: University of Chicago Press, 1996), 201–3.

21. McFadden, "Septima P. Clark and the Struggle for Human Rights," 88, 89; Shaw, *What a Woman Ought to Be and to Do*, 203.

22. Clark, *Echo in My Soul*, 95–98; Brown, *Ready From Within*, 23–34; Hall Interview, SOHP-UNC, 63–69.

23. Barton Interview, RSS-SPC, 16–17, 21; Clark, *Echo in My Soul*, 119–20; Brown, *Ready From Within*, 30–31; Wigginton, *Refuse to Stand*, 240–41.

24. Ibid.

25. Brown, *Ready From Within*, 31–32.

26. Wigginton, *Refuse to Stand*, 240; Brown, *Ready From Within*, 31–34, 43–44; Barton, 23–24. For a discussion of the activism of black women in Montgomery, in particular the Women's Political Council, see Jo Ann Gibson Robinson, *The Montgomery Bus Boycott and the Women Who Started It* (Knoxville: University of Tennessee Press, 1987).

27. Wigginton, *Refuse to Stand*, 241.

28. Brown, *Ready From Within*, 67.

29. Ibid., 46.

30. Wigginton, *Refuse to Stand*, 190.

31. Sea Island Project, Part D, 26–29, Robert Scott Small Library, College of Charleston, SC.

32. Bettye Collier-Thomas and V. P. Franklin, *My Soul Is a Witness: A Chronology of the Civil Rights Era, 1954–1965* (New York: Henry Holt and Company, 2000), 48.

33. Wigginton, *Refuse to Stand*, 242; Barton Interview, RSS-SPC, 18–19.

34. Collier-Thomas and Franklin, *My Soul Is a Witness*, 31.

35. Clark, *Echo in My Soul*, 141; Wigginton, *Refuse to Stand*, 249; Sandra Brenneman Oldendorf, "Highlander Folk School and the South Carolina Sea Island Citizenship Schools: Implications for the Social Studies" (Ed.D. diss., University of Kentucky, 1987), 1; Septima Clark, "Literacy and Liberation," *Freedomways* (First Quarter, 1964), 113–24; Paulo Freire, *Pedagogy of the Oppressed* (New York: Seabury Press, 1970).

36. Clark, *Echo in My Soul*, 141; Wigginton, 249; Oldendorf, "Highlander Folk School."

37. Wigginton, *Refuse to Stand*, 251.

38. Ibid., 253.

39. Brown, *Ready From Within*, 50–51.

40. Ibid., 55–63; Wiggington, *Refuse to Stand*, 264–72.

41. Taylor Branch, *Parting the Waters*, 575–76; Aldon Morris, *The Origins of the Civil Rights Movement: Black Communities Organizing for Change* (New York: The Free Press, 1984), 111–13; McFadden, "Septima P. Clark and the Struggle for Human Rights," 90; Brown, *Ready From Within*," 61–62; Robnett, *How Long?*, 9; For a discussion of Ella Baker's struggle to interest SCLC's ministerial leaders in citizenship classes to teach basic reading and writing skills, see Carol Mueller, "Ella Baker and the Origins of 'Participatory Democracy,'" in Crawford, Rouse, and Woods, eds., *Women in the Civil Rights Movement*, 58–59.

42. Septima P. Clark, "Literacy and Liberation," *Freedomways*, First Quarter 1964, 114.

43. Ibid., 124.

44. A Workshop for Volunteer Teachers in the Citizenship Education Program of SCLC, 1965, RSS-SPC.

45. In the development of the citizenship training program in South Carolina, Zilpha Horton had brought many folk songs to the people of Johns Island and they in turn had taught her their secular and sacred music. Music often stimulated and motivated people to organize and to persevere. Septima Clark, Interview by Eugene Walker, typescript, July 30, 1976, Atlanta, GA, 2–3, Southern Oral History Program, University of North Carolina Chapel Hill, RSS-SPC (hereafter cited as Walker Interview, SOHP-UNC).

46. Walker Interview, SOHP-UNC, 4.

47. Ibid.

48. Brown, *Ready From Within*, 70.

49. Walker Interview, SOHP-UNC, 5–6.

50. Citizenship Program of SCLC, 35–65; RSS-SPC.

51. Brown, *Ready From Within*, 68.

52. Robnett, *How Long?*, 140–45.

53. For discussion of the development of female networking in the era of slavery and after, see Deborah G. White, *Arn't I a Woman? Female Slaves in the Plantation South* (New York: Norton, 1987), and Stephanie J. Shaw, "Black Club Women and the Creation of the National Association of Colored Women," in Darlene Clark Hine, Wilma King, and Linda Reed, eds., *We Specialize in the Wholly Impossible: A Reader in Black Women's History* (Brooklyn, NY: Carlson Publishing, 1995), 433–48.

54. For a closer view of the lives of two such women, see *Making a Way Out of No Way*, a film on the life and activism of Modjeska M. Simkins of Columbia, South Carolina, produced by Beryl Sanders and the Public Television of South Carolina; and *Fundi*, a film on the life of Ella Baker, produced and narrated by JoAnn Grant.

55. Collier-Thomas and Franklin, *My Soul Is a Witness*, 195, 207, 213.

Chapter 8

African American Women in the Mississippi Freedom Democratic Party

Vicki Crawford

Historical accounts of the Civil Rights Movement of the 1950s and 1960s have generally focused on the roles and contributions of male leaders and the nationally oriented civil rights organizations that they led. It has been only within the past decade that historians turned to consider the important roles played by female activists in the struggle for social change. This has come about, in large part, as a result of women historians who have attempted to document women's roles in mobilizing and sustaining the movement.[1] The marginalization of black female activists has obscured our understanding of the movement's leadership and rank-and-file. While male leadership dominated at the national and regional levels of the twentieth-century black freedom struggle, women's activism was strongest on the local level where black women extended their roles within church communities and secular organizations to organize for political change. This essay seeks to explore the role of African American women in the Mississippi Freedom Democratic Party, one of the most significant grassroots political organizations to evolve in the southern Civil Rights Movement.

The Mississippi Freedom Democratic Party (MFDP) was formed in April 1964, as an outgrowth of a statewide effort to remedy the severe social and political repression of African Americans. In 1960, conditions in Mississippi were more oppressive than elsewhere in the South. Although Mississippi had a higher proportion of black people than any other state, structural barriers to black voting systematically disfranchised them. The intensity of white resistance in Mississippi evolved from a historical legacy of black oppression dating back to the post–Reconstruction era when the state was the first to disfranchise African Americans, in 1890, through a revised state constitution which included, among various measures, a literacy requirement as a precondition to registering to vote. Mississippi's discriminatory voter registration laws were supplemented by other denials of black equality. Socioeconomic conditions within the predominantly rural state trapped most African Americans in the sharecropping system. In 1960, the black median family income was $1,444, approximately 34 percent of that of whites, which was $4,209, and nearly 83 percent of black families had incomes below the poverty level. Roughly one-half of all blacks had completed only six years or less of schooling, and over 32,000 black adults had no formal education at all. By contrast, half of all white adults had completed eleven or more years of school. More than 40 percent of all employed black men were farm workers or laborers, and almost 65 percent of black women were employed as cooks, maids, servants, and in other service jobs.[2] The combination of disfranchisement, social and economic discrimination, and strong white resistance culminated in one of the most significant challenges to the power structure ever witnessed in the United States. The Mississippi Freedom Democratic Party (MFDP) was pivotal in the transformation of what some had come to call the "closed society."[3] Its impact on Mississippi politics would be far-reaching, radically altering the balance of power within the state.

Although there had been earlier attempts to organize people at the local level prior to the 1960s, the black freedom struggle did not coalesce until then. Understandably, the few earlier attempts were less successful given the extremely violent response that local residents were sure to suffer. In 1961, young, Harlem-born Robert Moses arrived in Mississippi at the request of local activist C. C. Bryant to initiate one of the first voter registration campaigns in the state. At this time, blacks comprised merely 3 percent of all registered voters throughout the state, and early mobilization of local communities was a difficult task.[4] Fear of economic reprisals and harassment and violence often prevented sharecropping families and the rural poor from actively joining the struggle. Following Moses' early campaign in the southwest town of McComb, in 1961, other young activists working through the Student Nonviolent Coordinating Committee (SNCC) arrived in Mississippi where they organized voter registration drives around the state. As the movement drew strength and momentum, the focus on voter registration accelerated. By this time, civil rights groups had created the Council of Federated Organizations (COFO) as an umbrella organization to unify their activities throughout the state.[5]

Two years following Moses' first voter registration campaign in the southwest town of McComb, he conceived the idea for a "freedom election" in 1963. This symbolic act would demonstrate the desire of Mississippi blacks to vote, and refute charges made by Mississippi Senator James O. Eastland that African Americans had no interest in the franchise. In June 1963, COFO held a mock "freedom election" which paralleled the election between the two Democratic candidates for governor that August. Over 27,000 blacks cast their votes in the mock election.[6] A second mock election was held in November to parallel the state's general election. This time, COFO ran two candidates of their own: veteran black activist Aaron Henry, and Reverend Edwin King, a white minister from Tougaloo College. Henry and King were write-in candidates for governor and attorney general. Between 80,000 and 90,000 votes were cast in this parallel election, which symbolically demonstrated that, if blacks had been able to vote, they would prove a decisive factor in election outcomes. Moreover, the significance of the freedom vote was that it paved the way for the formation of the Mississippi Freedom Democratic Party (MFDP), a year later.[7]

Mississippi Freedom Summer and the MFDP

By 1964, the COFO officers had conceived the idea for the Freedom Summer Project. In spite of the freedom vote a year earlier, by this time, only 6.7 percent of Mississippi's black adults had succeeded in signing up to vote.[8] Moreover, the U.S. Supreme Court's *Brown v. Board of Education* decision had mandated the desegregation of public schools ten years earlier, yet in all districts across the state, schools remained segregated, as did other public accommodations such as restaurants, theaters, motels, and recreational facilities. The Freedom Summer Project was conceived by Robert Moses and Allard Lowenstein, a white civil rights activist, with support from local activists, notably Fannie Lou Hamer and Lawrence Guyot.[9]

After earlier voter registration efforts yielded meager results, Moses and the others agreed that a more intensive campaign had to be devised. According to Moses, they "decided that outside intervention alone would make possible a significant breakthrough in voter registration in Mississippi and that this intervention could come about only with greater national publicity regarding Mississippi civil rights activities."[10] The architects of Freedom Summer recruited and brought in a massive influx of northern black and white college students to Mississippi, where they registered potential voters in an effort to dramatize conditions in the state. It was an attempt on the part of the project's planners to force the federal government to intervene in the state. More importantly, another goal of Freedom Summer was to develop grassroots leadership which would sustain itself long after the college students had left. In addition to the massive, statewide voter registration campaign, other Freedom Summer activities included the establishment of Freedom Schools and community centers where literacy training was provided. Perhaps the most significant development that grew out of Freedom Summer, however, was the creation of an independent, third political party of farmers, former sharecroppers, and other grassroots people.

The Mississippi Freedom Democratic Party (MFDP) was formed to supplant the state's regular Democratic party, which had excluded black voters, openly defended segregation in party planks, and repudiated national party platforms. The MFDP sought to gain recognition from the national party as the official Democratic party within the state, inclusive of black voters and in support of the major platforms and the presidential candidate of the national party. The process by which the MFDP sought to establish its legitimacy was based on legal arguments and political activities which would demonstrate the desire of the state's large black population to acquire the right to vote. The party did not realize its goal of wresting control from the state's all-white "regular" Democratic party; however, the process politicized black communities throughout the state and paved the way for the later election of black public officials statewide. By 1994, Mississippi had 751 black elected officials, more than any other state.[11]

The major campaigns launched by the MFDP included the challenge to the Mississippi delegation to the 1964 Democratic National Convention, the challenge to Mississippi's congressional delegation, and the protest against the nomination of former Mississippi governor James P. Coleman to a judgeship on the Fifth Federal Circuit Court. The congressional and convention challenges attacked the systematic exclusion of potential black voters, and the protest of Coleman's nomination was a response to his record as a staunch defender of segregation. Among the key founders and leaders of the MFDP were three African American women—Fannie Lou Hamer, Annie Devine, and Victoria Gray—who were at the center of power within the grassroots party where they influenced decision making and helped to develop the party's strategies and tactics. The leadership and rank-and-file of the MFDP were working class, a significant shift from traditional black leadership in the state, which primarily consisted of ministers and prominent local business leaders. In addition, the MFDP had strong female representation within its ranks which resulted in egalitarian participation among the party's activists. By 1964, Hamer, Devine, and Gray were seasoned civil rights veterans, having organized the movement in their own respective towns and communities.

Fannie Lou Hamer

Fannie Lou Hamer was the child of sharecroppers, born in 1917, in Montgomery County, Mississippi. She was typical of most rural, poor black women in background and circumstances, yet indisputably extraordinary in her courageous stand against racism and economic injustice. By the time she became involved in the movement, in 1962, Hamer had long suffered Mississippi's racism and rural poverty. That year, Hamer responded to an appeal by SNCC workers who had come to Sunflower County to organize local residents; she was among the few local people to volunteer to go to the courthouse and attempt to register. Upon her return to the plantation where she and her husband, Pap, had sharecropped for more than eighteen years, Hamer was told to leave. From that moment on, Fannie Lou Hamer courageously committed herself to the freedom struggle, where she rose to national prominence in the fight against racial and economic injustice.

Fannie Lou Hamer went back to the county courthouse repeatedly until she was finally registered on January 10, 1963. She became one of the first of the county's approximately 30,000 black residents to register. In June 1963, Hamer suffered a brutal beating which left her permanently scarred. After returning from a voter registration workshop, Hamer, along with several others, was arrested, jailed, and brutally beaten in Winona, Mississippi. She recalled that she paid for that beating every day of her life. Fannie Lou Hamer's source of strength derived from her strong religious beliefs, which sustained her activism in the most difficult of circumstances.

For Mrs. Hamer, civil rights activism was a natural expression of her spirituality in practice. She quoted the Bible frequently in her challenges to white supremacy and appealed to the moral conscience of white Americans. In one of her many speeches before a mass civil rights meeting, she warned how the continuation of racism threatened the moral fabric of American society:

> A house divided against itself cannot stand. America is divided against itself and without them considering us as human beings, one day America will crumble! Because God is not pleased. God is not pleased with all the murdering, and all the brutality and all the killings for no reason at all. God is not pleased that the Negro children in the state of Mississippi are suffering from malnutrition . . . And, then how can they say that in ten years time, we will force every Negro out of the state of Mississippi. But, I want these people to take a good look at themselves, and after they have sent the Chinese back to China, the Jews back to Jerusalem and give the Indians their land back; they take the Mayflower back from where it came, the Negro will still be in Mississippi.[12]

Not only was Mrs. Hamer a powerful orator, but her singing inspired many a civil rights meeting. One activist recalled that "when Mrs. Hamer finishes singing a few freedom songs, one is aware that he has truly heard a fine political speech, stripped of the usual rhetoric and filled with the anger and determination of the civil rights movement."[13]

Annie Devine

Annie Devine was born in Mobile, Alabama, and while still a child moved to Canton, Mississippi, where she was reared by her mother's sister. She grew up in Canton and later worked at various jobs throughout her teenage and early adult years. She married, had four children, and eventually divorced after ten years of marriage. Mrs. Devine attended Tougaloo College for two years and taught elementary school briefly in Flora, Mississippi. By the 1960s, she held a job as a debit manager for the black-owned Security Life Insurance Company. Mrs. Devine had a wide sphere of influence within the black community of Canton, where she was a committed and highly respected church worker. By 1961, the Congress of Racial Equality (CORE) had begun organizing in Canton and young activists sought her out. They realized that Mrs. Devine could be pivotal in lending credibility to civil rights activities and in encouraging local people to join the struggle. The first step to building mass support was, of course, involving persons in the community whom others looked to for advice and counsel. CORE activist Matthew Suarez recalled that Annie Devine was a stabilizing force among the young activists who had come to Canton:

> She directed us to blacks who were trustworthy in the community, told us what blacks would do and what they wouldn't, how to address them. In many ways, she acted like a go-between with black, male leaders [notably preachers] and young folks [who resisted their authority]. We were saying to leadership, "You ought to be ashamed not to be doing this and that for our people, and [Mrs. Devine] was saying you ought to do this because of what has happened." She could draw on her lived experience. She was the backbone, a part of the strategists. She understood clearly how we should handle and conduct ourselves in Canton. We came in like we're here to save you folks and Mrs. Devine instructed CORE that this was the wrong approach. You can't relate to people in this community using this approach. Mrs. Devine was a country diplomat.[14]

Annie Devine joined CORE, and became one of the founders of the MFDP in 1964.

Victoria Gray

Victoria Gray joined the black freedom struggle shortly after young SNCC workers Curtis Hayes and Hollis Watkins arrived in the southeast town of Hattiesburg in 1962. Mrs. Gray was one of the few local people who was willing to commit to the movement in its early stages, and her involvement was critical to getting voter registration under way in Forrest County. By this time, she was a middle-aged wife and mother of three children as well as a successful businesswoman.

Victoria Gray grew up in the tiny village of Palmer's Crossing, an all-black community of independent farmers and landowners situated just outside of Hattiesburg, Mississippi. Following the death of her mother when Victoria was three years old, she was reared by her paternal grandparents who instilled in her their own sense of independence and self-sufficiency. Gray's grandparents were proud people, successful farmers who owned property and were economically independent of local whites. After high school, Victoria Gray attended Wilberforce University, in Ohio, for three years and later taught school briefly before the regimentation of teaching became a "bother." In the meantime, she married and traveled to Germany, where she spent three years with her husband who was in the U.S. military. After returning to the United States, they were stationed in Fort Meade, Maryland, for several years. During this time, Gray became a successful sales representative for a black-owned beauty products firm called Beauty Queen. She excelled in business, though her marriage was breaking apart. Eventually, she divorced and returned to her native community of Palmer's Crossing, where she moved into the homeplace left by her grandparents in 1955. Here, Victoria Gray opened up a local office selling Beauty Queen products and recruited two additional sales agents. Within a few years, she had a sales force of more than twenty-five agents.

Once young SNCC workers arrived in Hattiesburg in 1961, they searched about for a local church to hold mass meetings. Several ministers had already turned them down. One day, when Curtis Hayes and Hollis Watkins happened by the shop of Gray's brother, a television and electronics operator, they began discussing the reluctance of local ministers to open up the churches. Gray's brother suggested that they contact his sister, Victoria, who could be influential in encouraging the minister of St. John Methodist Church to let the activists use its facilities. From here, St. John's became a movement church and Victoria Gray was among the key advocates in a drive to register black voters.

Gray later attended a Southern Christian Leadership Conference (SCLC) workshop in Dorchester, Georgia, where she met South Carolina activist Septima Clark who pioneered the innovative citizenship education program. The goal of citizenship education was to teach adult literacy skills as a means of personal empowerment and preparation for voter registration. Historically, the literacy requirement had been a major roadblock to black suffrage since many African Americans in the state could not read or write. Following a week of intensive training under Clark, Victoria Gray returned to Hattiesburg where she launched citizenship education in that community. She recalled that the model program initiated by Septima Clark proved highly effective in Mississippi:

> It really gave people the information that gave them the courage to say I am going to become a registered voter. When they understood the relevance and the connectedness between being registered to vote and righting a lot of the other things that were wrong in the community, that's where the courage came from to say let's do it. Everywhere there was a really effective movement in Mississippi, at the heart of that movement was the people who had taken the citizenship education program.[15]

Even though the citizenship training program was primarily implemented by activists working for SCLC, Gray never allowed organizational differences to restrict her movement activities; she later worked for CORE, SNCC, the Delta Ministry, and MFDP. Perhaps Gray's ability to rise above some of the organizational rifts that sometimes separated other civil rights groups came from what she called her "faith connection" and broader vision of the movement's goals. She stated:

> It doesn't matter what area I am in, my faith connection is my mainstay. My faith connection has been with me in all that I've ever done, whether it was in the community at large, whether it was in the political arena. I came to appreciate the importance of people being involved in the political arena. I think people who are involved in the political arena who do not have a spiritual base are the people who want to build bigger and bigger jails, spend more and more on defense, and get people off of welfare onto workfare, but they don't have any jobs for them to work on. The lack of a spiritual base on which one functions is just so destructive as opposed to those who have one.[16]

By 1964, Victoria Gray had become fully involved in the black freedom struggle, though she does not recall exactly "when the switch came." To be sure, the spiritual and moral teachings of her upbringing laid the foundation for social activism. She remembered that, "I was born into a community where there was no separation between the spiritual and the secular. There's never been a time in my life when there was a separation of who I am and what I do and why I do what I do." She further explained that once civil rights activities got under way in the Hattiesburg community, she responded to the teachings of her youth, which called for acting on one's spiritual principles. Gray stated, "I had been reared with the sense that you have a responsibility to respond to a need, that coupled with the training for as long as I can remember that 'be ye doers of the word and not hearers only.'"

What Gray terms her "faith connection" began with the teachings of her grandmother, who quoted scripture to Victoria throughout her childhood and teenage years. "It was not just a verse she said, but an act in cooperation that made that thing consistent in your life."[17]

Prior to the events of Freedom Summer in 1964, Victoria Gray, Fannie Lou Hamer, and Annie Devine had not known one another personally. But, Victoria Gray recalls that

> one thing we have in common, we're deeply spiritual people; that is one common denominator. We come from three totally different places; three totally different environments; never had heard of each other before the movement, and somehow, as we journeyed, our paths came together and remained so, throughout and continues. And, the black woman was the only one who could do it and live.[18]

The MFDP Convention Challenge

The Mississippi Freedom Democratic Party (MFDP) was formed in April 1964 to mount opposition to the state's traditional Democratic party, which excluded blacks from participation. It was a well-devised, tactically conceived structure which would parallel the pyramid-like process for selecting precinct and state representatives who would then be elected to attend the Democratic National Convention to be held in Atlantic City, New Jersey. In June 1964, the traditional Democrats predictably excluded blacks from the delegate selection process. In a calculated response, the MFDP organized an executive committee which established parallel precinct meetings, county conventions, and a statewide convention. Over 800 delegates attended the state convention of the MFDP which convened on August 6, 1964, in Jackson, Mississippi. The keynote speaker was veteran activist Ella Baker, who urged the delegates to move forward in their plans to challenge the all-white regulars. They elected sixty-eight delegates and chose the party's national representatives. Among them were Victoria Gray, serving as a national committeewoman, Fannie Lou Hamer as Vice-Chair of the delegation, and Annie Devine as secretary of the delegation, along with Lawrence Guyot who was the newly elected chairman of the MFDP. To build additional support for the MFDP and its convention challenge in Atlantic City, the organization held a "freedom registration" campaign designed to offer further evidence in the disparity between black and white voting patterns in the state. By 1964, official registration figures showed that only 20,000 blacks were registered as compared to 500,000 whites. This constituted less than 7 percent of the 435,000 blacks in Mississippi 21 years and older who were eligible to vote.[19]

Prior to the convention that August, the MFDP managed to garner support from other civil rights groups, labor unions, and some liberal Democratic party leaders. In the months preceding the national meeting, a few state Democratic conventions had passed resolutions in support of the MFDP challenge. Once the sixty-eight delegates arrived in Atlantic City that August, they were guardedly optimistic about defeating the Mississippi "regulars"; however, it would soon be evident that the national party leadership would attempt to sell them out. The very presence of grassroots people at the convention was significant in itself. As one observer noted, "The MFDP sent to Atlantic City for the Democratic National Convention was probably the first delegation in generations to have been selected by the 'people,' in the politically meaningful sense of the term."[20]

The first step to unseating the regular delegation entailed an appearance before the Credentials Committee on Saturday, August 23, 1964. The MFDP was aware that the Credentials Committee might decide on four possible outcomes: the regular delegation could be seated; the MFDP could be seated; both could be seated; or neither could be seated. At the Credentials Committee hearings, the MFDP offered compelling evidence of the brutality and violence in Mississippi and the disfranchisement of the state's black citizens. National civil rights leaders were present as well. Roy Wilkins of the NAACP, James Farmer of CORE, and Dr. Martin Luther King, Jr. of SCLC were among those who testified in support of the MFDP. However, it was Hamer's heartrending account of conditions for African

Americans in Mississippi that captured the attention of the nation-wide audience. In the midst of her testimony, President Lyndon Johnson pre-empted her and announced an emergency televised news conference. But the nation had heard and witnessed Fannie Lou Hamer, loud and clear.

Ultimately, the MFDP challenge resulted in the offer of a compromise proposed by the party's national leaders. President Johnson, up for re-election, feared that recognition of the MFDP would cost him southern votes and result in a convention walkout by southern white delegates if the MFDP were seated. Johnson gave the job of orchestrating a compromise to vice-presidential hopeful, Senator Hubert Humphrey, along with other liberal Democratic leaders, the result of which was the offer of two at-large seats at the convention to the entire MFDP delegation.[21] Along with this token gesture, the compromise would still allow the seating of the regular delegation from Mississippi. Furthermore, to add insult to injury, it specifically named the at-large delegates to be chosen: Reverend Ed King and state NAACP president Aaron Henry. Ultimately, the MFDP rejected the compromise in toto, but not until the delegates debated bitterly among themselves. One faction within the ranks argued for acceptance of the compromise, while another, led by Fannie Lou Hamer, Annie Devine, and Victoria Gray, emphatically urged rejection on the grounds that it was an empty offer. Annie Devine remarked that "the compromise left us right where we were. It didn't give us any leverage at all."[22] Mrs. Hamer summed up the MFDP response most emphatically when she stated, "We didn't come all this way for no two seats."[23] Despite the defeat, the convention challenge did, in effect, result in some reforms within the national Democratic party. It revised its rules so that by the 1968 national convention, the party had adopted a nondiscrimination clause in its requirements for delegate selection, making that convention more racially inclusive than ever before.

The MFDP Congressional Challenge

Following the convention defeat, the MFDP returned to Mississippi to challenge the state's representatives to the U.S. Congress which convened in January 1965. Again, the MFDP argued that the five white congressmen from Mississippi had been illegally elected since black voters were excluded from the franchise. By this time, the MFDP had gathered mounting evidence of black exclusion from voting—over 15,000 pages of sworn testimony documenting the harassment, reign of terror, and violence aimed at potential black voters. Fannie Lou Hamer, Annie Devine, and Victoria Gray were selected to challenge the congressional representatives from their respective districts. All three women were middle-aged mothers who juggled household responsibilities, along with their commitment to political activism. They were assisted by attorneys, a national support committee, and MFDP representatives who lobbied Congress to unseat the state's regular delegation. In articulating the significance of this action, Mrs. Hamer stated, "The challenge is not simply a challenge to the Congressmen, but a case of deciding between right and wrong. I want to see if the U.S. Constitution has any meaning for Negroes."[24]

When Congress opened session in January 1965, the three women and their supporters traveled to Washington to state their case. They were told that it would be eight months before the Credentials Committee could hear their testimony. Meanwhile, the three activists rented an apartment in Washington, where they continued to press for a hearing date. Finally, the MFDP challenge was heard on September 17, 1965. Fannie Lou Hamer, Annie Devine, and Victoria Gray became the first black women in the United States to be seated on the floor of the U.S. House of Representatives as they offered testimony and presented credentials to challenge the regular white Mississippi congressmen. The challenge was summarily dismissed by congressional vote.[25] According to Annie Devine's recollection of the hearing, Mrs. Hamer gave yet another compelling speech.

> She said that no matter how the nation looked on this challenge, we weren't there to play. We were there because we wanted the nation to know it was sick. Everything we testified to was true. "I hope," Mrs. Hamer said, "I live long enough to see some changes made, some hearts soften, some people begin to do some right things in Mississippi."[26]

Conclusion

In the aftermath of the convention and congressional defeats, the MFDP concentrated its efforts on local and statewide voter registration, demonstrations, and various other civil rights projects. In 1965, it organized a campaign in opposition to the appointment of former Mississippi governor James P. Coleman to the Fifth Federal Circuit Court, the main tribunal for the South, extending from Texas to Florida. The appointment of Coleman, a staunch segregationist, was a setback for the region since the Fifth Circuit Court of Appeals reviewed and rendered final decisions on most civil rights litigation in the South.

The activism of the MFDP helped to reshape the course of local politics in the state. For the first time, black residents were drawn into the political process, and their electoral power could no longer be ignored. In the years that followed the formation of the MFDP, black candidates ran successfully for a number of local offices throughout the state. By 1967, Holmes County resident, Robert Clark, was elected as Mississippi's first black representative to the U.S. Congress since Reconstruction.[27]

Clearly, the most enduring aspect of the MFDP was the empowerment of black Mississippians and the model it set for other communities throughout the South. Moreover, the massive evidence presented in the convention and congressional challenges along with the compelling testimony of Fannie Lou Hamer and others helped to generate support for passage of the Voting Rights Act of 1965. This legislation outlawed several discriminatory practices in voter registration, such as the use of literacy tests, poll tax requirements, and other measures aimed at disfranchising African Americans. In Mississippi, after passage of the Act, federal registrars supervised local elections and as a result, over 235,000 black citizens were added to the registration rolls from August 1965, when it was signed into law, to September 1967.[28] In a dramatic change of events, Mississippi's black voter registration rose from 6.7 percent to an estimated 59.8 percent within two years.[29] Undoubtedly, without the activism of the MFDP and the important roles of women within the organization, this would not have been possible.

In the final analysis, the leadership and activism of African American women were central to the cultivation of indigenous leadership and the significant changes in Mississippi society. The systematic use of violence and terrorism and the legacy of black exclusion were formidable forces to overcome, yet black women were pivotal in mobilizing and sustaining the movement in local communities across the state. Perhaps their effective roles as agents of social change derived from a confluence of factors, including their experiences with race, gender, and class. Fannie Lou Hamer, Annie Devine, and Victoria Gray had long histories as community and church workers before they entered the political sphere. Their skills and leadership abilities positioned them at the center of local community networks, which was essential to the movement's success. Sociologist Belinda Robnett's incisive analysis of women's activism suggests some explanations for the exclusion of women from formal positions of leadership within traditional civil rights organizations. She argues that "the exclusion of women from formal leadership positions created an exceptionally qualified leadership tier in the area of micromobilization."[30] This middle layer of leadership has been often overlooked at the expense of analyses which focus on the movement's national leaders and institutions. When the emphasis takes into account the intermediate layer of leadership, women's participation comes into fuller view. Robnett characterizes women who occupy this position as bridge leaders, those who serve as a go-between with formal leaders and the movement's rank-and-file.

In the case of the Mississippi Freedom Democratic Party, it is clear that the structure of the organization, from its inception, created more expansive opportunities for female leadership and participation. In a radical departure from older, established organizations such as the NAACP, women were founding members of the MFDP, were elected as vice-chairs and comprised a large faction of the party's delegates. The grassroots nature of the MFDP and its decentralized style of decision making paralleled the Student Nonviolent Coordinating Committee (SNCC). This structure diminished the gender and class divisions which typified the older, more established civil rights organizations.

In addition, it appears as though generational factors account for the inclusiveness of women within the ranks of the MFDP. Younger men, such as Lawrence Guyot, Bob Moses, and others, clearly recognized the radical potential of women in developing strategy and tactics and in mobilizing local residents. Their comments suggest that older women were frequently sought out in establishing the movement in communities throughout the state. As long-time community activists, women were influential in the informal expansion of the movement when more established leaders were sometimes less willing to step out. Through church and secular networks, women persuaded friends, relatives, and others to challenge the status quo.

Their own activism was a model, in itself, in helping local residents overcome fear.

One of the main sources for the courage and fearlessness exhibited by women such as Fannie Lou Hamer, Annie Devine, and Victoria Gray was their spiritual foundation and the ways in which they appropriated religious teachings in challenging authority and confronting injustice. The spiritual dimension in understanding and assessing black women's political action or "praxis of liberation" deserves much more exploration. It fostered self-dignity, an ethic of community responsibility and sustained risk taking in the most extreme circumstances. Black women's spirituality was an important source for personal transformation and radical action.

NOTES

1. Several recent studies that examine women's involvement in the Civil Rights Movement include Belinda Robnett, *How Long? How Long? African-American Women in the Struggle for Civil Rights* (New York: Oxford University Press, 1997); Joanne Grant, *Ella Baker: Freedom Bound* (New York: John Wiley and Sons, 1998); Cynthia Griggs Fleming, *Soon We Will Not Cry: The Liberation of Ruby Doris Smith Robinson* (Lanham, MD: Rowman and Littlefield, 1998); Vicki Crawford, Jacqueline Anne Rouse and Barbara Woods, eds., *Women in the Civil Rights Movement: Trailblazers and Torchbearers, 1941–1965* (Bloomington: Indiana University Press, 1993); Constance Curry, *Silver Rights* (Chapel Hill: Algonquin Books, 1995); Bernice Barnett, "Invisible Southern Black Women Leaders in the Civil Rights Movement: The Triple Constraints of Gender, Race and Class," *Gender and Society* 7 (June 1993): 162–82; Cynthia Stokes Brown, ed., *Ready from Within: Septima Clark and the Civil Rights Movement* (Navarro, CA: Wild Tree Press, 1986); Dianetta Gail Bryan, "Her Story Unsilenced: Black Female Activists in the Civil Rights Movement," *SAGE* 2 (Fall 1988): 60–63. Also, several personal accounts include Endesha Ida Mae Holland, *From the Mississippi Delta: A Memoir* (New York: Simon and Schuster, 1997); Mary King, *Freedom Song: A Personal Story of the 1960's Civil Rights Movement* (New York: William Morrow, 1987); Casey Hayden, "A Nurturing Movement: Nonviolence, SNCC and Feminism," *Southern Exposure* (Summer 1988): 48–53. Also, several entries on individual activists are included in Darlene Clark Hine, ed., *Black Women in United States History* (Brooklyn, NY: Carlson Press, 1990).

2. U.S. Bureau of the Census. *1960 Census of Population*. 1: *Characteristics of the Population, Part 26, Mississippi* (Washington, DC: Government Printing Office, 1963).

3. In a first-hand account, Mississippi Professor James Silver used this term to characterize the totalitarian nature of repression in Mississippi in his book, *The Closed Society,* (New York: Harcourt, Brace and World, 1966).

4. Mississippi Freedom Democratic Party Papers, *The Mississippi Freedom Democratic Party* (Summer 1964); microfilm edition.

5. For information on the Council of Federated Organizations' activities in Mississippi, see Charles Payne, *I've Got the Light of Freedom: The Organizing Tradition and the Mississippi Freedom Struggle* (Berkeley: University of California Press, 1995).

6. Leslie Burl McLemore, "The Mississippi Freedom Democratic Party: A Case Study of Grassroots Politics," Ph.D. diss., University of Massachusetts, Amherst, 1971, 101; John Dittmer, *Local People: The Struggle for Civil Rights in Mississippi* (Urbana: University of Illinois Press, 1994), 272–302.

7. McLemore, "The Mississippi Freedom Democratic Party": 102–3.

8. U.S. Commission on Civil Rights, *Hearings Held in Jackson, Mississippi, February 16–20, 1965* (Washington, DC: Government Printing Office, 1965).

9. Frank Parker, *Turning Point: The 1964 Mississippi Freedom Summer* (Washington DC: Joint Center for Political and Economic Studies, 1994).

10. Quoted in Clayborne Carson, *In Struggle: SNCC and the Black Awakening of the 1960's* (Cambridge: Harvard University Press, 1981), 97–100.

11. Parker, *Turning Point,* 9.

12. Fannie Lou Hamer, audio recording, Greenwood, Mississippi, Moses Moon Collection in the African-American Culture Archives. National Museum of American History, Smithsonian Institution, Washington, DC, 1963.

13. Quoted in Jon Michael Spencer, "Freedom Songs of the Civil Rights Movement," *Journal of Black Sacred Music* (Fall 1987): 14.

14. Matthew Suarez, oral history interview, August 17, 1978. Tom Dent Oral History Collection, Amistad Research Center, Tulane University.

15. Victoria Gray Adams, interview with the author, July 26, 1995, Petersburg, Virginia.

16. Ibid.

17. Ibid.

18. Ibid.

19. McLemore, "The Mississippi Freedom Democratic Party," 106–17; Lawrence Guyot and Michael Thelwell, "The Politics of Necessity and Survival in Mississippi," *Freedomways* 5 (Spring 1966): 120–32.

20. McLemore, "The Mississippi Freedom Democratic Party," 125.

21. Arthur Waskow, MFDP Papers, "Notes on the Democratic National Convention," August 1967.

22. Tom Dent, "Annie Devine Remembers," *Freedomways* 22 (Winter 1982): 89.

23. Frank Parker, *Black Votes Count: Political Empowerment in Mississippi After 1965* (Chapel Hill: University of North Carolina Press), 25–26.

24. Quoted in Mississippi Freedom Democratic Party Newsletter, April 3, 1965, MFDP Papers, microfilm edition.

25. MFDP Papers, microfilm edition; McLemore, "The Mississippi Freedom Democratic Party," 169–80.

26. Dent, "Annie Devine Remembers," 90.

27. McLemore, "The Mississippi Freedom Democratic Party," 339–45.

28. Parker, *Black Votes Count*, 30–31.

29. Ibid., 31.

30. Robnett, *How Long? How Long?* 191.

Chapter 9

Anger, Memory, and Personal Power
Fannie Lou Hamer and Civil Rights Leadership

Chana Kai Lee

By revisiting in this essay the familiar parts of Hamer's story—the first voter registration attempts, the eviction from the plantation, and the Winona beating—I highlight the usefulness of categories like personal memory and anger. More to the point regarding the value of this approach for black women's civil rights history, this way of thinking about leadership really should push us to take seriously the matter of black women's subjectivity. What was it like for these women to live their lives? How did they think about what they were doing? How did they think about themselves, their public and private lives? How did they perceive and conceive of their relationship to larger forces—to histories of racial violence and racial exclusion; the persistence of black women's devaluation? How did they think about their particular circumstances (in this case, the Civil Rights Movement)? What language did they rely on to convey understanding and conscious purpose to each other and posterity? As I have argued elsewhere about reconstructing histories of black women, I can think of few exercises as profitable and instructive as reflection over the meaning of their lives for those who lived those lives. How can we not think about this in our effort to yield a more complete measure of a life and a movement?

Still, I appreciate the temptation to do otherwise exclusively. More often than not, through public commemorations, in written work, at conferences and in other ways, we understand and recall what their lives meant for us, the living. This is understandable, if also insufficient. Let's face it: history is property; it is currency. Among other uses, we claim it to shape identities. We appropriate it to speak to contemporary political circumstances and to make our own history. And, we just plain use it to feed our curiosity. But to state the obvious and the too often unstated, the subjective experience informs public, political activism at every turn. This was certainly true in the case of activist Fannie Lou Hamer.

Born in 1917, Fannie Lou Hamer was a Mississippi sharecropper who emerged as a compelling grassroots leader during the Civil Rights Movement. She entered the movement in the summer of 1962 after attending a Ruleville, Mississippi mass meeting sponsored by the Student Nonviolent Coordinating Committee (SNCC). In 1964, she spoke before the National Democratic Party Convention in Atlantic City, New Jersey. Soon after, she rose to national prominence as a member of the Mississippi Freedom Democratic Party (MFDP). Throughout her fifteen-year public career, Hamer endured beatings, imprisonment, poverty, and disease to make her place in history. In 1977, she succumbed to cancer and heart disease, but not before registering thousands to vote, traveling to West Africa in 1964, creating a farm cooperative in 1967, leading a school desegregation movement in 1968, running for political office several times, creating a women's organization in 1971, and teaching thousands about activism and freedom.

Hamer's leadership during the civil rights era is best understood as an evolving process. As such, her leadership was an effective, if sometimes conflicting, blend of personal qualities, boundless vision, and thoughtful strategizing. The primary political mission for Hamer was the end of racial *and* economic injustice. Indeed, as a product of the Jim Crow South, she was a race woman, but she was also a very poor woman, and she remained so throughout her life. These two conditions—racism and poverty—shaped her political aspirations. Consistent with these priorities, she conceived institutions and solutions that focused attention on the local scene in the Mississippi Delta. Hamer was forever impatient and angry, and in her speeches and daily organizing, she transformed this anger into formidable personal power. Indeed, her individual example was a contribution unto itself.

Memory, anger, and history were the tools that she used to craft a public persona and mobilize her needy contemporaries in the Delta and beyond. In her public recollections, Hamer situated herself in a historical legacy routinely passed on to her by an attentive mother and a far-sighted grandmother. Significantly, racial and sexual vulnerability were recurrent themes in Hamer's autobiographical accounts. Any understanding of the meaning and impact of Hamer's leadership must begin with her consistent use of a painful personal and collective past to transform an oppressive present.

Registration and Eviction

In August 1962, SNCC came to Ruleville, and forty-four-year-old Hamer attempted to vote for the first time. From that point on her life changed dramatically. On Monday, August 27, she attended the first mass meeting in her town. At this meeting, SNCC schooled the citizens about their rights and the process of voter registration. Hamer, in reflecting on that fateful moment, noted, "Until then I'd never heard of no mass meeting and I didn't know that a Negro could register and vote."[1] Eager and committed, Hamer and others learned to fill out registration applications at the meeting. When SNCC members asked who would be willing to go to the county courthouse in Indianola the following day to secure this most precious of rights, eighteen people raised their hands and expressed an interest in testing a longstanding practice of excluding blacks from southern politics.

Among the courageous eighteen, Hamer emerged as the leader. It was a logical extension of her role as a timekeeper on a local plantation; she was already a community leader. During the mass meeting, Hamer was not only among the first to commit to go, but, through an impromptu, inspirational speech that underscored her own deepening devotion to change, she also encouraged others to make that choice. Indeed, Hamer already sensed that change was on the horizon, and her decision to be among the "Indianola 18" was undoubtedly influenced by the excitement she felt at the possibility of realizing a better life—a life defined by something more than suffering and neglect. In reflecting on that defining moment, Hamer recalled:

> I could just see myself voting people outa office that I know was wrong and didn't do nothin' to help the poor. I said, you know, that's sumpin' I really wanna be involved in, and finally at the end of that rally, I had made up my mind that I was gonna come out there when they said you could go down that Friday to try to register.[2]

Like its meaning for most individuals, the vote symbolized hope for Hamer and other Deltans. It represented a way out of grim circumstances that seemed unrelentingly permanent. Thus, Hamer's decision to get involved in voter registration work was not, as she put it, a "bolt out of the blue." Casting a ballot was a concrete response to the perpetual injustice that filled the lives of the southern poor. It was a practical answer for a very practical, no-nonsense woman who was exceedingly impatient for something better. In the fields, Hamer had long pondered, in anger and frustration, bringing a change in conditions for herself and those around her. Before SNCC came, she talked so much about this that some called her the "one . . . [who] didn't have real good sense," much in the same way that folks talked about her mother.[3]

After the town meeting, Hamer and seventeen other defiant Ruleville citizens climbed aboard an old bus chartered by SNCC and rode twenty-six miles to the county seat in Indianola.[4] As the bus pulled into Indianola, Hamer noticed a crowd forming near the bus as the vehicle pulled up to its final destination. Outside the courthouse, there was a wild scene indeed. Hostile white men and women had gathered around the courthouse en masse. In spite of the advice and warnings of the younger, more experienced activists and the record of her own experiences, Hamer was momentarily shocked by the scene. A minute or two passed before she realized that she and the others were the center of attention. Still, they continued on their mission.

As the Ruleville citizens marched up to the courthouse, they encountered antagonistic circuit clerk, Cecil B. Campbell, who snapped, "What do you want?" Without missing a beat, Hamer replied, "We are here to register."[5] Campbell then directed them to leave the courthouse and re-enter in pairs. Hamer and Ernest Davis stayed inside while the others left the courthouse and waited to be called.[6] After Hamer and Davis provided their full names, the registrar directed them to answer twenty-one more questions on their place of employment, employer, place of residence, and even the date of the application itself. Campbell then administered a literacy test, a test that Hamer described as being "rough."

Hamer "flunked" the test, which she simply referred to as an "ordeal." She and the others walked back toward the bus and climbed aboard in noticeable anticipation of the late afternoon trip back to Ruleville. Little did they know that a state highway patrolman was following the bus. A few miles and minutes into the trip, the patrolman, joined by local policemen, confronted the group with the consequences of its actions. He stopped the bus and threatened the driver with arrest if he did not pay a fine for driving a bright yellow bus that could be mistaken for a school bus.[7] Everyone knew that this was Jim Crow subterfuge at its best. The same vehicle had never been stopped when it was used to transport cotton migrant workers out of state.

Indianola marked a turning point in the evolution of Hamer's leadership. After this first registration attempt, Hamer moved beyond "resistance" as everyday, individual acts of survival. She began taking initiatives to promote collective struggle for real power. As she began resisting on a different level during her SNCC years and after, the stakes and positive consequences grew in direct proportion. Her actions were having larger consequences, partly because more people were benefitting from them. But Indianola was hardly the beginning of Hamer's real troubles. It was a replay of the kind of injustice that marred her childhood and adolescent years. This new experience with injustice resulted from Hamer's effort to realize empowerment on different terms, precisely through exercising her right to the franchise, which she clearly saw as having great potential for transformation. Yet she knew that the process would be no easy achievement. She was a forty-four-year-old woman who had intimate knowledge of the racist ways of white Mississippi. Still, she was constantly amazed at the lengths to which some would go to keep blacks powerless.

The Indianola experience also helped Hamer realize the potential strength in numbers through community action. For Hamer and others, the "Indianola 18" was now a collective, an easily identifiable unit of folk bound by common concerns and committed to certain political objectives. And Hamer had a distinctive place in this collective entity, not simply because of her longstanding membership in the Ruleville community, but also because slowly she began seeing herself as the embodiment of both injustice and empowerment. By leading the group up to the courthouse and deciding to enter first, Hamer performed an act of leadership that others in the group were expected to follow. Coming out of the fields and boldly walking into a courthouse was unimaginable for these individuals before August 31, 1962. In this regard, the Indianola voter registration attempt was anything but an insignificant gesture. In 1960, blacks comprised more than 61 percent of the voting age population in Sunflower County, yet they made up only 1.2 percent of registered voters.[8]

Indeed, Indianola represented something more than a small group's one-time attempt to challenge the political boundaries of Jim Crow. It also marked a significant turning point in group consciousness: Local folk now began believing that they had it in their power to change what they once viewed as permanently unchangeable. Certainly, the mass meeting the night before bolstered such a transformation—the music, the enthusiastic appeals of the young, predominantly SNCC-led group. For others, this change extended beyond learning a method of action with which they could imagine a new future; more fundamentally, it led some to believe that they simply deserved better, and no less. Such a transformation for Hamer actually began with the teachings of her mother. Lou Ella Townsend insisted that her daughter develop a steadfast love of self that would protect her against the random, debilitating insults hurled by an invalidating society. Certainly her mother's early lessons eased her passage into leadership for the movement.[9] And she used her memories of them to remind herself and others of their relationship to a longer history. This is especially true for the experiences that followed—her eviction and brief experience on the run.

After her first registration at Indianola, Hamer stepped up the pace with her newly acquired political obligations, and the harassment increased accordingly. By September 1962, apparent guardians of Jim Crow launched a wave of politically motivated attacks on her life and livelihood, and this seemed to have the opposite effect of what was intended. Ever indignant, Hamer seemed to feed off each new attack or threat of attack; she appeared to resist with renewed commitment to the cause. To be sure, this quality of her leadership soon convinced others to align themselves with the cause.[10]

Upon returning home after the Indianola journey, Hamer greeted her daughter Dorothy and her husband's cousin, who had run out to deliver some news. As writer June Jordan put it, it was only a matter of minutes before "trouble fell into [Hamer's] life like a hammer smashing on her head."[11] According to the girls, the plantation owner, W. D. Marlow, was "blazing mad and raising sand." He demanded that Hamer return to the courthouse and withdraw her voter registration application. If she refused, she had another option: leave the plantation immediately, without her husband "Pap" and their belongings. Marlow insisted that Pap remain behind in order to clear the couple's outstanding debt. This lasted but for so long. Soon, Pap found himself looking for another job as well.[12]

As the youngsters delivered the threat, Hamer listened without responding and then proceeded to enter the house, where she sat down on one of the girls' beds. Meanwhile, Pap remained outside, and no sooner had Hamer walked inside than Marlow arrived, demanding to know whether his message had been passed along to Fannie Lou. "So did you tell her what I said?" Pap replied a stiff, "Yes, sir." Marlow added swiftly, "I mean that she got to go back and withdraw her registration or she'll have to leave?" Hamer, overhearing the exchange between Pap and Marlow, got up from the bed and stepped outside. Just as Marlow noticed her presence, he asked: "Did Pap tell you what I said?" Hamer calmly replied, "Yes, sir, he did." Evidently unable to restrain the paternalist impulse within, Marlow continued,

> Well I mean that you going to have to tell me whether you going back and withdraw your registration [application] or you going [to] have to leave here. We're not going to have this in Mississippi, and you will have to withdraw. I am looking for your answer, yea or nay?

For a moment Hamer simply stared at him. Marlow then added, "I'll give you until tomorrow morning. And if you don't withdraw you will have to leave."[13] Apparently having had about as much as she could take from Marlow, Hamer began thinking about how unfair he was being in light of all that she had done for him:

> I just thought to myself, "What does he really care about us?" I had been workin' there for eighteen years. I had baked cakes and sent them overseas to him during the war. I had nursed his family, cleaned his house, stayed with his kids. I had handled his time book and his payroll. Yet he wanted me out. I made up my mind I was grown, and I was tired.[14]

Undoubtedly, Hamer had a few reasons to be beside herself about Marlow's reactions. The political significance of his effort to keep sharecroppers disfranchised was certainly not lost on her. But, on a more personal level, Hamer was just plain outraged and insulted that Marlow would be so unappreciative and selfish. She had expected some degree of decency and consideration. She found none and was highly offended that he refused to acknowledge that, for once, she wanted to do something—anything—to better her own condition. In spite of the very human ways she had acted toward him—like baking and sending cakes to him overseas during World War II—Marlow could not bring himself to see her need to do something for herself. It was almost as if she had expected him to put aside momentarily the racist constraints and customs of Jim Crow Mississippi.

In a 1968 interview about her showdown with Marlow, Hamer recalled her final response, "Mr. Dee, I didn't go down there to register for you. I went there to register for myself."[15] With the help of other civil rights workers she moved out that night, leaving home and family for the freedom to act in her own best interest.

On the Run

Surely Hamer must have had some doubts and fears about leaving the plantation. As was often the case, she probably revised her memories later, editing out details that contradicted the image of her as forever bold and daring. Her 1968 recollection of this moment leaves the impression that she acted with little regret or hesitation, which was probably not entirely the case given that leaving meant separation and difficult times for the family she left behind. Pap had to stay on until the end of the harvesting season.[16] There was simply no way he could leave in light of the family's fragile economic circumstances, which surely worsened without Fannie Lou's contribution. To add insult to injury, Marlow fired Pap anyway at the end of the harvest and confiscated the furniture and car, for which he was claiming the family still owed an outstanding debt of $300. Mean and vengeful to the very end of their relationship, a self-satisfied Marlow had gotten the best of the Hamers.[17]

Leaving that night must have taken a lot out of Hamer, and it was certainly hard for her family to accept. In walking away from her position as plantation timekeeper, Hamer gave up a preferred position for black sharecroppers. It allowed a degree of leverage, control, and discretion. Although the timekeeper was subjected to exploitation as well, the position was slightly above that of an ordinary sharecropper. Irrespective of her relatively privileged position, Hamer found leaving difficult simply because she had no alternative source of income and no idea how long it would take to find support, either through donations or another job. Although Marlow expressed his demand as a choice including two options, Hamer's leaving was hardly an exercise in free will. In departing that night, she merely anticipated what would surely follow the next morning, and perhaps wisely so in light of the persecution she soon faced.

On the night of her eviction, Hamer left her home, husband, and children to go stay with friends in Ruleville, stopping first at the home of neighbors, Mary and Robert Tucker, a local couple known for housing voter registration activists.[18] Only a matter of days after Hamer arrived at the Tuckers, a reign of terror was touched off in the small town of Ruleville, and Hamer was among the leading candidates for persecution. Ten days after her eviction, on September 10, 1963, sixteen bullets were fired into the Tucker home. Fortunately, no one was injured.[19]

The shooting and Hamer's recent move were more than a matter of mere coincidence. Keepers of the Jim Crow South were after Hamer— the new troublemaker on the block in the eyes of the many who feared and loathed the new boldness of local blacks. The Indianola visit—as well as SNCC's activities throughout other parts of the Delta—stirred up a lot of controversy in the small town of Ruleville, and soon Hamer and her local co-workers came to symbolize that trouble to those determined to preserve the old order.

After another shooting that involved critical injuries to two Jackson State students, Hamer fled Ruleville.[20] Throughout her brief time on the run, Hamer received much-needed charitable support from Ruleville citizens, oftentimes across class boundaries. For example, black school teachers sympathetic to her plight made sure that she ate.[21]

After becoming a virtual fugitive, Hamer stayed with friends and family in Ruleville, but ultimately, she and her husband decided that it would be best that she leave the town altogether since the violence continued unabated. This decision was prompted by a curious scene that Pap observed in the Marlow plantation office. A little more than a week after Hamer's eviction, he casually strolled into the plantation maintenance shop, where he noticed some plastic-covered buckshot shells sitting on top of the table. Instantly, he grew suspicious and hurried out to the Tuckers' home, where his wife was staying. Pap told Hamer what he had seen in the shop and suggested that he should take her out to their niece's place in Tallahatchie County, just northeast of Sunflower.[22] And his concern was anything but unfounded fear. She remembered that he reasoned to her, "I believe something going to happen because a man don't buy no buck shot shells this early in the year, you know, not for rabbits or something like [that]." So Hamer and her two adopted girls proceeded to Tallahatchie, where they picked cotton to support themselves. They ended up staying until late October.

During her two months in Tallahatchie, Hamer experienced a significant change of heart and attitude. She thought long and hard about her circumstances, especially the feeling of being on the run. It occurred to her that she should no longer live a life in virtual exile. After considering her own history and that of her family and community, she decided that running away did a disservice to her sense of self and to the struggles of others who meant so very much to her. She decided that she would run away no longer. One Saturday morning Hamer arose and began preparing to leave the house. Somehow understanding that Hamer was not dressing to go out to work that morning, her niece asked where she was headed. Hamer replied, "Back to Ruleville." Although this announcement rattled the girls, Hamer had done a lot of reasoning with herself and concluded that it served no one to live in fear, neither her deceased foreparents nor posterity.[23] She rejected the notion that she was a criminal who needed to act as if she had done something wrong. When one of the daughters raised the possibility of something happening upon her return, Hamer told them, "But this what you got to look at. I'm not a criminal. I hadn't done one thing to nobody, I went down to register for myself and I got a right to live in Ruleville because its [sic] people there have done way more thing[s] than that, they still here, and I'm going back to Ruleville regardless."[24]

In fact, her bold decision to return involved much more than being treated like a criminal. It also had to do with the familiar theme of economic exploitation. Few unjust conditions enraged Hamer so much as the continued (and unacknowledged) devaluation of her labor and that of her forebears. Her return was symbolic reclamation. In her explanation to the girls she added, "My parents helped to make this town and this county what it is today, because it was out of their sweat, tears, and blood that they [white landowners] got as much land that they have here; and I [have] a right to stay here."[25] Although fearing for their caretaker's life, the girls accompanied Hamer back to Ruleville.

This change of heart for Hamer signaled a transition moment slightly

Ella Baker. Courtesy of Schomburg Center for Research in Black Culture.

Hamilton Holmes and Charlayne Hunter Gault. Courtesy of Schomburg Center for Research in Black Culture.

Septima Poinsette Clark and Rosa Parks at Highlander Folk School. Courtesy of Highlander Research and Education Center.

Ruby Doris Robinson Smith with son Toure. Courtesy of Cynthia Griggs Fleming.

Shirley Chisholm with Bettye Collier-Thomas and T. Peter Davis. Courtesy of Bettye Collier-Thomas.

Dorothy I. Height with Roy Wilkins, Floyd McKissick, A. Philip Randolph, Whitney Young, and Martin Luther King. Courtesy of Bethune Council House National Historic Site.

Mary McLeod Bethune at entrance to the White House. Courtesy of Bethune Council House National Historic Site.

Above: Black Panther Party women at "Clothes Giveaway." Courtesy of Jack Franklin Collection, African American Museum in Philadelphia.

Left: Thomasina Johnson Norford, Director of AKA Non-Partisan Council. Courtesy of Moorland-Spingarn Research Center.

Above: Gloria Richardson and members of the Cambridge Nonviolent Action Committee confronted by the Maryland National Guard. Courtesy of Black Star Publishers.

Right: Fannie Lou Hamer. Courtesy of Moorland-Spingarn Research Center.

akin to a conversion experience. While in Tallahatchie, Hamer had a very searching and reflective moment that led her to rethink her responses to danger, displacement, and uncertainty.[26] Although Hamer was resolute about her part at the Indianola courthouse, she still trod with caution upon her immediate return to Ruleville. Eventually, she and Pap concluded that she had gone as far as she could go in testing the limits of racist reaction. By the time she returned from Tallahatchie, Hamer had decided that such challenges, however life-threatening, must be met with an equally resolute, more principled reaction. Christian faith, indignation, and emotional memories of her foreparents undoubtedly inspired such a changed outlook.

Throughout the fall of 1962, Hamer participated in more movement-sponsored activities. She set about the business of defining an activist role for herself. At the invitation of Robert Moses, she attended a SNCC leadership training conference at Fisk University. Nashville activist Charles McLaurin traveled to Tallahatchie and escorted her back from Nashville.[27] Before signing on officially with SNCC after the Fisk conference, Hamer returned home and continued voter registration canvassing as a field secretary-at-large under the sponsorship of the Council of Federated Organizations (COFO), a state-wide coalition of civil rights organizations.[28] Unquestionably, the admiration between Hamer and SNCC was mutual. Although Hamer did a little work with SCLC, she preferred working with SNCC.

After her initial voter registration attempt, SNCC members readily identified Hamer as the "perfect prospect" for local leadership. From SNCC's perspective, contacting Hamer was a way of tapping into the community of the needy because she had served as a leader on the plantation during her tenure as timekeeper, which meant that she often served as a go-between for black laborers and white "boss men" or landowners. Many in the small town of 1,100 knew Hamer. Among other occasions when she kept herself rooted and in touch, her residence was often an after-work gathering place for members of the community.[29] Locally she had plenty stature. According to scholars of the movement, Hamer was a readily identifiable type in a social movement context. She was anthropologist Karen Sacks's "centerwoman" and sociologist Belinda Robnett's "bridge leader." Charles Payne has also singled her out as a familiar type to the movement: the charismatic, intellectually tough-minded woman leader.[30] Indeed, Hamer stood at a pivotal place in her relationship to the folk she sought to organize, and over time her charisma enhanced her stature immeasurably. She knew them, they knew her, and mutual trust prevailed, for the most part. As her movement years passed, she would prove to be the respected, spiritual and political advisor, the daunting mobilizer, of folks whom others simply chose to ignore. And, as with most "bridge leaders," women and men, Hamer did not have the level of national visibility held by similarly influential male leaders, particularly men of the cloth. Still, her leadership mattered, and not every local or national "leader" could make such a claim. SNCC discovered early on that Hamer's legitimacy was rooted in her authenticity and her proximity to the folk, not on her ability to bridge formal leaders and organizations with the masses. In this sense, the notion of Hamer as a bridge leader is too limiting. Her legitimacy rested squarely on her ability to bridge local communities to their local organizations. Her individual relationship as leader to formal, national personalities and organizations did not define Hamer's roles or vision.

Not long after Indianola, Hamer became one of the organization's leading spokespersons in the Mississippi Delta. She traveled across the South, stirring many audiences with her dramatic descriptions of the tragic plight of Afro-Mississippians. She combined her clever, anecdotal speeches with extemporaneous singing to become an effective fundraiser for the Mississippi movement. Hamer worked throughout the Delta, but her main center of activity was Greenwood, Mississippi, the SNCC field headquarters.[31] Wherever she found herself doing movement work, she acquired a reputation for being hardworking and deeply committed. Each day one could pass by a church and hear her singing and preaching about the need to join the movement. She was also widely respected for her knowledge of the Bible and her outspokenness. She often challenged pastors in their own churches, calling on them to address the immediate obstacles hampering black life and to embrace the movement in whatever way possible.

According to former SNCC activist and Greenwood native, June Johnson, "See [laughter] you really ain't supposed to ask no preacher no questions in the middle of a sermon. But see Mrs. Hamer would get up and disrupt the sermon and want to know certain things that he didn't talk about in terms of how it related to our daily survival."[32] By 1964, Greenwood had become a hotbed of civil rights activities in the Delta, and Hamer's role in this was certainly not lost on SNCC. As recorded in the minutes from a staff meeting in October, James Jones pointed out, "In G'wood, people are beginning to relate to each other, i.e., to Mrs. Hamer, etc., . . ."[33] To be sure, Greenwood citizens became more active as a consequence of Hamer's presence.

Winona: Sexualized Racial Violence

Along with increased responsibility and authority, Hamer's early movement work also brought sustained attention from local law enforcement officials bent on intimidating activists. On Monday, June 10, 1963, Hamer was arrested in Winona, Mississippi, sixty miles east of Indianola. With seven other activists, she was returning from a voter registration workshop in Charleston, South Carolina. Members of the group were taken to jail, where they were brutally beaten and detained for three days. Hamer would live to tell this story, and she would tell it repeatedly until the day she died. In an interview given three days after the incident, Hamer recalled:

> So, then I had to get over there on the bed flat on my stomach, and that man beat me—that man beat me until he give out. And by me screamin', it made one of the other ones—plainclothes fellow [Charles Perkins], he didn't have on nothing like a uniform—he got so hot and worked up off it, he just run [over] there you know and started hittin' me on the back of my head. Well, my hand—I was trying to guard some of the licks [from a weaker left side due to polio] you see—and my hands, they beat my hands till they turned blue, and after he had finished, my clothes . . . quite naturally, being beaten like that, my clothes come up, and I tried to pull them down, you know. It was just pitiful. And then he—one of the other white fellows—just taken my clothes and just snatched them up, and this Negro, when he had just beat me until I know he was just [going to] give out, well, then, this state patrolman told the other Negro to take it. So he taken over from there. And they just beat. . . . That's when I started screaming and working my feet 'cause I couldn't help it. The patrolman told the first Negro that had beat me to sit on my feet. I had to hug around the mattress to keep the sound from coming out. Finally they carried me back to my cell.[34]

As the two black prisoners beat Hamer, the white officers continued name-calling and taunting her. At one point they jokingly asked had she seen Martin Luther King, Jr. that day. The blows started getting so unbearable that Hamer began wishing that the two men would strike that "one lick that could have ended [her] misery." Her torment was experienced by the others. They heard Hamer crying out for mercy as she prayed for an end to what she later referred to as "the mos' horrifying experience I have ever had in my life."[35]

The beating left Hamer in an unbearable physical state. Some three days after her release, she was still unable to lie on her face while asleep because it felt "hard as bone," as did her entire body, especially her fingers, which she could not bend. Sadly, some injuries were permanent: she lost sight in her left eye, and she suffered irreparable damage to her kidneys. What is more, the beating also exacerbated a limp that had plagued Hamer since a childhood bout with polio. She knew she could never really forget this experience, if only because the physical reminders were all too prominent. "Every day of my life I pay with the misery of this beatin," she once observed ruefully.[36] After her beating the police considered beating Hamer's cell mate, teenage Euvester Simpson, but there was concern about her bruises providing unquestionable evidence since she was lighter in skin complexion than her co-workers. The police were clearly concerned about being investigated, especially by federal authorities, and they did not want to leave any unnecessary physical evidence of their wrongdoing.[37] They did not show such concern for the remaining activists, a few of whom were beaten beyond recognition. Dark-complected Annelle Ponder was beaten so severely that she could only whisper a single word to another activist: "freedom."

Although unknown to the arrested members at the time, some civil rights people had come down to the jail to inquire about their whereabouts and condition, only to be arrested themselves and subjected to the same degree of mental and physical torture. Included among them was Lawrence Guyot, a twenty-three-year-old Mississippi native and Tougaloo College graduate who had his own impressive record of activism. When he arrived at the jail, Guyot introduced himself to the officers and indicated that he came to post bond for the group. Sheriff Earle Patridge immediately ordered him "to get out of Winona and stay gone." Just as Guyot was making his way out of the jail, highway patrolman John Basinger knocked him down for refusing to say "sir" to Patridge. Other officers then joined in beating Guyot inside the sheriff's office before locking him up in a cell. Guyot's harrowing experience included being transported to nearby Carroll County, where he was brutally beaten by a group of klansmen. Afterwards they returned him to Winona, where his co-workers remained in detention.[38]

During Guyot's brief imprisonment in Winona, Hamer caught a glimpse of him through a large door that she had convinced the jailer to leave open because the heat had become unbearable inside what she later described as a "dungeon." She noticed something disturbing about Guyot's appearance. His characteristic beaming grin was missing and he appeared woeful. According to Hamer, "Guyot looked like he was in a bad shape and it was on my nerve, too, because that was the first time I had seen him . . . not smiling."[39] The group later discovered the reasons for Guyot's grim look. The authorities had "forcefully disrobed" him before administering his beating. But there was more. As Hamer put it in a 1968 interview, his sadistic assailants had also "taken a piece of paper and tried to burn Guyot's private."[40] He was detained until some time after the larger group was released. When he was reunited with his fellow civil rights activists, the bruises across his face and body did more to describe his experiences than mere words could have.

Although Winona represented the most painful tragedy of Hamer's life, it later served her well as she set out to draw attention to the plight of Afro-Mississippians. As strange and horrible as that experience was, she managed to squeeze some political capital out of the horror and her subsequent suffering. Nearly all of her many political speeches and public appeals after June 1963 contained a moving, vivid account of that gruesome night. The most notable was her presentation at the 1964 Democratic Party National Convention.

In public accounts, Hamer underscored carefully the racial motives behind the attack. But in private, Hamer reflected on the other sensitive dimensions of the beating. Historian Jacquelyn Dowd Hall has described the function of violence in the indiscriminate lynching of black men in terms of the specter of "ritual [sexual] violence in service of racial control."[41] To be sure, Hamer readily identified the purpose of racial control, but in private Hamer considered whether her attackers experienced some sexual gratification from their violent behavior and her agony. She read something in their facial expressions. Her unremitting pain appeared to be her assailants' pleasure—sexual pleasure as far as Hamer was concerned.[42] In fact, it is difficult to ignore the many sexual elements of the Winona beating: the repeated raising of Hamer's dress; the forced undressing of another activist, teenage June Johnson; and the most egregious example, the attempted burning of Guyot's penis. But Hamer never emphasized the sexual aspects of the beating in her political speeches. The racial violence held a larger and more consistent place in her sharing about Winona. Undoubtedly, the emotional difficulties of talking about the sexual violence weighed heavily on Hamer, the granddaughter of a rape victim. Still, Winona remained a staple experience in Hamer's memory. Time and again, she used it to her advantage. What emerged for movement participants was a deeper conviction in the need for the movement and in the authenticity and suitability of Hamer's leadership.

Local Organizing: Feeding and Clothing the Needy

The year 1964 was just as challenging for Hamer as 1962 and 1963 had been. During the first seven months of 1964, she strengthened her grassroots support by directing a food and clothing drive, encouraging voter registration, and running for political office. She gained a lot of organizing experience for large projects. She also learned social movement crisis management, which was hardly an easy task. In return she offered an example of bravery, resilience, and stamina. Appropriately, her fellow Deltans and other activists responded with unwavering support. All of these steps proved necessary before Hamer could play a role in the ill-fated challenge at the 1964 Democratic National Convention in Atlantic City, New Jersey—the event that ultimately gave her a place in history. Through it all, the racial inequities of her home state gradually became the focus of national attention, and this was one important goal of the movement for 1964.

For Hamer, a meaningful social movement was one that addressed the everyday needs of people. It made little sense to recruit the disfranchised to go into a courthouse and register to vote when they were worried about eating or having shoes to wear. While most black Deltans were effectively excluded from the political mainstream, they were also without the basic necessities—food and clothing. In most economic categories for their class, black farmers were at the bottom. According to a 1964 USDA report, black Deltan median income was

$456 a year as compared to $968 for whites in the Delta. Black Deltans were poor even in comparison to other blacks statewide. The average black Mississippi income was $606 and the white statewide average was more than three times as much at $2,030.[43] Infant mortality figures also indicated a struggle for basic necessities. A black baby was two times more likely to die in infancy than a white infant. In this category, Afro-Deltans were at the bottom again, with the chances of a black baby dying its first year twice that of a white baby.[44] Housing conditions also reflected need. In 1965, over 90 percent of black homes in rural Mississippi had no flush toilet, bathtub, or shower.[45]

The needs of Mississippi's poor remained at the center of Hamer's attention throughout her public career. After all, she, too, was extremely poor. From the very beginning, she embraced "moral pragmatism" as a spiritually based political perspective. She defined her social change agenda by focusing on whatever needed to done and wherever it needed to be done because this was only right. If there was a need in a community for food, clothing, or housing, the moral pragmatist in the Civil Rights Movement directly addressed those needs alongside the effort to dismantle Jim Crow. In a word, the most pressing community needs determined one's political agenda. Hamer's moral pragmatist approach was based on her sense of community allegiance and Christian obligation. Dire need and religious duty shaped one's politics. Accordingly, a pragmatic Hamer kept her attention trained on conditions in the local communities of the Delta.

Beginning in 1964, Hamer's local activities included organizing and overseeing food and clothing distribution for Ruleville and other Delta towns in need. Churches, civic clubs, and trade unions sent food and clothing from as far as New York and Boston. Other movement organizations (for instance, the Southern Conference Educational Fund in New Orleans) solicited donations through their own networks.[46] Hamer often distributed the goods from her home, which was quite an obligation since shipments often included as much as 10,000–30,000 pounds of food.[47] Distribution work was always tiring and even occasionally disappointing. Sometimes crowds around distribution sites grew as large as 200, and often distributors ran out of clothing before all needs were met. More than a few SNCC field reports contained messages from Hamer requesting more and more clothing.

Hamer and SNCC also used food and clothing distribution as an effective way of mobilizing citizens for voter registration. People often left distribution sites with a commitment to register after hearing one of Hamer's impromptu speeches. In March 1964, Boston Friends of SNCC donated 10,000 pounds of food, among other necessities, and 60 people responded by going down to the county courthouse and attempting to register.[48]

Sometimes, drawing the link between food and voter registration involved confrontation and bluntness on Hamer's part, a recourse that she definitely thought was okay. Sometimes neighbors and peers were less than enthusiastic about participating in any other movement-sponsored activities, although they were quick to come for food and clothing. Hamer saw some of them as ingrates, and she did not take this too well. On one occasion, Hamer interrupted a freedom school session and demanded that the adult participants go to Indianola and register.[49] On another occasion, Hamer absolutely refused to give clothes and food to women who had lined up in her yard at seven o'clock in the morning to receive commodities. She shamed them by referring to them as "a pack of them women [who] never even been once to Indianola to try and register to help themselves!"[50] In her mind, it was only right and necessary that everyone attempt voter registration before receiving donations. It boiled down to taking advantage of all opportunities to help one's self, especially an opportunity to "keep pounding on that registrar's door." To those in fear of losing their jobs or lives, Hamer reassured that the movement would take care of them, no matter the consequences. That morning she announced that "no food and no clothes was goin' to be distributed till all the cars come back from Indianola."[51] She borrowed a car and drove women to Indianola. Hamer got additional drivers to bring more groups of women. At the end of that morning, Hamer made sure thirty women had registered. A little after two o'clock that afternoon, they returned to Ruleville. In her characteristic spirited style, she made these remarks to a crowd gathered at her porch:

> These thirty women know that the way we're goin' to change things here in the Delta, here in Mississippi, is by gettin' the vote. Folks up North want to help us free ourselves, and that's why they send these boxes. Anybody who loses his job because he tries to register to vote is goin' to be helped. Anybody who tries to help by standin' up—goin' to Indianola—is goin' to be helped.[52]

Just as there were those who attempted registration at the prodding of Hamer, there also were those few who took the food and clothing, and for whatever reason, chose not to make the most of the "opportunity."[53] This small minority notwithstanding, most were beginning to identify with Hamer and her work. Although some may have felt some kind of pressure or obligation (to Hamer or northern donors) to attempt registration, there were also those who, like Hamer, believed that the food and clothing represented the beginning of even better times. Hope was in the air, due in no small way to Hamer's energy and persistence. What also added to this heightened sense of possibility was an ambitious voter registration and educational effort known as "Freedom Summer."

Freedom Summer

Hamer played more than one pivotal role in Freedom Summer. She was quite active and visible throughout. She also did not stray far from internal controversy and conflict, especially if it had something to do with young people and the politics of race and gender. The most controversial aspect of the Freedom Summer plan was the decision to involve an estimated 1,000 volunteers from the North, many of whom were white students.[54] Movement activists argued that the white student involvement was needed to attract federal attention and to compel some action, especially against racial violence and other harassment. For so long blacks had been victims of violence, but their experiences never occasioned federal intervention, even when such was requested, which historically had been loud and often throughout the twentieth century. The presence of white women students, however, raised the danger threshold considerably, owing to the southern taboo against the social mingling of white women and black men.[55]

Perceived reckless behavior of some white women activists had Hamer unusually distressed during Freedom Summer. Her concerns stretched back to the Freedom Summer training sessions in Oxford, Ohio, held in June of the same year. She questioned the women's youthfulness, especially their naivete about race and southern mores. On one occasion during that summer, Hamer noticed a car of white female volunteers driving around her neighborhood. She had reason to be on alert. An old white associate in town had called the matter to her attention: "Fannie Lou, the town is getting upset. There's going to be real trouble if those girls aren't careful."[56] As she stood on the porch watching the women ride around the neighborhood, she observed to Pap, "They're goin' past the [Freedom Summer Community] center again . . . that's the third time those white women have passed this house in the last hour."

Hamer was not the only one disturbed about this irresponsible behavior. A number of individuals in SNCC, black and white, women and men, frequently noted in meetings (and later in personal remembrances) problems caused by interracial commingling, especially among white women and black men. Hamer and others feared that clear violation of southern race–sex taboos was just begging for a violent reaction that would stifle the movement. Her patience was wearing thin. She had warned the women well in advance of their arrival in Ruleville. In a conversation with local activist Charles McLaurin, Hamer fumed, "Those cars out there cruisin' up and down, lookin' so hard, is full of women!"[57] Annoyed and beyond consolation, she ranted:

> McLaurin, I spent a whole week with those girls in Ohio. I told them frankly what they had to expect. That just bein' in the Delta was goin' to be a red flag to the whites, let alone livin' here in the quarter [Ruleville's black section]. "When you ain't workin'," I'd say, "stay inside. Don't go wanderin' into town. It's askin' for trouble!" I told 'em and told 'em. "It ain't gonna be like home." They're good kids, and they seemed to understand. But they get down here and nobody's settin' their house on fire, so they act like they're visitin' their boyfriends on college week end [sic]!"[58]

Hamer recognized the consequences of this sort of behavior. It compromised the safety of certain black Ruleville citizens and jeopardized the outcome of the movement. She warned: "If some whites laid hands on one of those young girls, every Negro man in Ruleville would be in trouble. That kind of trouble kills people in Mississippi. And what would become of the Movement then?"[59]

Hamer's focus on black men reflected her realistic understanding of who was most endangered by interracial liaisons for her time and place. The southern racial and sexual hierarchy almost always demanded that black men be targeted first and foremost for blame and punishment in cases where sex/race taboos were violated. In line with the dictates of "southern chivalry," white southern men deemed white women prized possessions to be honored and protected from "the uncontrollable sexual appetites" of black men. Hamer's family history told her that the opposite was not true of black women and white male liaisons, regardless of the circumstances. This, too, probably accounted for her anger. In oral history accounts passed down to her while a young girl, Hamer learned that her maternal grandmother, Liza Bramlett, gave birth to twenty-three children, only three of whom were fathered by a black man. Bramlett told her granddaughters that the other twenty were the result of rape at the hands of white men. There was a point to Bramlett's sharing; she wanted her grandchildren to have some appreciation for the dangers they faced in the South. As Hamer witnessed the young white women driving around carelessly, she must have also thought about the lack of protection for vulnerable southern black women like herself and her foremothers.

Hamer reached an uncommon level of angst. Her display of extreme concern over white female involvement in Freedom Summer was rare for the usually unflappable Hamer. She watched the women's every move and just grew incensed with their violation of southern taboos:

> It's just as if I never said nothin' to them at Oxford! They sit out under trees in the back yard playin' cards with the Negro boys. Why, that back yard faces the hospital! Or they stand around in the front in groups, chattin' and laughin'! Some of them even wave at cars as they drive by! They cut through white property to get to town. And they go to town to buy curlers and cokes![60]

Vexed and nearly forsaken, Hamer eventually revealed to McLaurin that she was "worried sick." She questioned whether "all of this [life in the American South] just [wasn't] real for them yet." In a state of high frustration, she declared, "Then, if they can't obey the rules, call their mothers and tell them to send down their sons instead!"[61] To be sure, Hamer was agitated as never before. As she reacted to the white women volunteers, she was also responding to a historical circumstance: the monumental position of race and sex in her personal life history and that of most black Mississippians. With its delicate mixture of race and sex, Freedom Summer, then, left Hamer worn and worried, but only temporarily. What resulted was one of those rare moments when Hamer was more flustered than energized by the convergence of historical memory and present circumstances. She was drained, and not simply in response to the behavior of an ingenuous group of young adults. External troubles and challenges for the movement remained a serious fact of life. She eventually got beyond this moment and continued mobilizing and seizing nearly every opportunity to use historical memory to propel others forward.

Going National: 1964

Hamer's movement work in 1964 included exposing the ugly side of Mississippi life to a broader audience. She did so by highlighting her personal experiences with violence, and as a result, her local and national appeal increased substantially. She gave one personal testimony after another in official hearings and investigations. If politicians and other officials needed to be shown how bad things really were, she presented herself as the personification of suffering and struggle. And she shared generously and with seemingly little regard for the usual reprisals that awaited those who simply refused to stay in their place. Mostly she talked about the example of Winona. On other occasions she talked about how, as a young girl, a local white man murdered her family's animals in order to punish the Hamers for having an unusually decent sharecropping year. She also talked about the infamous lynchings that took place in and around her county, like the shooting and burning of Joe Pulliam, an upstanding citizen and hardworking sharecropper whose only "crime" was to insist on his fair share.[62]

The Magnolia State was hardly a safe place for people like Hamer, and she intended to tell all who would listen. During the movement, civil rights activists arranged a number of public hearings for the purpose of giving voice to local folks and their concerns. These hearings usually included panels comprised of sympathetic individuals who were deemed influential Americans. They usually included professionals, philanthropists, entertainers, politicians, and others. On June 8, 1964, Fannie Lou Hamer participated in a public hearing held at the National Theatre in Washington, DC. She and twenty-four other Mississippians, including Elizabeth Allen, the wife of slain federal witness, Louis Allen, spoke to a panel of prominent Americans about increased violence and intimidation in Mississippi.[63]

In her testimony, Hamer began with her first voter registration attempt in Indianola and her subsequent eviction. After summarizing these two experiences and the shooting that occurred soon after, she turned to the Winona experience, emphasizing all of its horrors in great detail, including the humiliating experience of having her dress raised and listening to her co-workers get beaten. This public recounting of Winona marked one of Hamer's rare public attempts to work through the private humiliation of the experience. On one tape-recorded version of her presentation, Hamer sobbed as she carefully recounted the details, pausing occasionally to collect herself. In spite of her pain (or maybe because of it), she forged ahead to the end of her story, concluding in an angry tone that typified her public manner. Undoubtedly, reliving the horror was excruciating for the Winona survivors. But this was necessary in Hamer's eyes, and it was also completely consistent with her leadership style, her public way of being. More than any single incident associated with Hamer, Winona justified the immediate presence of federal officials to make democracy a reality in Mississippi.

At the National Theatre hearing, Hamer did not stop at Winona in using her memories for political purposes. Another injustice weighed heavily on her mind, again for political and personal reasons. Hamer's last comment to the panel was among her first public statements on forced sterilizations of rural women:

> One of the other things that happened in Sunflower County, the North Sunflower County Hospital, I would say about 6 out of the 10 Negro women that go to the hospital are sterilized with the tubes tied. They are getting up a law said if a woman has an illegitimate baby and then a second one, they could draw time for 6 months or a $500 fine. What they didn't tell is that they are already doing these things, not only to single women but to married women.[64]

Hamer seized the moment to call attention to Mississippi's inhumane 1964 sterilization bill, which many activists immediately recognized as the legislature's pathetic attempt to repress the movement by scaring local folk, especially women. SNCC leaders called it the "genocide bill" and rightly argued that it targeted black Mississippians in general and local civil rights participants in particular.[65] The timing of its introduction coincided perfectly with the spring campaign of local candidates who were supported by civil rights organizations. In

calling attention to the proposed law during the hearing, Hamer de-
nounced the immediate evil intent of the bill. She specifically condemned it as yet another example of Mississippi's ill regard for black
life. If anyone could speak to the sterilization issue, it was Hamer,
herself a victim of forced sterilization.

In 1961, Hamer was given a hysterectomy without her knowledge
and consent. She went into the hospital expecting to have a cyst removed from her stomach. After the procedure, she awakened to discover that her uterus had been removed. Even though Hamer was ap-
proaching the end of her reproductive years in 1961, the experience still
became another instance of loss and dispossession in her life. The 1964
sterilization bill represented the same, although symbolically for her
and realistically for others yet to experience such a violation. During the
hearings, Hamer raised this issue as if it were the last point on her mind,
as if it were truly an afterthought. However, she may have raised it last
because it was something that bothered her most out of all the other
horrible experiences that typified her life. It stands out among the rest
of her testimony, for not everyone in the movement regarded sterilization as a political concern of their work in Mississippi. Clearly Hamer
did, and thus she spoke about it. Again she summoned personal memory to create a larger context and meaning for a contemporary political
moment. Struggle was historical and continuous.

In spring 1964, Hamer and other movement leaders formed the
Mississippi Freedom Democratic Party (MFDP), a grassroots political
party formed after blacks had tried unsuccessfully to participate in
the affairs of the "regular" state party, which was all white. In August
of that year, Hamer joined sixty-eight other Freedom Democrats at
the National Democratic Party Convention in Atlantic City, New Jersey. She was vice-chairperson of her delegation. As they had planned,
the Freedom Democrats turned the 1964 Democratic Convention into
a political contest of high drama. Unfortunately, in the end the historic moment occasioned both victory and defeat for Hamer and the
Mississippi movement. During the week-long convention proceedings, the Mississippi civil rights activists challenged the seating of the
"regular" Mississippi delegation by charging that its members were
not the legitimate representatives of the state since it excluded blacks.
Blacks were intimidated and kept from registering, some even losing
their lives, and others losing their homes and jobs. In addition, blacks
were not allowed to attend precinct meetings or to engage in other of-

ficial party business at the state level. The Freedom Democrats appealed to the Credentials Committee of the convention based on a set of principles that centered on democracy, equality, accessibility, and lawfulness—all creeds that were apparently foreign to the Mississippi state party.

After a great deal of negotiating and meetings, the Freedom Democrats were offered the infamous compromise, which allowed them two seats at large on the convention floor, but which still allowed the seating of the all-white delegation. Hamer was out front in her rejection and criticism of such a compromise. She remarked, "We didn't come all this way for no two seats."[66] The highlight of the convention came when Hamer presented a moving account of the Winona experience. The support she received was enormous; numerous letters and phone calls followed. As a result of her appearance, she won tremendous national support for the Mississippi civil rights cause. Her message was as eloquent as it was incisive and passionate. Still, Hamer and other Freedom Democrats could not help feeling defeated. They had traveled a long distance that summer, expended a lot of energy, and generated much hope. There had been no federal commitment to their cause. Hamer came away from the convention proceedings thoroughly disabused of the idea that federal attention would automatically lead to liberty and justice for all. Her use of memory and personal tragedy in this instance was less effective; it did not move the party that has since become so closely identified with civil rights reform.

The end result of her travels to Atlantic City included a number of important lessons and significant turning points. Indeed, the 1964 Democratic Convention was a watershed moment for Hamer. Once again she used survival of personal tragedy to instill others with a sense of outrage and an abiding commitment to doing anything to make change. While some may have doubted the importance of her symbolism, most believed that her mere presence could galvanize a social movement that had its major ups and downs from time to time. In a word, her personal example of courage and dignity counted for something. She was an inspirational leader who stilled troubled waters in times of uncertainty, even as she attempted to make sense of her own doubt and profound disappointment with those who appeared not to want freedom as badly as she did. In August 1964, the entire nation experienced her sense of possibility and deep commitment to making America a better place.

The challenge was also important for Hamer's evolution as a leader. From her defeat Hamer learned in clear and definite terms that appeals to the federal government did not always bring about the necessary remedy. The challenge and its defeat also marked the beginning of deteriorating relations between Hamer and middle-class movement leaders. Consequently, she became more interested in working exclusively to build strong local institutions for the problems that plagued her community. While she came away from the challenge quite bitter and disillusioned, she ultimately became more resolved to press her main objective: the poor would and should have a voice in their own destiny through meaningful franchise. Ironically, she also came away from this defeat in a better position to assist the movement financially due to the broader audience she won over with her dramatic testimony about the horrible 1963 Winona beating. Despite (or perhaps because of) the MFDP's defeat and her subsequent bitterness, Hamer continued her grassroots political work by recruiting prospective voters and preaching about the powers of the ballot and other crucial issues.

Beyond 1964

Although the convention was a blow to her morale, Hamer kept up her pace, traveling and speaking regularly in 1964 and 1965. She was fully committed to launching a full-scale attack on poverty at the local level. She refused to slow up, and neither did her hardship. Political disappointment and personal tragedy shadowed her at every turn between 1966 and 1968. She broke with SNCC over black separatism, and she suffered a family's worst nightmare: her teenage daughter died tragically from a cerebral hemorrhage.[67] Eventually she resumed her work, but with considerable sadness and fatigue. However, her proudest moment was yet to come: the building of the Freedom Farm Corporation.

The farm was Hamer's most complete institutional attempt to broaden the meaning of civil rights activism. It was an elaborate effort to bring economic self-sufficiency to Mississippi's poor. A focus on poverty was hardly a shift in Hamer's agenda. She had always, since her first official civil rights activity in 1962, envisioned her political work in this extensive way. Ending human suffering was a political obsession for Hamer, and this included suffering caused by decades of poverty. But even as Hamer devoted herself to eradicating poverty, she still kept one eye on the political mainstream. Throughout the late sixties and early seventies, she continued her political activities, including a 1971 run for the Mississippi State Senate and various large-scale voter registration efforts. Unknown to many, however, Hamer's active political days were nearing an end. It was not a waning commitment or a surrender to the opposition that would stop her. By the early 1970s, Hamer's body and mind started to betray her. Depression, hypertension, diabetes, and heart disease were starting to get the best of her, and by 1976, breast cancer began hastening her demise. On March, 14, 1977, she died at age fifty-nine.

Among the institutions she created and the thousands of people she fed or registered was another aspect of her legacy—self-conscious creation of her public identities and her deft use of personal tragedy. As I have focused on Hamer's subjectivity and her self-conscious creation of her public identities, I have kept one eye on her public record of human service through what we call the Civil Rights Movement. It is, however, precisely the meaning of her life for her that has given her historical presence. This is the ultimate significance of her centering personal pain, anger, and the difficult memories to affect the course of history—hers and ours.

NOTES

1. Fannie Lou Hamer, interview with Robert Wright, August 9, 1968, Civil Rights Documentation Project (CRDP), Moorland-Spingarn Collection, Howard University, Washington, DC; Fannie Lou Hamer, *To Praise Our Bridges* (Jackson, Mississippi: KIPCO, 1967), 12; Howell Raines, *My Soul Is Rested* (New York: Penguin Books, 1977), 249; Phyl Garland, "Builders of a New South," *Ebony* 21 (August 1966): 29; Chana Kai Lee, *For Freedom's Sake: The Life of Fannie Lou Hamer* (Urbana: University of Illinois Press, 1999), 23–25.

2. Raines, *My Soul Is Rested*, 249.

3. Ibid., 255.

4. Jerry Demuth, "Tired of Being Sick and Tired," *The Nation* 198, no. 23 (June 1, 1964): 549.

5. Fannie Lou Hamer, interview with Robert Wright, CRDP; Susan Kling, *Fannie Lou Hamer: A Biography* (Chicago: Women for Racial and Economic Equality, 1979), 17. Hamer sued Cecil B. Campbell three years later for

unlawful interference with the elections held in Sunflower and Moorhead, Mississippi.

6. John Egerton, *A Mind to Stay Here: Profiles from the South* (New York: Macmillan, 1970), 97; Fannie Lou Hamer, interview with Robert Wright, CRDP; "Fannie Lou Hamer Speech," Gainesville, Florida, n.d., in author's possession. Thanks to David Chalmers for sharing a copy of this tape.

7. Fannie Lou Hamer, interview with Robert Wright, CRDP; Raines, *My Soul Is Rested*, 250; Demuth, "Tired of Being Sick and Tired," 550.

8. U.S. Commission on Civil Rights, *Political Participation* (Washington, DC: Government Printing Office, 1968), 246; "Registration Efforts in Mississippi Continue Despite Violence and Terror," *The Student Voice*, October, 1962. Voter registration figures for groups in the nonwhite category are hard to come by for the Delta before 1964. Compare these Sunflower County figures with those for the entire state: blacks represented 36 percent of the statewide voting age population but comprised only 5.3 percent of the registered voters. See also U.S. Commission on Civil Rights, *Voting in Mississippi* (Washington, DC: Government Printing Office, 1965), 70–71; and Pat Watters and Reese Cleghorn, *Climbing Jacob's Ladder, The Arrival of Negroes in Southern Politics* (New York: Harcourt, Brace & World, 1967), Appendix II.

9. Hamer's mother, Lou Ella Townsend, often told her young daughter, I want you to respect yourself as a Black child, and as you get older, you respect yourself as a Black woman. If you respect yourself enough, other people will have to respect you. See "Fannie Lou Hamer Speaks Out," *Essence* (October 1971): 53.

10. "Marked for Murder," *Sepia* 14, no. 4 (April 1965): 28–33.

11. June Jordan, *Fannie Lou Hamer* (New York: Crowell, 1972), 22.

12. Fannie Lou Hamer, interview with Robert Wright, CRDP; Demuth, "Tired of Being Sick and Tired," 550; Raines, *My Soul Is Rested*, 250–51.

13. Besides Hamer's insolence, another factor that seemed to weigh heavily on Marlow's mind was the thought of being singled out for allowing an "agitator" to remain on his property. During his exchange with Hamer, he also pointed out: "They gon' worry me tonight. They gon' worry the hell outa me, and I'm gon' worry hell outa you. You got 'til in the mornin' to tell me." Although he never identifies who "they" are, Hamer assumed he is referring to men in the White Citizens Council or the Ku Klux Klan. See Raines, *My Soul Is Rested*, 251.

14. Egerton, *A Mind to Stay Here*, 97–98.

15. Fannie Lou Hamer, interview with Robert Wright, CRDP; Hamer, *To Praise Our Bridges*, 12–13; Kling, *Fannie Lou Hamer*, 19; Raines, *My Soul Is Rested*, 251; Egerton, *A Mind to Stay Here*, 97–98.

16. Andrew Young, "Eulogy for Mrs. Hamer," Fannie Lou Hamer Funeral (March 1977), videotape, Mississippi Department of Archives and His-

tory, Jackson, Mississippi; Kling, *Fannie Lou Hamer*, 19; Jordan, *Fannie Lou Hamer*, 22.

17. Kay Mills, *This Little Light of Mine: The Life of Fannie Lou Hamer* (New York: Dutton, 1993), 38–40; George Sewell, "Fannie Lou Hamer's Light Still Shines," *Encore American & Worldwide News* (July 18, 1977), 3; Kling, *Fannie Lou Hamer*, 20.

18. Hamer, *To Praise Our Bridges*, 13; Raines, *My Soul Is Rested*, 251; Taylor Branch, *Parting the Waters: America During the King Years, 1954–63* (New York: Simon and Schuster, 1988), 636.

19. Hamer, *To Praise Our Bridges*, 13; Raines, *My Soul Is Rested*, 245–48, 251; "Fannie Lou Hamer Speech," Gainesville, Florida.

20. Raines, *My Soul Is Rested*, 245–46.

21. Fannie Lou Hamer, interview with Robert Wright, CRDP.

22. Raines, *My Soul Is Rested*, 251.

23. Ibid.

24. Ibid.

25. Ibid.

26. The conversion motif abounds in Western and non-Western life-writing. See, for example, Robert Elbaz, *The Changing Nature of the Self* (Iowa City: University of Iowa Press, 1987); Theodore Rosengarten, *All God's Dangers: The Life of Nate Shaw* (New York: Alfred A. Knopf, 1974); Nellie Y. McKay, "Nineteenth-Century Black Women's Spiritual Autobiographies: Religious Faith and Self-Empowerment," in Personal Narratives Group, ed., *Interpreting Women's Lives: Feminist Theory and Personal Narratives* (Urbana: University of Illinois Press, 1989), 137–54. Perhaps the best-known example in African American life-writing is Malcolm X (with Alex Haley), *The Autobiography of Malcolm X* (New York: Grove Press, 1965).

27. Charles McLaurin, "Memories of Fannie Lou Hamer," *Jackson Advocate* (February 26–March 4, 1981), 1, Section C. On SNCC's Fall Institute and Hamer's participation, see the following: Memo from Charles McDew on Combination Fall Coordinating Committee Meeting and Leadership Training Institute, n.d., SNCC Papers, microfilm edition, reel 11; 1962 Fall Coordinating Committee Meeting Leadership Training Institute application for Fannie Lou Hamer, SNCC Papers, reel 11; Politics and Voting Workshop sign-up sheet for Leadership Training Institute [longhand], SNCC Papers, reel 11. The Institute hoped to achieve the following: "students, the nation over, shall have an opportunity to communicate problems and solutions to each other and to dramatize the comprehensive unity of *the Movement* [emphasis original]. It is hoped that the students . . . will return to their respective tasks with additional information, with a revitalized commitment and with a new sense of community and good will."

28. Other organizations included: the Southern Christian Leadership

Conference (SCLC), the Congress of Racial Equality (CORE), the National As-socation for the Advancement of Colored People (NAACP), and the National Urban League (NUL). See Steven F. Lawson, *Black Ballots: Voting Rights in the South* (New York: Columbia University Press, 1976), 263–65; Watters and Cleghorn, *Climbing Jacob's Ladder,* 48–49; Minion K. C. Morrison, *Black Political Mobilization, Leadership, Power, and Mass Behavior* (Albany: State University of New York Press, 1987), 47–49.

29. Garland, "Builders of a New South," 30.

30. Belinda Robnett, *How Long? How Long? African American Women in the Struggle for Civil Rights* (New York: Oxford University Press, 1997), 157–71; Karen Brodkin Sacks, *Caring By the Hour: Women, Work, and Organizing at Duke Medical Center* (Urbana: University of Illinois Press, 1988), 120–21; Charles Payne, *I've Got the Light of Freedom: The Organizing Tradition and the Mississippi Freedom Struggle* (Berkeley: University of California Press, 1995), 194.

31. On Greenwood as an active spot in the Delta, see Payne, *I've Got the Light of Freedom,* and Branch, *Parting the Waters,* 708–55.

32. Fannie Lou Hamer, interview with June Johnson, July 22, 1979, Tom Dent Oral History Collection (TDC), Tougaloo Civil Rights Collection, Tougaloo College, Jackson, Mississippi. On Hamer's important influence on the Greenwood movement, see Payne, *I've Got the Light of Freedom,* 242, 258, 260–61.

33. Minutes from SNCC Staff Meeting, October 11, 1964, SNCC Papers, microfilm reel 3.

34. "The Winona Incident, An Interview with Annelle Ponder and Fannie Lou Hamer, June 1963," in Watters and Cleghorn, eds., *Climbing Jacob's Ladder,* Appendix I, 364; See also U.S. Congress, Hearing before a Select Panel on Mississippi and Civil Rights, *Congressional Record* (Washington, DC: Government Printing Office), 14002.

35. Raines, *My Soul Is Rested,* 253; Branch, *Parting the Waters,* 819.

36. Kling, *Fannie Lou Hamer,* 22–23; Sewell, "Fannie Lou Hamer's Light Still Shines," 3.

37. Fannie Lou Hamer, interview with June Johnson, TDC; Howard Zinn, *SNCC: New Abolitionists* (Boston: Beacon Press, 1964), 95.

38. "Jury Frees Officers," *The Student Voice* (December 9, 1963), 2.

39. "The Winona Incident," 374; Demuth, "Tired of Being Sick and Tired," 550; Hamer, *To Praise Our Bridges,* 14.

40. Fannie Lou Hamer, interview with Robert Wright, CRDP.

41. Jacquelyn Dowd Hall, "The Mind That Burns in Each Body: Women, Rape, and Racial Violence," in Ann Snitow, Christine Stansell, and Sharon Thompson, eds., *Powers of Desire: The Politics of Sexuality* (New York: Monthly Review Press, 1983), 329.

42. Sylvia Townsend (Hamer's cousin and confidante), interview with the author, May 18, 1990, New York City.

43. Nationally, the median incomes of blacks and whites were $1,362 and $2,088 respectively. U.S. Department of Commerce, *Statistical Abstract of the United States, 1966* (Washington, DC: Government Printing Office, 1966), 338; U.S. Department of Commerce, Bureau of the Census, *Population Reports* (Washington, DC: Government Printing Office, 1964), Series P-20, no. 145 and Series P-60, no. 47; U.S. Department of Agriculture, *Statistical Bulletin*, 1964 (Washington, DC: Government Printing Office, 1964), no. 339.

44. U.S. Bureau of the Census, *Statistical Abstract of the United States: 1967* (Washington, DC: Government Printing Office, 1967).

45. Ibid.

46. Action Memo from [James A.] Jim Dombrowski, Executive Director, Southern Conference Educational Fund, Inc., to Friends Everywhere, January 23, 1964, SNCC Papers, microfilm reel 9. The participation of the Southern Conference Educational Fund (SCEF) in economic assistance projects during the movement was entirely consistent with SCEF's mission. SCEF was set up in 1948 as a tax-exempt organization to the Southern Conference of Human Welfare, a southern white liberal organization founded in 1938. The SCHW championed racial equality and fairness by taking on inequality of pay and conditions between black and white schools and teachers. SCHW also championed the cause of black and white tenant farmers. An interracial organization, SCHW was bent on uplifting the South economically by eradicating racial inequality, which it believed retarded the progress of the South as a whole. See Linda Reed, *Simple Decency and Common Sense: The Southern Conference Movement, 1938–1963* (Bloomington: Indiana University Press, 1991); Thomas Krueger, *And Promises to Keep: The Southern Conference for Human Welfare, 1938–1948* (Nashville: Vanderbilt University Press, 1967).

47. WATS Report, March 13, 1964, Ruleville, SNCC Papers, reel 15.

48. Ibid.

49. The freedom schools were among the key institutions established, along with community centers and voter registration projects, during the Freedom Summer campaign. They were formed to redress inequalities in Mississippi's public education and to empower students by encouraging them to ask and answer questions about their immediate surroundings.

50. Tracy Sugarman, *Stranger at the Gates: A Summer in Mississippi* (New York: Hill and Wang, 1966), 117.

51. Ibid.

52. Ibid., 119.

53. Some received food and clothing through theft.

54. "Freedom Summer Planned in Miss.," *The Student Voice* (Special Issue, Spring 1964), in Clayborne Carson, ed., *The Student Voice, 1960–1965: Periodical of the Student Nonviolent Coordinating Committee* (Westport, CT: Meckler Corporation, 1990), 133.

55. Doug McAdam, *Freedom Summer* (New York: Oxford University Press, 1988), 7, 66–69; John Dittmer, *Local People: The Struggle for Civil Rights in Mississippi* (Urbana: University of Illinois, 1994), 207–11, 242–71.

56. Sugarman, *Stranger at the Gates*, 113.

57. Ibid., 113.

58. Ibid.

59. Ibid., 114.

60. Ibid.

61. Ibid.

62. Regarding these other early experiences, see Mills, *This Little Light of Mine*, 6–14.

63. Louis Allen was the key witness to the 1961 murder of Herbert Lee, a voter registration worker brutally slain by a Mississippi state representative, E. H. Hurst. Hurst claimed to a grand jury that he killed Lee in self-defense because Lee was threatening him with a fire iron. Initially, fearing for his life, Allen corroborated Hurst's version of the incident. However, just after the jury freed Hurst, Allen signed a statement charging that Hurst murdered Lee "without provocation." Allen was subsequently warned to leave his home town of Liberty, Mississippi. After the threats and an encounter with a deputy sheriff which resulted in his jaw being broken, Allen asked for federal protection, but to no avail. Allen finally decided to leave Mississippi for Milwaukee, but twelve hours before he was scheduled to leave, he was shot down in his front yard (reportedly, his head was blown off), while his terrified wife and children witnessed the incident from inside the Allen house. For a full account of the Lee and Allen murders, see Clayborne Carson, *In Struggle: SNCC and the Black Awakening of the 1960s* (Cambridge: Harvard University Press, 1981), 48–49.

64. Ibid.

65. "Genocide in Mississippi," SNCC Papers, reel 19.

66. Fannie Lou Hamer, interview with Anne Romaine, November 1966 (transcript), 222, 228, Anne Romaine Papers, Martin Luther King, Jr. Center for Nonviolent Social Change, Atlanta, Georgia; Fannie Lou Hamer, interview with Robert Wright, CRDP.

67. On the split with SNCC, see Carson, *In Struggle*, 191–211, 240; and Payne, *I've Got the Light of Freedom*, 368, 372. On the death of Hamer's teenage daughter, Dorothy, see Mills, *This Little Light of Mine*, 191.

From Civil Rights to Black Power
African American Women and Nationalism

The essays in Part IV examine the role of black women during the period of transition from the emphasis on civil rights to the more militant demands for "Black Power." These essays offer new perspectives on the participation and leadership of African American women within organizations and campaigns that were previously characterized as "male-centered" and "male-dominated." Rather than working behind the scenes as "bridge leaders," as was the case in various civil rights campaigns, African American women in the Black Power movement were highly visible, more outspoken, and often militant in the pursuit of black equality. They sometimes placed themselves in dangerous positions and questioned nonviolence as the most appropriate strategy to bring about social change. At the same time, however, in a movement full of contradictions about "proper" gender roles, the talents of many women were underutilized and unappreciated.

Sharon Harley's essay, "'Chronicle of a Death Foretold': Gloria Richardson, the Cambridge Movement, and the Radical Black Activist Tradition," examines the personal background and leadership style of Gloria Richardson, the chair of the Cambridge Nonviolent Action Committee (CNAC). While Gloria Richardson has been the subject of several recent studies of African American women in civil rights campaigns, neither she nor the movement she led is mentioned in the major studies of the Civil Rights Movement authored by Robert Brisbane, Adam Fairclough, Juan Williams, Manning Marable, Jack Bloom, Robert Weisbrot, and others (see Selected Bibliography). Harley argues that the major reason why Richardson and the Cambridge Movement have not been included in the general histories is because Richardson's militant leadership of a civil rights campaign that sometimes turned violent did not fit their paradigm for the Martin Luther King-led, nonviolent civil rights campaigns of the early

1960s. Harley demonstrates that Gloria Richardson and the leadership she provided were part of the radical black activist tradition in the United States that would take center stage in black protests in the late 1960s.

In her essay, "Black Women and Black Power: The Case of Ruby Doris Smith Robinson and the Student Nonviolent Coordinating Committee," Cynthia Griggs Fleming describes the impact of the increasing black militancy on one of the most influential women in SNCC. Robinson had joined SNCC in 1961, participated in the Freedom Rides and numerous other demonstrations, and rose to the position of Executive Secretary in 1966. In its early years SNCC was relatively egalitarian, but Fleming points out that to some outside observers the administrative structure may have appeared male-dominated. Ruby Doris Smith Robinson held formal leadership positions in SNCC, and Fleming documents the fact that with the coming of Black Power in 1966, Robinson and other black women activists initially accepted certain notions of "black male assertiveness," even with all its contradictions. However, before her untimely death in 1967 at the age of twenty-five, Robinson had begun to deconstruct the unsubstantiated claims of male Black Power advocates that women in leadership positions were doing "a man's job."

Farah Jasmine Griffin, in "'Ironies of the Saint': Malcolm X, Black Women, and the Price of Protection," examines the legacy of Malcolm X for African American women. While Malcolm was and is still revered by many black women for holding out the "promise of protection," there were aspects of his rhetoric that reflected the patriarchal attitudes and values of that period. Malcolm became well known for the significant changes he made throughout his life. Griffin argues that "beyond wondering how Malcolm's view of women might have changed" had he lived, we must also engage in the task of deconstructing and revising the ideological formations he left us that may contribute to our own oppression.

In "'No One Ever Asks What a Man's Role in the Revolution Is': Gender Politics and Leadership in the Black Panther Party, 1966–71," Tracye A. Matthews examines the dominant gender ideologies in the 1960s and compares those espoused by the Black Panther leadership with the views and perspectives found in the Moynihan Report (1966), and among black cultural nationalists and white feminists. Matthews also presents a detailed analysis of the impact that African

American women in leadership positions had on the evolution of gender beliefs and practices within the Black Panther Party and concludes that this significant ideological transformation must be considered one aspect of a larger, dynamic social process.

Chapter 10

"Chronicle of a Death Foretold"

Gloria Richardson, the Cambridge Movement, and the Radical Black Activist Tradition

Sharon Harley

> The Winchester rifle should have a place of honor in every home.
>
> —Ida Wells Barnett (1892)

> The choice that Cambridge and the rest of the nation finally faces is between progress and anarchy, between witnessing change and experiencing destruction.
>
> —Gloria Richardson (1964)

> It never once entered my head that women could not be civil rights leaders or organizers.
>
> —Kathleen Cleaver (1997)[1]

Gloria St. Clair Richardson was a militant black leader, who in her refusal in 1963 and 1964 to accept nonviolence as the primary strategy in civil rights protests, foretold the death of the nonviolent Civil Rights Movement most closely associated with Martin Luther King, Jr. However, Richardson, who became one of the most feared and militant "up-south" black leaders in the early 1960s, has largely been a marginalized figure in early published accounts of the modern Civil Rights Movement, written for the most part by male scholars and former activists. Although in recent years discussions of Gloria Richardson and her "militant" grassroots movement in Cambridge, Maryland have appeared in texts devoted to the role of women and gender politics in the modern Civil Rights Movement, these studies have been written mainly by women scholars.

Several scholarly articles and encyclopedia entries have examined the civil rights activities of Gloria Richardson, and she was one of the women activists discussed in Paula Giddings' *When and Where I Enter: The Impact of Black Women on Race and Sex in America* (1984), *Women in the Civil Rights Movement: Trailblazers and Torchbearers, 1941–1965* (1990), edited by Vicki Crawford, Jacqueline Rouse, and Barbara Woods; and sociologist Belinda Robnett's *How Long? How Long? African-American Women in the Struggle for Civil Rights* (1997). These writers have begun the process of establishing Richardson as a major figure in the 1960s Civil Rights Movement. Unfortunately, some of these authors tell (and even retell) Richardson's story through the lens of her critics, white and black, and restate conclusions drawn by others rather than conducting their own independent research. For example, in the articles "Gloria Richardson: Breaking the Mold" (1996) by Anita K. Foeman and "Recasting Civil Rights Leadership: Gloria Richardson and the Cambridge Movement" (1996) by Sandra Y. Millner, we find critical assessments of Richardson that focus primarily on her social class background and "uncompromising" political stances. In coming to these conclusions, Foeman and Millner rely almost exclusively on secondary sources. Only in the studies by Edward Trever, Anita Brock, and Paula Giddings was the attempt made to situate Richardson within the radical black female activist tradition.[2]

In arguing that Gloria Richardson's actions created a *"new* image of the Black woman in America, an image that move[d] beyond that of long-suffering martyr and took the shape of a woman as warrior," Anita Foeman ignored a rich history of political activism among African American women dating back to the antebellum period in the United States.[3] Harriet Tubman, Ida Wells Barnett, Amy Jacques Garvey, Gloria Richardson, Fannie Lou Hamer, and Angela Davis are among the best known black female leaders, but there are and were "hundreds" of local, often "unknown," black women leaders and activists.[4] In an extended examination of "Civil War on Race Street: The Black Freedom Sruggle and White Resistance in Cambridge, Maryland, 1960–1964," Peter B. Levy focused primarily on the political and economic conditions in the city, rather than women in general and Gloria Richardson in particular, as leaders in local civil rights campaigns.[5] More recently, however, Jenny Walker attacked Paula Giddings for describing Gloria Richardson as a "gun-toting militant" who should be considered a "feminist icon." Unfortunately, in her zeal to expose Giddings' "distortions and misrepresentations," Walker failed to examine Richardson's connections with other "civil rights militants" and organizations that were part of the black radical tradition in the United States.[6] This essay focuses on Richardson's radical political ideology and leadership style, and reveals how this courageous grassroots woman foresaw the arrival of militant Black Power campaigns that emerged in the late 1960s.

Sociologist Belinda Robnett in her gendered analysis of the modern Civil Rights Movement moved beyond traditional definitions and sites of leadership to develop a women's leadership topology within the movement. She is to be commended for identifying these leadership types, although in the case of Gloria Richardson there appears to be some inconsistency in the historical analysis. But Robnett's expansive concept of a "woman bridge leader" simultaneously encompasses and excludes Richardson's leadership style and practice. As with other bridge leaders, Richardson's allegiance was primarily to her local constituency, but she did not function as a "bridge" to national or regional institutions and organizations, even with her affiliations with the Student Nonviolent Coordinating Committee (SNCC), the National Association for the Advancement of Colored People (NAACP), and the Congress of Racial Equality (CORE). Robnett also claimed that Richardson became chair of the Cambridge Non-Violent Action Committee (CNAC) "because no man was willing or able to do the job," but offered no evidence to support this assertion.[7] Indeed, Robnett contradicted her own claim in presenting Richardson's assessment of how and why she became the leader of CNAC. Richardson recalled that "there were community meetings and people really asked me to . . . represent them because they felt that I was furthest removed from economic reprisal at the time because my uncle and my mother would support me and my family at that period, whereas other people . . . [had] to, I guess, moderate their lives."[8] Similarly, there is no evidence to support Robnett's assertions that, in the case of Richardson, when she assumed her leadership position and "exercised . . . power to the fullest, [she was] either ignored and overridden or lost credibility" or, quoting Anita Foeman, that "Richardson had no true constituency."[9] Robnett's assessment raises several questions: By whom was she ignored? (Certainly not by local white officials, the national media, ranking federal officials, or her fellow grassroots activists.) With whom did she lose credibility? (Certainly not with her black working-class followers in Cambridge, who, as Cleveland Sellers wrote, "had nothing but praise for her.")[10] It appears that Robnett relied too heavily on Foeman's and Brock's conclusions about the nature of Richardson's political activism and leadership.[11] At the same time, if Gloria St. Clair Hayes Richardson (later Dandridge) was not a consistent "bridge leader," or the *premier* black female "warrior" and "uncompromising militant" her white critics suggested, then who was this woman who garnered the respect and praise of thousands of poor black Eastern Shore residents, the anger of high-ranking federal and local officials, and the silent treatment from middle-class Cambridge residents and earlier civil rights historians?

The story of Gloria St. Clair Hayes Richardson Dandridge's civil rights activism must be told in at least two parts: first, it is necessary to document her political activism and leadership during an intense two-year period of public protests and racial strife (with occasional violent outbursts) in the Eastern Shore town of Cambridge, Maryland; and second, there is the need to reconcile the intense media coverage of Richardson's militant activism from 1962 to 1964 with her marginalization (indeed, erasure) in many published accounts of the modern Civil Rights Movement. As attorney and former Black Panther leader Kathleen Neal Cleaver observed, "The visual record documents the presence of women, but in the printed texts of academic accounts, women's participation tends to fade." Central to understanding the silence around Gloria Richardson's radical political activism is the hidden history of gender identity and ideologies in black communities, as well as Richardson's self-imposed silence and her unwillingness to "tell her own story."[12]

Recently, when I asked some black and white Marylanders what they knew or thought about Gloria Richardson, most (including a Cambridge, Maryland native) responded: "I don't know who she is." Others responded that they thought she was dead. Yet, she is alive and well, living and working in New York City. Quite possibly those who believed she was deceased may have seen her photograph in a March 1982 issue of the *Baltimore Afro-American* with the caption: "The *late* Gloria Richardson as she appeared during the height of the struggle in 1963."[13]

This essay offers a different rendering of Gloria Richardson's life and leadership role in the Cambridge Movement—one that includes, but extends beyond, her class identity; one that focuses less on how the white and black media viewed her, and more on her actual role and self-professed motivation in one of the most significant protest movements outside the Deep South—the first to be led by a woman. And finally, one that reveals how and why she (not unlike other female leaders and grassroots activists in general) until very recently has been rendered invisible in the history of the civil rights struggles in the United States.

Cambridge, Maryland: "Picturesque" and Poor

Contributing paradoxically to both Richardson's activist commitment and her subsequent obscurity was the geographic and social landscape of the Eastern Shore of Maryland. Its isolated communities with their run-down, dilapidated housing and mundane forms of racial subordination recalled an earlier time. The extreme economic dependency of many of the black and white residents made it appear as if time had stood still. Cambridge, located in Dorchester County in the southern section of the Eastern Shore, is approximately 16 miles east of the Chesapeake Bay Bridge, built in 1954. Regardless of the side one took in the debates over the building of the bridge, it was universally recognized that the new bridge would bring outsiders to the "picturesque" Eastern Shore communities. This change was noted in Cambridge's tricentennial retrospective in 1969 when the author observed that this small town on the Choptank River "was isolated and secure until about fifteen years ago. Then they built a bridge and across it came the whole upsetting twentieth century."[14] In the 1960s (and today) the pristine, picturesque scenery visible from the one-lane roads and two-lane highways as one travels to and from Chesapeake Bay beaches obscures sites of intense poverty—backyard outhouses, dilapidated housing, and inhumane workhouses, more reminiscent of impoverished nineteenth-century rural communities or what one might encounter in a poverty-stricken, developing country today. According to more than one observer, the poor housing that many blacks and some whites occupied was "not even originally built for human habitation. . . . [B]lacks rented 'chicken shack' homes, buildings originally built to raise chicken."[15] In Cambridge, the majority of the employed blacks and whites worked in oyster, poultry, tobacco, and canning factories, or as farmhands. In 1964, nearly 30 percent of Cambridge's black residents was chronically unemployed, and another 30 percent was seasonally employed. Two thirds of all black families earned less than $3,000 per year. Low wages, coupled with high unemployment (blacks were five times more likely than whites to be unemployed), and underemployment resulted in an acutely impoverished way of life for many Cambridge residents. The city's few black middle-class residents, including Gloria Richardson, could hardly ignore the deplorable conditions in Cambridge, even if they only cruised by in air-conditioned automobiles.[16]

The depressed living conditions in Cambridge and other communities were not solely responsible for Richardson's likening Maryland's Eastern Shore communities to Mississippi. Certainly, the similarities in the racial climate were equally, if not more, compelling bases for the unfavorable comparisons between life in Mississippi and in Cambridge, Maryland in the 1960s. As in other parts of the South, black citizens in Cambridge, Maryland could buy clothes, but not try them on in the stores; could buy carry-out food, but not eat in the restaurants; and could buy movie theater tickets, but were confined to the balconies of segregated theaters and, later, to the last rows of the segregated balconies. Blacks lived in segregated communities and attended segregated schools, despite local officials' claims that Cambridge schools were "integrated" in accordance with the 1954 Supreme Court public school desegregation decision. Furthermore, blacks and whites in Cambridge and other Eastern Shore communities fully understood, as Richardson recounted, that "there were certain places blacks after sundown were not expected to go, certain areas of the town that they did not want to see you in."[17] In that regard, Cambridge rivaled the most segregated cities in the Deep South, and Richardson felt that the practices in the town represented all that was "wrong with America" at that time.[18]

A lifetime of living without indoor plumbing and hot water, as well as routine mistreatment and segregation at work, in public recreational facilities and restaurants built up deep resentment among blacks, especially in Cambridge's segregated Second Ward. There was no simple solution to their sense of economic and political powerlessness. As Second Ward resident Goldie Freeman proclaimed,

"When we don't say anything, they say we're happy. When we do, they say we're racists, extremists, agitators. You can't win."[19]

Growing Up in "A Very Political Family"

It was in this Eastern Shore community and under these circumstances that Gloria St. Clair Hayes (later, Richardson Dandridge) came of age. Born in Baltimore, Maryland in 1922 into a well-known, educated middle-class Cambridge family, Gloria's early life differed in some (but not all) ways from most early twentieth-century Eastern Shore blacks. Her grandfather, Herbert Maynadier St. Clair, was an elected member of the Cambridge City Council, a position he held for some thirty-four years. When St. Clair was first elected in 1912, his ward was evenly divided between black and white residents; by the 1960s, the ward was predominantly black and referred to as the "Negro ghetto."[20]

As Gloria matured, the youthful joys of being the granddaughter of a well-known public figure were mixed with feelings of guilt and pain. The cozy relationship her grandfather enjoyed with the Phillips Packing Company, known for their substandard wages, inhumane work conditions, and its complicity in maintaining the racial status quo, was as troubling to Richardson as the personal mistreatment her grandfather experienced in their racially divided, economically depressed community. Barred by racial custom from attending the yearly councilmen's banquet, Councilman St. Clair's dinner reportedly was "sent to him on a plate to be eaten at home." Eventually, her grandfather's patient and gradual approach to effecting social, political, and economic change prompted Cambridge blacks, and even Gloria, to brand him a "gradualist." The differences in their approaches and political agendas were the root of a number of arguments between Gloria Richardson and her grandfather. Regardless of their differences, the roots of her activism were being laid because as she declared, "I grew up in a very political family."[21]

It was not lost on Richardson that her grandfather's political notoriety and social class position could not protect them from the quotidian racial indignities and segregationist practices so deeply ingrained in the very fabric of Eastern Shore cultural, political, and social life.

"Regardless of my background," she recalled, "I experienced the same kinds of things all other Blacks did in Cambridge."

> My father died because he could not go to the hospital most of the time. My people had to travel to Johns Hopkins' segregated clinic. I was not able to get a job of any kind since I didn't want to teach. I could not go into the restaurants if I wanted to. So I was a victim as well as the rest of the Blacks in Cambridge.[22]

Although Gloria Richardson was not alone in her victimization, she likely viewed racism with a more critical eye than other Second Ward residents, a perspective she may have developed while an undergraduate student at Howard University. There Richardson, a 1941 graduate, studied under such black intellectual luminaries as historian Rayford W. Logan, theologian Howard Thurman, and poet and literary scholar Sterling Brown. These and other Howard University professors taught and published extensively on how race influenced and determined the life experiences and the socioeconomic conditions for blacks in the United States, the Caribbean, and Africa. It was also at Howard where Gloria joined fellow classmates in picketing in front of Woolworth's Five and Ten Cent Store in Washington, DC to protest its discriminatory hiring practices; this experience provided her with more than a textbook understanding of direct political activism.

Following her graduation from Howard University, Gloria St. Clair Hayes worked for the federal government for two years. Afterward, she returned home to Cambridge to be near her family (her grandfather "didn't like his family being spread all over the place") and to work. While there she married a Cambridge school teacher and had a daughter, Donna. All the while, it never occurred to her (or any one else for that matter) that eventually she would be the leader of a grassroots struggle for racial and economic justice that would garner major media attention and the ire of national and local public officials.

For its college-educated black residents like Gloria Richardson, the racially segregated Eastern Shore job market offered only a few teaching positions in black public schools. For most blacks and a fair number of whites, educated or not, shucking oysters, farming (skinning tomatoes), working in a local cannery, or poultry work were the only employment options available. With limited job prospects, Gloria turned for employment to the pharmacy her family had previously owned in downtown Cambridge, an option obviously unavailable to most of Cambridge's black and white residents. As a single mother, Richardson became even more conscious and personally aware of the economic plight of Eastern Shore blacks. By the early 1960s, Richardson's anger at the severely limited job prospects for blacks (including herself), combined with the economically depressed living conditions in Cambridge, had reached a boiling point. And she was not alone.

While working as the manager of the pharmacy, Richardson's personal contact with the pharmacy's mostly working-class black clientele helped to define the nature and style of her leadership. The middle-class Richardson developed an affinity for the black working class which her family had promoted for years. Furthermore, in paying their bills on time, as Richardson was told by her father ("unlike the middle class"), the ordinary working people of Cambridge were responsible for keeping the pharmacy in business and thus for providing the financial support for her family. This early identification with the working class not only greatly influenced Richardson's leadership style, but also her political and economic agenda.[23]

Earlier writers' preoccupation with Richardson's social class background has often prevented scholars from more fully appreciating her courageous role in one of the most violent civil rights struggles of the early 1960s. Richardson's social background did not differ from that of other black male or female civil rights leaders, including Martin Luther King, Roy Wilkins, Whitney Young, Ella Baker, or James Farmer. Mississippi SNCC activist Joyce Ladner also suggested that the reluctance of male leaders and writers to accord courageous black female activists a greater place in histories of civil rights struggles might have been due to these women exhibiting characteristics defined as exclusively male.[24]

Disturbing to Some, Praised by Others: Gloria the Militant

Like scores of civil rights leaders in the 1960s, Gloria St. Clair Hayes Richardson had not set out to become a civil rights activist. Like many of them, Richardson's involvement in the Cambridge Movement followed that of the youthful activists (junior and senior high school students) who were among its initial organizers, participants, and leaders.

In Richardson's case, it was her daughter Donna Hayes Richardson and other SNCC organizers who encouraged her participation.

The young people's style of organizing resonated with Gloria Richardson. In particular, she found it to be more refreshing, immediate, and compelling than the formal, deliberate leadership style of the established civil rights organizations, such as the National Association for the Advancement of Colored People (NAACP), Southern Christian Leadership Conference (SCLC), and the Congress of Racial Equality (CORE). Proclaiming that "there was something direct, something real about the way the kids waged nonviolent war," Richardson recalled that for "the first time I saw a vehicle I could work with."[25]

As in most social reform movements, it was the convergence of these varied factors that led the thirty-nine-year-old Gloria St. Clair Hayes Richardson to join the Cambridge Movement in 1962 and to be appointed chair. At that time, nineteen-year-old Enez Grubb, a Cambridge native, served as her co-chair for the Cambridge Nonviolent Action Committee (CNAC), the local SNCC affiliate. Grubb had also held this position under Gloria's cousin and predecessor Freddie St. Clair. Grubb, who is currently an ordained minister and pastor of Mount Olive AME Church in Salisbury, Maryland, recalled that there was no opposition to them because they were women: "it just did not come up."[26] At the height of the Cambridge Movement from 1962 to 1964, Richardson, Enez Grubb, and other Cambridge residents from high schoolers to the elderly, along with students and activists from outside the region, regularly sat-in at movie theaters, bowling alleys, restaurants, and other public places; marched in the streets of Cambridge; picketed downtown businesses; wrote letters to newspaper editors; and occasionally responded to violent attacks with violence of their own. During that two-year period, the only times Richardson was absent from the picket lines was when she was in jail for her protests, and the struggles continued in her absence. Between 1962 and 1964 as chair of CNAC, Gloria Hayes Richardson was both praised and vilified (mainly in the white press) for her militant leadership and for her public dismissal of expected (female) middle-class behavior.

Armed with first-hand knowledge of the ineffectiveness of the gradualist approach to politics through her grandfather's years on the local city council, and a clear understanding of the pervasive nature of racial oppression in Cambridge, Richardson advocated a more aggressive approach to social change. As Gloria and other members of her family became more deeply committed to the protest campaigns, her family's pharmacy building and the house where she lived (also owned by her family) frequently bustled with the sights and sounds of organizers and activists of the "Cambridge Movement."[27]

The Cambridge Movement: Foretelling a Shifting Paradigm

When Richardson appeared as a leader of the Cambridge Movement before the Cambridge City Council in March 1963, she demanded an immediate end to the city's segregationist practices. When it was not forthcoming, Richardson and Grubb followed up (as promised) a few days later with a series of public protests and demonstrations. This pattern of militant demands followed by sit-ins, boycotts, and picketing became characteristic of the Cambridge Movement. Gloria Hayes Richardson and the Cambridge Movement became virtually synonymous, and the town and its courageous grassroots leader garnered considerable state and national attention from the news media.

On May 14, 1963, Gloria Richardson, her mother, Mable St. Clair Booth, and her teenage daughter, Donna Richardson, were arrested for their involvement with a series of civil rights demonstrations that took place that day. Donna was arrested at a sit-in at the lobby of Cambridge's segregated Dorset Theater. That same day, Gloria and her mother sat down on the sidewalk in front of the Dizzyland Restaurant after they were refused service. The women were part of a group of sixty-two protestors who were arrested on May 14. In response, Cambridge's Chief of Police ordered in reinforcements, including K-9 dogs and state police officers, in a futile attempt to discourage further demonstrations.[28]

Gloria Richardson was unique among early 1960s civil rights leaders because she combined the campaign for racial equality with the demand for economic justice.[29] Racial injustices in Cambridge were apparent at the economic as well as at the political and social levels. Widespread poverty, low wages, unemployment, and the absence of labor unions forced many black and poor white Eastern Shore residents into substandard living conditions. Richardson declared that "most people weren't really concerned about the social interchange but were concerned for the quality of their lifestyle, their jobs, their health, their education."[30] Consequently, economic improvement was a central aspect of Richardson's Cambridge Movement in the early 1960s, forecasting the emphasis in the major northern and southern civil rights campaigns in the late 1960s.

By the mid-1960s, Martin Luther King had become more concerned with the economic plight of African American communities. In December 1967, King was forced to admit that the dream he had so eloquently spoken of in the summer of 1963 had turned into a nightmare as he "moved through the ghettoes of the nation and saw black brothers and sisters perishing on a lonely island of poverty in the midst of a vast ocean of material prosperity, and saw the nation doing nothing to grapple with the Negroes' problem of poverty." Sounding more like Gloria Richardson and even Malcolm X, in 1966 King had asserted that "There must be a better distribution of wealth, and maybe America must move toward a Democratic Socialism."[31] The economic issues that brought King to Memphis, Tennessee in support of striking garbage workers in March and April 1968 had been a part of Richardson's civil rights agenda in the early 1960s, and that of A. Philip Randolph and other northern protest leaders from the 1940s.

Ironically, Gloria Richardson and Martin Luther King had a major falling out in 1963 when she refused to encourage African Americans in Cambridge to vote for a referendum aimed at the desegregation of public accommodations. Richardson opposed this measure because she believed that equality had already been guaranteed by the U.S. Constitution. In addition, Richardson pointed out to King that African Americans in Cambridge had been participating in elections for nearly one hundred years and it had not significantly changed the quality of their life. Harlem Congressman Rev. Adam Clayton Powell, but few local NAACP officials or church leaders, shared Richardson's views about the referendum. Many African Americans, following Richardson's advice, boycotted the election and the measure failed to pass. Richardson's critics lambasted her for not supporting the referendum, accusing her of "grandstanding" and even worse, of being a "Communist."[32]

State and federal support in the form of food, housing, and employment assistance, in addition to state and federal ordinances requiring the immediate desegregation of the schools and other public facilities, were critical to improving the depressed socioeconomic conditions for blacks and poor whites. The failure to alleviate these conditions ultimately led to violent protests. By the spring of 1963, Cambridge was more than a smoldering tinderbox of racial tension, it was a full-blown series of brush fires—in many ways, the fulfillment of James Baldwin's predictions of racial unrest outlined in his 1963 book, *The Fire Next Time*. The intensity and number of public demonstrations, including sit-ins, mass arrests, and occasional violent outbreaks, meant that Cambridge, Maryland differed little from Birmingham, Alabama and other hotbeds of racial conflict that spring. However, as the head of the Cambridge Movement for economic, racial, and social justice, Richardson was different from most early 1960s civil rights leaders in that she was a woman *and* confrontational and unequivocal in her demand for an end to segregated public accommodations and job discrimination.

Given her militancy and uncompromising positions and the violence that erupted in June 1963, newspaper headlines not only announced that "3 Shot, 4 Hurt, 3 Places Burned in Racial Violence in Cambridge" (*Baltimore Evening Sun*, June 12, 1963); but also proclaimed "Mrs. Richardson True Segregationist" (*Boston Herald*, June 19, 1963). In the article in the *Boston Herald*, the reporter George Frazier depicted Richardson as "far, far more than even the most militant racist, is the true segregationist, alienating even the moderates who devoutly wish an end to strife. . . . [I]t would be an injustice to the decent residents of this town, colored and white alike, not to deplore the demagoguery of such as Mrs. Richardson." Frazier continued,

> One feels sure that her late grandfather, Mannie St. Clair, who was a respected city councilman, would have shared these misgivings. . . . That the Negro must march is a simple truth. But the trouble with Mrs. Richardson, her riffraff and rowdies, is that, in this town that sincerely wishes integration, they are rebels without a cause.[33]

The black citizens who participated in the nonviolent protests organized by the Cambridge Movement, and acted in self-defense to protect themselves from the unprovoked attacks by local whites reinforced by the state and local police, would disagree with this assessment of Richardson's leadership, and remained loyal to her. In August 1963, either as a testament to her national notoriety, or Cambridge's close proximity to the march site, Gloria Richardson was one of the few black women activists officially invited (at the last minute) and introduced at the 1963 March on Washington. Like the rest, she was offered neither a speaking part nor any official role.

Richardson continued in her leadership role in the following year. The May 1964 visit of one of the nation's most prominent self-proclaimed segregationists, Alabama Governor George Wallace, certainly stoked the embers of racial conflict. Again, Richardson's fear of racial violence in the aftermath of Wallace's visit prompted her to issue a bold public warning that "somebody could be killed" if something was not done and soon. Richardson appealed to both President John F. Kennedy and the U.S. Attorney General Robert Kennedy for immediate federal assistance to combat a rapidly deteriorating racial situation. Unfortunately, Richardson's dire predictions proved justified. The situation worsened to the point that the National Guard considered using "live" ammunition (instead of dummy bullets and bayonets) to quell the demonstrations.[34]

The July 1964 issue of *Ebony* Magazine featured an article on Gloria Richardson and in bold print dubbed her "The Lady General of Civil Rights." The unidentified author described Richardson in terms stereotypically applied to women, but seldom used in referring to men. Richardson was "cordial with family and friends, sharp-tongued at the conference table, a tigress in street demonstrations." But the article also revealed how far Richardson and her followers were willing to go to obtain racial justice. The journalist reported that

> unlike other civil rights fighters, talking big and praying softly, Gloria and her followers have been preparing for war with local police, the national guard and federal troops, if necessary, in an all-out battle for their rights. Negro National Guard Capt. William (Box) Harris, sent into the community on a scouting mission, reported seeing one house with several shotguns ready for firing.[35]

In fact, the writer continued: "No one really talks seriously about practicing non-violence in Cambridge" on either side of the racial divide. Whites were equally likely to attack blacks as blacks were to shoot at whites and to destroy white-owned businesses in the town of Cambridge, where the black and white sections of town were divided ironically along "Race" Street. More importantly, although local, state, and national officials criticized Richardson for her "militant, uncompromising leadership," she was frequently called upon when demonstrations turned violent and they wanted to negotiate. General George C. Gelston of the National Guard was quoted as having said "She is the only person who can control things"; Audry Thompson, the segregationist spokesperson for the Dorchester White Citizens Council, remarked, "We can't deal with her and we can't deal without her."[36]

Gloria Richardson's major leadership position, along with her co-chair Enez Grubb, can be attributed to the fact that this was largely a local grassroots effort with considerable youth and working-class involvement *and* limited ministerial input. In its refusal to fully accept the nonviolent strategies and tactics of the King-led Southern Christian Leadership Conference (SCLC) and with women at its helm, the Cambridge Movement did not draw upon the Eastern Shore's middle-of-the-road, middle class, male-dominated NAACP or the conservative black clergy.

Consequently, without the presence of a male-dominated church leadership, the Cambridge Movement and Richardson escaped some of the obstacles that Ella Baker, Septima Clark, and other black women activists experienced in assuming leadership roles in the SCLC, NAACP, and the Congress of Racial Equality (CORE). In these civil rights groups, men exercised much of the authority, while women assumed leadership largely in the behind-the-scenes support roles. Among the women who earned official positions (not the major ones) such as NAACP and SCLC organizer Ella Baker, the message was clear that this was a male-led movement.

Ella Baker expressed a widely shared but frequently unrecorded sentiment about women in the upper echelon of the civil rights leadership when she declared: "I knew from the beginning that as a woman, an older woman, in a group of ministers who are accustomed to having women largely as supporters, there was no place for me to have come into a leadership role." In specific reference to King's SCLC, she added, "having a woman be an executive of SCLC was not something that would go over with the male-dominated leadership. And then, of course, my personality wasn't right, in the sense that I was not afraid to disagree with the higher authorities. I wasn't one to say, yes, because it came from the Reverend King."[37]

Black women who assumed leadership positions traditionally occupied by black men were often subjected to criticism, even ridicule, within black institutions and communities. This tendency to denigrate the contributions of African American women to black freedom struggles to some extent helps to explain their absence from many historical accounts of these movements. Despite the fact that she received nearly daily front-page coverage in local and national newspapers in 1963 and 1964, Gloria Richardson and the Cambridge Movement were not mentioned by the authors of the leading studies of the Civil Rights Movement.[38] However, Gloria Richardson's story is somewhat different from that of other women leaders and grassroots organizers. While the significant contributions to civil rights protests made by African American and other women may be missing from the historical accounts because of male bias on the part of the historians, there may be other reasons why civil rights scholars have failed to include discussions of the Cambridge Movement. Given the violent nature of the Cambridge protests in 1963 and 1964, this protest campaign did not fit well into the story of the "nonviolent" Civil Rights Movement that these historians were recounting.

Gloria Richardson and the Black Radical Activist Tradition

As a result of her experiences in Cambridge, Maryland, Gloria Richardson and many of her supporters questioned in action and deeds the nonviolent philosophy and approach that characterized the civil rights campaigns in the early 1960s. Cambridge activists recognized that decades of sustained, multidimensional racial and economic injustices had produced violent reactions, a virtual "civil war" in Cambridge. Prefiguring the disenchantment with the nonviolent, integrationist, church-led Civil Rights Movement of the early 1960s and the rise of militant Black Power struggles, Richardson questioned nonviolence as the primary tactic to further racial progress. Jenny Walker was very likely correct to point out that during the Cambridge protests, Gloria Richardson should not be described as a "gun-toting militant," since Richardson later maintained in an interview that she did not even know how to shoot a gun at that time. However, researchers who have claimed that Richardson became disenchanted with nonviolence as a tactic for black advancement are not engaging in a "disingenuous use of existing literature," but are coming to the same conclusions based on Richardson's statements and actions from as early as November 1963.[39]

Jenny Walker made no mention in her essay of Gloria Richardson's participation in the Northern Negro Grass Roots Leadership Conference, organized by Reverend Albert Cleage in Detroit in November 1963. After Reverend C. L. Franklin and NAACP leaders moved to exclude black nationalist supporters of Malcolm X and the Freedom Now Party from the Northern Negro Leadership Conference held in Detroit on November 9–10, 1963, Rev. Cleage organized the meeting of grassroots leaders that took place at the same time. Rev. Cleage's conference attracted "civil rights militants," including Reverend Milton Galamison and Jesse Gray, who organized school boycotts and rent strikes in New York City; Lawrence Landry, who had organized the successful school boycotts in Chicago; Stanley Branche, head of the "Committee for Freedom Now" in Chester, Pennsylvania; Gloria Richardson, and others. At that meeting Malcolm X was the featured speaker and he delivered his now-famous "Message to the Grass Roots."[40]

At that leadership conference Gloria Richardson announced publicly her support for strategies other than nonviolent protests to obtain social justice and political advancement for African Americans. Gloria Richardson and others believed that Malcolm's address signaled his break with Elijah Muhammad and the Nation of Islam and foreshadowed the movement from the "Negro revolution" to the "Black revolution." While Richardson and the other civil rights militants did not endorse Malcolm's references to the need to "resort to firearms" to bring about black freedom and advancement, they fully supported his calls for armed self-defense by African Americans taking a stand for their civil rights.[41]

Early in 1964, Gloria Richardson joined with Lawrence Landry, Stanley E. Branche, and other militant activists to form ACT (not an acronym) and to support the principle that African Americans will and should "do whatever is necessary to be free." Richardson believed that "the resisting white community takes advantage of our commitment to nonviolence and uses this against us." Besides, she stated, "Self-defense may actually be a deterrent to further violence. Hitherto, the government has moved into conflict situations only when matters approach the level of insurrection."[42] At the height of the civil rights campaigns in 1963 and 1964, there was growing distance between Dr. Martin Luther King, Jr. and the militant activists who refused to accept his nonviolent approaches and strategies unequivocally. In the rush to tell Martin Luther King's story and that of respectable Rosa Parks—who made the King story possible—there was no place for an uncompromising female activist who sided with those more militant activists who openly questioned the efficacy of nonviolence. These histories of the male-dominated, moderate civil rights campaigns failed to discuss the militant activities of Gloria Richardson, who wrote in a 1964 essay:

> To some Negroes it must be proved that nonviolence can win, that you cannot fight evil with evil. They are not concerned with the philosophy of Gandhi. . . . After all, America trained them to kill and to be immune to death in order to win for an ideal-democracy. The white power structure ignores this because it is not concerned with the reality of masses of Negroes in action. . . . The choice that Cambridge and the rest of the nation finally faces is between progress and anarchy, between witnessing change and experiencing destruction.[43]

The limited scholarship on the Cambridge Movement, Gloria Richardson, or other black female activists should not blind us to the rich activist tradition among women, men, and children in African American and other racially oppressed communities nor to the fact that the political work and ideas of Richardson and other women activists were often as important as the political struggles of black male leaders.

Although Richardson and her grassroots movement did not inspire scholars to write about them until recently, their actions did inspire the next generation of black activists who took center stage in the late 1960s and early 1970s. Former Black Panther Angela D. LeBlanc-Ernest declared that "women who later became members of the Black Panther Party followed the legacy of radical African-American female activists of the early 1960s, such as Gloria Richardson." Former Panther leader Kathleen Cleaver connected Richardson's activities to a long tradition of black female activism. Cleaver explained:

> I learned what heroism and leadership meant from Diane Nash, who led student demonstrations in Nashville, Tennessee, and later organized Freedom Rides, from Gloria Richardson, who mobilized the black community to fight segregation in Cambridge, Maryland, and from Ruby Doris Robinson, who helped coordinate the 1964 Mississippi Summer project. It never once entered my head that women could not be civil rights leaders or organizers.[44]

Neither the marginalization of her political work in early studies of the Civil Rights Movement nor her heroic stature among black women activists meant as much to Richardson as the recognition that her activism was better "than skinning tomatoes and shucking oysters."[45] In many ways Gloria Richardson and the Cambridge Movement's militant responses in the early 1960s to social, economic, and political injustices prefigured the violent resistance of black residents in Watts, Detroit, Newark, and other northern and southern cities in the second half of that turbulent decade. This suggests that the story of Gloria Richardson and the Cambridge Movement must be considered the "Chronicle of a Death Foretold."[46]

NOTES

1. Wells Barnett's quote is cited in Paula Giddings, *When and Where I Enter: The Impact of Black Women on Race and Sex in America* (New York: William Morrow, 1984), 23. Wells Barnett and Gloria Richardson are examples of radical black female activists who have claimed the right to defend themselves and their communities. Kathleen Cleaver, "Racism, Civil Rights, and Feminism," in Adrien Katherine Wing, ed., *Critical Race Feminism: A Reader* (New York: New York University Press, 1997), 36.

2. Cleveland Sellers (with Robert Terrell), *The River of No Return: The Autobiography of a Black Militant and the Life and Death of SNCC* (Jackson: University of Mississippi Press, 1973) wrote about Richardson's courageous leadership of the Cambridge movement. However, in one of the two pages in which Clayborne Carson mentions Gloria Richardson, she appears as part of a larger discussion of SNCC organizer Bill Hall. See Carson's *In Struggle: SNCC and the Black Awakening of the 1960s* (Cambridge: Harvard University Press, 1981), 72. A fuller account of Richardson's civil rights activism appears in two recent publications devoted exclusively to the role of black women in the Civil Rights Movement, including Belinda Robnett, *How Long? How Long? African-American Women in the Struggle for Civil Rights* (New York: Oxford University Press, 1997) and Annette K. Brock, "Gloria Richardson and the Cambridge Movement" in Vicki L. Crawford, Jacqueline A. Rouse, and Barbara Woods, eds., *Women in the Civil Rights Movement: Trailblazers and Torchbearers, 1941–1965* (Bloomington: Indiana University Press, 1993), 121–44; and Edward Trever, "Gloria Richardson and the Cambridge Civil Rights Movement, 1962–1964" (M.A. thesis, Morgan State University, 1994). Biographical entries and short essays about Richardson include: Kathleen Thompson, "Gloria Richardson," in Darlene Clark Hine, Elsa Barkley Brown, and Rosalyn Terborg-Penn, eds., *Black Women in America: An Historical Encyclopedia* (Brooklyn, NY: Carlson Publishing, 1993), II, 980–82; Annette K. Brock, "Gloria Richardson" in Jessie Carney Smith, ed., *Notable Black American Women* (Detroit, MI: Gale Research, 1992), 938–40; Melanie B.Cook, "Gloria Richardson: Her Life and Work in SNCC," *Sage: A Scholarly Journal on Black Women,*

Student Supplement (1998): 51–53; Anita K. Foeman, "Gloria Richardson: Breaking the Mold," *Journal of Black Studies* 26 (May 1996): 604–15; and Sandra Y. Millner, "Recasting Civil Rights Leadership: Gloria Richardson and the Cambridge Movement," *Journal of Black Studies* 26 (July 1996): 668–87.

3. Foeman, "Gloria Richardson," 604–5.

4. Historian Gerda Lerner documented the history of black female activism beginning in the early nineteenth century in *Black Women in White America: A Documentary History* (New York: Random House, 1972). Black female activism is explored in Sharon Harley and Rosalyn Terborg-Penn, eds., *The Afro-American Woman: Struggles and Images*, 2d ed., (Baltimore, MD: Black Classic Press, 1998), and Paula Giddings, *When and Where I Enter*, passim.

5. Peter B. Levy, "Civil War on Race Street: The Black Freedom Struggle and White Resistance in Cambridge, Maryland, 1960–1964," *Maryland Historical Magazine* 89 (Fall 1994): 291–318.

6. Jenny Walker, "The 'Gun-Toting' Gloria Richardson: Black Violence in Cambridge, Maryland," in Peter J. Ling and Sharon Monteith, eds., *Gender and the Civil Rights Movement* (New York: Garland Publishing, 1999), 169–86.

7. See Robnett, *How Long? How Long?*, 19–23, 111–14, 161–65, quote on p. 161. In a published interview in 1994, Richardson added that her cousin, Frederick St. Clair, resigned as CNAC's chair because he felt there was a conflict between providing bail for jailed demonstrators and leading the movement. People asked her to serve as chair because they trusted her and because she was in a less vulnerable economic position. In the community organizing movement, the people who organized and represented the wards and districts in Cambridge constituted CNAC's executive board. See Peter S. Szabo, "An Interview with Gloria Richardson Dandridge," *Maryland Historical Magazine* 89 (Fall 1994): 349. Enez S. Grubb, her co-chair, confirmed Richardson's recollections of the selection process and insisted that the question of their gender never surfaced. Enez Grubb, interview with the author, September 1999, Cambridge, Maryland.

8. Robnett, *How Long? How Long?*, 161. Gloria Richardson made the same point in Gloria Richardson, interview with the author, January 17, 1998, New York City.

9. Robnett, *How Long? How Long?*, 165; Foeman's quote taken from Gloria Richardson, 612.

10. Sellers, *There Is No River*, 69, quoted in Trever, "Gloria Richardson and the Cambridge Movement."

11. Foeman, Gloria Richardson, 611–12, cited in Robnett, *How Long? How Long?*, 164.

12. Cleaver, "Racism, Civil Rights, and Feminism," in Wing, *Critical Race Feminism*, 36.

13. *Baltimore Afro-American*, March 2, 1982.

14. "Sunday Magazine," *The Washington Star*, July 12, 1969, in the Vertical File—Cambridge, Maryland Room, McKeldin Library, University of Maryland, College Park.

15. Walter R. Dean, Jr., *Baltimore Afro-American*, August 28, 1962, quoted in Trever, "Gloria Richardson and the Cambridge Civil Rights Movement," 9.

16. Sellers, *There Is No River*, 68, quoted in Trever, "Gloria Richardson and the Cambridge Movement," 6.

17. Quote from a transcribed interview, Gloria Richardson with Joyce Ladner (1978). In Ladner's possession. The system of "preferred choice" effectively maintained a segregated school system in Cambridge and most Eastern shore communities.

18. Unsigned article, "Gloria Richardson: Lady General of Civil Rights," *Ebony* 19 (July 1964): 23.

19. "Who Speaks for Cambridge," *Baltimore Afro-American*, January 27, 1962, quoted in Trever, "Gloria Richardson and the Cambridge Civil Rights Movement, 1962–1964," 17.

20. Thompson, "Gloria Richardson," 980.

21. Gloria Richardson, interview with the author, January 17, 1998.

22. Quotes taken from an interview with Gloria Richardson by Annette Brock cited in Cook's "Gloria Richardson," 22.

23. Gloria Richardson, interview with the author, January 17, 1998. See also Brock, "Gloria Richardson and the Civil Rights Movement," 122.

24. Gloria Richardson, interview with Joyce Ladner.

25. Gloria Richardson, interview with Gil Noble, cited in Brock, "Gloria Richardson," 125.

26. At the time the thirty-nine-year-old Richardson became CNAC chair, the nineteen-year-old Grubb was serving as co-chair, a position she continued to hold. A Cambridge native and current resident, Grubb, an ordained AME minister, comes from a long line of activist ministers. Enez Grubb, telephone interview with the author, September 27, 1999, Cambridge, Maryland.

27. Gloria Richardson, interview with the author, January 17, 1998; Brock, "Gloria Richardson and the Civil Rights Movement," 122–23; and Szabo, "Gloria Richardson," 349–50.

28. "62 Jailed Tuesday in Protests," *The Daily Banner*, May 15, 1963; Bettye Collier-Thomas and V. P. Franklin, *My Soul Is a Witness: A Chronology of the Civil Rights Era, 1954–1965* (New York: Henry Holt and Company, 2000), 198. See also Wayne E. Page, "H. Rap Brown and the Cambridge Incident: A Case Study" (M.A. thesis, University of Maryland, College Park, 1970); and Brock, "Gloria Richardson and the Cambridge Movement," 121–43.

29. See, for instance, Brailsford Brazeal, *The Brotherhood of Sleeping Car Porters: Its Origin and Development* (New York: Harper and Brothers, 1946);

and Melinda Chateauvert, *Marching Together: Women of the Brotherhood of Sleeping Car Porters* (Urbana: University of Illinois Press, 1998).

30. Quote from Gloria Richardson's interview with Joyce Ladner, 1978. In the transcribed interview, Richardson noted that, with the assistance of two SNCC field secretaries, Reginald Robinson and Bill Hansen (considered "the first white student to join SNCC"), they conducted a survey in which they "asked people to prioritize what their concerns were and it was at that point that we moved from public accommodations into what they called bread and butter issues, [such as] housing, jobs, segregation in the hospital, segregation in the school," Ladner interview, 12.

31. King's quotes taken from James H. Cone, *Martin & Malcolm & America: A Dream or a Nightmare* (Maryknoll, NY: Orbis Books, 1991), 213, 272. See also Cone's discussion of the increasing similarities in 1964 between Martin's and Malcolm's philosophical positions, 253–59.

32. Brock, "Gloria Richardson and the Cambridge Movement," 121–43; Carson, *In Struggle*, 94.

33. Quote appears in *Boston Herald*, June 19, 1963.

34. "Lady General of Civil Rights," *Ebony*, 24.

35. Ibid., 23.

36. Ibid., 25.

37. Ella Baker quoted in Ellen Cantarow, Susan G. O. Malley, and Sharon H. Strom, *Moving the Mountain* (Old Westbury: The Feminist Press, 1980), 84.

38. For major studies on the Civil Rights Movement that do not include Gloria Richardson, see Robert Brisbane, *Black Activism: Racial Revolution in the United States, 1954–1970* (Valley Forge, PA: Judson Press, 1971); Adam Fairclough, *'To Redeem the Soul of America': The Southern Christian Leadership Conference and Martin Luther King, Jr.* (Athens: University of Georgia Press, 1987); Juan Williams, *Eyes on the Prize: America's Civil Rights Years, 1954–1965* (New York: Viking Press, 1987); Manning Marable, *Race, Reform and Rebellion: The Second Reconstruction in Black America, 1945–1982* (Jackson: University Press of Mississippi, 1991); Jack Bloom, *Class, Race, and the Civil Rights Movement: The Political Economy of Southern Racism* (Bloomington: Indiana University Press, 1987); Robert Weisbrot, *Freedom Bound: A History of America's Civil Rights Movement* (New York: Norton, 1990); Taylor Branch in *Parting the Waters: America in the King Years 1954–63* (New York: Simon and Schuster, 1988), 916, 991; and in *Pillar of Fire: America in the King Years 1963–65* (New York: Simon and Schuster, 1998), 310, mentions Gloria Richardson, but provides no discussion of her leadership of the Cambridge movement.

39. Walker, "The 'Gun-Toting' Gloria Richardson," 179.

40. Malcolm X, "Message to the Grass Roots," (1963), reprinted in Clayborne Carson, et al., eds., *The Eyes on the Prize Civil Rights Reader* (New York:

Penguin Books, 1991), 248–61. See also Cone, *Martin & Malcolm & America*, 201–3.

41. Cone, *Martin & Malcolm & America*, 200–1.

42. "Lady General of Civil Rights," *Ebony*, 25, quoted in Cone, *Martin & Malcolm & America*, 202. For information on the new militant organization ACT, see the *New York Times*, April 17, 19, 1964.

43. Gloria Richardson, "Focus on Cambridge," *Freedomways* 4, no. 1 (Winter 1964): 34, found in the Vertical File, MD, Cambridge Civil Rights, 1964, Cambridge, Maryland Public Library.

44. Angela LeBlanc–Ernest, "'The Most Qualified Person to Handle the Job': Black Panther Party Women, 1966–1982," in Charles E. Jones, ed., *The Black Panther Party Reconsidered* (Baltimore, MD: Black Classic Press, 1998), 307.

45. Gloria Richardson quoted in the *Washington Post*, June 12, 1963, see Vertical File—Maryland (State) Biography, Maryland Room, McKeldin Library, University of Maryland, College Park.

46. Gabriel García Márquez, *Chronicle of a Death Foretold* (New York: Plume Books, 1982).

Chapter 11

Black Women and Black Power

*The Case of Ruby Doris Smith Robinson and the
Student Nonviolent Coordinating Committee*

Cynthia Griggs Fleming

In June 1966, James Meredith, the first black student ever to enroll
at the University of Mississippi, began his historic march against
fear across the state of Mississippi. Just a few days after the march
began, Meredith was shot by a sniper and had to be hospitalized. The
leaders of the major civil rights organizations—the Congress of Racial
Equality (CORE), the Student Nonviolent Coordinating Committee
(SNCC), the Southern Christian Leadership Conference (SCLC), and
the National Association for the Advancement of Colored People
(NAACP)—all decided to send representatives to continue the march.
As the marchers made their way across the state, they were greeted
by enthusiastic crowds of black Mississippians who voiced their encouragement as the marchers passed. But mixed in with the shouts of
encouragement was an undertone of frustration. Like so many others,
black Mississippians had heard government promises of better conditions. Yet it seemed that their lives had not changed. Most were tired
of waiting and they made their impatience known.

Black Power Emerges

Many members of SNCC who had been working for these changes
mirrored the crowd's impatience and frustration. It was in that atmosphere that the cry of Black Power first surfaced. It all started when
the marchers arrived in Greenwood on June 16. Stokley Carmichael,

SNCC's chairman, was arrested for attempting to defy a police order. Meanwhile, a crowd of well wishers that had gathered to hear Carmichael speak became angry when they got word that he had been arrested. As they milled around in the hot June sunshine, many soon began to perspire and their collective resentment grew as their level of discomfort rose. Why had local authorities arrested Carmichael, they demanded to know. After all, they reasoned, they were just trying to hold a peaceful assembly. It seemed that the white folks were determined to interfere with every aspect of their lives. As the crowd became increasingly restless, Carmichael suddenly appeared after being bailed out of jail. A hush fell over the gathering as they waited expectantly.

Carmichael began speaking slowly and deliberately at first, but then his words came out faster and the level of his voice rose, building to a dramatic crescendo. In a clear, lilting voice that was heavy with emotion and just a hint of his Trinidadian accent, Carmichael told the waiting rally: "This is the twenty-seventh time I have been arrested. I ain't going to jail no more."[1] "What we gonna start saying now," he cried, "is black power."[2] The crowd roared back, "BLACK POWER."

Standing there in the crowd that day was Ruby Doris Smith Robinson, a young black Atlantan who had just recently been elected to the post of Executive Secretary in SNCC. As she raised her fist and shouted "Black Power," Ruby could feel the excitement of the crowd all around her. She knew that this was an historic occasion, and she was sure that the civil rights struggle could never be the same again. But what did it all mean, Ruby wondered. Always the practical strategist, she worried about how this new slogan would be defined, and what impact it would have on the civil rights struggle.

In a short time, young black activists offered definitions that would provide substance for this new slogan. Most agreed with Carmichael's assertion that

> It [Black Power] is a call for black people in this country to unite, to recognize their heritage, to build a sense of community. It is a call for black people to begin to define their own goals, to lead their own organizations, and to support those organizations. It is a call to reject the racist institutions and values of this society.[3]

Carmichael went on to insist that "the concept of Black Power rests on a fundamental premise: Before a group can enter the open society, it must first close ranks."[4]

Most in SNCC agreed that these definitions made sense. But what about their practical application? Increasingly, after 1966, this insistence on black solidarity ushered in an era of male chauvinism. Such a development was particularly ironic in light of SNCC's tradition of developing male and female leadership. As far back as SNCC's founding meeting, women had played a critical role in the leadership and the membership of the group. As the organization grew and developed, women were important participants in those critical events that defined the group's early direction.

The SNCC action in Rock Hill, South Carolina in February 1961 clearly illustrates this reality. Rock Hill was a turning point for SNCC because up until that time the group had functioned more as a coordinating body for local movements. But by early 1961, many SNCC members became concerned about the increasing number of sit-in demonstrators being bailed out of jail. They were worried that the large amount of bail money required was putting a severe financial strain on black communities all over the South. Many argued that student demonstrators should refuse bail and serve their full sentences. To inaugurate their new policy they decided to send a delegation to Rock Hill, South Carolina to support a group of Friendship College students who had already refused to post bail after they were arrested for sitting-in. Significantly, that delegation was composed of equal numbers of men and women. Charles Sherrod and Charles Jones, the two men, were accompanied by Diane Nash and eighteen-year-old Ruby Doris Smith.

Ruby Doris Smith—The Activist

This action was a turning point for SNCC, and it also marked the start of Ruby Doris Smith's activist career with the organization. An examination of Ruby's career clearly reveals the possibilities for female leadership in early SNCC. After serving thirty days in the York County Jail in South Carolina, Ruby went on to join the Freedom Rides. The rides were initiated in May 1961 by the Congress of Racial Equality to test compliance with the Supreme Court's desegregation rulings affecting interstate travel. CORE's recruits were brutalized by a white mob as they were leaving their bus in Birmingham, Alabama, and it looked like the Freedom Rides would be suspended.

At this point, SNCC's Diane Nash took the initiative and recruited additional riders. She explained to James Farmer, the head of CORE, that if they let violence stop the Freedom Rides, "the movement is dead."[5] With Farmer's blessing, Diane Nash's SNCC recruits left Nashville, Tennessee in the early morning hours of May 17 aboard a bus bound for Birmingham. Birmingham's police chief Eugene "Bull" Conner and some of his officers intercepted the bus before it even reached the city limits. The policemen placed the riders in "protective custody" over night. The next morning the officers roughly pushed the freedom riders into waiting patrol cars that took off at top speed with a screech of their tires. Right after they crossed the state line into Tennessee, the policemen put the group out on the side of the road and sped away. The riders quickly made their way back to Nashville, and they soon boarded a bus bound for Birmingham.

In the meantime, Ruby Doris was in Atlanta trying to raise enough money for her ticket so that she could join the other riders. By the time the SNCC recruits were on their way to Birmingham for the second time, Ruby had enough money. She flew from Atlanta to Birmingham, and she went straight to the bus station to meet the others. She described the scene when she arrived:

> I was alone. When I got to Birmingham, I went to the bus terminal and joined the seventeen from Nashville. We waited all night trying to get a bus to Montgomery. Every time we got on a bus the driver said no, he wouldn't risk his life. The terminal kept crowding up with passengers who were stranded because the buses wouldn't go on. The Justice Department then promised Diane that the driver of the 4:00 A.M. bus would go on to Montgomery. But when he arrived he came off the bus and said to us: I have only one life to give, and I'm not going to give it to the NAACP or CORE.[6]

Throughout the night, tension ran high in the Birmingham terminal. Ruby and the others were acutely aware of the violence that had plagued the CORE-sponsored ride that preceded their effort, and they were also aware that they could not expect any aid or protection from the federal government. While the riders waited, they occupied themselves by singing freedom songs. As Ruby and the others clapped and sang, the words provided comfort and solace. Their voices swelled and reinforced each other. "Stand up and rejoice, a great day is here. We're fighting Jim Crow and the victr'y is near," they sang. Then they followed with the chorus, "Hallelujah, I'm a traveling, hallelujah ain't it fine, hallelujah, I'm a traveling down freedom's main line." Ruby and the other riders sang verse after verse, sometimes improvising on the spot. "I'm paying my fare on the Greyhound bus line. I'm riding the front seat to Montgomery this time."[7] The students continued their singing into the early hours of the morning. The songs bolstered their courage and helped chase away their fatigue.

Finally, the bus company found a driver, the students boarded the bus, and it departed for Montgomery. Before they made it through Alabama, however, the freedom riders faced mob violence and police hostility. Finally, they prepared to leave Alabama and enter Mississippi. Even though conditions in Alabama had been tough, everyone expected Mississippi to be tougher. James Farmer succinctly summed it up: "If Alabama had been purgatory, Mississippi would be hell."[8] As the bus sped deeper into Mississippi territory, many began to feel a sense of impending doom. The riders' commitment did not wane, but their anxiety level certainly increased. In the midst of this tense atmosphere, fellow freedom rider John Lewis recalls that Ruby Doris "had this sense of wanting to know about the different participants. How were people doing, were you all right or not. She had this sense of caring about the different individuals. . . . She wanted everybody to be all right."[9] Smith's SNCC colleagues noticed and appreciated the caring and concern she felt for them. They also appreciated the calm courage that she demonstrated when they were protesting together. A graphic illustration of Ruby's courage occurred during a demonstration at Atlanta's Grady Hospital. Grady was a public facility that admitted both black and white patients, but it had segregated entrances and segregated areas within the hospital. Throughout late 1961 and into early 1962 Ruby Doris, along with other Atlanta students, staged a series of protests at the hospital. Movement colleague Julian Bond vividly recalls one demonstration when black students went in the hospital's white entrance. As they approached the door, the students felt butterflies in their stomachs. They knew their presence inside the white entrance would cause quite a stir, and they wondered about the reaction. They did not have to wonder long, however, because as soon as they stepped inside, the looks of surprise on the faces of white patrons quickly gave way to icy stares, and a startled white receptionist immediately told them they could not use that entrance. "And besides," she insisted in a hostile voice dripping with sarcasm, "You're not sick anyway." The woman's hostile challenge stopped the students right in their tracks like a cold slap in the face. As they milled around in confusion, Ruby Doris separated herself from the group and boldly walked up to the receptionist's desk, looked her in the eye, bent over and vomited all over the desk, straightened up and demanded to know, "Is that sick enough for you?"[10] The receptionist's hostility quickly turned to a paralyzing confusion that rendered her speechless.

Ruby Doris Smith—The Administrator

Ruby Doris Smith's bold and daring exploits on the picket line earned her the respect of her SNCC co-workers. At the same time, she began to spend more and more time volunteering in SNCC's Atlanta office. In a short time she became James Forman's assistant and she began to assume a great deal of the responsibility for administering the organization. Recollections of Ruby's administrative style are quite varied, and that variety suggests that her style was multifaceted, flexible, and not easily characterized. A flexible and creative approach was necessary because of the different types of situations, problems, and individuals who regularly confronted her. At times she appeared to be an uncompromising task master who was especially tough whenever it appeared that staff people were trying to take unfair advantage of the organization's resources. Stanley Wise, who would later succeed Smith as SNCC's Executive Secretary, clearly recalls her attitude.

> She absolutely did not tolerate any nonsense. I remember some people came in there [the Atlanta Central Office] from Mississippi. They had driven their car over there and they said they needed new tires. And she pulled out [a card] from her little file. She said "listen, I've given you sixteen tires in the last four months . . . I've sent you four batteries, you had two motors in the car. You're not getting another thing. Now take that car out of here and go on back to Mississippi." That's what she told them.[11]

Wise remembered how amazed he was at the extent of Ruby's knowledge about the history of this one car, given the size of the SNCC fleet.

One of the most important vehicles for raising funds for SNCC's organizing campaigns was the group known as the Freedom Singers, which included Bernice Johnson, Cordell Reagon, Rutha Mae Harris, Charles Jones, and Matthew Jones.[12] SNCC freedom singer Matthew Jones recalls that his brother, another member of the freedom singers, was also a target of Ruby's wrath because she thought he was being wasteful. When the group performed on the West Coast, Ruby arranged round-trip transportation for them by automobile because she determined it to be the most economical. The group had an un-eventful trip out to the West Coast, and gave a successful concert, but when they assembled for the return trip, Jones's brother arrived too late. The cars had already left. He immediately called Ruby to explain that he was stranded in Los Angeles, but she refused to send him the money for a plane, train, or bus ticket. She reasoned that since Jones should have been responsible enough to meet the prearranged trans-portation at the appointed time, the organization should not have to pay for his mistake. Ruby's parting advice to Jones as she hung up the phone? "Well, walk back."[13] Irresponsibility did have its conse-quences. Reginald Robinson remembers that Ruby could also be un-compromising about procedure. "When she became in charge of the payroll and you had reports to do—you had expense accounts to turn [in]. Well if you didn't do what you were supposed to do, Big Mama [Ruby] would cut your money."[14] Charles Jones succinctly sums up Ruby Doris's no-nonsense approach: "You didn't run any games on her."[15] Jack Minnis, a member of SNCC's research staff, offers an even more blunt appraisal: "She had a 100 percent effective shit detector."[16]

All of Ruby Doris's SNCC colleagues agree that her primary ad-ministrative goal was the effective functioning of the Student Nonvi-olent Coordinating Committee. She had very definite ideas about how SNCC should be administered, and she never failed to stand up for her beliefs whether others agreed with her or not. As SNCC col-league Worth Long puts it, "she's set in her ways, and she's mostly right. . . . She would take a principle[d] stand. . . . She'd argue, and she'd huff and puff too. . . ."[17] During the free-wheeling discussions in SNCC about organizational policy, Long remembers Ruby as "a formidable opponent. I wouldn't want to play poker with her."[18] Co-worker Curtis Hayes particularly recalls her demeanor in meetings. "I guarantee if you ever see a picture of Ruby in a meeting . . . she'll be on the end of the chair. You'll never see her sitting back like this." Hayes was struck by Ruby's intensity: "Whoever's talking, she'll be leaning into them. And her eyes will be right into them." He also re-members how forcefully Ruby expressed her opinions. "And when you got to that point she don't agree with? She was all over you."[19]

The Importance of Gender in SNCC

In this relatively egalitarian atmosphere in which Ruby operated, many black women in SNCC did not feel that their actions or aspira-tions were circumscribed because of their gender. For example, SNCC staffer Martha Norman recalls, "I think there was no way I could have had an image of being limited as a woman."[20] SNCC colleague Dorie Ladner's view clearly corroborates Norman's assessment. She explains, "I did not feel that there was a role that someone could carve out for me and describe for me to fall into. So when I started out, I started as an equal partner with my fellow comrades, and that's where I remained."[21] Co-worker Michael Sayer readily agrees with Ladner's view. In fact, he used Ruby Doris as an example when he addressed the issue of male chauvinism in SNCC. He observed, "Be-cause you couldn't have known Ruby Doris; you couldn't have worked alongside or behind Ruby Doris and then asked the question, 'how come women don't play a leadership role in the movement?'"[22]

Jean Wheeler Smith, campus traveler and SNCC staff member, re-calls that the organization may have appeared to be sexist to outside observers because "admittedly the structure, the administrative structure on paper was men." But, she argues, "the women had ac-cess to whatever resources and decision making that they needed to have or wanted to have and I don't remember being impeded in this."[23] Joyce Ladner agrees with Smith's assessment. But Ladner goes on to argue that part of the organization's response was shaped by the actions and mindset of the women—particularly the black women—who joined the group. She recalled,

> None of these women I began to meet knew they were oppressed be-cause of their gender. No one had ever told them that. They had grown up in a culture where they had the opportunity to use all of their skills and all of their talents to fight racial and class oppression-more racially than anything else. They took their sexuality for granted, for it was not as problematic to them as their race and their poverty.[24]

Thus, it would seem that in SNCC's fluid atmosphere, some stereotypical notions of gender roles existed, but they existed alongside the shared assumption that people had the right to challenge them. Indeed, one movement scholar insists that in comparison to the larger society around it, SNCC was relatively egalitarian: "Rarely did women expect or receive any special protection in demonstrations or jails. Frequently, direct action teams were divided equally between women and men, sometimes on the theory that the presence of women might lessen the violent reaction."[25]

Because of that egalitarian atmosphere, most in SNCC did not see Ruby's role as a female administrator to be the least bit extraordinary. So many of these student activists had grown up in families with strong black women who worked outside the home and exercised authority inside the home, that black female authority figures seemed quite normal. In fact, because SNCC staffer Michael Simmons grew up with this reality, he was convinced that Ruby's administrative position was actually a traditionally female job.[26] Curtis Hayes agrees and insists that "she [Ruby] was a normal figure for me."[27] Thus, female leadership was accepted and even expected by many in SNCC.

Ruby Doris Smith Robinson and Black Power

But what happened when Black Power appeared on the scene? The black power slogan was exciting for some, frightening for others, and confusing to many. It seemed that those words meant different things to different people, and colleagues have differing memories of Ruby's ideas about the meaning of this powerful slogan. Her husband Clifford remembers that Ruby's acceptance of Black Power prompted her to reconsider her views on integration and embrace a certain amount of black separatism. On the other hand, movement co-worker John Lewis recalls another part of Ruby's ideas about Black Power. He explains, "She accepted the idea of black consciousness and the need of black people to be proud and have an appreciation for blackness."[28] Worth Long insists that Ruby's notions of Black Power transcended national boundaries; and she felt that all people of African descent should unite in their efforts to battle racist oppression.[29] Stokley Carmichael remembers that Ruby Doris supported notions of Black

206 CYNTHIA GRIGGS FLEMING

Power "150 percent."[30] She even taught her young son to say Black Power when he was only a year old. Regardless of Ruby's enthusiasm though, she refused to let her support for Black Power circumscribe her vision on the basis of race. Jim Forman clearly recalls that, "Ruby was one of the people who consistently upheld the position, as I did . . . that the problem was not just racial." On the contrary, she reasoned, racism spawned economic oppression which reinforced African American powerlessness.[31]

Just two months after Black Power's historic introduction, an exhausted Ruby granted an interview to *Ebony* magazine. Her observations about the direction of the movement and the role of women in the struggle are quite revealing. She argued that even though African American women were uniquely assertive, and they had been effective leaders in the civil rights struggle so far, black men should be given more leadership responsibility. She went on to suggest that the crusade for racial justice was really men's work after all; but since black men had been so victimized by American society, they were not yet ready to shoulder the whole burden. Ruby observed that increasing numbers of black men were becoming involved; and she optimistically predicted that in the future, women would not be needed for movement work anymore. But she was sure that change would come very slowly. She explained, "But, I don't believe the Negro man will be able to assume his full role until the struggle has progressed to a point that can't even be foreseen—maybe in the next century or so."[32]

The views Ruby expressed in this interview are quite curious in light of her unique position as a powerful female administrator in SNCC. But at the same time, her views are remarkably similar to the perceptions of the other black female civil rights veterans who were featured in the *Ebony* article. For example, SNCC staffer Jennifer Lawson observed, "Often women might prefer *not* to lead, but there's a responsibility to black people at this time that must be met, and it overshadows this business of being a man or a woman."[33] Carolyn Rivers, a New Yorker working in the Alabama Black Belt, agreed. But she went on to insist that, "If Negro men were able to assert themselves fully, they'd be willing to send all the women back home." Rivers did not say whether she thought the women would be willing to go.[34] Finally, Mrs. Fannie Lou Hamer explained, "But as women, we feel we have done many things that have enabled us to open doors for our men and to show them that when they get their chance, we will be there to back them up all the way."[35]

This advocacy of male leadership by Ruby and the other women is quite curious since it seems to contradict the example that each of them set. Any attempt to explain this apparent contradiction must examine the difficult reality these women faced. Ruby and the others were undoubtedly suffering from exhaustion and frustration as they tried to juggle their traditional female family responsibilities with their leadership commitments. At the same time, both the popular press and scholars of the black experience were popularizing the notion that because black men had somehow been more victimized than black women, the women were obligated to support male assertiveness. Above all, race loyalty undoubtedly overshadowed gender issues in the minds of most African American female civil rights activists of this era. They wanted to lead but they did not wish to assert themselves at the expense of their men. Such a position was fraught with contradictions.

Black Power Collides with Female Assertiveness

As Ruby and her colleagues wrestled with the issue of gender roles in the latter years of the Civil Rights Movement, their views were filtered through the prism of male chauvinism that accompanied the rise of Black Power. One of the distinctive tenets of the Black Power philosophy was the belief in black male dominance. For so long, Black Power advocates argued, black men had been virtually emasculated by white American society. Thus, they must assume leadership roles and reclaim their masculinity as a prerequisite to the empowerment of all black people. Some reasoned that men could only assume their rightful place, though, if women would step aside and stop interfering. Such a negative judgment of black female leadership was inextricably bound to a twisted assessment of black female self-reliance. This fallacious assessment blamed black women for the emasculation of their men because of their willingness to assume dominant roles.

As this attitude became increasingly prevalent among advocates of Black Power and black nationalism, African American women leaders were subjected to tremendous and often unpleasant pressures.

Well-known activist Angela Davis experienced some of those pressures when she organized a rally in San Diego, California in 1967. She recalled,

> I ran headlong into a situation which was to become a constant problem in my political life. I was criticized very heavily, especially by male members of [Ron] Karenga's [US] organization, for doing a "man's job." Women should not play leadership roles, they insisted. A woman has to "inspire" her man and educate his children.[36]

Davis reasoned that this male attitude was particularly ironic since "much of what I was doing had fallen to me by default." This was only the beginning of such problems. By 1968, Davis was obliged to confront similar male attitudes in the Los Angeles chapter of SNCC where both men and women served on the central office staff. She clearly describes the circumstances:

> Some of the brothers came around only for staff meetings (Sometimes), and whenever we women were involved in something important, they began to talk about "women taking over the organization"—calling it a matriarchal coup d'etat. All the myths about black women surfaced. (We) were too domineering; we were trying to control everything, including the men—which meant by extension that we wanted to rob them of their manhood. By playing such a leadership role in the organization, some of them insisted, we were aiding and abetting the enemy, who wanted to see black men weak and unable to hold their own.[37]

Other strong African American women leaders experienced similar problems. Kathleen Cleaver, an officer in the Black Panther Party, was particularly frustrated by the males' refusal to respect her ideas. She recalled that, "If I suggested them, the suggestion might be rejected; if they were suggested by a man, the suggestion would be implemented."[38] Gloria Richardson, the undisputed leader of the Cambridge movement in Maryland, faced a forceful show of male chauvinism at a Cambridge rally in the late 1960s. When Richardson attempted to address the crowd, male members of CORE shouted her down and called her a "castrator."[39]

This blatant sexism also became an integral part of the emerging cultural nationalism of the era. Cultural nationalists sought to define and popularize a black value system that would promote a positive self image—at least for some. An important part of this value system was an emphasis on black male strength, which was defined in the context of an idealized image of a submissive black woman. Imamu Amiri Baraka, noted author and activist, clearly explained the cultural nationalist view in 1967 of the black woman's character. As he put it, "Nature . . . made woman submissive, she must submit to man's creation in order for it to exist."[40] Fellow cultural nationalist Ron Karenga agreed with this assessment. He wrote, "What makes a woman appealing is femininity and she can't be feminine without being submissive."[41] The teachings of these cultural nationalists clearly implied that black women who refused to submit to male authority could prevent their men from properly developing a strong male personality. With this in mind, black cultural nationalists demanded that women conform to certain standards of behavior. For example, they thought black women should not use birth control devices since having more children was the most strategically important service to the struggle that women could perform. They reasoned, "For us to speak in favor of birth control for Afro-Americans would be comparable to speaking in favor of genocide."[42]

Even as many of the cultural nationalists were calling for black women to have more children, there were some in the scholarly establishment who claimed that black mothers were crippling their sons. For example, psychiatrists William Grier and Price Cobbs insisted that black mothers did this both through example and direct interaction. They argued that:

> Black men develop considerable hostility toward black women as the inhibiting instruments of an oppressive system. The woman has more power, more accessibility into the system, and therefore she is more feared, while at the same time envied. And it is her lot in life to suppress masculine assertiveness in her sons.[43]

It seems, then, that black women were being blamed and chastised by many—both inside and outside the movement. The debate was sharp, emotional, and exhausting. Strength and self-reliance had been part of the black female role and persona for generations, stretching all the way back into slavery. More recently, African American women had been the leaders and the backbone of the Civil Rights Movement. But now they were being told that they had stepped out of bounds and the black freedom struggle could not succeed until they returned to their "proper places."

During these unsettling and uncertain times in the latter years of the civil rights struggle, Ruby Doris remained the practical strategist who refused to be persuaded by concepts she thought were impractical or slogans without substance. She always tried to take the most workable ideas and incorporate them into her thinking. In fact, Ruby's practical approach prompted her to offer her opinion to advocates of cultural nationalism who became enthralled with the romantic rhetoric of blackness that became so popular during the era. Stanley Wise clearly recalls her reaction to his "conversion." He explains, "I remember I became very, very nationalistic in the organization and was lauding the praises of why we ought to become Africans and had to go back to Africa for our roots and she said, 'Stanley [is] just walking on the deep end, don't worry about him. He'll be all right next week.'"[44]

There were others besides Wise whose declarations of blackness were also closely scrutinized by Ruby. SNCC colleague Freddie Greene Biddle explains the basis of that scrutiny.

> As far as Ruby was concerned . . . she had always been black first. . . . And that's basically the issue that she raised with all the people—with the Johnny come latelies who . . . [had] their strong black power thing. . . . That was probably what Ruby used to define as the northern blacks who had been so white until all of a sudden they became so black conscious.[45]

But, just as SNCC faced this difficult transition to the era of Black Power and black nationalism, the voice of its most powerful female administrator, Ruby Doris Smith Robinson, was silenced. Just months after Black Power's historic introduction in Greenwood, Mississippi, Ruby Doris was diagnosed with a rare form of cancer, lympho sarcoma. She languished in a New York hospital during the early months of 1967. Then during the summer she returned to Atlanta, where she spent her last days surrounded by family members and movement colleagues. Tragically, she never got a chance to confront the most problematic aspects of Black Power: she died on October 7, 1967 at the age of twenty-five. Some charge that the unique stresses to which she was subjected because of her status as a powerful female administrator in SNCC actually contributed to her death. As one put it,

> Ruby Doris died at the age of twenty-[five] and she died of exhaustion . . . I don't think it was necessary to assassinate her. What killed Ruby Doris was the constant outpouring of work, work, work, work with being married, having a child, the constant conflicts, the constant struggle that she was subjected to because she was a woman. She was destroyed by the movement.[46]

Ruby Doris Smith Robinson in Retrospect

In the years since Ruby's death, an increasing number of scholars have begun to write about the role of African American women in the Civil Rights Movement. A number of the works produced by these scholars are biographies which focus on the life of a particular individual. Such works are quite useful since they help students of the movement to understand the complexities of movement leadership and activity in the context of the life of a particular individual. Other recent works examine major civil rights organizations and major movement events, and they pinpoint the roles played by black women in these circumstances.[47]

One recent book, however, Belinda Robnett's *How Long? How Long? African-American Women in the Struggle for Civil Rights*, constructs an analytical framework that allows us to compare black female movement roles across organizational lines. Robnett sees most of the African American women movement leaders as bridge leaders—that is, leaders who did not usually hold formal leadership positions, but rather grassroots leaders who formed a bridge between the community and more formalized organizations.[48] Because of their unique position, bridge leaders could encourage and channel community emotion to complement the activities and goals of the formal (male) leadership within organized groups. According to Robnett's analysis, Ruby Doris Smith Robinson was clearly a bridge leader during her early days with the Atlanta Student Movement, and the Student Nonviolent Coordinating Committee. However, with her election to a titled position in SNCC in 1966 she made the leap from bridge leadership to formal leadership—an extremely rare feat for any woman in the movement. Clearly, by everyone's standards, Ruby Doris Smith Robinson stood out—even among the extraordinary women leaders in the Civil Rights Movement.

NOTES

1. Clayborne Carson, *In Struggle: SNCC and the Black Awakening of the 1960s* (Cambridge: Harvard University Press, 1981), 209.

2. Ibid., 209–10.

3. Kwame Toure (Stokley Carmichael) and Charles V. Hamilton, *Black Power: The Politics of Liberation in America* (New York: Vintage Books, 1992), 44.

4. Ibid., 44.

5. James Farmer, *Lay Bare the Heart: An Autobiography of the Civil Rights Movement* (New York: New American Library, 1985), 203.

6. Ibid.

7. Howard Zinn, *SNCC—The New Abolitionists* (Boston: Beacon Press, 1964), 45–46.

8. Pete Seeger and Bob Reiser, *Everybody Say Freedom, A History of the Civil Rights Movement in Songs and Pictures* (New York: Norton, 1989), 62.

9. Farmer, *Lay Bare the Heart*, 2.

10. John Lewis, interview with the author, April 24, 1989, Knoxville, Tennessee.

11. Julian Bond, interview with the author, December 16, 1988, Washington, DC.

12. Stanley Wise, interview with the author, November 11, 1988, Atlanta, Georgia.

13. Rutha Mae Harris, one of the original SNCC Freedom Singers, discussed the significance of music to the Civil Rights Movement at the "African American Women in the Civil Rights–Black Power Movement" conference at Temple University, November 21, 1997.

14. Matthew Jones, Jr., interview with the author, April 24, 1989, Knoxville, Tennessee.

15. Charles Jones and Reginald Robinson, interview with the author, June 28, 1991, McComb, Mississippi.

16. Ibid.

17. Jack Minnis, interview with the author, November 4, 1990, New Orleans, Louisiana.

18. Worth Long, interview with the author, February 8, 1991, Atlanta, Georgia.

19. Ibid.

20. Curtis Hayes, interview with the author, June 29, 1991, McComb, Mississippi.

21. Martha Prescod Norman, interview with the author, December 30, 1988, Detroit, Michigan.

22. Dorie Ladner, interview with the author, May 18, 1991, Washington, DC.

23. Michael Sayer, interview with the author, May 5, 1990, New Market, Tennessee.

24. Women's Panel, SNCC Conference at Trinity College, Hartford, Connecticut, 1988.

25. Ibid.

26. Sara Evans, *Personal Politics: The Roots of Women's Liberation in the Civil Rights Movement and the New Left* (New York: Vintage Books, 1979), 41.

27. Michael Simmons, interview with the author, May 16, 1991, Philadelphia, Pennsylvania.

28. Hayes interview.

29. Lewis interview.

30. Long interview.

31. Stokley Carmichael, interview with the author, March 14, 1990, Knoxville, Tennessee.

32. James Forman, interview with the author, May 15, 1991, Washington, DC.

33. Phyl Garland, "Builders of a New South," *Ebony,* August 1966, 35, 36.

34. Ibid., 37.

35. Ibid.

36. Ibid.

37. Paula Giddings, *When and Where I Enter: The Impact of Black Women on Race and Sex in America* (New York: Bantam Books, 1984), 316.

38. Ibid.

39. Ibid., 317.

40. Ibid.

41. Ibid., 318.

42. Ibid.

43. Ibid.

44. William Grier and Price Cobbs, *Black Rage* (New York: Basic Books, 1968), 63.

45. Wise interview.

46. Freddie Greene Biddle, interview with the author, June 29, 1991, McComb, Mississippi.

47. Giddings, *When and Where I Enter,* 315.

48. See Carson, *In Struggle;* James Forman, *The Making of Black Revolutionaries: A Personal Account* (New York: Macmillan, 1972); Taylor Branch, *Parting the Waters: America in the King Years,* 1954–63 (New York: Simon & Schuster, 1988); Fred Powledge, *Free at Last? The Civil Rights Movement and the People Who Made It* (New York: Harper Collins, 1992); John Dittmer, *Local People, The Struggle for Civil Rights in Mississippi* (Chicago: University of Illinois Press, 1994); Belinda Robnett, *How Long? How Long? African–American Women in the Struggle for Civil Rights* (New York: Oxford University Press, 1997), 19.

Chapter 12

"Ironies of the Saint"
Malcolm X, Black Women, and the Price of Protection

Farah Jasmine Griffin

This essay grows out of two concerns: First, the re-rise of what I want to call a "promise of protection" as a more progressive counter discourse to elements of misogyny in black popular culture; second, my feeling that the emergence of Malcolm X as an icon of younger African Americans requires a serious and sustained examination and engagement of all aspects of his legacy. Malcolm X has not been the subject of a black feminist critique in the way that Richard Wright or Miles Davis have been. When I looked to black feminist thinkers who have written on Malcolm, few of them were as critical of his views on women as I had expected. Patricia Hill Collins, Barbara Ransby, and Tracye Matthews are among the few to call attention to Malcolm's gender politics.[1]

Black women are reluctant of being critical of Malcolm X: theirs is a reluctance born from the desire not to have such a critique co-opted by those who already hold him in contempt and disdain and a reluctance grounded in the genuine love, respect, and reverence that many black women have for Malcolm. I must admit that even as I write this essay, I share this reluctance, for there are few black male leaders whom I hold in as much esteem as I do Malcolm. Nonetheless, while I recognize Malcolm to be a man of his times and a man with tremendous capacity for growth, I am disturbed by any tendency to uncritically adopt his political and rhetorical stance, particularly around gender.

In this essay I will articulate some of the reasons why so many black women, even black feminists, appreciate and revere Malcolm and his legacy. Then I hope to offer a reading of his position on women, not as a means of discrediting the esteem in which we hold him, but as a means to move us beyond the oppressive gender politics embedded in his rhetoric. Malcolm X offered black women a promise of protection, an acknowledgment of the significance of white racist assaults on black beauty and an affirmation of black features, particularly hair and color. In the remainder of this essay, I will examine these two important aspects of his legacy.

The Promise of Protection

> Her head is more regularly beaten than any woman's and by her own man; she is the scapegoat for Mr. Charlie; she is forced to stark realism and chided if caught dreaming; her aspirations for her and hers are, for sanity's sake, stunted; her physical image has been criminally maligned, assaulted, and negated; she's the first to be called ugly, yet never beautiful, and as a consequence is forced to see her man . . . brainwashed and wallowing in self-loathing, pick for his own the physical antithesis of her. . . . Then to add insult to injury, she . . . stands accused as emasculator of the only thing she has ever cared for, her black man. . . Who will revere the black woman? Who will keep our neighborhood safe for black innocent womanhood? . . . black womanhood cries for dignity and restitution and salvation. black womanhood wants and needs protection and keeping and holding. . . . Who will keep her precious and pure? Who will glorify and proclaim her beautiful image? To whom will she cry rape?
>
> —Abbey Lincoln[2]

Malcolm X's appeal to a broad range of black women lay first in his courage and commitment to black liberation and second in his attempt to address the call sent out by Abbey Lincoln and cited above; a call that had been voiced many times prior to Lincoln's articulation of it: "Who will revere the black woman? Who will keep her precious and pure? Who will keep our neighborhoods safe for innocent black womanhood? Who will glorify and proclaim her beautiful image?" The terms "precious," "pure," "innocent," "beautiful," and "revere" were (and in many instances, continue to be) particularly important to African American women. Each of these terms has been equated with white womanhood and thereby with femininity—both privileged spheres in our society; spheres where black women have historically been denied access. Poor and working black women, and dark-skinned black women especially, have been excluded from the discourse of the precious, pure, and protected.

However, as appealing as the promise of protection and the guarantee of purity are, they are also intensely problematic: These are the very same terms used by white American men, particularly white Southern men, to repress white women and to systematically brutalize black men—all in the name of protection and (race) purity.

My term "promise of protection" is influenced by Jacquelyn Dowd Hall's term, "rhetoric of protection." Hall uses the phrase to describe the discourses of a pure and protected white womanhood in the American South. According to Hall, "the rhetoric of protection [was] reflective of a power struggle between men." She continues, "the right of the southern lady to protection presupposed her obligation to obey."[3] I have chosen not to use the word "rhetoric" because I want to avoid the implications of the word that suggest a discourse lacking in conviction or earnest feeling. Malcolm's desire to "protect" black women grew out of a sincere concern for their emotional, psychic, and physical safety; it was also reflective of the power struggle between black and white men and black men and women. Furthermore, the pure and protected black woman of his vision was also obligated to obey her protector—the black man. The exchange is as follows: The woman gets protection; the man acquires a possession.

Nonetheless, many black women were willing to accept the terms of this contract. Barbara Omolade explains, "The extremes of American patriarchy, particularly under slavery, pushed black women outside traditional patriarchal protection." Consequently, the promise of patriarchal protection was certainly much better than the methodical abuse suffered by black women throughout much of their history in the New World. As had been the case a century earlier with their recently freed foremothers, the assurance of their safety was a very appealing vision for many black women: It stood in direct opposition to the degrading images that bombarded them on a daily basis and the harsh reality of many of their lives. Omolade notes, "Most black women accepted traditional notions of patriarchy from black men because they viewed the Afro-Christian tradition of woman as mother and wife as personally desirable and politically necessary for black people's survival."[4]

Malcolm X's promise of protection comes from a long tradition in African American writing and organizing. The National Association of Colored Women was formed in 1896 in part to protect the name and image of black women. Leaders like W. E. B. Du Bois and Alexander Crummell both called for the protection of black women from rape, physical abuse, and economic poverty.[5] Large numbers of the urban women to whom Malcolm X spoke were the daughters of or were themselves women who fled the South in an attempt to escape the threat of rape from white males. Black women also found themselves the victims of economic exploitation, unfair employment practices, medical experimentation, and domestic violence. Who was deemed better to play the role of protector than black men? This, of course, is a role that had been denied black men throughout history.

Malcolm's promise of protection assumes a stance of victimization on the part of those who need to be protected without allowing much room for their agency in other spheres. It places the woman in the hands of her protector—who may protect her, but who also may decide to further victimize her. In either case her well-being is entirely dependent on his will and authority. Note Malcolm's words upon hearing the dynamic Fannie Lou Hamer speak of her experiences in Mississippi:

> When I listen to Mrs. Hamer, a black woman—could be my mother, my sister, my daughter—describe what they have done to her in Mississippi, I ask myself how in the world can we expect to be respected as *men* when we will allow something like that to be done to our women, and we do nothing about it? How can you and I be looked upon as men with black women being beaten and nothing being done about it? No, we don't deserve to be recognized and respected as men as long as our women can be brutalized in the manner that this woman described, and nothing being done about it, but we sit around singing "We shall overcome."[6]

Later, when introducing her at the Audubon, Malcolm would refer to her as "the country's number one freedom-fighting woman." However, the predominant tone of this passage refers to Hamer only as victim in need of protection—not the protection afforded to citizens by their governments (which the South and the nation at large did not provide) but the protection of a black man. Hamer's victimization makes black men the subject of Malcolm's comment. When read closely, the above statement is not a paragraph about Fannie Lou Hamer but about the questionable masculinity of black men, particularly those black men of the southern Civil Rights Movement such as Martin Luther King. If black men protected "their" women, then Ms. Hamer would not be a victim of such abuse. Nor would she be a freedom fighter—that would be a position monopolized by black male protectors.

According to Malcolm in his *Autobiography*, "All women by their nature are fragile and weak: they are attracted to the male in whom they see strength."[7] This assertion of the nature of black women leaves little room for women like Fannie Lou Hamer, Ella Baker, Septima Clark, Harriet Tubman, Mary McLeod Bethune, Ida B. Wells, or Angela Davis.

Malcolm's general understanding about the nature of women was acquired in childhood through witnessing the abusive actions of his father as well as from his days on the streets of Boston and New York. While the discourse of protection emerges from the Nation of Islam, it does not challenge Malcolm's earlier notions of women's nature. Instead, the Nation provides him with a framework that still accepts women's nature as fragile and weak, that also sees women as manipulative, but that encourages men to protect and respect instead of abuse them. Malcolm's mentor Elijah Muhammed shared his sense that the protection of the black woman guaranteed black men their manhood: "Until we learn to love and protect our woman, we will never be a fit and recognized people on earth. The white people here among you will never recognize you until you protect your woman."[8]

In all of the instances cited above, women are subordinate to men whether as the objects of abuse or protection. In the *Autobiography*, Malcolm notes:

> Islam has very strict laws and teachings about women, the core of them being that the true nature of man is to be strong, and a woman's true nature is to be weak, and while a man must at all times respect his woman, at the same time he needs to understand that he must control her if he expects to get her respect.[9]

Protection is not in and of itself a bad thing. Patriarchal societies such as ours foster misogyny from which all women need protection. A racist patriarchal society is particularly dangerous for black women. However, protection need not be equated with possession. Of course, until the day arrives when we no longer live in a patriarchal society, women need to be protected from misogyny and paternalism; however, instead of fighting simply to protect women from misogyny, we must all engage in the fight to eradicate patriarchy as well as racism. This dedication is nowhere apparent in Malcolm's writing. Finally, it is one thing to protect an individual so that she may actually live with a greater degree of freedom, that is, make our streets safe so that women may walk alone at night. It is another thing entirely to "protect" someone and in so doing to limit their freedom and mobility. We must be careful to distinguish offers of protection that are made in a context that places limitations on women's freedom.

In a brilliant Afro-centric feminist critique of African American nationalism, "Africa on My Mind: Gender, Counter Discourse and African-American Nationalism," E. Frances White argues that "black nationalism is an oppositional strategy that both counters racism and constructs utopian and repressive gender relations."[10] Herein lies the paradox of Malcolm's promise of protection. When considered only in contrast to the external discourse of white supremacy, Malcolm's proposal of protection seems to offer a radical stance on black womanhood. However, if we consider what his discourse shares with white sexist discourse, we see something altogether different. Again White warns:

> In making appeals to conservative notions of appropriate gender behavior, African-American nationalists reveal their ideological ties to other nationalist movements, including European and Euro-American bourgeois nationalists over the past 200 years . . . European and Euro-American nationalists turned to the ideology of respectability to help them impose the bourgeoisie manners and morals that attempted to control sexual behavior and gender relations.[11]

Malcolm X's promise of protection falls under the rubric of the "ideology of respectability." The protected woman is the "respectable" woman. The man who protects her is the respected man.

The Affirmation of Black Beauty

> I knew he loved me for my clear brown skin—it was very smooth. He liked my clear eyes. He liked my gleaming dark hair. I was very thin then and he liked my black beauty, my mind. He just liked me.
> —Betty Shabazz[12]

In addition to the promise of protection, Malcolm X also offered all black people, and black women in particular, an affirmation of black features and physical characteristics. In so doing, he followed the lead of Marcus Garvey and Elijah Muhammad. To many this may seem unimportant or shallow, but when considered in light of constant white supremacist assaults on notions of black beauty, it is of profound significance. From the minstrel caricatures to "serious scientific" studies, black difference has always been predicated on black bodies. Big black lips, nappy black hair, large black thighs and derrieres, black black skin, "oversized" black genitals.

Though African Americans always fought such assaults by establishing and maintaining their own sense of their humanity, dignity, capability, and beauty, perhaps in no realm have our oppressors been more successful than in convincing us of our own ugliness. Throughout our history on this continent, black Americans have accepted and revised white standards of beauty. Yet for large numbers of black women these standards continue to be oppressive, particularly when they are upheld by other African Americans. In 1925, Walter White observed: "Even among intelligent Negroes there has come into being the fallacious belief that black Negroes are less able to achieve success."[13] The color tension between Marcus Garvey and W. E. B. Du Bois is legendary. Garvey questioned Du Bois' credibility as a leader by accusing him of wanting to be "everything but black" and Du Bois referred to Garvey as "fat, black, and ugly."[14] Du Bois' comment is something of a floating trinity in black America. Like the floating blues lyric that appears in diverse songs and contexts, so too does the phrase, "fat, black and ugly"—readily available as an all too familiar taunt. Or, witness Colin Powell's statement in an interview with Henry Louis Gates—"I ain't that black."[15]

If black men have used color and features as weapons against each other, the impact of a color hierarchy on black women has been especially devastating. In a heterosexist society, standards of beauty always impact upon women more harshly than upon men. Because black women were always compared to "the white woman"—the standard bearer—in the eyes of mainstream society and in the eyes of far too many black men, they fell short of this ideal.[16]

By the time Malcolm X began speaking to black audiences, black women had suffered centuries of "humiliating and detested images of [them]selves imposed by other people."[17] Pages of black magazines were filled with advertisements for hair-straightening and skin-lightening products; most black sex symbols were café au lait at best: Lena Horne, Dorothy Dandridge, Eartha Kitt. As Malcolm gained notoriety, black audiences would see the emergence of darker beauties like Abbey Lincoln, Cicely Tyson, and Nina Simone, but these would still be rare. It is in this context that we must be aware of the appeal of Malcolm's affirmation of black features and color. Also, we must remain cognizant of the class connotations of a color hierarchy in black communities.

When Malcolm X spoke out against racist hierarchies of beauty, black women heard an admired and respected leader who finally took seriously an issue that had affected them profoundly—an issue that is often not given serious attention by black leaders and thinkers because it is not considered "political" and because it calls for a self-critique that few leaders have been willing to endure. This was not the case with Malcolm X: "Out in the world, later on, in Boston and New York, I was among the millions of Negroes who were insane enough to feel that it was some kind of status symbol to be light-complexioned—that one was actually fortunate to be born thus."[18]

Many black people, particularly women, welcomed Malcolm's willingness to break the silence around "the color thing." The issue of colorism, of distinctions based on grade of hair and keenness of features, tears at the very fabric of who we are as a people. In the way that certain feminist critiques of the nuclear family uncovered the sexist aspects of that institution, so too do critiques of white standards of beauty and desirability reveal hidden dimensions in black family life. Malcolm exposed this when he said, "I actually believe that as anti-white as my father was, he was subconsciously so afflicted with the white man's brainwashing of Negroes that he inclined to favor the light ones. . . . Most Negro parents . . . would almost instinctively treat any lighter children better than they did the darker ones."[19] With humor and pathos Malcolm taught black people to see the way they came to hate their color, their hair, their features. He also connected this understanding with their political awakening.

> You know yourself that we have been a people who hated our African characteristics. We hated our heads, we hated the shape of our nose, we wanted one of those long dog-like noses, you know; we hated the color of our skin, hated the blood of Africa that was in our veins. And in hating our features and our skin and our blood, why we had to end up hating ourselves.[20]

While contemporary black critics like Lisa Jones and Kobena Mer-cer[21] challenge the adequacy of the notion of self-hatred for under-standing the personal aesthetics of African Americans, Malcolm still has much to teach us about the way we have often uncritically adopted white supremacist standards. Although the black church has also been a sight of affirming black beauty, Malcolm went a step further and sug-gested that we rid ourselves of all remnants of the white supremacist legacy, including straightened hair. It is quite ironic that other members of the Nation would later charge the organization with its own brand of colorism. In a CBS documentary on Malcolm X, one member even claimed that Malcolm's ascendancy to a position of leadership was aided by his fair coloring.[22] In fact, Malcolm X is even somewhat oppo-sitional from the official Nation of Islam stance on issues like hair and color in his celebration of unstraightened black hair.[23]

For black women in Malcolm's audience, greetings like "My beau-tiful black brothers and sisters" with which he opened some of his talks, must have come as rare and welcome salutations.[24] In February 1992, *Essence* magazine ran a special issue on "Honoring Our He-roes." Malcolm was on the cover and one of the featured articles was an as-told-to narrative by his widow, Betty Shabazz. Audrey Edwards and Susan Taylor opened the narrative with the following: "He has come to embody the best in black men: strong and uncompromising, clear—committed to securing power 'by any means necessary.'"[25] In that quotation, Malcolm's wife Betty Shabazz recalls her own feeling of affirmation in Malcolm's aesthetic appreciation of her blackness.

Black women cherished Malcolm's willingness to affirm them as worthy of respect, love, and admiration. All hierarchies of beauty are ultimately oppressive. And yet in a context where black women have been constructed as ugly just because they are black, it has been nec-essary to affirm them by acknowledging the beauty of blackness in all of its various guises. Still, our challenge isn't to reverse this hierarchy but to redefine beauty while questioning it as the most important characteristic for a woman to possess. Finally, our goal ought to be to dismantle all such oppressive hierarchies altogether.

The appreciation of the variety and diversity of black beauty is nowhere more evident than in black nationalist movements. How-ever, this affirmation of black beauty rarely leads to a progressive gender politics. In fact, nationalist movements of all sorts also have been characterized by their patriarchal ambitions. At best black women can expect to be called black queens and we all know that where there are queens there are kings: a pairing that is rarely an equal one (not to mention the class and antidemocratic implications of such titles).

During his time, Malcolm's promise of protection and affirmation of black beauty were welcome and needed. However, even then they held evidence of a very problematic gender politics. Our task is to scrutinize this aspect of his legacy with a critical eye. Of course we must hold on to and value that which sought to affirm black women, but we must rid ourselves of and revise all elements of his philosophy that might be detrimental to them.

Womanist Malcolm?!

> do not speak to me of martyrdom
> of men who die to be remembered
> on some parish day.
> i don't believe in dying
> though i too shall die
> and violets like castanets
> will echo me.
>   —from "Malcolm" by Sonia Sanchez

It is quite significant that in spite of the profound sexism of some of his writing, Malcolm X continues to be a hero for many black women, even many black womanist critics, theorists, and artists, myself included. Most black women who had the opportunity to hear Malcolm never flocked to cover their bodies and hair, walk two steps behind their men, and join the Nation of Islam. Nevertheless, many of them appeared to have voiced their admiration and respect for his vision and for his commitment to black women and families. In my classes, it is most often white women who are the first to raise concerns about the sexist moments in the *Autobiography*, while many of my black women students immediately jump to Malcolm's defense, claiming him as a hero.

Black women thinkers like Angela Davis, bell hooks, and Alice Walker have all acknowledged his impact on their intellectual development and politicization. Davis and Walker have sought to rescue

224 FARAH JASMINE GRIFFIN

his legacy from the misogyny of those black leaders who followed him. hooks applauds his affirmation of blackness in the midst of a society that despises all that is black. Patricia Hill Collins is one of the few contemporary black feminist thinkers to provide a sustained critique of Malcolm's gender politics in an effort to make black nationalism more accountable to black women.[26] Perhaps Collins is able to launch such a critique because she shares Malcolm's black nationalist politics.

If black women critical thinkers have been reluctant to forward a critique of the sexism inherent in much of Malcolm's legacy, black women creative writers, particularly our poets, have praised him in terms that celebrate the very patriarchy of his masculinity and held that up as his value to us as a people. Sonia Sanchez, Lucille Clifton, Margaret Walker Alexander, Gwendolyn Brooks, and Alice Walker are all among the women who have written poems in honor of Malcolm X. In 1968, Brooks published "Malcolm X":

> Original.
> Ragged-round.
> Rich-robust.
>
> He had the hawk-man's eyes.
> We gasped. We saw the maleness.
> The maleness raking out and making guttural the air
> and pushing us to walls.
>
> and in a soft and fundamental hour
> a sorcery devout and vertical
> beguiled the world.
>
> He opened us—
> who was a key,
>
> who was a man.

Brooks's Malcolm is the one who is loved and revered by many black women: A BLACK MAN, MALE, MALCOLM who could protect us and "open" us as he was a key. The "us" of this poem is a feminized black people who are in need of a very masculinized black leader.

Some black women have pinned their hopes on "What might have been the direction of Malcolm's thinking on questions of gender had he not been so cruelly assassinated?" For some sense of this, we all turn to one statement in particular that has come to represent a kind of beacon light for us:

> One thing that I became aware of in my traveling recently through Africa and the Middle East in every country you go to, usually the degree of progress can never be separated from the woman. If you're in a country that is progressive, then woman is progressive. If you're in a country that reflects the consciousness toward the importance of education, it's because the woman is aware of the importance of education. But in every backward country you'll find the women are backward, and in every country where education is not stressed it's because the women don't have education. So one of the things I became thoroughly convinced of in my recent travels is the importance of giving freedom to the woman, giving her education, and giving her the incentive to get out there and put that same spirit and understanding in her children. And frankly I am proud of the contributions women have made in the struggle for freedom and I'm one person who's for giving them all the leeway possible because they've made a greater contribution than many of us men.[27]

This is the comment that leads some black women to say that Malcolm began to reconsider his stance on women, their nature, and their role in the black freedom struggle. It is seen as part of the overall growth and change he experienced following his travels through Africa and the Middle East. Patricia Hill Collins has pointed out that even here, women are not agents. They are given freedom and education so that they may better act upon their roles as mother.[28]

By the end of his life, it appears Malcolm not only changed his opinion about women's position in society, but he also began a much needed self-critique. In the important essay "Black Popular Culture and the Transcendence of Patriarchal Illusions," Barbara Ransby and Trayce Matthews cite the following excerpt from a letter Malcolm wrote to his cousin-in-law in 1965:

> I taught brothers not only to deal unintelligently with the devil or the white woman, but I also taught many brothers to spit acid at the sisters. They were kept in their places—you probably didn't notice this in action, but it is a fact. I taught these brothers to spit acid at the sisters. If the sisters decided a thing was wrong, they had to suffer it out. If the sister wanted to have her husband at home with her in the evening, I taught the brothers that the sisters were standing in their way; in the way of the Messenger, in the way of progress, in the way of God himself. I did these things brother. I must undo them.[29]

If Malcolm himself came to be aware of the need to "undo" the work of his teachings about women, certainly we must recognize this need as well. Beyond wondering how Malcolm's view of women might have changed, we are left with the task of critiquing and revising what he left us. The re-emergence of his popularity with young black people, the use of his discourse by present-day nationalist leaders requires us to provide a systematic critique of those elements of his thought that place limits on black women. Angela Davis suggests we concern ourselves with "the continuing influence of both those who see themselves as the political descendants of Malcolm and our historical memory of this man as shaped by social and technological forces that have frozen his memory, transforming it into a backward imprisoning memory rather than a forward looking impetus for creative political thinking and organizing."[30]

Just as there are some who want only to preserve the racial politics of the pre-Mecca Malcolm, so too are there those persons who want to freeze his pre–Mecca statements on women. We must move from Abbey Lincoln's call for a Malcolm-like black man who will revere and protect us in the traditional sense of these words. And we must imagine the possibility that Malcolm's legacy might lead to a celebration of the Malcolm X of Alice Walker's poem, "Malcolm":

> Those who say they knew you
> offer as proof
> an image stunted
> by perfection.
> Alert for signs of the man
> to claim, one must believe
> they did not know you at all
> nor can remember the small, less popular
> ironies of the Saint:
> that you learned to prefer
> all women free
> and enjoyed a joke
> and loved to laugh.
>
> —Alice Walker[31]

Walker's Malcolm is a man who "learned to love all women free." A mythical Malcolm, yes (for perhaps the real ironies of the Saint are that he loved black women—yet could not imagine them as equal partners and in this way he is no different than most men of his time), but no less mythical than the one who fuels contemporary images of him in popular culture and nationalist discourses.

Malcolm's tremendous capacity for self-reflection, growth, and revision can serve as an example for us. A serious and critical engagement with his words and thought leads us to the understanding that we must respect and acknowledge his continuing importance and significance while moving beyond the limitations of his vision.

NOTES

1. See Barbara Ransby and Tracye Matthews, "Black Popular Culture and the Transcendence of Patriarchal Illusions," in Beverly Guy-Sheftall, ed., *Words of Fire: An Anthology of African American Feminist Thought* (New York: The New Press, 1995), 526–35; and Patricia Hill Collins, "Learning to Think for Ourselves: Malcolm X's Black Nationalism Reconsidered," in Joe Wood, ed., *Malcolm X: In Our Own Image* (New York: Anchor Books, 1992), 59–85.

2. Abbey Lincoln, "Who Will Revere the Black Woman?" *Negro Digest* (September 1966), reprinted in Toni Cade, ed., *The Black Woman* (New York: Signet, 1970), 82–84.

3. Jacquelyn Dowd Hall, "The Mind That Burns in Each Body": Women, Rape, and Racial Violence," in Ann Snitow, Christine Stansell, and Sharon Thompson, eds., *Powers of Desire* (New York: Monthly Review Press, 1983), 335.

4. Barbara Omolade, "Hearts of Darkness," in Snitnow, *Powers of Desire,* 352

5. See Alexander Crummell, *Destiny and Race: Selected Writing, 1840–1898,* edited by Wilson Jeremiah Wilson (Amherst: University of Massachusetts Press, 1992); and W. E. B. Du Bois, "The Damnation of Women," in *Darkwater: Voices from Within the Veil* (New York: Harcourt, Brace, 1920), 164–85.

6. George Breitman, ed., *Malcolm X Speaks: Selected Speeches and Statements* (New York: Grove Weidenfeld, 1965), 107.

7. Malcolm X and Alex Haley, *The Autobiography of Malcolm X* (New York: Ballentine Books, 1990).

8. Again, here as with Malcolm, protection is really about manhood. It is quite significant that the editorial from which this statement is taken was recently republished in an edition of *The Final Call* devoted to black women. Reprinted in *The Final Call,* July 20, 1994, 18.

9. Malcolm X, *The Autobiography,* 226.

10. E. Frances White, "Africa On My Mind: Gender, Counter Discourse and African-American Nationalism," *Journal of Women's History,* 2, no. 1 (Spring 1990), 76.

11. Ibid.

12. Betty Shabazz, "Loving and Losing Malcolm," *Essence* (February 1992): 107.

13. Walter White, "Color Lines" *Survey Graphic* VI (March 1925): 682.

14. For an exploration of the color debate between Garvey and Du Bois, see V. P. Franklin, *Living Our Stories, Telling Our Truths: Autobiography and the Making of the African American Intellectual Tradition* (New York: Oxford University Press, 1996), 122–25.

15. See Henry Louis Gates, "The Powell Perplex," in *Thirteen Ways of Looking at a Black Man* (New York: Random House, 1997), 84.

16. Even today, more than twenty years after the "black is beautiful" sixties and the Afro-centric nineties, colorism continues to thrive among African Americans. As recently as 1994, psychologist Midge Wilson of DePaul University asserted, "Studies show that successful Black men are particularly likely to marry light-skinned women." Karen Grisby Bates, "The Color Thing," *Essence* (September 1994): 132. See also Kathy Russell, Midge Wilson, and Ronald Hall, *The Color Complex: The Politics of Skin Color Among African Americans* (New York: Anchor Books, 1992).

17. Editor's Statement from the first issue of *Essence*, April 1970.

18. Malcolm X, *The Autobiography*, 4

19. Ibid.

20. *Malcolm X on Afro-American History* (New York: Pathfinder, 1967), 86.

21. See Kobena Mercer, *Welcome to the Jungle: New Positions on Black Cultural Studies* (New York: Routledge, 1994); Lisa Jones, *Bulletproof Diva: Tales of Race, Sex and Hair* (New York: Doubleday, 1994).

22. See "The Real Malcolm X: An Intimate Portrait of the Man," CBS News Video, 1992. Executive Producer Andrew Lack, Producer, Brett Alexander.

23. See E. Frances White, "Listening to the Voices of Black Feminism" *Radical America*, 7–25.

24. Malcolm X, *The Autobiography*, 201.

25. Betty Shabazz as told to Audrey Edwards and Susan Taylor, "Loving and Losing Malcolm," *Essence* 22, no. 10 (February 1992): 50.

26. See bell hooks, "Sitting at the Feet of the Messenger: Remembering Malcolm X," in *Yearning: Race, Gender, and Cultural Politics* (Boston: South End Press, 1990), 87; Angela Y. Davis, "Meditations on the Legacy of Malcolm X" and Patricia Hill Collins, "Learning to Think for Ourselves: Malcolm X's Black Nationalism Reconsidered," in Joe Wood, ed., *Malcolm X: In Our Own Image* (New York: Anchor Books, 1992), 36–47, and 59–85.

27. Paris interview, November 1964.

28. Collins, "Learning to Think for Ourselves," 79.

29. I am grateful to Tracye Matthews for calling my attention to this letter. Letter cited in Guy-Sheftall, ed., *Words of Fire*, 530. It originally appeared in

an unpublished manuscript by Paul Lee, "Malcolm X's Evolved Views on the Role of Women in Society."

30. Davis, "Meditations on the Legacy of Malcolm X," 44–45.

31. Alice Walker, "Malcolm," in *Her Blue Body Everything We Know: Earthling Poems 1965–1990 Complete* (New York: Harcourt Brace Jovanovich, 1991), 291.

Chapter 13

"No One Ever Asks What a Man's Role in the Revolution Is"

Gender Politics and Leadership in the
Black Panther Party, 1966–71

Tracye A. Matthews

By the middle of the 1960s, young black people in the United States were growing weary of civil rights leaders telling them to turn the other cheek so that they could "overcome someday."[1] The inspiring eloquence of Martin Luther King, Jr. had been challenged, even ridiculed, by the fiery message of Malcolm X. For black youth, who increasingly found themselves trapped in overcrowded northern ghettos, many of the old movement slogans and ideas—particularly nonviolence as a philosophy—were becoming obsolete.[2] In spite of the gains of the southern black freedom movement, civil rights organizations and leaders, especially King, were slowly but surely becoming aware of growing dissatisfaction among blacks with the limitations of hard-won legislation, especially its failure to ensure economic gains and tackle seemingly intractable forms of southern and northern racism. The call for "Black Power" became the order of the day.

Beginning in 1964 and continuing each summer through 1968, disillusionment, frustration, and economic discrimination fueled urban rebellions in black communities across the country.[3] It was within this context that the Black Panther Party for Self Defense (BPP) formed and staked its claim for leadership of the black masses. In October 1966, Huey P. Newton and Bobby Seale officially founded the Party in Oakland, California, one of many U.S. cities noted for its racist and repressive police force. The main targets of their initial organizing efforts were disaffected urban black male youth, and their activities centered on addressing police brutality through armed self-defense. Although the actual size of their constituency and membership is open to debate, the Party had a significant impact on the ideological and political developments of the late 1960s and early 1970s both nationally and internationally.

Contemporary expressions of dissatisfaction with "traditional" political leaders, especially among young African Americans, are reminiscent of the sentiments that led to the revolutionary youth movement of the late 1960s in which the Panthers played a critical role. Yet, in spite of renewed popular interest, the political ideology and inner workings of the BPP still remain hidden from those most likely to take up the mantle of resistance in the current era. The first two years of the Black Panther Party's development have been fictionalized, romanticized, and popularized in the recent larger-that-life Hollywood film *Panther*, complete with a supporting cast that looks like a BET (Black Entertainment Television) top-forty countdown, a full line of Panther gear for the nineties, two "Panther inspired" CDs, and a "PANTHER 'Power to the People' Sweepstakes" in which the winner receives $1,000.00 personal empowerment cash.[4] However, the content (or lack thereof) of this and many of the other contemporary popular sources influencing our collective memory of the Panthers, including movies, hip-hop magazines and music, and mainstream newspapers, may in fact serve to reproduce rather than rectify mistakes and miscalculations of the past.

The goal of this essay is to provide a perspective on an often-ignored aspect of the history and legacy of the BPP, namely, its gender politics. The gender ideology of the BPP, both as formally stated and as exemplified by organizational practice, was as critical to its daily functioning as was the Party's analysis of race and class dynamics in black communities. Rather than the Party's gender politics being secondary to the "larger" struggle against racism and capitalism, I instead posit that the politics of gender were played out in most aspects of party activity and affected its ability to function as an effective political organization.

A comprehensive scholarly analysis of the ideology, activities, successes, and failures of the Black Panther Party has yet to be undertaken by historians. While there exist numerous first-hand accounts that were written during the late sixties, as well as several recently published autobiographies and memoirs, most of these sources are primarily descriptive and do not attempt a sustained investigation of the race, class, or gender politics of the Party.[5] My purpose here is to begin this process with an examination of the construction of gender ideology within the context of Panther Party politics from 1966 to 1971.[6] Gender struggle affected the Party's political ideology and positions taken on a variety of issues, relationships with the larger black and progressive political communities, daily working and living arrangements, and the organization's ability to defend itself from state-sponsored disruption. The Party's theory and praxis with regard to issues of gender and sexuality should be viewed as an ongoing, non-linear process that was affected by factors both internal and external to the organization. This analysis of gender ideology offers insights into the internal politics of black communities, especially relations of power between and among men and women, and the myriad ways in which these dynamics influence political movements and popular perceptions of them.

Although much of the public rhetoric of the BPP and other Black Power organizations tended to center on issues usually defined (by themselves and by scholars) as race and/or class concerns, contestation around the politics of gender formed a significant component of the "hidden (and not so hidden) transcript" in the intracommunity discourse.[7] Evelyn Brooks Higginbotham suggests that race functions as a metalanguage in Western culture and tends to subsume and obscure gender, class, and other social relations. In addition, she argues that scholarly works in women's studies and African American history that are premised on the assumption of racial, gender, and class homogeneity "preclude recognition and acknowledgment of intragroup social relations as relations of power," and overlook crucial micropolitical struggles in black communities.[8] In this essay, I wish to show how the imagery, rhetoric, and praxis of the BPP contain components of ongoing power struggles, overt and hidden, over gender identity and sexuality. These struggles in turn complicate and disrupt romanticized notions of "nation-building" and/or black unity, both historical and contemporary, that presume the existence of a monolithic black community and privilege male authority/dominance in the family, as well as in the political and cultural arenas.

In this analysis, gender is not to be understood as a discrete category unto itself, but one of several interacting factors, such as race, class, color, age, and sexual orientation, that together make up individual identities, as well as the social terrain upon which we experience our realities. To say that I am examining gender and the politics of the BPP does not mean that this work is solely about sexism in the Party, or women's experiences. Instead, a gendered analysis also encompasses the experiences of men; definitions of manhood and womanhood; the interconnections between gender, race, and class-based oppression; and the impact of all of these factors on the successes and shortcomings of the BPP.

The category of gender was not as fully politicized and theorized during the late 1960s as it is today, thus one must resist the temptation to impose current standards to measure the feminist, nationalist, or revolutionary credentials of the BPP. Each of these social theories and categories must be understood as being situationally and historically specific. What constitutes feminism or radicalism in one time period is not necessarily recognized as such in another. Nevertheless, it is useful to compare and contrast feminism and race-consciousness across historical periods, examining continuities and changes. In addition, it is possible to assess which theories and actions constitute a challenge to status quo relations of power in different eras, and thus to assess the merits of political organizations on their own terms and in their particular historical context.

Ideas about gender and gender roles were far from static within the BPP. As the Party spread numerically and geographically, class and gender diversity within its ranks increased. New members brought new (and old) ideas with them. Despite the initial self-conscious creation by the leadership of a masculine public identity for the Panthers, some women and men in the Party challenged the characterization of the struggle as one mainly for the redemption of black manhood, and worked within its constraints to serve the interests of the entire black community. The stories of the BPP cannot be reduced to a monolithic party line on "the woman question," or a linear progression from an overtly and overwhelmingly sexist organization to a pro-black feminist/womanist one. Instead, one must pay attention to internal conflict as well as agreement, overt as well as covert manifestations of this dialogue, change over time, diversity of individual experiences, and internal as well as external influences. While it can justifiably be argued that the BPP at various points in its history was a male-centered, male-dominated organization, this point should not negate the important ideological and practical contributions of its female members or of the men who resisted chauvinistic and sexist tendencies. Indeed, the diversity, both in terms of geography and personnel, of an organization whose existence spanned from Oakland to Algiers and from 1966 to 1982, cannot be understood and appreciated through simplistic explanations or superficial head counts of official leadership roles. As will be shown, black women were critical players in the BPP, and the Party overall had a significant impact on the political life of many youths and adults outside its ranks.

In this essay I present an overview of the larger sociopolitical context with regard to gender ideology in which the BPP functioned. I also present some examples of BPP theory in action in an attempt to assess the day-to-day gender struggle and its implications for the lives of party members and the life of the Party.

Competing Gender Ideologies

The designation, conscious or otherwise, of specific gender-based roles for women and men within the Black Panther Party began with the Party's inception. Of course, this process did not happen in a vacuum. Thus, it will be helpful first to briefly examine the gendered context in which the Panthers operated. In addition to having their own ideas about the roles men and women should play in society and within the Party, the founders and members were also influenced by competing ideologies, and vice versa. These competing ideologies could be either supportive of or opposed to the status quo of American society. Three such ideologies that bear mentioning because of their enormous impact on the period are cultural nationalism, feminism, and the black matriarchy/tangle of pathology thesis.[9] These three ideological discourses illustrate historian E. Frances White's contention that "counter discourse struggles against both dominant and competing oppositional discourses."[10] In other words, the oppositional rhetoric of the BPP challenged and was challenged by other "alternative" as well as mainstream perspectives. There were, of course, many other important hegemonic and counterhegemonic theoretical constructs vying for prominence. These three are highlighted because of their impact on the evolving black consciousness of the period in general and on the BPP specifically.

One of the most popular proponents of black cultural nationalism, at least on the West Coast in the late 1960s, was the Los Angeles–based US organization headed by Maulana Karenga. The US organization stressed the necessity for cultural awareness among blacks to be gained primarily through the revival of African traditions—real or invented—of dress, language, religion, and familial arrangements as well as the rejection of white supremacy. The relationship between Karenga, the US organization, and the BPP changed over time just as the Panthers' own ideological positions changed. In the early years of the Party, Karenga participated in meetings and rallies in support of the BPP.[11] However, over time as their respective ideologies were clarified and contradictions were exposed, the BPP became scathingly critical of the US organization. Chiefly, the Party's critique was based on the fact that Karenga's group promoted cultural nationalism and black capitalism. Drawing on the theories of Frantz Fanon, the Panthers repeatedly asserted that cultural pride was a necessary phase in black people's political development, but it did not guarantee liberation, nor did black skin necessarily identify one as an automatic ally.[12] The open conflict between the two organizations came to a head in January 1969 when two prominent Panthers, John (Jon) Huggins and Alprentice "Bunchy" Carter, were killed by US members in a shoot-out at a Black Student Union meeting on the UCLA campus.[13] This incident sparked numerous articles and political cartoons in *The Black Panther* that criticized cultural nationalism in general and Karenga in particular. There were even charges leveled that Karenga himself was on the payroll of the FBI and/or various other police and government agencies.[14]

One major component of US rhetoric called for women's submission to traditional male "authority," and promoted the notion of complementary gender roles. According to Karenga's teachings,

> What makes a woman appealing is femininity and she can't be feminine without being submissive. A man has to be a leader and he has to be a man who bases his leadership on knowledge, wisdom and understanding. There is no virtue in independence. The only virtue is in interdependence. . . . The role of the woman is to inspire her man, educate their children, and participate in social development. . . . We say male supremacy is based on three things: tradition, acceptance, and reason. Equality is false; it's the devil's concept. Our concept is complementary. Complementary means you complete or make perfect that which is imperfect.[15]

Karenga and other proponents of complementary gender roles for men and women rarely addressed the power imbalances between the respective roles prescribed. These theories also tended to rely heavily on biological determinism and notions of "natural order" in assessing and assigning separate roles for black women and men. In practice, complementary theory often led to ridiculous incidents between black women activists and members of US, such as when Panther Elaine Brown was told she had to wait to eat until after the male "warriors" had been fed, and, on another occasion, when Angela Davis was discouraged or prevented from taking on a leadership role because it was deemed a "man's job."[16]

E. Frances White's important article "Africa on My Mind: Gender, Counter Discourse, and African-American Nationalism" provides a thorough critique of various strains of cultural nationalism, including Karenga's, that "can be radical and progressive in relation to white racism and conservative and repressive in relation to the internal organization of the black community." As White points out, Karenga and other nationalists construct "collective political memories of African culture . . . that both counter racism . . . and construct utopian and repressive gender relations." In particular, she argues that in "building off conservative concepts of 'traditional' African gender relations before colonial rule, [Karenga] argues that the collective needs of black families depend on women's complementary and unequal roles."[17]

Although BPP members themselves invoked complementary theory early in the organization's development, the unapologetic male supremacist policies and practices of the US organization exacerbated the already tenuous relationship between the two organizations.[18] Bobby Seale included the issue of male chauvinism in his public opposition to cultural nationalism in a 1970 interview. He stated that "[c]ultural nationalists like Karenga, are male chauvinists as well. What they do is oppress the black woman. Their black racism leads them to theories of male domination."[19] For Seale, the link between racism and sexism was that both were practices of domination that fed upon each other through some unspecified process. He presented the BPP as a viable alternative to US and cultural nationalism on the basis of the Panthers' ostensibly more progressive party line on "the gender question." The timing of Seale's statement reflected ongoing, internal Party struggles to reconcile the existence of male chauvinism within its ranks and refine its gender ideology. It may also have been an attempt to deflect negative attention away from the Party's own contradictions on these issues.

A second ideological trend that influenced the social and political terrain of the 1960s is contained under the rubric of feminism and the predominantly white Women's Liberation Movement (WLM). Many young white women who eventually played leadership roles in the second wave of the feminist movement in the United States had been previously politically involved and developed their budding gender consciousness in the southern Black Freedom Movement and the New Left.[20] For example, in 1965, responding to a buildup of gender tensions within Students for a Democratic Society (SDS) and a heightened recognition of their own capabilities, women in the organization pressed that group to issue a statement on women's roles in the student movement and women's liberation.[21] The growth of various factions in the women's movement, such as radical feminism, lesbian separatism, and women of color caucuses, continued throughout the decade and into the 1970s.[22] Although early proponents of the WLM professed to encompass the issues, needs, and demands of all women, its initial definition of the term *feminism*, and its strategies, ideology, tactics, and membership, were dominated by white middle-class women.

The rise in visibility of a feminist women's movement in the mid to late sixties is portrayed as the exclusive domain of white women in most historical texts. While the proliferation of explicitly feminist organizations among white women cannot be denied, some of the earliest stirrings of an incipient gender consciousness can be found in the activities of black women, especially those in the Student Nonviolent Coordinating Committee (SNCC).[23] Black women in black (mixed-gender) organizations did not necessarily relate to the label *feminist* as defined by the theories and activities of the predominantly white WLM organizations. However, this lack of identification with the terms "feminist" or "women's lib" should not preclude the recognition that black women who organized on issues, such as police brutality, racism, poverty, imperialism, and black women's liberation, had a significant impact on the development of gender consciousness during this time.[24] In fact, their involvement and leadership in these arenas represented a challenge to the black community to view all of these issues as indeed black women's issues, as well as concerns for the community as a whole. Their presence in black organizations eventually forced a recognition of the sexism in some of those organizations and of the racism and middle-class biases of many white women's groups. Historian Deborah King reminds us that "black feminist concerns . . . have existed well over a century. In other words, black women did not just become feminists in the 1970s."[25] Nor did they need to rely on white women's organizations and theories to define the terms of their womanhood or political interests.

The Black Panther Party came into direct contact with various predominantly white women's liberating groups. The level of these interactions differed between chapters and even varied from person to person. In some areas, local WLM groups organized fundraisers and rallies for Panther political prisoners. For example, an article in *The Black Panther* newspaper reported the attendance of more than five thousand people at a rally in support of the Panther New Haven 14 and in protest of the particularly cruel treatment of imprisoned Panther women. According to the author of that article:

> Black Panther Party Chapters and Branches, and Women's Liberation groups from Massachusetts, Connecticut, New York, New Jersey, Pennsylvania, Maryland, and Washington, D.C. participated in the march and rally. Organized by the New Haven Chapter of the Black Panther party, and Women's Liberation groups mostly from New York, the action exposed the blatantly fascist acts of the Connecticut pigs . . . against the people's servants—the Black Panther Party.[26]

The Party did not have an official position on the ideologies and tactics of WLM organizations until Huey P. Newton's statement, "The Women's Liberation and Gay Liberation Movements" in August 1970, calling for the formation of working coalitions with the revolutionary factions of both movements.[27] Prior to this pronouncement, individual Party members had a variety of critical perspectives. Some of the most thorough and thoughtful critiques of the WLM were forthcoming from Panther women. Panther women (and men) eventually came to the conclusion that the struggle for women's liberation was a part of the struggle against capitalism and as such should be waged by men and women together. According to one former member, there was never a position taken that women's liberation was not a part of black liberation struggle, but the Party felt the need to make more formal pronouncements on the issue in part because of the growth and visibility of the WLM.[28]

Panther sisters stated in a 1969 interview that to the extent that women's organizations did not address themselves to the class struggle or to national liberation campaigns they were not really furthering the women's liberation movement, because in order for women to be truly emancipated in this country there would have to be a socialist revolution. This critique of various women's lib organizations grew from their basic premise that the WLM viewed "the contradictions among men and women as one of the major contradictions in capitalist society . . . and develop[ed] it into an antagonistic contradiction, when actually it is a contradiction among people. It's not a contradiction between enemies."[29] Panther women also acknowledged that black women's relationship to black men was qualitatively different from gender relations between whites. In a 1971 interview, Kathleen Cleaver stated that

> the problems of black women and the problems of whites are so completely diverse they cannot possibly be solved in the same type of organization nor met by the same type of activity . . . I can understand how a white woman cannot relate to a white man. And I feel sorry for white women who have to deal with that type of [person].[30]

In addition to such theoretical differences, the BPP women interviewed also questioned the structure and practice of some women's liberation organizations. One sister rejected the anti-male and female separatist structures and strategies employed by some organizations as "illogical . . . because you can't solve the problem apart from the problem. You can't be liberated from male chauvinism if you don't even deal with it—if you run away from it."[31]

Although some of the women dismissed the usefulness of women's caucuses and separatist groups outright, others agreed that they should be judged by their practice and reserved commentary until they could assess whether those types of formations furthered the struggle for socialism. Although women in the BPP generally chose not to work in female-only organizations, and most did not think of themselves as feminists, this did not necessarily mean that they accepted male chauvinism or sexism. Most expected to be treated as equals, as revolutionary comrades, by their male counterparts. And some did engage the WLM as well as the men (and other women) in the BPP on issues of gender and black women's roles in the movement.

A final important piece of the ideological landscape of this period that influenced thinking about gender concerned the alleged structural and cultural deficiencies of the black family. Daniel Patrick Moynihan's *The Negro Family: A Case for National Action*, published in March 1965 under the auspices of the U.S. Department of Labor, became a cornerstone of intense debate in a variety of settings. Moynihan's report used sociological, historical, anecdotal, and statistical information regarding the status of black families to draw the conclusions that black families were matriarchal, that black men were unable to fulfill the roles required of men in a patriarchal society, and that the resulting pattern of female-headed households was largely responsible for the "tangle of pathology" in which black people found themselves. According to Moynihan, "the Negro community has been forced into a matriarchal structure which, because it is so out of line with the rest of the American society, seriously retards the progress of the group as a whole and imposes a crushing burden on the Negro male, and in consequence, on a great many Negro women as well."[32]

The ideas presented in this report, which suggested a change in focus for the government's civil rights policies, were eventually made public. Responses to Moynihan came from all sectors of black communities, including academics, grassroots activists, politicians, service providers, artists, and independent intellectuals.[33] While the implications of the Moynihan report on the internal debate in the black community were important, this should not be considered the beginning of such discussions about a black matriarchy, black male castration, and the like. Moynihan inserted himself, and by extension, the federal government and the media, into previously existing discussions within black communities. Moynihan built upon earlier works on black family structure to buttress his claims, especially E. Franklin Frazier's *The Negro Family in the United States*.[34]

Direct references to the Moynihan report in BPP literature are few. However, engagements of its major theses can be found in writings by Panthers on black family structure, slavery, and the sexual politics of black–white relations. In the 1967 essay "Fear and Doubt," Huey P. Newton wrote that

> he [the black man] feels that he is something less than a man. . . . Often his wife (who is able to secure a job as a maid, cleaning for white people) is the breadwinner. He is, therefore, viewed as quite worthless by his wife and children. He is ineffectual both in and out of the home. He

cannot provide for, or protect his family. . . . Society will not acknowledge him as a man.[35]

Newton was not far from Moynihan in his assessment of the dilem-
mas of black manhood in general, and black men's seeming inability
to live up to the patriarchal norms of the larger society in particular.
In this instance, Newton failed to challenge the notion of men as sole
providers for and protectors of black families while corroborating the
opinion that black women devalued, disrespected, and dominated
black men, and were privileged with economic advantages at the expense of black manhood.

Discussions within the Party regarding gender roles and relations
responded to the thesis of black matriarchy and cultural pathology in
varied and sometimes contradictory ways. Panthers could condemn
the racism of the larger society in its assessment of black families and
reject the notion that black culture is inherently pathological, while at
the same time affirming an ideal of male-dominated gender relations.
To complicate matters further, Newton's own questioning of the va-
lidity and usefulness of "the bourgeois family," which he described as
"an imprisoning, enslaving, and suffocating experience," eventually
led the Party to experiment with communal living and communal
sexual relationships. Although this challenge to traditional nuclear
family structures might be perceived as radical, an acceptance of male
dominance within these alternative arrangements could diminish
their revolutionary potential. This point serves to further illustrate E.
Frances White's analysis of the "interrelationship between dominant
and counter discourse." She points out that "as part of the same dialectic, counter discourses operate on the same ground as dominant
ideology."[36] While the BPP offered fundamental critiques of U.S. society, Party members were socialized by and accepted many of its hegemonic norms.

Although cultural nationalism, feminism, and the black matriarchy thesis were not the only prominent ideological and popular discourses in the late 1960s and early 1970s, their impact was felt nationally (and internationally). Individual Panther chapters may or may
not have had direct contact with organizations or individuals espousing any of these perspectives. Yet their ideas and activities were critical threads in the cultural fabric of this period. As such, they formed
a part of the larger framework of competing gender ideologies in

which the party functioned, and their impact was represented in a variety of cultural forms, including fiction, films, scholarly literature, and poetry.[37]

It should also be noted that the official gender ideology espoused by the Panther leaders, including Huey Newton, Bobby Seale, and Eldridge Cleaver, shifted over time. Initially the emphasis was placed on linking black liberation to the regaining of "black manhood." However, by the early 1970s as one of the "8 Points of Attention" to be recited and memorized by Panther recruits, point 7 read "Do not take liberties with women."[38] This evolution in the gender ideology of the Panther leadership was also reflected in the statements and actions of the rank-and-file male members, who often abandoned overtly sexist and male chauvinist behaviors as a result of their interactions with Panther women, particularly those in leadership positions. While the popular image of the BPP, both in the 1960s and currently, is that of a male-dominated, macho cult, Panther rhetoric and realities deserve a more nuanced description; one must take into account the diverse individual experiences of Party members as well as the subtle ideological shifts made by the male leaders.[39]

Observation and Participation: Quotidian Gender Struggle in Ideology and Practice

Huey P. Newton was often quoted as saying that many people learned primarily through observation and participation, a point which supports the argument that the events of everyday life were important in shaping the consciousness and practice of Party members.[40] It is critical, then, that we begin to explore the daily struggles over gender and definitions of black manhood and womanhood and not just moments of extraordinary rupture and conflict (although these, too, are important). I do not mean to suggest that the BPP was a hotbed of critical inquiry on gender issues in the academic sense. Instead, many of these dialogic interactions played themselves out in the daily acts of living and working together. In other words, the actions of Party members often represented their theory.[41] A few examples drawn from the experiences of women in the Party will serve to illustrate the impact of gender politics and power dynamics on everyday life.

The late Connie Matthews, who worked in both the international chapter and Oakland headquarters, recounts that

> [I]n theory, the Panther party was for equality of the sexes . . . on a day-to-day struggle with rank-and-file brothers, you got a lot of disrespect, you know. . . . Because, I mean, it's one thing to get up and talk about ideologically you believe this. But you're asking people to change attitudes and lifestyles overnight, which is not just possible. So I would say that there was a lot of struggle and there was a lot of male chauvinism. . . . But I would say all in all, in terms of equality . . . that women had very, very strong leadership roles and were respected as such. It didn't mean it came automatically.[42]

Matthews acknowledges the existence of sexism in the Party, but at the same time highlights the existence of struggle on the part of women (and men) to grapple with the disparities between Party rhetoric and the concrete reality of daily working and living arrangements. She confirms an awareness of the influence of socialization on Party members' ideas and behavior. Yet her quote leaves some ambiguity as to whether she saw chauvinistic "attitudes and lifestyles" as being generated from within, or from outside of black communities, or both. She also hints at her opinion of the way in which class differences may have affected gender relations in her reference to the "rank-and-file" brothers as being particularly disrespectful.

Statements by Assata Shakur corroborate Matthews' acknowledgments of the daily struggles of women for respect in the Party. According to Shakur,

> [A] lot of us [women] adopted that kind of macho type style in order to survive in the Black Panther Party. It was very difficult to say "well listen brother, I think that . . . we should do this and this." [I]n order to be listened to, you had to just say, "look mothafucka," you know. You had to develop this whole arrogant kind of macho style in order to be heard. . . . We were just involved in those day to day battles for respect in the Black Panther Party.[43]

Here, Shakur presents one strategy employed by some women in the BPP to exert authority-participation by assuming supposedly masculine styles of behavior and posturing. This approach to political organizing is more authoritarian than democratic and was criticized elsewhere by Shakur.[44] However, black women's presumption of a style, actions, and words associated with male prerogative potentially un-dermined the notion of men's inherent aggressiveness or innate lead-ership abilities that were the basis of masculinist gender ideologies, including some of the BPP's earlier formulations. While this macho posturing by women may have reinforced the notion of black women as domineering, it also challenged the idea that only black men should lead and "protect" black women. That some women had to modify their public persona in order to be respected is indicative of the extent to which gendered power dynamics pervaded the lives of Party members.

Such intracommunal struggles, which Matthews and Shakur de-scribe, directly affected the organization's culture and ability to func-tion, yet are hidden in analyses that fail to look at gender relations as relations of power. The ways in which women and men understood their respective roles, and the relative exercise of power they brought to bear on their relationships, were not merely personal dynamics, but also political interactions and choices made in the context of the movement. Although on a very practical level the dialogue on gender in the Party was affected by the presence of increasing numbers of women, it was, more importantly, the impact of these women's ac-tions that demanded a certain level of respect and recognition from male members.

Female Panthers often tested and stretched the boundaries of the largely masculinized Party structure. Many of these women held low or no formal positions of rank. Yet their heroic actions thrust them into positions of prominence inside and outside of the Party. Women, such as Joan Bird, Afeni Shakur, and numerous other unnamed rank-and-file members, fought figuratively and literally for the revolution-ary principles and platform of the Party. Many were involved in armed confrontation with police authorities alongside Panther men.[45] By so doing, they challenged old Party notions of community defense being a man's job. The brutal treatment of these women by police au-thorities made it clear to them as well as the entire black community that they could expect no comfort or benefits from stereotypes of women as fragile and weak and needing to be protected. After all, this construction of womanhood historically had never been applied to black women by the larger society (even though some nationalists adapted their own variation). Nor could the idea (propagated by Moynihan and even some Panthers), that black women somehow received special treatment from government agencies or U.S. society in general, remain intact.

Once these black women, involved in militant organizing efforts, stepped outside of roles traditionally assigned to women or African Americans, their treatment more closely resembled the experiences of their black male comrades than those of white women. Racist and sexist government agencies and a racist and sexist mainstream polity responded to Black Panther women as black people who did not "know their place" with respect to their gender, race, or class.

The above examples attest to the ability of some black women to carve out a space for their own empowerment within the context of a formally male-dominated organization, often in the face of extreme male chauvinism and harassment from within and without. In her recognition of women as strong leaders in the Party, Connie Matthews legitimizes women's contributions as crucial to the survival of the organization. In so doing, she not only pays respect to the leadership abilities of the well-known (and higher ranking) women in the BPP, such as Ericka Huggins, Kathleen Cleaver, and Elaine Brown, but also to local female rank-and-file members.

Matthews' claim that women held key leadership roles is echoed in other accounts. Many former Panthers recall that women were responsible in terms of both leadership and personnel for key Party programs, such as the free breakfast programs, liberation schools, and medical clinics; yet the media image of the Party was and is male-centered. The Party also recruited non-Panther "welfare mothers, grandmothers and guardians in the black community" to help staff breakfast programs in particular.[46] As former Panther Malika Adams pointed out,

> [W]omen ran the BPP pretty much. I don't know how it got to be a male's party or thought of as being a male's party. Because those things, when you really look at it in terms of society, those things are looked on as being woman things, you know, feeding children, taking care of the sick and uh, so. Yeah, we did that. We actually ran the BPP's programs.[47]

Her assessment of the prominence of women not only provides us with the standard participatory history or "women were there too" analysis, but on an even more significant level, argues for new definitions of leadership and politics. As Adams indicates, the types of activities prescribed in these community survival programs often represented an extension of "traditional" roles for women in the family: nurturers, caretakers of children, transmitters of morals, etc. Yet Panther men as well as women staffed the programs, thus potentially challenging narrowly defined male gender roles. These types of movement jobs are often categorized by historians and activists alike as "support work," or "community service," as opposed to "real" political activism.[48] These tasks were the lifeblood of the organization and as such should be understood more accurately as forms of political leadership. Given the context of state repression, these activities took on an explicitly political and public function and were often the sites of intense struggle with state authorities. Thus, public speaking abilities and formal titles were not the sole markers of leadership abilities, a point not missed by the FBI.

Panther survival programs were an ideological and practical counter to the misinformation and destruction campaign being waged against the BPP. In fact, many of the FBI's activities against the Party were designed to undermine the free breakfast for children operations and other community based "survival programs." An FBI memo from Director J. Edgar Hoover in 1969 described the free breakfast program as "the best and most influential activity going for the BPP and as such, is potentially the greatest threat to efforts by authorities . . . to neutralize the BPP and destroy what it stands for."[49]

The experiences of Brooklyn-branch member Janet Cyril further illuminate this point. As one of the founding members of that branch, she eventually became citywide coordinator of the free breakfast programs. In the meantime, she was expelled from the Party no less than four times. She argues that this was in part due to her generally anti-authoritarian attitude, which, in her assessment, was even less tolerable because she is a woman. One of her expulsions was for refusing to have sex with a very high-ranking member of the Central Committee of the Party: "[He] thought he was gon' sleep in my bed with me. And uh, that was not happening. And I was given several direct orders which I disobeyed quite directly (laugh). And then to top it off, the street I lived on had alternate side of the street parking and their car got towed in the morning because they overslept."[50]

After this episode, Cyril was expelled for sabotage. She later found out through research in the FBI's Counter Intelligence Program (COINTELPRO) files that the FBI deliberately planted misinformation by using an actual informant, which made it appear that Cyril was the informant. This particular tactic was called "bad-jacketing" or "snitch-jacketing."[51] An FBI internal agency memorandum, she recalls, stated that she should be targeted for "neutralization" because of her effectiveness as an organizer.

This example points to the significance of the community service programs in lending credibility and longevity to the BPP, which was precisely why the FBI made such determined efforts to undermine them. It also gives a concrete example of the power relations embedded in sexual interactions in that Cyril was expelled at least once for refusing to participate in what some Party members referred to as "socialistic fucking," or engaging in sexual relations ostensibly as a revolutionary duty.[52] In this case, the political impact of the attempted power play by the male leader actually served the interests of the oppressive state apparatus and helped to undermine the effectiveness of one of the Party's key local leaders and programs. Here, the contradictions between the theory and practice of the national leadership with regard to sexual relationships and sexual self-determination directly and adversely affected the Panthers' capacity to function as a viable political organization.

Conclusions

The ideological development of Party members was an ongoing process, ripe with contradiction, and shaped by the material and cultural conditions of the late 1960s and early 1970s. The increasing numbers of women in the Party as rank-and-file members and as leaders and the severity of state repression directed at all Panthers provided the pressure-cooker setting for testing out their new ideas about gender and revolution.

The members of the BPP were themselves products of the larger society. Thus, the terrain on which intracommunal debates over gender, class, and race took place was influenced by the terms of the so-called dominant culture and its agents. The Party was both critic and purveyor of American culture and politics. Panthers decried the class and gender biases of their contemporaries and the larger white society, but at the same time they re-affirmed many of those same shortcomings. A former female member of the Party's Brooklyn branch recalled,

> [W]e could talk about this stuff [gender and sexism]. We could talk about it just as we talked about capitalism and imperialism. But I don't know that we internalized it. I think we saw that our Party line was that there was no difference [between men and women]. We tried to be progressive in our thinking. But I think what we didn't realize was that we were just as much victims of a social condition that perpetuated it and that we carried these traits with us.[53]

She acknowledges that men and women engaged each other in discussions about gender issues, yet basic contradictions remained between theory and practice. Most still did not have full command of the contemporary language and theory of gender politics that was being developed, revised, and disseminated during this period. Many of their shortcomings arose from the lack of experience addressing such concerns in an explicitly political context. This was probably especially true for those who had no previous activist involvement. Their contradictions were part and parcel of the dialectic between hegemonic norms, which reinforced unequal gender roles and power relations between men and women, and intracommunal struggles, which attempted to redefine the terms of this discourse both internally and externally.

Despite their limitations (or perhaps because of them) and the generally dire circumstances in which they found themselves, the BPP was still often ahead of most other black nationalist organizations and many white leftist and mainstream organizations in their progress toward addressing (at least rhetorically) "the woman question." According to Assata Shakur,

> The BPP was the most progressive organization at that time [and] had the most positive images in terms of . . . the position of women in the propaganda . . . I felt it was the most positive thing that I could do because many of the other organizations at the time were so sexist, I mean to the extreme. . . . There was a whole saturation of the whole climate with this quest for manhood . . . even though that might be oppressive to you as a human being. . . . For me joining the BPP was one of the best options at the time.[54]

Thus, for Shakur and many other black women seeking involvement in the Black Power Movement and grassroots organizing, the Party presented a viable option. The programmatic focus of the Party after

1968 directly addressed the needs of poor black women, especially those who were primarily responsible for childrearing. BPP membership could also offer women and men a sense of control over their lives outside the Party. Many, probably for the first time in their lives, were able to contest directly the larger society's representations and perceptions of them and to fight for better treatment from the state apparatus that imposed its policies on their lives and their communities. Through its ideology, rhetoric, imagery, and praxis, the BPP engaged the dominant culture in a debate about the parameters of black racial and sexual identity and its impact on politics and policy. This was particularly significant given the history of struggles by black people to be recognized as respectable, fully human beings.[55] They also engaged each other and the larger black community about what it meant to be a black woman, man, comrade, revolutionary—not in the abstract—but in the heat of political struggle.

The insidious attempts by the U.S. government to destroy the organization and individual members restricted the development of a more self-reflective theory and practice by BPP members. Party members did not always have the luxury or the space to reflect and revise past errors. Nonetheless, it is somewhat paradoxical and instructive that a movement that was initially so thoroughly male centered in many ways broke ground for subsequent explicitly feminist/womanist activism by black women and, in some ways, engaged in more nuanced discussions of gender roles than those found currently in social movements, academic texts, and popular culture.

For example, the movie *Panther* fails to treat in any substantial manner the role of women in the Party, not to mention the internal struggles over gender roles and sexist/misogynistic behavior, a point made by many reviewers of the film. However, some of these same cultural critics replicate this error of omission by making summary comments, such as in the sixties "it was believed that the greatest threat to the nation was a black man with a gun,"[56] and that the film is a "stirring affirmation of black masculinity, an image of what the Panthers could have, and maybe should have, been.[57] Statements like these justify and excuse the movie's inattention to gender politics as critical to the story of the Party and, in effect, further the notion that the central actors and focus of black struggle should be black men and manhood. Through an emphasis on "gun barrel politics" in both the film and the reviews, the critical presence and actions of female Panthers are virtually ignored, while the complexities of black masculinity are constrained by romanticized, flat images of angry, hard bodies with guns.[58]

Many of the intracommunal debates raised by the Black Panther Party have resurfaced once again in the context of a resurgent cultural nationalism in black communities in the United States Unfortunately, both the language and the content of many contemporary discussions reflect little if any recognition of the historical depth of these issues, nor of the progress made, however limited, in addressing them in the past. Black men are once again talked about and talk about themselves as castrated or as "endangered species." Black women are often cited as being complicit in this process or as succeeding at the expense of black men. The most popular formulations blame poor, working-class black women for their alleged inability to raise black boys/men, and accuse black women in general of being the willing recipients of alleged special treatment and unearned entitlements from white society. To paraphrase the official recruitment literature from the Million Man March, black men need to resume their rightful place as patriarchs of black families and communities.[59]

The interrelationship between the ways black people are targeted for gender-, class-, and sexual-orientation-specific attacks are unrecognized in our acceptance of linear, "either/or" analyses of problems facing black communities as a whole. For the sake of so-called black unity, we often sacrifice or ignore the needs of some of the most oppressed and marginalized sectors of our communities to the detriment of us all. Those who dare to assert our heterogeneity and identify oppressive practices within and between black communities are silenced and assailed as divisive or assimilationist, as race traitors, or worst of all, as just not authentically, purely black enough. Witness the virtual gag order and public attacks against those within the community, particularly black women such as Angela Davis, who disagreed with the Million Man March's gender politics, focus, and agenda (or lack thereof).

We would all benefit from a closer, more complex interrogation and public discussion of historical struggles over these same issues, from slavery to the present, one that does not gloss over mistakes or internal differences, to aid us in redefining our roles and relationships in ways that can nurture and sustain the community and build a progressive black movement for the twenty-first century.

NOTES

1. An earlier version of this essay was first presented at "African American Women in the Civil Rights–Black Power Movement," a conference sponsored by the Temple University Center for African American History and Culture, on November 20–21, 1997.

2. There is a lengthy history of armed resistance among Black communities in the United States. Several studies have noted that many Civil Rights Movement participants practiced nonviolence as a strategy, not a philosophy, while at the same time engaging in armed self-defense tactics. For evidence of this, see Gene Marine, *The Black Panthers* (New York: Signet, 1969), 36; Clayborne Carson, *In Struggle: SNCC and the Black Awakening of the 1960s* (Cambridge: Harvard University Press, 1981); Aldon Morris, *Origins of the Civil Rights Movement: Black Communities Organizing for Change* (New York: The Free Press, 1984), 19; Akinyele Umoja, "Eye for an Eye: The Role of Armed Resistance in the Mississippi Freedom Movement, 1955–1980" (Ph.D. diss., Emory University, 1996); and Timothy B. Tyson, *Radio Free Dixie: Robert F. Williams and the Roots of Black Power* (Chapel Hill: University of North Carolina Press, 1999).

3. *Report of the National Advisory Commission on Civil Disorders [The Kerner Report]* (New York: Bantam Books, 1968; Pantheon Books, 1988), 35–41.

4. The film *Panther* (Gramercy), written by Mario Van Peebles and directed by his father, Melvin Van Peebles, opened to mixed reviews from critics and former Panthers alike. For sweepstakes information, see *Young Sisters and Brothers Magazine* 4,8 (May 1995): 40.

5. For examples of primary sources written in the 1960s and 1970s, see Gene Marine, *The Black Panthers*, and Huey P. Newton, *Revolutionary Suicide* (New York: Harcourt Brace Jovanovich, 1973); G. Louis Heath, ed., *Off the Pigs: The History and Literature of the Black Panther Party* (Metuchen, NJ: Scarecrow Press, 1976); and Philip S. Foner, ed., *The Black Panthers Speak, The Manifesto of the Party: The First Documentary Record of the Panthers Program* (Philadelphia: Lippincott, 1970). For brief scholarly treatments, see Robert Allen, *Black Awakening in Capitalist America* (Garden City, NY: Doubleday and Co., 1969), and Manning Marable, *How Capitalism Underdeveloped Black America* (Boston: South End Press, 1983). There are government hearings and reports on BPP activity such as U.S. Senate, *Final Report of the Select Committee to Study Government Operations with Respect to Intelligence Activities*, 94th Cong., 2d sess., 1976, S. Rept. 94–755. There are also more recently published specialized texts, such as those on FBI repression, which are cited below.

6. The time period examined in this essay does not include the period during and following the major division within the Party over matters of ideology, practice, and leadership, and its decline as a national organization. Many

important shifts occurred after the split, especially in terms of the numbers of formally recognized female leaders. Some former Panthers believe that the "original" BPP ended in 1970 or 1971; others saw themselves as being part of the BPP until 1981, when the Oakland Community School closed.

7. Most scholarly texts on the Civil Rights Movement, (White) Women's liberation movement, and Black Power movement neglect or minimize any analysis of the issues of gender politics in the Black Power movement or BPP.

8. Evelyn Brooks Higginbotham, "African-American Women's History and the Metalanguage of Race," *Signs* 17, 2 (Winter 1992): 225, 274. Here she draws on James C. Scott's notions of the infrapolitics and hidden transcripts of everyday resistance in his book, *Domination and the Arts of Resistance: Hidden Transcripts* (New Haven: Yale University Press, 1990). Higginbotham adds to this a discussion of hierarchies and power struggles within oppressed communities. See also Robin D. G. Kelley, *Race Rebels: Culture, Politics, and the Black Working Class* (New York: The Free Press, 1994), for a nuanced discussion of infrapolitics and intraracial power dynamics in black communities.

9. Daniel Patrick Moynihan, *The Negro Family: The Case for National Action* (Office of Policy Planning and Research, U.S. Department of Labor, March 1965).

10. E. Frances White, "Africa on My Mind: Gender, Counter Discourse and African-American Nationalism," *Journal of Women's History* 2, 1 (Spring 1990): 80.

11. US was a member of the Black Congress, an umbrella organization in Los Angeles organized around the principle of operational unity. The Congress supported Free Huey movement activities. See *Harambee* 11, 1 (November 17, 1967): 1–2, 8.

12. Two examples of Panther critiques of cultural nationalism are Linda Harrison, "On Cultural Nationalism," *The Black Panther*, February 2, 1969, and George Mason Murray, "Cultural Nationalism," *The Black Panther*, March 3, 1969.

13. Ward Churchill and Jim Vander Wall, *Agents of Repression: The FBI's Secret Wars Against the Black Panther Party and the American Indian Movement* (Boston: South End Press, 1988). Evidence shows that this shooting was probably instigated by FBI agents within US and through counterintelligence propaganda circulated between the two organizations. The authors quote a 1968 FBI memo from J. Edgar Hoover encouraging agents to "fully capitalize upon BPP and US differences as well as to exploit all avenues of creating further dissension within the ranks of the BPP," 42.

14. For example, see *The Black Panther*, February 2, 1969, 3; and March 3, 1969, 4; Newton, *Revolutionary Suicide*, 255; and Louis Tackwood and The Citizens Research and Investigation Committee, *The Glass House Tapes* (New York: Avon Books, 1973), 105.

15. Clyde Halisi, ed., *The Quotable Karenga* (Los Angeles: US Organization, 1967), 27–28.

16. Elaine Brown, *A Taste of Power: A Black Woman's Story* (New York: Pantheon Books, 1992), 109; Angela Davis, *Angela Davis: An Autobiography* (New York International Publishers, 1974, 1988), 161. At the time of this incident in 1967, Davis was a founding member of the Black Student Union at the University of California at San Diego.

17. White, "Africa on My Mind," 73–77. The BPP and US subscribed to revolutionary nationalism and cultural nationalism respectively and thus had widely divergent political perspectives and programs for action. The BPP identified themselves variously as revolutionary nationalists, Marxist-Leninists, and Intercommunalists at different points in time. Despite the diversity of nationalist ideologies, aspects of White's critique are applicable to both organizations.

18. Panthers' critiques of cultural nationalism may have varied regionally. Both my own and sociologist David Maurrasse's interviews with former Party members suggest that New York–based Panthers considered themselves more nationalistic or more rooted in African culture than West Coast Panthers.

19. Bobby Seale, "Bobby Seale Explains Panther Politics," *The Guardian*, February 1970, 4, US's anti-white polemics were interpreted as "black racism" by the BPP.

20. Sara Evans, *Personal Politics: The Roots of Women's Liberation in the Civil Rights Movement and the New Left* (New York: Vintage Books, 1979), 57, 193–95.

21. Alice Echols, *Daring to Be Bad: Radical Feminism in America*, 1967–1975 (Minneapolis: University of Minnesota Press, 1989), 34–35.

22. See Echols, *Daring to Be Bad*, for an excellent account of the politics and activities of white radical and cultural feminists.

23. See Robin Morgan, ed., *Sisterhood Is Powerful* (New York: Vintage Books, 1970), xxi. Several key women in the BPP were former members of SNCC, including Kathleen Cleaver and Connie Matthews.

24. Several earlier studies analyze the political activities of black women in the 1960s through an either/or framework—either they were feminists or Black Power sympathizers. This does not account for the activities of black women that incorporated race, gender, and class simultaneously. See, for example, Evans, *Personal Politics*, 101; Paula Giddings, *When and Where I Enter: The Impact of Black Women on Race and Sex in America* (New York: Bantam Books, 1984), 311, 323; and Echols, *Daring to Be Bad*, 106.

25. Deborah King, "Multiple Jeopardy, Multiple Consciousness: The Context of a Black Feminist Ideology," *Signs* 14, 1 (Autumn 1988). For examples of black women's writings on the issues of gender and race in this period, see Toni Cade, ed., *The Black Woman: An Anthology* (New York: Mentor, The New American Library, 1970).

26. Cappy Pinderhughes, "Free Our Sisters," *The Black Panther*, December 6, 1969, 2. Bobby Seale and Ericka Huggins, along with twelve other New Haven BPP members, were charged with the kidnapping, murder, and torture of fellow Party member Alex Rackley, who had been falsely identified as an informant by an actual police infiltrator, George Sams. Two Panthers and Sams were convicted. For more on this case, see Ward Churchill and Jim Vander Wall, *The COINTELPRO Papers: Documents from the FBI's Secret War Against Dissent in the United States* (Boston: South End Press, 1990), 146–47, 360.

27. Huey Newton, "The Women's Liberation and Gay Liberation Movements: August 15, 1970," in *To Die for the People: The Writings of Huey Newton* (New York: Vintage Books, 1972), 152–55.

28. Kathleen Cleaver in a telephone conversation with the author, November 27, 1994.

29. Anonymous, "Black Panther Sisters Talk about Women's Liberation," pamphlet reprinted from *The Movement* (September 1969). The same interview appears as "Panther Sisters on Women's Liberation," in Heath, *Off the Pigs!*, 339–50. Quote from 344. Originally appeared as "Sisters," *The Black Panther*, September 13, 1969, 12.

30. "Black Scholar Interviews Kathleen Cleaver," *Black Scholar* 2 (December 1971): 56.

31. Anon., "Panther Sisters on Women's Liberation," in Heath, *Off the Pigs!*, 348; "Sisters," *The Black Panther*, 12.

32. Lee Rainwater and William L. Yancey, *The Moynihan Report and the Politics of Controversy* (Cambridge, MA: MIT Press, 1967), 75.

33. In this period, cultural productions by black people directly addressed gender, race, and class issues as they were manifest in all areas of black life. See Abby Arthur Johnson and Ronald Mayberry Johnson, *Propaganda and Aesthetics: The Literary Politics of African-American Magazines in the Twentieth Century* (Amherst: University of Massachusetts Press, 1979, 1991), especially chapter 6; and William L. Van Deburg, *New Day in Babylon: The Black Power Movement and American Culture, 1965–1975* (Chicago: University of Chicago Press, 1992); and Madhu Dubey, *Black Women Novelists and the Nationalist Aesthetic* (Bloomington: Indiana University Press, 1994).

34. E. Franklin Frazier, *The Negro Family in the United States* (Chicago: University of Chicago Press, 1939, 1948, 1966).

35. Newton, *To Die for the People*, 81.

36. White, "Africa on My Mind," 79.

37. For an analysis of the cultural components and impact of the Black Power movement, see Van Deburg, *New Day in Babylon*.

38. See Appendix B, "8 Points of Attention," reprinted in Foner, *The Black Panthers Speak*, 98–99.

39. For additional information on Panther leaders and rank-and-file male

members' rhetoric on gender relations, see Tracye Matthews, "'No One Ever Asks What a Man's Place in the Revolution Is': Gender and Sexual Politics in the Black Panther Party, 1966–1971" (unpublished Ph.D. diss., University of Michigan), 1998.

40. Newton, *To Die for the People*, 15.

41. Elsa Barkley Brown, "Womanist Consciousness: Maggie Lena Walker and the Independent Order of St. Luke," in Michelene R. Malson, et al., eds., *Black Women in America: Social Science Perspectives* (Chicago: University of Chicago Press, 1990), 194.

42. Connie Matthews, interview with the author, June 26, 1991, Kingston, Jamaica.

43. Assata Shakur, interview with the author, July 30, 1993, Havana, Cuba; Assata Shakur, *Assata: An Autobiography* (Westport, CT: Lawrence Hill and Company, 1987), 204.

44. Shakur, *Assata*, 204.

45. For specific mainstream media articles about Joan Bird, see *New York Post*, May 14, July 7, December 1970; and *New York Times*, July 7 and 15, 1970; For information about Afeni Shakur, see *New York Times*, July 15, 1970. About Ericka Huggins, see *New York Times*, December 2, 1969, and March 22, 1970.

46. Heath, *Off the Pigs!*, 100; See also *The Black Panther*, September 7, 1986, 7.

47. Frankye Malika Adams, interview with the author, September 29, 1994, Harlem, New York.

48. Ibid.; Adams stresses that although men also participated in these programs, women organized and led them.

49. "FBI Airtel from Director to SAC's in 27 field offices," May 15, 1969, cited in Huey P. Newton, "War Against the Panthers: A Study of Repression in America" (Ph.D. Diss., University of California, June 1980), 109.

50. Janet Cyril, interview with the author, September 29, 1994, Brooklyn, NY.

51. For additional definitions of these terms, see Churchill and Vander Wall, *Agents of Repression*, 49–51.

52. Frankye Malika Adams, interview with the author, September 29, 1994, Harlem, New York.

53. Ibid.

54. Assata Shakur, interview with the author, July 30, 1993, Havana, Cuba.

55. In my dissertation "'No One Ever Asks What a Man's Place in the Revolution Is,'" I explore the construction of black Civil Rights Movement participants as noble, respectable, asexual, and peaceful in juxtaposition to notions of black urban youth as a riot-prone, extremist, hypersexual menace. This is one of many oppositional dichotomies imposed by mainstream discourses and reinforced by some activists and by many academic studies of this period, such as the now almost obsolete Malcolm-versus-Martin Dyad, nonviolence versus self-defense, accommodation versus resistance, theories. On

intracommunal struggle and challenges to these types of false dichotomies, see Robin Kelley, *Race Rebels*. On the topic of respectability and racialized constructions of sexuality, see Evelyn Higginbotham, "African-American Women's History and the Metalanguage of Race," *Signs* 17 (Winter 1992): 251–74.

56. Michael Eric Dyson, "The Panthers, Still Untamed, Roars Back," review of Gramercy film, *New York Times*, April 30, 1995, 17, 25.

57. Michael Robinson, "The Van Peebleses Prowl Through the Panthers' History," *American Visions*, 10, 2 (April/May 1995): 16–18.

58. The chronology of events and emphasis on guns in the Black Panther Party closely resembles the structure and content of an anti-Panther government report that summarizes House Committee on Internal Security public hearings on the BPP conducted in 1970 and gives an analysis of the origins, politics, tactics, successes, and failures of the Party. The report also details the anticapitalist ideology of the BPP, a point easily missed in the film. See House Committee on Internal Security, "Gun Barrel Politics: The Black Panther Party, 1966–1971," 92d Cong., 1st sess., 1971, H. Rept. 92–470.

59. Frightening parallels can be drawn between this strain of black thought and current reactionary discourses on the evils of affirmative action and black single motherhood.

Part V

Law, Feminism, and Politics

The essays in Part V examine the aftermath and legacies of the Civil Rights–Black Power Movement. Many African American women learned important lessons from their experiences in the movement and applied them in the social and political arenas. In the first half of the century there was little conflict between African American women's racial identity and feminist ideologies. However, after the emergence of Black Power and the increase in the male chauvinist and sexist attitudes and practices within civil rights organizations, as well as the rise of the Women's Liberation Movement, African American women became more aware of the potential for conflict between their racial consciousness and feminist values, and began to organize around issues and topics that reinforced their sense of "sisterhood."

Genna Rae McNeil presents a case study in the development of sisterhood among African American women. In 1974 Joan Little, an African American woman, killed her white prison guard in North Carolina when he attempted to assault her sexually. She fled the prison, but later turned herself in to the FBI. When news of Little's incarceration on charges of first-degree murder was publicized, it galvanized African American women who were veterans of the Civil Rights and Women's Liberation Movements. Little's confrontation with the criminal justice system dramatized women's and African Americans' right to resist state-sponsored oppression. In "'Joanne Is You and Joanne Is Me': A Consideration of African American Women and the 'Free Joan Little' Movement," McNeill documents the efforts of various women's groups and individuals from diverse social class and ideological backgrounds to obtain freedom for Joan Little. Participation in the Free Joanne Little Movement demonstrated to many African American women that "sisterhood is powerful."

Duchess Harris's essay, "From the Kennedy Commission to the Combahee Collective: Black Feminist Organizing, 1960–80," compares and contrasts the ideological positions and political agendas of black women involved in the President's Commission on the Status of Women (PCSW) in 1961 with those of the National Black Feminist Organization (NBFO) and the Combahee River Collective (CRC) in the 1970s. While the African American women appointed to the President's Commission emphasized the racial dimensions of their oppression in American society, the women who organized the NBFO and CRC were interested in attacking the problems of racism, sexism, and homophobia. Harris argues that each group's ideological positions were more radical than the group that preceded it, and during those years African American women became more aware of the complex relationships between racial identity and gender politics, and between sexual identity and feminist consciousness.

In the final essay, Linda Faye Williams examines "The Civil Rights–Black Power Legacy: Black Women Elected Officials at the Local, State, and National Levels." Using statistical and other types of data, Williams argues that despite black women's success in obtaining elective office, they are still underrepresented in local, state, and national legislative bodies given their proportion of the American population. Williams also points out that African American women seeking political office benefitted from the social changes brought about by the Civil Rights–Black Power and Women's Liberation Movements. Both movements taught women to be politically active and to take seriously their civic responsibilities. These movements laid the foundation for black women's entrance into mainstream politics; however, Williams also found that African American women legislators who came of age after the 1960s generally did not engage in civil rights and social welfare issues as did their predecessors. Focusing specifically on the political activism of Fannie Lou Hamer within the Democratic Party, and Elaine Brown, who served as chairperson for the Black Panther Party in the 1970s, Williams argues that for the future, African American women need to engage in mainstream, system-oriented politics as well as protests and demonstrations to bring about social, economic, and political advancement for African Americans in the twenty-first century.

Chapter 14

"Joanne Is You and Joanne Is Me"

A Consideration of African American Women and the "Free Joan Little" Movement, 1974–75

Genna Rae McNeil

> Joanne Little, she's my sister
> Joanne Little, she's our mama . . .
> Joanne's the woman
> Who's gonna carry your child . . .
> Joanne is you and
> Joanne is me
> Our prison is
> This whole society.
> —Bernice Johnson Reagon[1]

Joan Little, a twenty-year-old inmate in North Carolina's Beaufort County jail, stabbed Clarence Alligood. And in the early morning hours of August 27, 1974, she ran. About 5 feet 3 inches tall, weighing barely 120 pounds, Joan (pronounced Jo-Ann) Little was black, female, and poor. Clarence Alligood, who was closer to 5 feet 10 inches tall and weighed over 200 pounds, was Little's sixty-two-year-old white jailer. Little would later explain that the stabbing of Alligood was an act of resistance and self-defense. Moreover, she insisted that when she fled the jail she did not realize Alligood was dying. Little later testified that Alligood had come to the Beaufort County jail cell, where Little was being held awaiting disposition of a breaking and entering charge, and there her jailer, Alligood, forced her to perform oral sex. Alligood coerced her with an icepick, Little recounted. She made it a weapon of defense; then, she escaped. The memory of an injured Alligood yet vivid, Little hid in Washington, North Carolina, until she could decide what to do. Later coming to the jail, a colleague of Alligood discovered a bloody, partially nude Alligood dead with multiple stab wounds and a dried stream of semen on his thigh.

Declared a fugitive and suspected murderer, Little's life was particularly in jeopardy at the beginning of September 1974 because of an application from the authorities for the use of a Reconstruction era "Outlaw" statute. Contemplating a pending "shoot on sight" order and having read newspaper accounts of an intentional "brutal murder" of a night jailer who was acting "in the line of duty," Joan Little decided to seek assistance so that she might surrender somewhere outside of Beaufort County. On September 3, 1974, accompanied by supporters and attorneys, Jerry Paul and Karen Bethea Galloway, Little surrendered to the North Carolina State Bureau of Investigation (SBI). Following her surrender, rejecting Little's account of her act of resistance, the grand jury handed down an indictment of first-degree murder. Joan Little faced a penalty of death by execution.[2]

In the next year, Joan Little and her case slowly became a *cause celebre*. Lawyers and nonlawyers collaborated as a defense team to save Joan Little from execution. Mounting the most effective defense included devising a unique defense strategy. The controversy over the indictment further polarized eastern North Carolina racially; this required a change of venue. The attorneys viewed several other tasks as necessary and urgent, including selecting more scientifically a jury committed to the verdict of innocence unless guilt was proven beyond a reasonable doubt, reducing the charge from first-degree murder, and obtaining a lesser penalty than death by execution. In the sociopolitical context of the early 1970s, the legal team also understood that unless the public's consciousness was raised about the multiple injustices inherent in this case, Joan Little was at even greater risk. Support from the public at large could not be guaranteed by legal maneuvers alone. Therefore, attorneys Jerry Paul and Karen Galloway encouraged the development of a statewide, regional, and ultimately national movement to promote a fair trial, to raise funds for Little's defense, and "to free Joan Little." After a five-week trial, on August 15, 1975, Joan Little was acquitted by a jury of six African Americans and six whites.

Unprecedented in North Carolina's history, *State vs. Joan Little* es-

tablished a woman's right of self-defense against sexual assault and a
defendant's right to have a change of venue beyond the boundaries of
contiguous counties. It underscored, as well, the need for further
scrutiny of the law that gave police the power to slay a suspected
law-breaker. Within a few years, North Carolina's "Outlaw" statute
would be struck down.[3] For thousands of supporters and sympathizers, however, Joan Little's acquittal substantially represented the effective mobilization of progressive social organizations, networks of
activists, and movements for justice.[4]

Despite the prominence of Joan Little's case between the summer
of 1974 and 1975 and its discussion in both James Reston, Jr.'s *The Innocence of Joan Little* (New York, 1977) and Fred Harwell's *A True Deliverance* (New York, 1979), Joan Little's ordeal and the movement that
formed in response to her experiences of August 1974 have not been
the subject of a book-length historical study.[5] Such a study is a larger
work in progress.[6] This essay undertakes a more limited discussion of
Joan Little, African American women activists, conceptions of sisterhood, and the "Free Joan Little" Movement.

Joan Little, Self-Awareness, and Issues of Identity

> During my confinement . . . I've
> become more aware of myself than ever before.
> This means more than anything to me.
> —Joan Little[7]

When Joan Little decided to stand trial in North Carolina for the stabbing death of Clarence Alligood rather than go into exile, it committed her to both the fight of her life and fight for her life. From the moment of the media's coverage of Little's surrender and the inclusion
of photographs of this twenty-year-old black girl-woman, the question became "who is this girl and what is she to you?"[8]

Seeing her picture in North Carolina's newspapers, some could not
help but recognize that Joan Little was the embodiment of a particular intersection of race, sex, and class—namely, her African descent,
femaleness, and poverty—which constituted distinct disadvantages
in the United States, despite the presumption of innocence. Joan Little
illustrates historically what Karla Holloway maintained in *Codes of*

Conduct: Race, Ethics, and the Color of Our Character. "Giving [African-American women's] bodies . . . voices is a troubled enterprise."[9] It would be difficult for many observers to configure the truth and effectively move beyond the physical body to the holistic sense of personhood, when confronted with the image and reality of Joan Little. Indeed, any authentic awareness of Little's complexity and humanity was likely to develop only among her supporters, the defense team, and selected members of a jury.

Hearing about Little on the radio or seeing her image in the print media, some wondered aloud if Joan Little was to be considered a political prisoner, like the recently acquitted Angela Davis, or activists like the "Wilmington Ten," and the local civil rights leader Golden Frinks, whose protests frequently landed him in jail. Neither at the height of the national Civil Rights–Black Power Movement, which had experienced serious decline by the early 1970s, nor during the numerous civil rights confrontations in North Carolina, where attempts to end defacto segregation continued to come under attack, was Joan Little involved in civil rights activism.

Outside of organized protest movements, however, Joan Little chose to assert her right to equal treatment and the sanctity of her person. Although she did not become a political activist, in one important sense she engaged in a "political" act, the consequences of which reached far beyond her intent or personal ideology. As Robin D. G. Kelley argues, "'[p]olitics' comprises the many battles to roll back constraints and exercise some power over, or create some space within, the institutions and social relationships that dominate our lives."[10]

Joan Little mentally—and to some extent emotionally—had already created some space in her life for the exercise of a degree of freedom. Having made the decision to surrender on terms she and her lawyers established after her initial flight, Little was also taking steps to wrest some modicum of control from the oppressive white male authorities. Nevertheless, Little found herself physically confined again. This time, having been indicted for first-degree murder, she was held in Raleigh's correctional facility for women with bail set at $100,000. Joan Little would reflect upon her plight from behind bars throughout the fall of 1974 and into the winter of 1975.[11] During that same time, several groups began to mobilize for her defense and to gain better treatment for Little while incarcerated. The groups included the Free Joan Little Committee, the JoAnn Little Defense

Fund, the Commission for Racial Justice of the United Church of Christ (UCC), the Southern Christian Leadership Conference (SCLC), the Concerned Women for Fairness to JoAnn Little which later became the Concerned Women for Justice (CWJ), and the Southern Poverty Law Center (SPLC). A *Wall Street Journal* reporter covering the story witnessed the proliferation of support groups associated with Little, the many controversies that developed among them, and their varying approaches to soliciting support, and declared: "Differences of opinion over Miss Little's case are so wide, there isn't even agreement on how to spell or pronounce her name."[12]

The reporter's observation was cleverly phrased, but overly simplistic. One can effectively support a fair trial for an incarcerated person without knowing how that individual spelled her name or how she pronounced it. Even Joan and her mother Jessie Ruth Little gave voice to differences over the pronunciation of Joan's name. As that same journalist explained, "her mother says it's Joan, pronounced to rhyme with 'loan.'"[13] Perhaps the difference in the pronunciation of "Joan" may have been a manifestation of differences and distances that had developed over the years between mother and daughter.

Troubled Crossings: Joan Little's Personal Background

Joan Little was born on May 8, 1954 in Washington, North Carolina to Jessie Ruth Little and Willis Williams. While still a teenager, Jessie Little fell in love with Willis Williams, a young black man who worked as a laborer. Before that relationship soured, Jessie Little and Willis Williams had four children. The two eventually separated, and soon afterward Jessie Little married Arthur Williams (no relation), a lumber man. They had four children. Unfortunately, Arthur Williams was an alcoholic who contributed little to the family income. As a result, Jessie Little Williams was forced to work long hours outside the home as a factory or domestic worker. As she became older, Joan Little was expected to take care of her seven siblings, and although she was close to her mother, Joan resented her strict parenting style, and also was disturbed by Arthur Williams's drinking. By November 1968, truancy and rebelliousness on Joan's part prompted her mother Jessie Little Williams to request that a Beaufort County court send Joan to Dobb's Farm, a minimum security training school for youth, located outside of Washington, North Carolina. When Joan ran away from Dobb's Farm, her mother decided to seek her release and allowed her to move to the North with relatives to attend school in Philadelphia, Pennsylvania and Newark, New Jersey. Unfortunately, when Joan returned to North Carolina in 1970, her northern school records were not available. Rather than be placed in a grade she believed was below her level of attainment, Little dropped out of school.[14]

By the age of eighteen, Joan Little was on her own and working at low-paying jobs in eastern North Carolina. Falling in with the wrong crowd, she ran afoul of the law, and was arrested and charged with shoplifting and larceny, but was not convicted. Although she was employed at various jobs on and off, Little was arrested again, this time in 1974 in Greenville, North Carolina with her brother Jerome Little, on charges of breaking and entering. While out on bail she fled, but was later apprehended, and was being held in the Beaufort County jail, where she was attacked by her jailer Clarence Alligood.

By September 1974, Little had surrendered to the authorities in Raleigh, North Carolina. Having been charged with murder in Alligood's death, Joan Little concentrated on trying to make sense of where she was in light of whom she understood herself to be. Letters and conversations, testimony and statements to the press in 1974 and 1975 came from "Jo," "Joan," and "JoAnne." Placards of demonstrators, solicitations from fundraising committees, and supporters' written and mass-produced appeals exhibited similar variety in the spelling of Little's first name.[15] Naming is an important act; determining the name to which she would answer was important as well. Joan Little's frequent changing of the spelling of her name was telling, particularly when writing or preparing something to be read in public in support of her case. It suggested that despite some stubbornness, she was really a malleable young woman.

By the time of her Raleigh incarceration, Little had reached the point in her life when she wanted to be called JoAnne, not simply "Joan." She introduced herself with this pronunciation of her name and even wrote an important piece for the movement in her behalf over a signature that would assure her being called by the name she preferred. Joan Little, with Karen Galloway by her side, did handle the mainstream and alternative press extraordinarily well prior to the trial, and prior to any coaching for her testimony in court. This could be accounted for, according to Galloway, by understanding that Joan Little "spoke from the heart," was a smart young woman, and possessed obvious gifts, identifiable in her writing and in her voice when she articulated her own feelings and concerns.[16]

Thus, in the January 1975 issue of the alternative women's newspaper *off our backs*, Joan Little wrote about her growing self-awareness.

> During my confinement at [the] N[orth] C[arolina] C[orrectional] C[enter] [for] W[omen] and also while I was incarcerated in Beaufort County I've found that I've become more aware of myself than ever before. This means more than anything to me. I do a lot of reading and creative writing, also poetry and painting and drawing. . . . There are still times when all of this won't block the loneliness and anguish I feel, but there are others who are far worse off than I. . . . I have adequate time to get just that much closer to God. . . . It is people like you at *[off our backs]* and around the country that have given me the strength to go on.[17]

In the closing statement, she wrote, "In Sisterhood and the Struggle," and signed her name "JoAnne Little."

Little also published in that issue of *off our backs*, just below her letter, a "non-poem." It revealed even more about Little and her concerns:

> Do we need Life/death matter/criticized and laughed at? . . . /What's funny about no jobs and living/in roach filled two room shacks?. . . Life isn't what the man says on T.V. The people who have the power to change things aren't doing a thing. Drug traffic and conditions that breed/drug usage could be stopped . . . the lack of human dignity and respect . . . /A better life with better conditions and/opportunities for people don't have to be/just talk. . . . With a little effort this could/easily be reality. . . . This is not a poem but only facts.[18]

Little was concerned not only about reality and facts as she experienced them, but also about the "life and death matter" in which she had become both subject and object. She was vocal about several things in 1974, including her family, mother, and siblings, which helped to shaped her identity and constituted defining relationships. Little believed in the importance of being heard on the subject of the August 1974 incident and her upcoming trial.[19]

Little also felt that she was the best one to communicate the meaning of her actions in the jail and her subsequent escape. In *off our backs* she wrote, "though now it has been almost 4 months since the incident on the 27th of August and the death of Mr. Clarence Alligood: . . . I really feel bad . . . but what could I have done? . . . I acted on instinct. . . . I had no other choice."[20]

Sisterhood—"Any Woman Any Where"

My memory is, . . . when I said "Joanne is you/Joanne is me/Our prison is this whole society," it was like something had been unleashed in the culture. Women would just scream on that line . . .

Joan Little really showed me where my voice was on the issue. And when it happened she was in a situation of a Black woman with a white man. But what she opened for me was *any woman any where* who is violated.

—Bernice Reagon[21]

Joan Little, insistent upon her right to defend herself and to have a voice in discussions about her life, became a catalyst for the continuing movement toward African American and women's liberation. Whether explored, contested, assumed, celebrated, or detested, talk of "sisterhood" could not be completely ignored in 1974 and 1975. For African Americans, sisterhood presented challenges and opportunities. The realities of disadvantage and oppression in a society that privileged white males were becoming more apparent and less tolerable for women, regardless of race, ethnicity, class, or sexual orientation. When Joan Little's ordeal came to national attention, it was in the wake of continued FBI assaults upon civil rights and militant Black Power advocates and African American liberation groups, and only eight years after the founding of the National Organization for Women (NOW). In the same period, African Americans convened the National Black Political Convention. American citizens experienced other events relevant to women's issues and blacks' rights: the introduction of the Equal Rights Amendment (ERA), and a campaign for its ratification; the arrest, trial, and acquittal of Angela Davis; the Supreme Court decision in *Roe v. Wade* legalizing abortions; the founding of the National Black Feminist Organization; and a multiplicity of local struggles to eradicate racial oppression through desegregation, equal protection of the laws, equal opportunity in litigation, affirmative action, and nonviolent direct action protest.[22]

In significant numbers, women, African Americans, and non–African Americans, conscious of systemic racism and patriarchal dominance, were becoming aware of the need to develop appropriate analyses, consider different ideologies, and make concerted efforts to raise their own and others' political consciousness. Some women had been active participants in the Civil Rights–Black Power Movement, while others in the late 1960s and early 1970s took up the struggle against sexism and joined the emerging women's liberation movement. Still other women came to view Joan Little's plight as an authentic opportunity to consider the possibilities of "sisterhood" across racial and class lines through the development of an integrated women's alliance.[23]

An investigation of sisterhood provides rather obvious but also nuanced understandings of the contemporary relationships among women. Clearly, Little and other African American women could experience a "sisterhood" because their common history and experiences personified the intersection of race, gender, and class. Non–African American women, who perceived themselves as oppressed on account of sex, used the language of sisterhood to foster interracial participation in the women's liberation movement and to signify attempts to engage in a praxis of mutual interest and equality. As women's organizations interacted with one another within the context of the Free Joan Little (FJL) Movement, group leaders had to reexamine the concept of "sisterhood" in light of *State vs. Joan Little*. As a result, self-conscious recognition of *difference* created varying degrees of solidarity among women of diverse racial, socioeconomic, and personal backgrounds.

Forging the solidarity among African American women and the exploration of sisterhood with women regardless of race were not the primary goals of the "Free Joan Little" Movement. In the process of fighting for Joan Little's life, fair trial, and freedom, however, five African American women activists who had begun their political activism in the Civil Rights–Black Power Movement arrived at new interpretations of sisterhood.[24]

One of the first activists to recognize the importance of understanding and embracing the reality of sisterhood with Joan Little was Karen Bethea Galloway, a young Duke University Law School graduate and new member of Jerry Paul's Durham law firm who was assigned to the case. Shortly after agreeing to handle Little's case with Jerry Paul on a *pro bono* basis, Galloway quickly learned that public support and voices of experience were vital to Little's defense. Accordingly, not only Karen Galloway, but also the recently acquitted political prisoner Angela Davis, former SNCC activist Bernice Johnson Reagon, the radical leader of the National Alliance Against Racist and Political Repression (NARPR) Charlene Mitchell, and local civil rights organizer Christine Strudwick, each demonstrated in vital ways what they deemed "sisterly" in this situation.[25]

Karen Galloway related to Joan in two different ways. Initially, they had more of a "sibling relationship" than one of lawyer-client. Karen Galloway was only a few years older than Joan Little and about the same size. After being mistaken for Joan Little several times, Karen Galloway grew accustomed to serving her client by identifying as closely as she could with Little. Karen recalled readily that she felt "Joan was like a sister," in part because they were both African American women and also because they were close in age. Galloway was convinced that, but for her parents and the privileges of her upbringing, she could have been in Joan's place.[26]

Angela Davis was among the many African American women, including Charlene Mitchell and Bernice Johnson Reagon, who were compelled on ideological and personal grounds to demand the freedom of Joan Little and view Little's plight as symptomatic of societal ills stemming from racist, sexist, and economic discrimination. Davis was committed to these causes because of her sense of gratitude to those who had championed her cause as a political prisoner only a few years before. Davis also had a desire to participate in struggles to clarify her own ideological stance and to engage in an ongoing critique of her political activism. Davis, Charlene Mitchell, and Bernice Johnson Reagon were long-time opponents of racial injustice and were then developing their stances on the problem of sexual oppression, and they saw in the Little case several social justice issues that deserved greater attention. Initially coming to the case primarily out of ideological concerns, Davis had the opportunity to get to know Joan Little personally. Davis had been asked to help Little prepare for the trial and was able to offer invaluable assistance.[27]

> I found out about the case from Reverend Ben Chavis in 1974. We discovered in the course of doing work around the 'Wilmington 10' case that North Carolina had the largest proportion of imprisoned people, the largest number—proportionately speaking—of people on death row, the largest number of political prisoners. And it was in the midst

of doing this work, focusing on North Carolina that we learned about the Joan Little case.

For some time I had been interested in finding ways of raising issues of gender in connection with the antiracist work that we were doing. And, of course, in a way that did not reflect the tendency to absolutize gender that was apparent in the white middle class women's movement.

Although Angela Davis had been concerned about the role of sexual assault and violence against women in history, and addressed those issues in articles about Joan Little, she commented that

I can't say that was the reason why I was attracted to the case. *It was a sister who obviously was in need of assistance* and because of the successful outcome of my case, I had committed myself to doing whatever I could to help organize movements around the case of other individuals. So I wasn't thinking . . . that there's the case that allows us to deal with all these issues together. That became clear after having basically made a commitment to do work around the case.[28]

Within the context of the failure of a white jailer to maintain a professional distance and meet professional responsibilities in the Beaufort County jail, Little, although a victim, refused on August 27, 1974 to be further victimized. This time, regardless of her incarceration, her past, others' view of her actions, or the value placed on her life, Davis believed that Little had resisted sexual assault and had a right to do so. "It was very important to me to use whatever influence I had that largely developed from the movement organized by people in support of my freedom to use that in a sisterly way" in the case of Joan Little. In addition, despite differences in background and adult experiences, Angela Davis developed a personal relationship with Joan Little. "I felt it was important to try and cross boundaries, and not only be a spokesperson for Joan Little, but to develop a relationship with her."[29]

It should be noted that the personal relationship Angela Davis shared with Joan Little did not in isolation affect Little's representation of herself in the courtroom or preparation for her trial. Attorneys Jerry Paul and Karen Galloway had agreed that Angela Davis's assistance should be enlisted because each was concerned about not only securing a "not guilty" verdict, but also assuring that Little's presentation of her identity would help, not hinder them, in obtaining such a verdict. Paul and Galloway understood the performative elements of a trial and the political as well as racial nature of such a public sphere. Paul emphasized adequate (but not excessive) rehearsal and some emulation of Karen Galloway's demeanor by a defendant, whose identity was to some extent a work in progress and whose very body and image could be seen as contesting her testimony.[30]

Galloway, although somewhat uncomfortable with her status as "role model," both sympathized and empathized with Joan Little. In fact, Karen Galloway (Bethea-Shields) years later recalled relating to Joan Little in several ways. The initial "sibling relationship" later gave way to a more difficult lawyer-client encounter because Galloway had the serious responsibility, with the other lawyers and Angela Davis, of preparing Little for a first-degree murder trial. The easy give and take of two young African American women, who sometimes were mistaken for one another, of necessity came to an end as the trial date approached. Galloway had professional responsibilities to her client that required a "no-nonsense" approach. Little experienced Galloway during the summer of 1975 as "demanding," while Galloway as attorney recognized that Little's life literally depended upon the assistance she could render for the defense team and Little's growing number of supporters.[31]

One of Joan Little's most vocal supporters was Bernice Johnson Reagon, former Student Nonviolent Coordinating Committee (SNCC) activist and founder of the musical group "Sweet Honey in the Rock." Reagon discovered that the various incidents that led to her involvement in the Civil Rights Movement provided her with startling insights into Joan Little's identity and a special sympathy for her plight. Joan Little's act of resistance as a woman revealed to Reagon the commonalities of all women in that their bodies have the potential to be both sites of conquest and effective instruments of resistance to violation. Reagon first met Joan Little in Washington, DC, where Sweet Honey in the Rock had been invited to a rally to sing the song "Joanne Little." Bernice Reagon recalled that Little spoke about being hunted for the murder of the jailer, who was described as having acted "in the line of duty." "Little talked about being between the mattresses in a house when the sheriff came in, when they were looking for her. And I thought, 'Oh God, this is really something.'"[32] Yet Reagon also remembered that "we sang the song and Joan Little came up. . . . She was this little woman and she . . . told us to 'help Jerry.' It was like she was saying help Jerry because

Jerry is helping me. . . . And she was not quite yet standing on the ground her experience had placed her."[33]

Bernice Reagon became involved in the political work to "Free Joan Little." Bernice Reagon wrote and performed the song, "Joanne Little," which became the anthem for the Free Joan Little Movement. Reagon recalled that

> people seemed to plug into the part of the song in that second verse, which is like the declaration of stance. "What did she do to deserve this name? Killed a man that thought she was fair game. When I heard the news I screamed inside. Lost my cool. My anger I could not hide. Joanne is you. Joanne is me. Our prison is this whole society." It was like something had been unleashed in the culture.[34]

The particular genius of Bernice Reagon's song, "Joanne Little," was its capacity to galvanize all of Little's supporters, regardless of their degree of political consciousness or sophistication. This narrative and its refrain implicitly gave recognition to sisterhood in various manifestations, especially for persons of African descent and for women, regardless of race. It allowed the singer/activist to create for herself and others a space that could be occupied with Joan Little, the victim and resister. Reagon's lyrics contained progressive and critically conscious meanings that served to establish linkages and relationships among activists. The lyrics offered a way of understanding commonalities and sisterhood through personal identification.[35]

"Sisterhood" manifested itself in ways that were different, but indispensable, to the FJL Movement. The relationship between the Concerned Women for Justice (CWJ), a grassroots civil and human rights organization, and the National Alliance Against Racist and Political Repression (NAARPR) also deserves scrutiny. While the CWJ was predominantly African American female and Christian, the NAARPR was an interracial, ideologically diverse network of experienced activists ranging from old-fashioned liberals to communists, and was headed by an African American woman, Charlene Mitchell. The CWJ's official history noted the group's earlier name, "Concerned Women for Fairness to JoAnn Little," that was changed in November 1974 to "Concerned Women for Justice."[36]

After several meetings in 1974 with Joan Little and one with her mother Jessie Williams, Mrs. Christine Strudwick, later CWJ's second vice president, recalled that she felt an indisputable closeness to Joan, a young "sister" who was victimized by harsh conditions of life, but one for whom there was still hope and a future. "I kind of felt like Joan could have been one of my daughters and was caught up in a situation, that she really had no control, as far as finance was concerned."[37] Strudwick enthusiastically supported CWJ's goals as expressed by Armenta Eaton, a founding member and secretary to the N.C.–VA branch of the United Church of Christ's Commission on Racial Justice. The CWJ's objectives were to "raise money, give some to the legal defense, [and] some to the mobilization. To give Joan moral support, write and visit her when we could, and help [her mother] Jessie Williams."[38]

The members of CWJ, led by another founder, Velma Hopkins, viewed Little as a sister and/or daughter for whom they had some responsibility. They recognized that the difficulties of living in poverty, being African American and young, without adequate education or a well-paying job, were compounded by the family's poverty and desperate need for the income that Joan, as the eldest daughter, could provide. They also felt a special kinship with Joan's mother, Jessie Williams, since so many CWJ members themselves were close to her age and also had daughters. Beyond this, they felt it consistent with their Christian duty to visit and aid women at the Central Women's Correctional Facility of North Carolina.[39] Sisterhood was familiar and even comfortable for these women, who easily related to other African American women as "sisters" because of their common racial and religious backgrounds.[40]

In contrast, the NAARPR placed little emphasis on religion and focused primarily on race insofar as racism contributed to repression and oppression in the United States. Interestingly, the first director of the NAARPR was Charlene Mitchell, an African American woman, a political radical, and close friend of Angela Davis. Mitchell's relationship with Angela Davis, and the NAARPR's on going political activity in North Carolina, made the case of Joan Little attractive for the group. Mitchell's identification with yet another African American woman and the compelling issues involved made Little's case perfect for the alliance.[41]

Charlene Mitchell traveled to North Carolina in 1974 to discuss the matter with Jerry Paul and Karen Galloway, and later recalled that "When we [in the Alliance] heard about the Joan Little case, it came in the midst of this whole thing of assault on African Americans in North Carolina. And we were trying to determine our position on the death penalty." Mitchell believed that

> the charge that Joan Little had killed her jailer brought together [many issues]: the prison system, how women were treated, the right of guards and sheriffs to rape their prisoners without fear of themselves being tried for it; the whole way in which racism worked in this whole process; that white men were never convicted of raping Black women; you know it just went on and on.

The prosecution had suggested that Little had given her consent to the sexual relationship with the jailer. Mitchell flatly disagreed.

> No one can ever consent to have anything to do with their jailer. Any relationship is one of unequals and therefore consent is out of the question. And so we weren't dealing with whether the problem is that she was having sex with agreement or not. That wasn't the point. There was a weapon involved and this man was doing something that he had no business doing and he ended up dead, and it was his fault. Therefore she could not be accused of murder.[42]

Within the context of defining "sisterhood," public support and financial resources for Joan Little also came from members of the organized lesbian and feminist communities. Many women viewed oppression as the common concern; moreover, some lesbians, regardless of race, identified their oppression due to sexual orientation as an additional motive for political organization. Lesbian groups, such as the Alliance of Lesbian Feminists of Atlanta (ALFA) and North Carolina's Triangle Area Lesbian Feminists, found it politically beneficial to include themselves among the active supporters of Joan Little. In 1966, African American women, including politician Shirley Chisholm and attorney Pauli Murray, were among the founders of the leading feminist organization, the National Organization for Women (NOW); and in 1975, it was NOW's Rape Task Force leader, Mary Ann Largen, who enthusiastically supported Joan Little's cause. After making contact with attorney Karen Galloway, Largen organized NOW's special solicitations on Little's behalf.[43]

A demonstrated sisterhood forged through a common commitment to civil and human rights did not alone bring women together in Little's defense. Angela Davis's article in *Ms.* magazine in June 1975 openly challenged men and women—regardless of race—to recognize their relationship to Joan Little. Writing at the invitation of the magazine's editor Gloria Steinem, Angela Davis's article "JoAnne Little: The Dialectics of Rape" generated new and important interest in the case, particularly among women's groups throughout the country. In the article Davis presented a nuanced, antiracist, and inclusive argument on Little's behalf, and ended with a call to action.

> If justice is to prevail, there must be a struggle. And the only force powerful enough to reverse the normal repressive course of events is the organized might of great numbers of people. Protests have already erupted. Mass actions have been organized in North Carolina—both by black community groups and women's organizations. The North Carolina Alliance Against Racist and Political Repression and the Southern Poverty Law Center . . . [are] vigorously supporting Sister JoAnne.[44]

Davis also maintained that

> rape is not one dimensional and homogeneous; but one feature that does remain constant is the overt and flagrant treatment of women, through rape, as property. . . . The oppression of women is a vital and integral component of a larger network of oppression . . . so male supremacy is . . . essential to its smooth operation. It is in the interest of the ruling class to cultivate the patriarchal domination of women.

Davis forcefully concluded

> JoAnne Little may not only have been the victim of a rape attempt by a white racist jailer, she has truly been raped and wronged many times over by the exploitation and discriminatory institutions of this society. All people who see themselves as members of existing communities of struggle for justice, equality, and progress have a responsibility to fulfill toward Joanne Little.[45]

The wide range of organizations supporting and working to free Joan Little proved critical to the progress of the defense and her eventual acquittal. Among women it was significant that Little was supported by Concerned Women for Justice (CWJ) as well as the National Organization for Women (NOW). At the same time, many African Americans became aware that Joan Little's defense movement encompassed a broad range of black organizations, including black church congregations, women's church groups, the Southern Christian Leadership Conference (SCLC), members of the black press, cultural nationalists and their organizations, such as Haki Madhubuti, Maulana (Ron)

Karenga, Amiri Baraka, Bibi Amina Baraka, and the Black Women's United Front, as well as revolutionary nationalists in the Black Panther Party.[46]

Organizations must transform individuals' feelings and ideologies into purposeful collective actions to bring about social and political change. The significance of *State vs. Joan Little*, Joan Little, and the Free Joan Little Movement for understanding the Civil Rights–Black Power Movement is inextricably linked to her symbolic representation of the right to resist oppression. The fluidity of the identification, unbound by a particular ideology, allowed a host of activists and organizations to coalesce around her cause and the movement for her freedom. For many African American women, Joan Little was the dramatic symbol, and the Free Joan Little Movement became the appropriate site, for raising feminist consciousness and strengthening the bonds of sisterhood.

> Joanne Little, she's my sister . . .
> Joanne Little, she's our mama . . .
> Joanne is you and
> Joanne is me.

NOTES

1. Excerpts from Bernice Johnson Reagon, "Joanne Little," song recorded for the album *Give Your Hands to Struggle* (Brooklyn, ca. 1975); later rerecorded and released on a 45 RPM recording to raise funds for the Joanne Little Defense Fund. "Recording in Prisons," Box 25, Archives of Atlanta Lesbian Feminist Alliance [ALFA], Special Collections Library, Duke University, Durham, NC.

2. Jerry Alligood, "Police Seek Woman in Jail Slaying," *Raleigh News and Observer* (hereinafter N&O), August 28, 1974, 49; and Ashley Futrell, "Brutal Murder" (editorial commentary), *Washington (North Carolina) Daily News*, August 28, 1974; see Joan Little, "Testimony on Direct and Re-direct Examination," *State vs. Joan Little*, transcript (hereafter Trial Transcript), Papers of James Reston, Southern Historical Collection (SHC), University of North Carolina at Chapel Hill (UNC-CH). See also Fred Harwell, *A True Deliverance* (New York: Alfred A. Knopf, 1980, 86–89; and James Reston, Jr., *The Innocence of Joan Little: A Southern Mystery* (New York: Times Books, 1977); and Julian Bond, former president (1974–75) Southern Poverty Law Center, interview with the author, February 23, 1996, Washington, D.C.

3. Jerry Paul, interview with the author, Virginia Beach, VA, March 29,

276 GENNA RAE McNEIL

1996; Marvin Miller, interview with the author, April 1, 1996, Alexandria, VA; Karen Bethea Galloway-Shields, interview with the author, March 2, 1993, April 21, 1994, March 21, 1996 and August 8, 1996, Durham, NC. For contemporary press discussions, see, e.g., "Jury Verdict Based on Evidence" (editorial), (N&O), August 17, 1975 (clipping), Papers of Hamilton H. Hobgood, SHC, UNC-CH. Regarding the "Outlaw" Statute of North Carolina originally passed in 1866, it was struck down by a three-judge federal panel in 1975; see Neal Yancey, "Outlaw Statute Struck Down," *Spectator*, October 1, 1981.

4. See, for example, "Message sent to Joann [sic] after her victory" and press release issued by National Office of National Organization for Women (NOW) following Little's acquittal, Carton 31, Public Information Office, Subject: Little, Joan case, NOW Papers, Schlesinger Library, Radcliffe College; and "Alliance Hails Joann Little Verdict as Peoples' Victory," press release, August 15, 1975, Archives of National Alliance Against Racist and Political Repression, New York. See also Angela Y. Davis, interview with the author, June 7, 1994, Santa Cruz, CA; Armenta Eaton (United Church of Christ [UCC] and Concerned Women for Justice [CWJ]), interview with the author, April 25, 1996, Louisburg, NC; Golden Frinks, Southern Christian Leadership Conference, (SCLC) interview with the author, March 28, 1996, Edenton, NC; Bennie Rountree, interview with the author, March 28, 1996, Greenville, NC; Christine Strudwick (CWJ), interview with the author, March 19, 1996, Durham, NC; and Leon White, Commission for Racial Justice, UCC, interview with the author, July 17, 1996, Raleigh, NC.

5. See Melton McLaurin's *Celia a Slave* (Athens: University of Georgia Press, 1991); and A. Leon Higginbotham, "Race, Sex, Education and Missouri Jurisprudence," *Washington University Law Quarterly* 67, no. 3 (1989): 680–96.

6. This essay is part of a larger study, which will explore in considerable detail three interrelated topics. First, the multiplicative nature of African American female identities and relationships, resulting from the intersection of race, class, culture, and gender that function as "axes of stratification." Second, it will examine the case of *State* vs. *Joan Little* and the "Free Joan Little" Movement and their contribution to an historical explanation of African Americans' pattern of resort to the courts to seek justice. I argue that such conduct affirmed African Americans' self-definition through a cultural critique rooted in their unique experience and history. Third, the study will focus on the symbolic construction of a nonrevolutionary social movement, Joan Little as a symbol, *State* vs. *Joan Little* as a *cause celebre*, and the importance of social and cultural processes in community formation.

7. JoAnne [sic] Little, "Self-aware" Dec. 29, 1974, *off our backs* (January 1975), Newspaper Clippings, Joan Little series, Hobgood Papers, SHC, UNC-CH.

8. Excerpt from Bernice Johnson Reagon, "JoAnne Little," 45 RPM Recording, "Recording in Prisons" file, ALFA Archives.

9. Karla Holloway, *Codes of Conduct: Race, Ethics, and the Color of Our Character* (New Brunswick: Rutgers University Press, 1995), 48.

10. Robin D. G. Kelley, *Race Rebels: Culture, Politics, and the Black Working Class* (New York: Free Press, 1994), 9–10.

11. See Wayne King, "Killing of Carolina Jailer, Charged to Woman, Raises Question of Abuse of Inmates," *New York Times*, December 1, 1974, 41.

12. Bernard E. Garnett, "Black Woman's Trial in North Carolina Splits Rights Groups," *Wall Street Journal*, April 18, 1975, 1.

13. Ibid.

14. See Harwell, *A True Deliverance*, 21–34; Karen Bethea Galloway-Shields, interview with the author, March 2, 1993, April 21, 1994, and March 21, 1996; Jerry Paul, interview with the author, March 29, 1996; Reston, *The Innocence of Joan Little*, 281–93; Christine Strudwick, interview with the author, March 19, 1996; Bennie Rountree, interview with the author, March 28, 1996; and see also Angela Y. Davis, "Forum: Joanne Little—the Dialectics of Rape," *Ms.* 3, no. 12 (June 1975): 74–77.

15. Karen Bethea Galloway-Shields, interviews with the author, March 21 and August 8, 1996; Reston, *The Innocence of Joan Little*, 112–13; and Harwell, *A True Deliverance*.

16. Karen Bethea Galloway-Shields, interviews with the author, March 21 and August 8, 1996. Bethea Galloway-Shields emphasized that Little was not told "what to say," but rather advised regarding that which would jeopardize her defense.

17. JoAnne Little, "Self-aware."

18. JoAnne Little, "Not a poem," in *off our backs* (January 1975), in "Newspaper Clippings," Joanne Little series, Hobgood Papers, SHC, UNC-CH.

19. Christine Strudwick, interview with the author, March 9, 1996 and Karen Bethea Galloway-Shields, interviews with the author, March 21, and August 8, 1996.

20. JoAnne Little, "Self-aware."

21. Bernice Johnson Reagon, interview with the author, July 28, 1994, Washington, DC.

22. See Manning Marable, *Race Reform and Rebellion: The Second Reconstruction in Black America, 1945–1990*, 2d rev. ed. (Jackson: University Press of Mississippi, 1991), 114–76; Mary Frances Berry, *Why ERA Failed: Politics, Women's Rights, and the Amending Process of the Constitution* (Bloomington: Indiana University Press, 1986), 56–89; Toni Carabillo et al., *Feminist Chronicles, 1953–1993* (Los Angeles: Women's Graphics, 1993), 48–73.

23. Paula Giddings, *When and Where I Enter: The Impact of Black Women on Race and Sex in America* (New York: William Morrow, 1984), 277–348; Berry, *Why ERA Failed*, 56–89; D. C. Hine and Kathleen Thompson, *A Shining Thread of Hope: The History of Black Women in America* (New York: Broadway Books, 1998),

296–319; Nancy Woloch, *Women and the American Experience*, vol. II, 2d ed. (New York: McGraw-Hill, 1994); and Sara Evans, *Personal Politics: The Roots of Women's Liberation in the Civil Rights Movement and the New Left* (New York: Vintage Books, 1980). See also Robin Morgan, *Sisterhood Is Powerful: An Anthology of Writings from the Women's Liberation Movement* (New York: Vintage Books, 1970).

24. Angela Davis, Karen Bethea Galloway-Shields, Bernice Johnson Reagon, Charlene Mitchell, and Christine Strudwick, interviews with author, cited above.

25. Karen Bethea Galloway-Shields, interviews with the author, March 2, 1993, April 21, 1994, March 21 and August 8, 1996; Jerry Paul, interview with the author, March 29, 1996; and Angela Y. Davis, interview with the author, June 7, 1994.

26. Karen Bethea Galloway-Shields, interviews with the author, March 2, 1993, April 24, 1994, March 21, 1996 and August 8, 1996; Bethea Galloway-Shields stressed her own identification with Little and the development of a bond "like sisters." She also mentioned that given the commonalties in black women's experiences, the defense team decided to rely in part on the particular history of African American women in developing the defense of Joan Little.

27. Angela Y. Davis, interview with the author, June 7, 1994. Davis was willing to help prepare Little for her testimony for reasons of "sisterhood," their common experience of incarceration, and her views on the rights of political prisoners.

28. Ibid.

29. Ibid.

30. Holloway, *Codes of Conduct*, 45, 41–46.

31. Contrary to discussions found in Harwell's *A True Deliverance* (185), and Reston's *The Innocence of Joan Little* (64), Karen Galloway neither played a mere "symbolic" role until the end of the trial, nor was she the prime mover in a "brainwashing" scheme developed by the Little's attorneys to support a self-defense argument. According to accounts of the attorneys on the defense team, Karen Galloway served as a confidante and "sister" to Joan, as well as lawyer and press handler. While Galloway's inexperience was somewhat of a disadvantage, her capacity to relate to Joan in multiple ways enabled the defense team to function more effectively. (At the time neither Galloway nor Paul was overly concerned about Little's inability to pay any fees. The firm was functioning well and another partner was handling other cases.)

32. Bernice Johnson Reagon, interview with the author, July 28, 1994.

33. Ibid.

34. Ibid.

35. Ibid.

36. "The History of Concerned Women for Justice, Inc. (CWJ)," n.d., typescript, 1, Papers of Rosanelle Eaton and Armenta Eaton.

37. Christine Strudwick, interview with the author, March 19, 1996.

38. Armenta Eaton, interview with the author, April 25, 1996.

39. Ibid., Christine Strudwick, interview with the author, March 19, 1996. See also "The History of Concerned Women."

40. Black Baptist women's relationships among themselves during an earlier era are discussed in Evelyn Brooks Higginbotham, *Righteous Discontent: The Women's Movement in the Black Baptist Church, 1880–1920* (Cambridge: Harvard University Press, 1993).

41. Charlene Mitchell, interview with the author, August 11, 1995.

42. Ibid.; see also Richard Ford Thompson, "The Boundaries of Race: Political Geography in Legal Analysis," in *Critical Race Theory: The Key Writings that Formed the Movement*, Kimberle Crenshaw et al., eds. (New York: The New Press, 1995), 456, 459.

43. ALFA Archives, Duke University, Durham, NC. For discussions of the women's movement and legal issues, see Jane S. DeHart, "The New Feminism and the Dynamics of Social Change," in *Women's America*, 5th ed. (New York: Oxford University Press, 2000), 589–617; and Joan Hoff-Wilson, *Law, Gender, and Injustice* (New York: New York University Press, 1991), and NOW Papers.

44. Davis, "Forum: Joanne Little—the Dialectics of Rape," 77, 107, 108. See Evelyn Brooks Higginbotham, "African-American Women's History and the Metalanguage of Race," *Signs* 17 (Winter 1992): 251–74, and "Sexual Harassment" in D. C. Hine, Rosalyn Terborg-Penn, and Elsa Barkley Brown, eds., *Black Women in America: An Historical Encyclopedia* (Brooklyn, NY: Carlson Publishing, 1993), 1023–26.

45. Davis, "Forum: Joanne Little—the Dialectics of Rape," 77.

46. For another view of the black activist supporters of the Free Joanne Little Movement, see Komozi Woodard, *A Nation Within a Nation: Amiri Baraka (LeRoi Jones) and Black Power Politics* (Chapel Hill: University of North Carolina Press, 1999), 181–84.

Chapter 15

From the Kennedy Commission to the Combahee Collective

Black Feminist Organizing, 1960–80

Duchess Harris

Black and Lavender

I am Black
  and lavender
 is the color
 that I wear (proudly)
 Inside my heart.
We are Black
  and lavender
 and remain against all rhyme
 and reason has no answer
 except—we love who we know
 and know who we love
We are the old gay bulldagger
 in Sunday-go-to-meetin' suit
 with pointed brown-toed shoes
 packing it big
 behind the straining zipper
We are the two poets who died of cancer
 leaving a legacy of words
 to heal
 our still, beating hearts
We are the author who is coming out
 slowly
 and the actress
 who hides behind the blessed vow
We are the bitch with attitude
 the shy folk singer

the female athletes
and the ordained bishop
We are a joyous woman, stirring
We black women
Who dare love women
We seem a mystery and
a contradiction
and our drums are
Beating . . . beating . . . beating . . .
—Margaret Sloan-Hunter, founding member,
National Black Feminist Organization[1]

Anna Julia Cooper, a nineteenth-century black public intellectual, coined a phrase that has been useful in analyzing "the intersectional experience of racism and sexism."[2] In *A Voice from the South*, Cooper criticized black leaders for claiming to speak for the race but failing to include black women. Referring to Martin Delany's public claims that where he was allowed to enter, the race entered with him, Cooper countered: "Only the Black woman can say, when and where I enter. . . . Then the Negro race enters with me."[3]

I use Anna Julia Cooper as my point of departure because Paula Giddings used the phrase "when and where I enter" as the title of one of the most influential works that situate black women within American and African American political discourse. In *When and Where I Enter: The Impact of Black Women on Race and Sex in America* (1984), Giddings explored the role of black women in the history and politics of black liberation from the era of slavery to the election of Shirley Chisholm to the U.S. Congress in 1968. Giddings pointed out that black men articulated a political agenda in 1963 at the March on Washington, and Betty Friedan's *The Feminine Mystique*, published in 1966, provided a political agenda for middle-class white women, and Giddings asked, "who has presented the political agenda for Black women?"[4] Giddings did not answer her own question, and thus this is when and where I enter.

This essay compares the ideological positions and political agendas of the black women who were appointed to the Fourth Consultation of President John F. Kennedy's Commission on the Status of

Women (PCSW) to those of the women in the National Black Feminist Organization (NBFO) and in the Combahee River Collective (CRC). In examining the ideological and political perspectives of these three black women's groups, we can document the evolution of black feminism from 1961 to 1980. The varied experiences of black women activists served as the crucible for the development of black feminist ideologies during that period. The first group was composed of financially and educationally privileged black women chosen by officials of the federal government to serve on a national commission on women, while the other two included middle- and working-class black women who had been active in civil rights and grassroots black organizations. This study examines the political activities of these black women and their organizations, and reveals that despite differences in education and social class background, they were aware of three overlapping realities: (1) there were inextricable links between gender and racial identity; (2) their socioeconomic status was overdetermined by gender and racial identity; and (3) there was a need to organize collectively on the basis of these realizations.

This research reveals that each group's ideological perspectives were more inclusive than those of their predecessors. The black women on the Kennedy Commission articulated more conservative notions about gender than the women of the National Black Feminist Organization (NBFO) who, in turn, articulated more conservative notions about female sexuality and the disadvantages of the capitalist system than the women of the Combahee River Collective. Unlike the women of the Kennedy Commission and the NBFO, those members of the Combahee River Collective recognized that one's sexual orientation was distinctive and separate from gender and racial identity, and they organized around that realization.

The black feminist movement can be seen as moving from the relatively liberal and univocal focus on gender of the Presidential Commission to the more radical and polyvocal focus on gender, race, class, and sexual orientation of the Combahee River Collective. This study makes it clear that the later groups existed as a result of the efforts of the earlier ones, and that there was significant overlap in membership. Moreover, the ideological development among black feminists coincided with the growth of the Civil Rights–Black Power and Women's Liberation movements, to which they made important contributions.

Also in contrast to their predecessors, the newer generation of black feminists were more radical, and created small consciousness-raising groups rather than large formal institutions. Many of these young women came from middle-class backgrounds and had worked in the South for the Student Nonviolent Coordinating Committee (SNCC). Some of these black feminists had been members of Students for a Democratic Society (SDS) and other radical student organizations in the North.

Oral History as Evidence

Oral histories and analyses of archival data are used to document these three groups. The minutes from the Negro Women's Consultation for the PCSW are located at the John F. Kennedy Library in Boston, and the minutes from the Combahee River Collective retreats were provided by Gloria Akasha Hull, along with the mission statements, pamphlets, and other published and unpublished materials. I also used the Pauli Murray Papers from the Schlesinger Library and material from the Black Women's Oral History Project, as well as secondary sources, journal articles, and newspapers. The archival data are important because they contain the public records of these groups; however, one limitation is that these public statements often do not indicate the personal experiences and responses of the people involved.

To fill in this gap, oral histories from eleven black women were collected. These interviews are important because black women's lived experience is treated as a primary source in the study. Albert Memmi has noted that what is central to "race theory" is the interpretation of difference and what inferences may be drawn from it.[5] Taking Memmi's suggestion, I asked for these women's interpretations of political organizing between 1960 and 1980 and drew my own inferences from the transcripts. Like historian Evelyn Brooks Higginbotham, I found that race served as a "metalanguage" for the construction and representation of other social and power relations, namely, those based on gender, class, and sexuality.[6] Oral history becomes an important source of evidence because it allows us to examine what theorists have described as the particular epistemological position of black women in American society, a position that feminist literary critic Patricia Hill Collins refers to as the "outsider within."[7] Using a black feminist theoretical framework to understand the roles of black women allows us to determine *whose* knowledge defines black women. According to C. S'thembile West, ontology is the essence of be-ing: "How I be; Who I be; What I be; not how I am or who I am or what I am"; and the black woman must decide how she defines herself. To outsiders this conjugation of the auxiliary verb appears to be "improper grammar," but West argues that only the black woman can tell you what is improper about her defining her be-ing.[8]

If black women reject others' definition of them, they must then define or redefine their own being and provide their own theories of being or ontologies. Historically, black women's being has depended on the balance between self and community, for without the individual there is no community, and with the community there is no individual. Black women's resistance to being defined by others can be documented through an examination of their personal narratives. Letters, autobiographies, oral histories, and personal narratives provide a rich source of data for understanding and interpreting black feminist ontologies. Research that reveals the social, political, and economic context for these narratives provides the historical background for explaining black feminist theory, which is thus grounded in black women's experiences.[9]

In this essay the narratives constructed by the members of three black women's groups, the Fourth Consultation of the PCSW, NBFO, and CRC, are used to examine the transformation in black feminist ideologies from the Civil Rights Era to the preoccupation with the politics of identity in the 1980s.[10]

The PCSW and NOW: Precursors to NBFO and Combahee

In 1961, several years before the emergence of a vigorous second wave of feminism in the United States, President John F. Kennedy established the President's Commission on the Status of Women. It met for two years and submitted its report in 1963. As Betty Friedan wrote in 1963, "the very existence of the President's Commission on the Status of Women, under Eleanor Roosevelt's leadership creates a climate where it is possible to recognize and do something about discrimination against women, in terms not only of pay, but of subtle barriers to opportunity."[11] In order to cover some areas in depth, the Kennedy

Commission designated four consultative bodies, one on private employment opportunities, a second on new patterns of volunteer work, a third on portrayals of women in the media, and the fourth on "the problems of Negro women."

The "Consultation on Negro Women," headed by the National Council of Negro Women president Dorothy I. Height, was the first occasion on which the executive branch of the federal government gave special attention to black women. The persons attending the fourth consulting group were educators, editors of black magazines, representatives of the National Urban League, and governmental officials. Although the black women who participated on the commission were in no way either economically or educationally representative of most black women at the time, their ideological perspectives were relevant and their political agendas were significant.[12]

Novelist Toni Morrison declared that professional, educated black women were considered by many to be "irrationality in the flesh," and were not recognized in the glossary of racial tropes.[13] Literary critic Rose Brewer suggested that this was a reflection of educated black women's "polyvocality of multiple social locations."[14] This notion of holding multiple social locations has meant that well-educated, middle-class black women, such as those appointed to the President's Commission for the Status of Women, often came from underprivileged backgrounds and thus could serve as advocates for the masses of black women who were among the working poor. For example, in the case of the black women on the Kennedy Commission, they raised strong objections to the idea of forcing the mothers in families receiving Aid to Families with Dependent Children (AFDC) to work outside the home. Although they were empathetic toward women and families in poverty, the black women on the PCSW believed that the solution to the economic problems facing poor black women was to eliminate employment discrimination against black men. Four years before Daniel Patrick Moynihan published his report on the "pathology of the Negro family," the black women on the PCSW acknowledged and voiced objections to the matriarchal family patterns forced on African Americans because of racial discrimination in the labor market. These women also called for more, black-controlled social welfare and community programs as well as the inclusion of African American history and culture in predominantly black elementary and secondary schools.[15]

The black women on the Kennedy Commission provided a racialized analysis of the social and economic conditions for women, which
at the time was considered radical, and anticipated the polyvocality
of groups, such as the National Black Feminist Organization and the
Combahee River Collective in the 1970s. Although the white women
on the PCSW recognized the special hardships of black women, they
rejected comparisons between discrimination based on sex and that
based on race, and believed that remedies for dealing with sexual
discrimination should be different from those aimed at ending racial
discrimination.[16]

The black women on the PCSW privileged race over gender and
class, and their notions about gender were fairly traditional. They
emphasized and accepted the view that women should be responsible for the family and that work was secondary; the preoccupation
with race made their perspective *univocal*. However, within a decade
this univocality would be supplanted by a polyvocality in the discourse over black women's position in American society. Despite the
privileging of race over gender, however, the Fourth Consultation
came up with several relevant suggestions for enhancing the economic conditions for black women in the United States, such as raising the minimum wage and expanding unionization among domestic
and other service workers. Unfortunately, when the PSCW's twenty-
four recommendations were reported on the front page of the *New
York Times* on October 12, 1963, none of the findings and conclusions
of the Negro Women's Consultation were included in the summaries;
indeed, the black women's conclusions were not mentioned at all.
This demonstrated that although black women's issues were making
their way from the margins of public policy, they still were not a central concern for federal policymakers.[17]

African American Women and NOW

Contrary to popular belief, there were several women of color involved in the creation of the National Organization for Women
(NOW). In fact, this new organization's membership overlapped with
that of the PCSW and the subsequent National Black Feminist Organization. Three black women—attorney Pauli Murray, who also had a
leadership role on the PCSW; union organizer Aileen Hernandez; and

Shirley Chisholm, who later became the first black U.S. Congress-woman—were involved in the founding of NOW. In 1966, NOW emerged out of the third annual conference, held in Washington DC, of the Commission on the Status of Women.[18] During that period white women who were veterans of the civil rights campaigns were being confronted by the demand for Black Power and decided to shift their energies to the struggle for women's rights. Many upper-middle class, educated white women drew an analogy between sexism and racism, and the founders of NOW declared that they wanted to form "an NAACP for Women."[19]

Pauli Murray was asked to be a founding member of NOW by Betty Friedan after Friedan received reports of Murray's statements delivered at the 1965 meeting of the National Council of Women. At the council meeting Murray had declared, "If it becomes necessary to march on Washington to assure equal job opportunities for all, I hope I will not back down from the fight."[20] Also in 1965, Pauli Murray published an important article in the *George Washington University Law Review* in which she pointed out that while the brutality that African Americans have endured was far worse than that which women have faced, this did not obscure the fact that the rights of both groups were "different phases of the fundamental and invisible issue of human rights."[21]

NOW's statement of purpose reflected many of the issues that the black women on the Kennedy Commission had explored earlier. NOW's objectives centered on education, employment, legal and po-litical rights, family life, poverty, and mass media images. There was no great emphasis placed on "consciousness raising," but on the con-crete political and legal changes needed to improve the economic sit-uation of mainly middle- and upper-middle class women. NOW be-came the most important organization in the emerging Women's Liberation Movement, and most black women fully subscribed to NOW's push for increased political power and representation for women. At the July 1971 meeting of the National Women's Political Caucus, Fannie Lou Hamer and Shirley Chisholm spoke out in favor of more women running for political office.[22]

While NOW members mobilized throughout the country to in-crease the number of women elected officials, and were successful in gaining legislation and other government regulations that mandated "affirmative action" in public and private employment, they were less concerned with the pressing social and economic issues facing white, black, or brown working-class women. The National Black Feminist Organization was formed in 1973 partly because NOW did not deal adequately with the issue of race and the particular concerns of working-class black women.

The National Black Feminist Organization

The National Black Feminist Organization (NBFD) was formed in August 1973. And in November 1973, the first Eastern Regional Conference on Black Feminism was held in New York City, attracting over 500 women from throughout the United States. Among those present were Shirley Chisholm, Alice Walker, Eleanor Holmes Norton, Flo Kennedy, and Margaret Sloan, NBFO's first and only president.[23] According to Sloan, "by organizing around our needs as Black women, we are making sure that we won't be left out . . . which was what was appearing to be happening in both the Black liberation and the women's liberation movements."[24]

Before and during this time, many black women felt frustrated by the treatment they received from black men involved in the Black Power Movement. According to Pauli Murray, "Black women began to sense that the struggle into which they had poured their energies, Black Liberation and the Civil Rights Movement, may not afford them rights they assumed would be theirs when the civil rights cause triumphed."[25] Many Black Power advocates exhibited male chauvinist attitudes and behavior, expecting black women to remain in their "traditional" roles, while the Women's Liberation Movement held out the promise of significant advancements, primarily for upper- and middle-class white women.

The NBFO focused on issues not addressed by male-dominated Black Power groups or white-controlled feminist organizations. Through the creation of several "Task Forces," NBFO engaged the issues that were needed for the advancement of the organization and generated information on topics important to its membership and to black women in general. The organization was concerned with welfare rights and reform, rights of domestic workers, reproductive freedom, and the problems of unwed mothers. Task forces were formed on the media images, drug addiction, women in prisons, rape, the arts, and the black lesbian as well as the ongoing structure for the organization, plans for a national conference, and relations with the national news media. NBFO educational forums were devoted to a broad range of subjects, including health care issues, unemployment, child care, the problem of forced sterilization, female sexuality, black women as consumers, sex role stereotyping, and the passage of the Equal Rights Amendment (ERA); and NBFO members engaged all classes of women in "consciousness raising."[26]

The NFBO challenged the belief current in black nationalist circles that the concept of "feminist" had little or no relevance to black people. Instead, the NFBO membership explored the multiple ways in which black women in the United States have suffered from the combined forces of racism and sexism, and exposed the myth of the black "matriarch," and other negative stereotypes and images of black women. They also argued that their presence would lend "enormous credibility" to the larger feminist movement. Unfortunately, feminism was not valued by many black men or women as a "serious political and economic revolutionary force"; however, this coming together of black feminists could strengthen the Black Power movement and encourage "all talents and creativity of Black women to emerge strong and beautiful."[27]

It is important to note that with regard to employment, black women have traditionally had more in common with black men than white women. In their task force on employment, the NBFO focused on domestic workers, of which in 1970, 97 percent were female, and of those, 64 percent were black. In supporting the efforts of black domestic workers to organize for their rights, the NBFO advocated pressuring the government to enact laws to guarantee the inclusion of domestic workers under the Fair Labor Standards Act. This would mean that they would be covered by all federal laws and would be guaranteed a minimum wage, sick pay, paid vacations, and would be covered by insurance and have the right to collective bargaining.[28]

In their discussions of economics and class, the NBFO leaders demonstrated their knowledge and understanding of the multifaceted nature of oppression. Although the NBFO leadership did not espouse socialism, as would be the case with the women in the Combahee River Collective, some of the positions NBFO supported could be considered socialistic. The black women in NBFO saw their oppression as having roots in the "classist, racist, sexist, capitalist-imperialist structures of this country." Their recommendations for eliminating economic distress included "income sharing, cooperative ventures, coalition politics, education and communication projects." These women also recognized the class prejudices of some of their membership, and actively encouraged black women from every socioeconomic class to become involved. They believed that "class distinctions must be abolished and classist attitudes and policies will not be tolerated within our ranks."[29]

The Equal Rights Amendment was also an important issue for the NBFO because a very high proportion of black women who worked outside the home were heads of households, and needed to be guaranteed equal employment opportunities. The NBFO leaders called for the ratification of the amendment by the states, and encouraged their members to lobby for its passage. They also endorsed the use of boycotts against a state's products to apply pressure to ratify the amendment.[30]

Birth control and a woman's right to choose when and how she would bear and raise children were extremely controversial issues during the 1970s. Within the Black Power movement, many of the male leaders were preaching against the use of birth control because they believed it was a tool of the white oppressor to decrease the size of the black population in the United States. Some black men suggested that black women needed to throw away the birth control pill and jump into bed "to breed Black revolutionaries." However, many black women felt this was just another excuse for black men to keep women in traditional roles. Novelist and social critic Toni Cade argued that the pill offered women a choice as to when they felt prepared emotionally, economically, and physically to have a child; and this did not mean that the woman would not necessarily want children sometime in the future. bell hooks went further and asked, "If birth control is truly the 'trick of the man' and the Black women needed to have revolutionary babies, why are there so many babies in Black orphanages? Black revolutionaries should adopt all these children until all the orphanages are empty if they want more Black revolutionaries."[31]

In their informational fact sheet on rape, the NBFO estimated that over 60 percent of rape victims were black, the majority of whom were young girls. Rape became an important issue for NBFO members and they advocated the elimination by all states of "collaboration laws," which required a witness to have been present at the time of the alleged rape. They also wanted to outlaw the use of a victim's previous sexual history as evidence in trials for rape. Oftentimes, the defendant's lawyer used scare tactics to intimidate the woman who was testifying against accused rapists; this approach tended to discourage other women from bringing rape charges to court. The NBFO membership also saw a need for change in laws that prohibited wives from bringing charges of rape against their husbands, and applied pressure on local government officials to create special police units that would be trained to deal with rape cases.[32]

For NBFO members consciousness raising was extremely important because it allowed the women to appreciate and celebrate their strengths. They saw it as a way to "establish a basis of trust and commitment to each other as individuals and to the organization as a whole." The goals of the consciousness-raising activities were developing love, trust, and sisterhood within the group; facilitating open and honest communication and positive confrontation (as opposed to negative squabbling); enabling women to deal with personal prejudices; and raising the feminist consciousness of black women.[33]

The NBFO disseminated information on how to reach out to black women, and how to educate them about feminism. The organization placed great emphasis on the need to include lesbians and incarcerated women in their educational and recruitment activities. This was very different from NOW, which had other priorities. The women of NBFO aimed their activities at the more personal and practical level rather than at the political mainstream. Given their lack of access to the larger political system, it is likely that they saw these issues and concerns as having more of a direct effect on most black women in the United States.[34]

The National Organization for Women continues to be an active force in the political arena and has developed chapters throughout the United States. NOW has gone through many leadership and programmatic changes, but has maintained and even strengthened its hierarchical structure. NOW leaders work within the political mainstream, while claiming they want significant changes and reforms that would advance the interests of women in general. Some of their statements can be interpreted as radical and inclusive of all women regardless of class, race, and sexuality, yet the rhetoric has often not been reflected in the realities. bell hooks suggested that the second wave of feminists were demanding a revolution, a change in the American social structure. Yet as they attempted to move feminism beyond the realm of radical rhetoric and to deal with the actual conditions for women in American society,

many of these younger, white middle- and upper-class women continued to regard women unlike themselves as "the other."[35]

The NBFO did not have the same fate as NOW, but instead disinte-
grated within four years of its founding. According to feminist critic
Michele Wallace, the NBFO "got bogged down in an array of ideological disputes" and "action became unthinkable." Wallace saw how
"women who had initiative and spirit usually attended one meeting,
were turned off by the hopelessness of ever getting anything accom-
plished, and never returned again."[36] Deborah Gray White, who examined the NBFO's activities in Chicago, concluded that

> the black feminists were accused of separating from the black movement
> and dividing the race. They were charged with aligning with the white
> women against black men. Their acceptance of homosexuality and the
> visibility of lesbian members fed man-hating charges, and their militant
> defense and support of black women revived images of matriarchy.[37]

As early as 1974, several NBFO members in the Boston chapter decided to form a new group altogether, the Combahee River Collective.

"All of Who I Am in the Same Place": The Women of the Combahee River Collective

> We are actively committed to struggling against racial, sexual, hetero-
> sexual, and class oppression and see as our particular task the develop-
> ment of integrated analysis and practice based upon the fact that major
> systems of oppression are interlocking. The synthesis of these oppres-
> sions creates the condition of our lives. As Black women we see Black
> feminism as the logical political movement to combat the manifold and
> simultaneous oppressions that all women of color face.
> —The Combahee River Collective Statement, 1977

The Combahee River Collective (CRC) began as the Boston chapter of
the NBFO, but these black women were more preoccupied with issues of sexual orientation and economic development. The group
came to define itself as anti-capitalist, socialist, and revolutionary.
During the six years of its existence, its members worked on a variety
of issues that affect black women, including racism in the women's
movement. The Combahee River Collective asserted the legitimacy of
black women's opposition to sexual exploitation and oppression, and

made a major contribution to the growth of black feminism in the United States. Its widely circulated "Combahee River Collective Statement" helped to lay the foundation for feminists of color organizing in the 1980s and the 1990s. Like the black women on the Kennedy Commission, the black women of Combahee had to work to get black women's experiences highlighted on the front pages of American newspapers. The Collective's most significant organizing effort was the mobilization of individuals and groups in the Boston area to protest the murders of twelve black women.[38]

In its first two years, the Collective was active in such projects as support work for Kenneth Edelin, a black doctor at Boston City Hospital who was arrested for manslaughter for performing a legal abortion. CRC members were involved in the case of Ella Ellison, a black woman who was accused of murder because she had been seen in the area where a murder had been committed. The CRC members also joined with the Third World Workers Coalition in picketing at the construction site for a new public school, protesting the absence of black and other minority workers.[39]

Re-entering the world of activism was something that Barbara Smith did not think she would ever do. Smith did her first political organizing in the Civil Rights Movement, but became disillusioned over the leaders' reformist, rather than revolutionary, objectives. After that disappointment, Smith did not believe that the black women's movement would be much different.

> I think one of the things that I was so happy about is that I had thought that I would never be involved in political work after I graduated from college because that was the height of Black Nationalism and I felt like I just wasn't permitted to be the kind of person I was in that context. I was supposed to marry someone or not marry them, who cared, but my job was to have babies for the Nation and to walk seven paces behind a man and basically be a maidservant. I didn't get involved in the women's movement for a few years after it became very visible because my perception was that it was entirely white.[40]

After attending the NBFO meeting in New York in November 1973, Smith felt she could accomplish more in the Boston community because she would be doing it from a black feminist base. When she returned from the NBFO conference, she met with several people and started trying to build a Boston NBFO chapter. Early in 1974, Smith met Demita Frazier and soon discovered that their vision for social change was more radical than that of the NBFO. Demita Frazier recalled that "we wanted to talk about radical economics." They were not only supportive of socialist approaches to economic change, they also wanted to make sure that "there would be a voice for lesbians in black women's organizations." Both knew that lesbians were involved in the formation of the NBFO, but "we weren't sure where NBFO was heading." After Barbara Smith attended the "Socialist Feminist Organizing Conference" held at Oberlin College in Ohio in 1974, Frazier noted that "we decided that we wanted to be a collective and not a hierarchial organization because it was antithetical to our beliefs about democracy and the need to share."[41]

The new organization got its name from Barbara Smith, who had read a small book by Earl Conrad, entitled *Harriet Tubman*. The Combahee River in South Carolina was where the abolitionist Harriet Tubman planned and led the only military campaign in U.S. history organized by a woman and where 750 slaves escaped to freedom. Smith liked the idea of naming the group for a collective action as opposed to one heroic person.[42]

In the summer of 1994, Barbara Smith was filmed while sitting on the shore of the Combahee River in South Carolina. When the filmmaker asked about the importance of the collective, she responded that

> [the] Combahee was really so wonderful because it was the first time that I could be *all of who I was in the same place*. That I didn't have to leave my feminism outside the door to be accepted as I would in a conservative Black political context. I didn't have to leave my lesbianism outside. . . . So it was just really wonderful to be able to be our whole selves and to be accepted in that way.

Smith recalled that in the early 1970s, "to be a Black lesbian feminist meant that you were a person of total courage. It was almost frightening. I spent a lot of time wondering if I would ever be able to come out because I didn't see any way that I could be Black and a feminist and a lesbian." Ultimately, these conditions and experiences led to the formation of the collective. "That is what Combahee created, a place where we could be ourselves and where we were valued. A place without homophobia, a place without racism, a place without sexism."[43]

The Combahee River Collective started with four black women sitting in Demita Frazier's living room discussing how they came to think of themselves as feminists. In the early 1970s, Boston was in turmoil over court-ordered busing to desegregate the public schools. Barbara Smith recalled the attack on attorney Ted Lanzvark in City Hall Plaza by white racists who used an American flag to beat him. "I don't know who was there on the spot with the camera, but that picture went out over the wire services all over the country, probably all over the world, to show what this country was all about." Smith also mentioned the shooting of a black high school student while he was playing football. "He was paralyzed for life. So that was the kind of atmosphere we lived in."[44]

Demita Frazier was from Chicago and brought issues of urban poverty to the Combahee Collective's discussions. When Frazier arrived in Boston, she intended to organize black women around feminist issues as well as the problems of the black poor, but it took about a year to find others who were interested in black feminist consciousness raising. "We were actually saying we were feminists. We were proud of that. We were not worried about flack from anybody else. It was a moment of power because I think we all recognized very quickly . . . that we were at the precipice of something really important."

Frazier emphasized the point: "That was literally how it started, sitting in someone's living room, having a discussion about the issues and it wasn't even the issues so much as getting to know one another and what our issues were, what brought us to think of ourselves as feminists. . . . It was really very different for me."[45]

Coming Together: The Combahee River Collective Retreats

The members of the Combahee River Collective held seven retreats in the northeast between 1977 and 1980. Held mostly in private homes, the members came together and shared with one another their thoughts, writings, hopes, and dreams about the social, economic, and political future of black women. Demita Frazier felt that the retreats "raised their political consciousness and fostered spiritual rejuvenation."[46] At the second retreat in November 1977 in Franklin Township, New Jersey, there were seven items on the agenda: (1) relations between lesbian and non-lesbian feminists; (2) socialism and a black feminist ideology; (3) lesbian separation and the black liberation struggle; (4) black feminist organization versus the black feminist movement; (5) black feminist scholarship; (6) class conflicts among black women; and (7) love between women—lesbian, non-lesbian, black, and white.[47] The participants were asked to bring something that would make a statement about themselves, a picture, a poem, or a journal excerpt. Demita Frazier recalled that the poet Audre Lorde was involved in the retreats.

> I had just met her and I asked her to come and she was thrilled and that is really how we got to become friends because we would see each other periodically at these retreats. We would call them retreats, but in fact they were political meetings that had lots of different elements. So it was a way for people who were separated to be in the same place and to engage in some political work with each other.[48]

During and after the third and fourth retreats in 1978, the participants were encouraged to write articles for the Third World women's issue of the journal *Conditions*, to be edited by Lorraine Bethel and Barbara Smith.[49] The importance of publishing was also emphasized in the fifth retreat, held in July 1979, and the members were advised to contribute articles for lesbian "herstory" issues of two journals, *Heresies* and *Frontiers*. The fifth retreat was also important because the participants surveyed the signs that black feminism had grown since 1977. In 1979, there were two black feminist groups in Boston, and in November of that year under the direction of Bettye Collier-Thomas, founding executive director of the Bethune Museum and Archives (BMA), "The First National Scholarly Research Conference on Black Women in America" was held, and BMA, the nation's first institution solely devoted to the collection, preservation, and exhibition of black women's history, was opened. In October 1979, black women historians organized a national group, the Association of Black Women Historians (ABWH). Also in 1979, Barbara Smith published *Sojourner: The Women's Forum*, a Third World women's studies research newsletter, and a group for black women in publishing was organizing art collaborations in New York City.[50]

Participants at the sixth retreat in November 1979 dealt with two literary events. They discussed articles in the May–June 1979 issue of *The Black Scholar*, entitled "the Black Sexism Debate," written in response to the article published in the previous issue by Robert Staples, "The Myth of Black Macho: A Response to Angry Black Feminists."[51] The participants also discussed the importance of writing to

Essence magazine in support of an article in the September 1979 issue entitled "I Am a Lesbian," by Chirlane McCray.[52] McCray was a Combahee member and at this time *Essence* began regularly publishing articles and fiction about lesbians. The group was hoping that their positive letters would counteract any homophobic letters that *Essence* might receive. Barbara Smith declared that

> the retreats were multidimensional, multimedia events. They were so many different things. Of course, it was a time to talk politics. It was a time to have parties. It was a time to flirt, for some. . . . What I really see is Black feminism as a building block. I think that we always felt a kinship, sisterhood, and solidarity with not just women of color, but with people of color, generally. That is articulated in the statement and certainly in the kinds of things that we worked on and did political work on; it was like building blocks.[53]

The Combahee River Collective and Community Activism

All of the Combahee women were involved in other civil rights and women's organizations. Several members belonged to the Committee to End Sterilization Abuse, while others worked for the establishment in Boston of Transition House, a shelter for battered women. The Collective members became involved in the case of Ella Ellison, a black woman who in defending herself against a sexual assault by a guard at Framingham State Prison ended up killing him. The case brought them within the circle of people in Massachusetts fighting the death penalty. This interaction helped the members to develop a coalition with other community groups and activists. Members of the Collective worked with religious groups, including the women's auxiliaries of local black Baptist churches. According to Barbara Smith, the Collective was very successful in working in the community, because even though the protests and demonstrations caused much disruption, they were really focusing on life and death, bread and butter issues. "And we just acted as if it were perfectly all right for us to be who we were and be respected for who we were. So we didn't have problems as a group going into situations like that which is not to say, as individuals we didn't have problems in the community. I never did."[54]

Boston had become notorious at the time for its poor treatment of African Americans. The busing controversy, the stabbing, with an

American flag, of a black attorney, the attack on a black high school football player, were reflections of the city's hostile racial climate. In addition, between January 28 and May 30, 1979, thirteen women, twelve black and one white, were murdered within a two-mile radius in the city of Boston. All but one of the victims were found in predominantly black neighborhoods in contiguous sections of Roxbury, Dorchester, and the South End. Many of the women were strangled, with bare hands or a scarf or cord, and some were stabbed. Two were buried after they were killed, and two were dismembered. Several of the women had been raped.[55]

In the January 30, 1979, edition of the *Boston Globe*, the report of the discovery of the bodies of the first two murder victims, then unidentified, was reported on page 30, beside the racing forms, in a four-paragraph description with the headline "Two Bodies Found in a Trash Bag." On January 31, 1979, the murder of Gwendolyn Yvette Stinson was reported on page 13 under the heading, "Dorchester Girl Found Dead." Karen Prater's death, on February 6, 1979, finally warranted a small block on the *Globe's* front page, followed by a confusing article about the growing community outrage and the absence of police resources. On February 7, on page 8 of its Metro Section, the *Globe* covered a community meeting held at the Lee Elementary School in Dorchester. Mayor Kevin White discussed the murders with more than 700 people in attendance.[56]

The *Globe* took no responsibility for its failure to draw public attention to the murders earlier. When the *Globe* did focus attention on the crimes, it was to denigrate the responses in the black community. The *Globe* remained silent about the crisis until February 21, when Daryl Ann Hargett was found strangled and lying on the bedroom floor in her apartment. This time the *Globe* reported the death of the fifth black woman in thirty days, printing the story inside a small box in the lower left-hand corner of the front page, misspelling Hargett's first name.[57] In contrast to the *Globe*, the *Bay State Banner*, the black community weekly, ran full coverage of the situation from the first of February 1979, and reported regularly on the black community's responses. The *Banner* provided detailed, front-page coverage of the murders throughout the year.[58]

On April 1, 1979, following the deaths of six black women, fifteen hundred people took to the streets to mourn the loss of their sisters, daughters, mothers, and friends. The memorial march commenced in

Boston's South End at the Harriet Tubman House and paused first at the Wellington Street apartment of Daryl Ann Hargett, the fifth victim. Barbara Smith recalled that "when the marchers reached the Stride Rite Factory on Lenox Street in Roxbury, where the bodies of the first two women were found, Lorraine Bethel whispered 'This is just horrible, we've got to do something.'"[59]

Smith and Bethel's anger and frustration over the speakers' failure at the rally to acknowledge sexism as a factor in the deaths of the women propelled them into action. Smith returned to her apartment in Roxbury and began developing a pamphlet that would speak to the fears of black women in Boston.

> I started writing a pamphlet that night and I thought of the title, "Six Black Women, Why Did They Die" and I wrote it up. . . . And by the next morning, it was basically done. I called other people in the Collective. . . . I read it to them and then I also called up Urban Planning Aid in Boston and went down there and got assistance with laying out the pamphlet.[60]

> We really wanted to get out a sexual and political analysis of these murders. We wanted to do some consciousness raising about what the murders meant. We also wanted to give women hope. So the pamphlet had the statement and the political analysis and it said that it had been prepared by the Combahee River Collective. That was a big risk for us, a big leap to identify ourselves in something that we know was going to be widely distributed. The pamphlet contained a list of things that women should do to protect themselves, especially self-defense methods.[61]

Smith and Bethel consulted with people in antiviolence organizations to make sure that the things they were recommending would be useful for women who were victimized by assault. The Collective received a great deal of support from white feminists as well. Barbara Smith recalled:

> It was a real opportunity to do some coalition building and we were able to mobilize hundreds and hundreds of people to come out and to speak out to talk about the issue. We were able to bring together very diverse groups of people around the issue of violence against women. And we never felt that it had lost the focus on the fact that the women were Black. One thing we did say though is that these are women who are being murdered. They could have been you. It could have been any of us.[62]

Conclusion: Defining the Politics of Identity

It appears that the Collective was most cohesive and active when it organized around the issue of the murders in Boston. Having a specific event to respond to and collectively organize around gave the members a cause on which to focus, leaving less time for in-fighting over power and authority or broken hearts. The eventual end of the Collective came about as a result of the movement of the members to other parts of the country. Physical disbursement, rather than frustration and disillusionment as was the case with the NBFO, brought about the end of the Combahee River Collective.[63]

The women of the CRC developed a political and ideological perspective which was more polyvocal than that espoused by the black women on the Kennedy Commission or in the National Black Feminist Organization. This perspective became very prominent in the 1980s and 1990s and became associated with the phrase "identity politics." Barbara Smith suggested that "we came up with the term 'identity politics.' I never really saw it anywhere else and I would suggest that people if they really want to find the origin of the term, that they try to find it in any place earlier than in the Combahee River Collective statement."

While the term came to define the activism of diverse racial, cultural, and gender groupings,

> what we meant by identity politics was a politics that grew out of our objective material experiences as Black women. This was the kind of politics that had never been done or practiced before to our knowledge, although we began to find out that there were Black feminists in the early part of this century and the latter part of the nineteenth century. But it had never been quite formulated in the way that we were trying to formulate it particularly because we were talking about homophobia and lesbian identity as well.

The polyvocal political expressions of the black feminists in the Combahee River Collective came to define the nature of identity politics in the 1980s and 1990s, and challenged earlier "essentialist" appeals and doctrines espoused by black and white nationalists or conservative women.

> We took on race, class, sexual orientation, and gender. And we said, instead of being bowled over by it and destroyed by it, we are going to

make it into something vital and inspiring. I have to say that I really did know what we were doing when we were doing it. I think that because I have such a grounding in Black history and in Black culture, I was quite aware that we were doing something new.[64]

The legacy of black feminist organizing from the President's Commission on the Status of Women to the Combahee River Collective can be found in the ideological formations that characterize "identity politics" in the United States in the 1980s and 1990s.[65]

NOTES

1. Margaret Sloan-Hunter, "Black and Lavender," *Black and Lavender* (Santa Cruz, CA: Talking Circles Press, 1995), 32–33.

2. Kimberle Crenshaw's theory of the "intersectional experience of racism and sexism" is meant to "account for the convergence of black and feminist critical issues within a paradigm that factors in both of these paradigms" and replaces what she referred to as "monocausal paradigms" that can only consider race at the expense of feminism, and vice versa. See "Beyond Racism and Misogyny," in Mari Matsuda, ed., *Words that Wound: Critical Race Theory, Assertive Speech, and the First Amendment* (Boulder, CO: Westview Press, 1993), 111–32.

3. Anna Julia Cooper, *A Voice from the South, By a Woman from the South* (1892, reprinted New York: Oxford University Press, 1988).

4. Paula Giddings, *When and Where I Enter: The Impact of Black Women on Race and Sex in America* (New York: William Morrow, 1984), 132.

5. Albert Memmi, *The Colonizer and the Colonized* (New York: Onion Press, 1965), 32.

6. Evelyn Brooks Higginbotham, "African-American Women's History and the Metalanguage of Race," in Darlene Clark Hine, Linda Reed, and Wilma King, eds., *"We Specialize in the Wholly Impossible": A Reader in Black Women's History* (Brooklyn, NY: Carlson Publishing, 1995), 3–24.

7. Patricia Hill Collins, *Black Feminist Thought: Knowledge, Consciousness, and the Politics of Empowerment* (New York: Routledge, 1990), 24.

8. C. S'thembile West, quoted in Barbara Omolade, *The Rising Song of the African American Women* (New York: Routledge, 1994), 35.

9. See, for example, Beverly Guy-Sheftall, ed., *Words of Fire: An Anthology of African-American Feminist Thought* (New York: New Press, 1995).

10. President's Commission on the Status of Women (PCSW), *Report of the Fourth Consultation* (Washington, DC: Government Printing Office, 1963); Deborah Gray White, *Too Heavy a Load: Black Women in Defense of Themselves*,

1894–1994 (New York: Norton, 1999), 17, 210–15, 242–53, 255–56. The NBFO maintained chapters in Chicago, Detroit, Atlanta, and Washington. With the exception of the Chicago branch, NBFO chapter records remain uncollected. The papers of the Chicago NBFO chapter, which later became known as the National Black Feminist Alliance, are located at the University of Illinois at Chicago, and at the Mary McLeod Bethune Council House National Historic Site, Washington, DC. Lorraine Bethel and Barbara Smith, eds., *Conditions: Five, The Black Women's Issue 2* No. 2 (Fall 1979); Gloria Hull, Patricia Bell Scott, and Barbara Smith, eds., *All the Women Are White, All the Men Are Black, But Some of Us Are Brave* (New York: The Feminist Press, 1982); and Barbara Smith, ed., *Home Girls: A Black Feminist Anthology* (New York: Kitchen Table, Women of Color Press, 1983).

11. Betty Friedan, *The Feminine Mystique*, 2d ed. (New York: Norton, 1974), 76.

12. The black women on the PCSW were Hilda Fortune, New York Urban League; Maude Gadsen, Beauty Shop Owners Association; Dorothy Height, National Council of Negro Women; Cenoria D. Johnson, National Urban League; Inabel Lindsey, Howard University; and Gerri Major, Johnson Publications.

13. Toni Morrison, *Playing in the Dark: Whiteness and the Literary Imagination* (New York: Vintage Books, 1990), 4.

14. Rose Brewer, "Theorizing Race, Class, and Gender: The New Scholarship of Black Feminist Intellectuals and Black Women's Labor," in Abena P. A. Busia and Stanlie M. James, eds., *Theorizing Black Feminism* (New York: Routledge, 1994), 13.

15. *Report of the Fourth Consultation*, 5; Daniel P. Moynihan, *The Negro Family: The Case for National Action* (Washington, DC: U.S. Department of Labor, 1965), reprinted in Lee Rainwater and William L. Yancey, *The Moynihan Report and the Politics of Controversy* (Cambridge, MA: MIT Press, 1967).

16. PCSW, *Report of the Fourth Consultation*, 7.

17. *New York Times*, October 12, 1963, 1. See also President's Commission on the Status of Women, *American Women: Report on the President's Commission on the Status of Women* (Washington, DC: Government Printing Office, 1963).

18. Toni Carabillo et al., eds., *Feminist Chronicles, 1953–1993* (Los Angeles: Women's Graphic, 1993).

19. For information on NOW's early years, see William Chafe, *The American Woman: Her Changing Social, Economic, and Political Roles, 1920–1970* (New York: Oxford University Press, 1972), 200–40; Andrew Sinclair, *The Emancipation of the American Woman* (New York: Harper & Row, 1965), 340–47; Jo Freeman, *The Politics of Women's Liberation: A Case Study of an Emerging Social Movement and Its Relation to the Social Policy Process* (New York: Longman, 1975), 3–55.

20. Pauli Murray quoted in Carabillo et al., *Feminist Chronicles*, 15.

21. Pauli Murray and Mary O. Eastwood, "Jane Crow and the Law: Sex Discrimination and Title VII," *George Washington University Law Review* 34, no. 2 (December 1965): 232–56.

22. For Fannie Lou Hamer, see Chana Kai Lee, *For Freedom's Sake: The Life of Fannie Lou Hamer* (Urbana: University of Illinois Press, 1999), 170–72; Shirley Chisholm, *Unbought and Unbossed* (Boston: Houghton Mifflin, 1970); and *The Good Fight* (New York: Harper & Row, 1973).

23. Guy-Sheftall, "Introduction," *Words of Fire*, 15; Margaret Sloan-Hunter, "National Black Feminist Organization," in Wilma Mankiller et al., eds., *The Reader's Companion to U.S. Women's History* (Boston: Houghton Mifflin, 1998), 393.

24. Margaret Sloan (Hunter), quoted in Carabillo, et al., *Feminist Chronicles*, 97.

25. Pauli Murray quoted in Gerda Lerner, *Black Women in White America: A Documentary History* (New York: Vintage Books, 1973), 595.

26. For information on the NBFO activities based on records of the Chicago chapter, see White, *Too Heavy a Load*, 242–56. See also Mary Frances Berry, *Why ERA Failed: Politics, Women's Rights, and the Amending Process of the Constitution* (Bloomington: Indiana University Press, 1986), 102–20.

27. Minutes of the National Black Feminist Organization, 1973–1977, New York chapter, hereafter cited as NBFO Minutes, are unpublished. Copies of the organization's minutes are in the possession of Duchess Harris.

28. Ibid.

29. Ibid.

30. Ibid.; Berry, *Why ERA Failed*, 116–19.

31. Toni Cade (Bambara) quoted in bell hooks, *Yearning: Race, Gender, and Cultural Politics* (Boston: South End Press, 1990), 64.

32. NBFO Minutes.

33. NBFO Minutes.

34. hooks, *Yearning*, 62.

35. Ibid., 121.

36. Michelle Wallace, *Invisibility Blues: From Pop to Theory* (London: Verso Press, 1990), 25.

37. White, *Too Heavy a Load*, 250–51.

38. For the Combahee River Collective Statement (1977), see Guy-Sheftall, *Words of Fire*, 232–40. For a discussion of the Combahee River Collective's objectives and impact on the development of black feminism, see Barbara Smith, "Black Feminism," in Mankiller, ed., *The Reader's Companion*, 203. There is no written history of the group. This essay relies on interviews with the founders and members conducted by Susan Levine Goodwillie in 1994 and Duchess Harris in 1995.

39. The Collective was made up of highly educated black lesbian feminists, six of whom were Barbara Smith, Demita Frazier, Cheryl Clark, Gloria Akasha Hull, Margo Okizawa Rey, and Sharon Page Ritchie.

40. Barbara Smith, interview with Susan Levine Goodwillie, 1994, Boston.

41. Demita Frazier, interview with Susan Levine Goodwillie, 1994, Boston.

42. Earl Conrad, *Harriet Tubman* (New York: P. S. Eriksson, 1969); Guy-Sheftall, ed., *Words of Fire*, 231.

43. Barbara Smith, interview with Susan Levine Goodwillie, 1994.

44. Ibid.

45. Demita Frazier, interview with Susan Levine Goodwillie, 1994.

46. Ibid.

47. Letter of Cheryl Clark and Cassie Alfonso to CRC members, August 25, 1977; copy in possession of Cheryl Clarke; Cheryl Clarke interview with the author, 1995, New Brunswick, NJ.

48. Demita Frazier, interview with Susan Levine Goodwillie, 1994.

49. Bethel and Smith, eds., *Conditions: Five* (Fall 1979).

50. *Sojourner: A Women's Forum* (Jamaica Plain, MA: Barbara Smith, 1979); For a history of BMA and "The First National Scholarly Conference on Black Women in America," see Bettye Collier-Thomas, "The Bethune Museum and Archives: Entering New Frontiers," *LEGACY*, 5, no. 1 (April 1996); for a history of ABWH, see Janice Sumler-Edmond, "Association of Black Women Historians, Inc.," in Darlene Clark Hine, Elsa Barkley Brown, and Rosalyn Terborg-Penn, eds., *Black Women in America: An Historical Encyclopedia* (Brooklyn, NY: Carlson Publishing, 1993), 48–49.

51. Robert Staples, "The Myth of Black Macho: A Response to Angry Black Feminists," *The Black Scholar* 10 (March–April 1979): 24–33; and "Black Feminism and the Cult of Masculinity: The Danger Within," in Robert Christman and Robert Allen, eds., "The Black Sexism Debate: Special Issue," *The Black Scholar* 10 (May–June 1979): 63–67.

52. Chirlane McCray, "I Am a Lesbian," *Essence* Magazine 10 (September 1979): 90–91.

53. Barbara Smith, interview with Susan Goodwillie, 1994.

54. Ibid.

55. Jamie Grant, "Who Is Killing Us?" (1979), unpublished essay in possession of Duchess Harris.

56. *Boston Globe*, January 30, 31, 1979; February 6, 7, 1979.

57. Ibid., February 21, 1979.

58. *Bay State Banner* (Boston, MA), February 1, 8, 15, 22, 1979.

59. Barbara Smith, interview with Susan Levine Goodwillie, 1994.

60. Ibid.

61. Ibid.

62. Ibid.

63. According to Margo Okizawa Rey, who was a graduate student at Harvard University in the late 1970s, this was a time when geographical disbursement of the members of the Collective was almost inevitable. Several members left Boston in the early 1980s to begin the next phase of their lives and careers. Most of the women continued the work of the Collective in their academic pursuits. Rey and Gloria Hull ended up in California teaching race and gender theory at San Francisco State and the University of California at Santa Cruz, respectively. Sharon Page Ritchie went to California to study clothing design. Cheryl Clarke is completing a Ph.D. dissertation at Rutgers University, where she is an administrator and advocate for gay, lesbian, and bisexual students on campus. Demita Frazier returned to Chicago to practice law. Barbara Smith has edited several volumes on gay and lesbian studies and is completing a history of gays and lesbians in the African American community; see Barbara Smith, "Introduction," *The Truth That Never Hurts: Writings on Race, Gender, and Freedom* (New Brunswick: Rutgers University Press, 1998), xi–xvi.

64. Barbara Smith, interview with Susan Levine Goodwillie, 1994.

65. The books on "identity politics" include Cherrié Moraga and Gloria Anzaldúa, eds., *This Bridge Called My Back: Writings by Radical Women of Color* (New York: Kitchen Table Press, 1981); Elly Bulkin, Minnie Pratt, and Barbara Smith, *Yours in Struggle: Three Feminist Perspectives on Anti-Semitism and Racism* (Ithaca, NY: Firebrand Books, 1984); Joseph F. Beam, ed., *In the Life: A Black Gay Anthology* (Boston: Alyson Publications, 1986); Judith Butler, *Gender Trouble: Feminism and the Subversion of Identity* (New York: Routledge, 1990); Essex Hemphill, ed., *Brother to Brother: New Writings by Black Gay Men* (Boston: Alyson Publications, 1991); Scott Bryson et al., eds., *Beyond Recognition: Representation, Power, and Culture* (Berkeley: University of California Press, 1992); Michael Awkward, *Negotiating Difference: Race, Gender, and the Politics of Positionality* (Chicago: University of Chicago Press, 1995); Philip Brian Harper, *Are We Not Men? Masculine Anxiety and the Problem of African-American Identity* (New York: Oxford University Press, 1996); Suzanne Pharr, *In the Time of the Right: Reflections on Liberation* (Berkeley, CA: Chardon Press, 1996), and *Homophobia: A Weapon of Sexism* (Berkeley, CA: Chardon Press, 1997); Andy Medhurst and Sally M. Munt, eds., *Lesbian and Gay Studies: A Critical Introduction* (London: Cassell Publishing, 1997); Smith, *The Truth That Never Hurts*; and Devon W. Carbado, ed., *Black Men on Race, Gender, and Sexuality: A Critical Reader* (New York: New York University Press, 1999).

Chapter 16

The Civil Rights–Black Power Legacy

Black Women Elected Officials at the Local, State, and National Levels

Linda Faye Williams

> African American women who come to government, come with the notion that government is not benevolent. . . . We come knowing that if we are going to take part in this process, we have to understand both the power and the limitations of the office. We really have to think very carefully about how we craft this thing called government. Our experience as African Americans has allowed us to develop very clear principles, focused on what we need to do.
> —Margaret Archie-Hudson, Assemblywoman, District 48 (Los Angeles)[1]

Arguably, one of the most potent legislative outcomes of the Civil Rights Movement of the 1950s and 1960s was the Voting Rights Act of 1965. While, for example, socioeconomic indicators such as the median income and the poverty rate demonstrate only murky progress at best in altering the relative condition of the black population as compared to the white population, the election of blacks to public office, largely as a result of the Voting Rights Act, demonstrates one straight line of upward growth (Figure 1).[2] From fewer than 500 black elected officials in the nation as a whole in 1965, the numbers have grown to more than 8,000.[3]

Black women have been no exception to this trend. Like their male

FIGURE 1

Comparison of Political and Socioeconomic Trends, Selected Years, 1965–1996

Number of Black Elected Officials (BEOs), Selected Years, 1965–1996

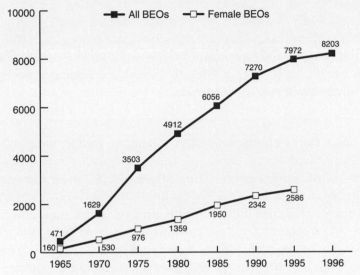

Socioeconomic Indicators: Female BEOs, Selected Years, 1965–1996

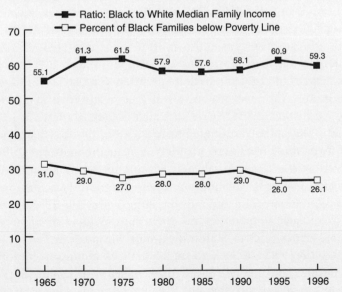

SOURCES: Joint Center for Political and Economic Studies, Washington, DC and U.S. Census Bureau

cohorts, since 1965 they too have won public office in greater and greater numbers. This essay first presents the relevant data on the extent of black women's success in winning public office at all levels of government; then discusses key factors that account for that progress—especially the role of politicization during the Civil Rights–Black Power Era. It then analyzes whether black women in public office are modifying their goals and priorities the more we move away from the Civil Rights Era; and finally introduces some prospects for the future of black women in politics.

The Rising Numbers of Black Women in Public Office

Since the heyday of the modern Civil Rights–Black Power Movement, the number of black female elected officials in the United States has grown impressively at all levels of government. For instance, in 1968, the first black woman (Shirley Chisholm, Democrat–New York) was elected to Congress; in 1975, there were four black women in Congress; and by 1997, thirteen black women served in the 105th Congress—including the first black female U.S. Senator, Carol Moseley Braun.[4]

The number of black female state elected officials has grown even more dramatically. In 1938, the first black woman was elected to a state legislature, Democrat Crystal Bird Fauset, elected to the Pennsylvania House of Representatives. In 1975, there were 35 black female elected state legislators, and by 1996, there were 179.[5]

Not surprisingly, given that there are more than 80,000 local governmental bodies, the most growth of all has occurred in black women holding local offices. In 1965, Constance Baker Motley, former New York City Manhattan Borough President, was the first black woman elected to hold a prominent position in a major metropolis; in 1975, there were twelve black female mayors; and in 1990, Sharon Pratt Kelly was elected mayor of Washington, D.C.—the first black female to become mayor of one of the nation's ten largest cities. By 1996, there were ninety-five black women mayors—including mayors of some nonmajority black cities, such as Sharon Becton of Minneapolis.[6]

All together, by 1996 there were 2,586 black female elected officials in the nation (31.5 percent of all black elected officials). This was a significant increase from the only 160 black female elected officials or 9.8 percent of the total in 1970, the first year data are available by gen-

TABLE 1

Black Female Elected Officials, 1975 and 1993

Office	1975	1996	% Growth Rate
U.S. Senators	0	1	—
U.S. Representatives	4	13	225
State Executives	0	1	—
State Senators	3	40	1233
State Representatives	32	139	334
County Supervisors and Council Members	25	95	280
Other County Officials	6	52	767
Mayors	12	95	692
Council Members	134	865	546
Other Municipal Officials	66	219	232
Judges, Justices, Magistrates	22	228	936
Police Chiefs, Sheriffs, and Marshals	6	2	−67
Other Law Enforcement Officials	8	24	200
State and College Board of Education Members	10	19	90
Local School Board Members	204	792	288
Other Education Officials	0	1	—

SOURCE: Joint Center for Political and Economic Studies

der on black elected officials (see Figure 1). As Table 1 shows, black women have made significant progress in winning public office at every level and in most types of offices, with the exception of police chiefs, sheriffs, and officers. There are now 147 black female county officials, 865 black female city council members, and 228 black female justices, judges, and magistrates.

Indeed, at the close of the twentieth century, the proportion of black elected officials who were women was greater than the proportion of white elected officials who were women. For instance, in 1993 (the latest year for which comparable data are available) African American women composed 22 percent of all African American mayors, but white women composed only 16 percent of all white mayors. Black women composed 29 percent of all black state legislators, while white women composed 25 percent of all white state legislators; and black women composed 23 percent of all black members of the U.S. House of Representatives, while white women composed only 10 percent of all white members of the House (Table 2). In short, if black elected officials are viewed as one group and whites another, then black women consistently form a larger proportion of black elected officials than white women do among white elected officials at all levels of public office. One must conclude that despite being disadvantaged by not only gender but race (and for most, class), black women have been able to overcome political disadvantage

TABLE 2
Women as a Percentage of White and Black Elected Officials,
Selected Years, 1976–1993

Year	Mayors		State Legislators		U.S. House Representatives	
	Black	White	Black	White	Black	White
1976	6.6	4.1	12.6*	7.8*	25.0*	3.5*
1977	7.4	5.8	15.6*	8.9*	26.6*	3.8*
1979	4.5	7.5	18.2*	9.9*	12.6	3.5
1981	10.7	7.8	18.9*	11.8*	11.7	4.7
1985	12.2	8.2	18.8*	14.5*	5.2	5.7
1993	22.2	16.1	29.4*	24.6*	23.1*	10.3*

* Racial differences significant at $p < .05$
SOURCES: Joint Center for Political and Economic Studies, National Women's Political Caucus, Center for the American Woman and Politics, and National Conference of State Legislators.

within the black community more quickly than white women in the white community. In sum, although black women have clearly not achieved descriptive representation in holding political office (they remain underrepresented compared to their share of the population at every level of government), their striking electoral progress is one clear legacy of the Civil Rights–Black Power Movement.

The "Puzzle" of Black Women's Success

How and why have black women, despite being caught in what Maya Angelou called "the tripartite crossfire of masculine prejudice, white illogical hate, and black lack of power,"[7] won and held a growing number of political offices?

The most obvious reason for the relative success of black women in running for and winning public office is, of course: "They got the votes!" Behind black women in Congress, state legislatures, mayoralties, and so forth are the millions of faceless voters—mostly black and heavily female—who supported their candidacies.[8] Indeed, the growth of black female voting power is another important political development. Although in 1956 black women's voter turnout rate (28 percent) was eighteen percentage points lower than black men's (46 percent),[9] data collected by the U.S. Census Bureau demonstrate a pattern of higher voter turnout for black women than for black men in every year since the mid-term elections of 1974.[10] In short, even before white women voted in higher proportions than white men (a trend beginning in 1980), black women outpaced black men in voting. By the 1992 presidential election, nearly two out of every three black voters were women. Although women continued to compose the majority of the black electorate in the 1994 mid-term elections, their proportion had fallen to 57 percent. Since black women compose only 52 percent of the black adult population, however, clearly a gender gap continued in black electoral participation rates.

Moreover, it appears that not only black women but black men are more supportive of women holding public office than either white women or white men. Table 3 presents a series of questions concerning

TABLE 3

Attitudes Toward Women in Politics, by Race, 1996

If your party nominated a woman for President, would you vote for her if she were qualified for the job?

	White women (%)	White men (%)	Black women (%)	Black men (%)
Yes	80.5	76.7	85.0	82.1
No	19.5	23.3	15.0	17.9

$p < .0005$
SOURCE: General Social Survey, 1996, National Opinion Research Center (NORC)

Most men are better suited emotionally for politics than are most women.

	White women (%)	White men (%)	Black women (%)	Black men (%)
Agree	43.2	47.8	39.3	41.1
Disagree	56.8	52.2	60.7	58.9

$p < .0450$
SOURCE: General Social Survey, 1996, National Opinion Research Center (NORC)

If half the leadership positions in this country were held by women leaders, do you think the country would be much better off, somewhat better off, somewhat worse off, or much worse off?

	White women (%)	Black women (%)
Better off (combined)	76.8	85.4
Worse off (combined)	8.4	8.3
No difference	14.7	6.3

$p < .05$
SOURCE: Women's Voices Survey, 1996

How important is it that more women be elected to the U.S. Senate?

	White women (%)	White men (%)	Black women (%)	Black men (%)
Very important	47.4	28.1	79.6	62.4
Somewhat important	30.5	31.2	18.3	25.2
Not very important	22.1	40.7	2.1	12.4

$p < .0005$
SOURCE: Voter News Service Exit Poll, 1996.

women in politics. In each instance, both black men and women provide more favorable responses than do white men and women toward women in politics or leadership positions. Blacks are more likely than whites to report they would vote for a woman for president, more likely to disagree with the view that men are better suited emotionally for politics, more likely to believe the country would be better off if half the leadership positions were held by women, and more likely to think it is important to elect more women to the Senate. According to these responses, black men are more supportive of having women in power than white women!

Other data show that most blacks clearly prefer an even playing field for black men and women in politics. For instance, the 1993–94 National Black Politics Survey found that 77 percent of African Americans want black women to "share equally in the political leadership of the black community."[11] Thus, the first piece of the puzzle to black women candidates' increasing success in politics is the strong support they find in black communities.

The efficacy of black voters' support for black female candidates has been facilitated by opportunities created by majority-minority redistricting. In fact, it is difficult to overestimate the influence of electoral redistricting (pursuant to the Voting Rights Act and subsequent challenges which led to the creation of majority-black districts) on the fortunes of black women candidates. New majority-black districts became essentially open seats in which blacks (including females) could contest an election without challenging a white male opponent. Since there were no incumbency advantages to overcome, many black females have won in these instances. For example, every black woman in Congress, with the exception of Senator Carol Moseley Braun (Democrat–Illinois) and Representatives Julia Carson (Democrat–Indiana) and Cynthia McKinney (Democrat–Georgia) represents a majority-minority jurisdiction, and it should be noted that McKinney's district was majority-black when she was first elected. Analysis of the racial composition of state legislative districts demonstrates that as late as 1992, three out of every four black female state legislators compared to two out of three black male state legislators represented majority-black districts.[12] In short, black women have been heavily dependent upon majority-black districting to win public office.

It is in this context that one understands the challenge posed to the future election of blacks—both male and female—by recent court cases attacking majority-minority redistricting. Comprehensive studies document how exceptional it remains for whites to vote for blacks of either gender.[13] This is especially true the more such candidates strive to genuinely represent the interests of blacks or any other group which does not benefit from the status quo. Abandoning race-conscious redistricting will come at great cost to black elected officials.

Yet this is precisely what recent U.S. Supreme Court decisions have been leaning toward. Beginning with *Shaw v. Reno* (a 1993 North Carolina case), followed by *Miller v. Johnson* (a Georgia case), *Louisiana v. Hays*, and *Bush v. Vera* (a Texas case), and so forth, the high Court's rulings in the 1990s have made it substantially harder to take race or ethnicity into account when drawing election district boundaries. In the wake of these rulings, even before the 1996 elections, seven majority-minority districts (six black and one Hispanic) were held to be unconstitutional and required to be redrawn. If the Supreme Court's decisions in *Shaw* and its progeny continue to produce a reduction in the number of majority-minority districts, then the number of African American (and Latino) representatives of both genders will decline as well. This negative development would mean that the era of relatively fast growth of black female elected officials was at an end. For the time being, however, the point here is that black women candidacies were greatly facilitated from 1970 through 1990 by majority-minority redistricting occurring after each decennial census.

Several other key hypotheses have been advanced to explain the increasing number of black women in public office, all turning on the view that black women are more politically ambitious than their white female counterparts. In turn, this heightened political ambition is attributed to: (1) socioeconomic factors; (2) double or triple consciousness as a result of race, gender, and class oppression; and (3) legacies of participatory modes developed or expanded in the Civil Rights–Black Power Era.

Regarding socioeconomic factors, several analyses have found that black women overcome the "double disadvantage" of race and gender by exceeding their racial and gender counterparts in certain preparatory background characteristics such as education and occupational prestige.[14] Table 4, based on analysis of data from all fifty states' bluebooks and/or legislative directories during 1995–1996, demonstrates the relevant data for more than 4,000 state legislators (including 140 black female ones) for which data on race, gender,

TABLE 4
Educational and Occupational Status of State Legislators by Race and Gender

	Percentages			
	Males		Females	
	White	Black	White	Black
Education (Number in sample)	(2,866)	(424)	(717)	(140)
High school or less	10.7	6.7	6.1	7.3
Post-secondary	17.4	20.4	23.4	15.7
College Graduate	28.8	21.6	37.3	21.8
Graduate/Professional Degree	43.1	51.3	33.2	55.2
Occupation (Number in sample)*	(2473)	(400)	(678)	(135)
High prestige	51.4	54.0	40.7	58.7
Moderate prestige	34.6	42.4	36.8	33.4
Low prestige	14.0	3.6	22.5	7.9

* Occupational prestige designations are adapted from General Social Surveys, Cumulative Codebook, 1996: High = Attorney, physician, engineer, professional, college professor; Moderate = School teacher, banker, businessperson, insurance, real estate, clergy; Low = Blue collar, farmer/rancher, housewife, student, other (Note: There is, perhaps, a gender bias in the occupational prestige analysis, given the classification of "housewife" as a "low-prestige" occupation.)
SOURCE: Calculations based on information in state blue books and legislative directories from all 50 states and/or the National Conference of State Legislators. The total number (4,147) of state legislators for which data were available compose more than half of all state legislators in the United States.

occupation, and education were available. This table shows that both black men and women have higher overall educational levels than white legislators and that black women have the highest educational levels of all four race-gender groups. In fact, among state legislators in the study, more black women (55.2 percent) held graduate degrees than did any other group. Although black women were only slightly more likely than black male state legislators (51.3 percent) to hold graduate degrees, they were substantially more likely than white female state legislators (33.2 percent) in this regard.

A similar situation obtains for occupational data. Again, a higher percentage of black women (58.7 percent) held jobs perceived to be "high prestige," followed by black males (54.0 percent), white males (51.4 percent), and white females (40.7 percent). Thus, black female state legislators are more likely to hold high prestige occupations and far less likely to hold low prestige occupations. In sum, the old adage black parents often tell their children, "You've got to work twice as hard to get half as far," seems to partially explain the puzzle of black women's success in winning public office.

What, however, of the hypothesis that black women's civic activism, especially as an outgrowth of the Civil Rights–Black Power Movement, helps to explain their relative success? The remainder of the essay takes up the analysis of this hypothesis. What is the legacy of the Civil Rights–Black Power Movement in shaping political participation and the priorities and actions of black women in public office?

The Civil Right–Black Power Movement—Legacies for Black Female Elected Officials

In what sense was the Civil Rights–Black Power Movement a stimulus for greater political ambition on the part of black women, and what are the legacies of the Movement for black women elected officials in the post–Civil Rights Era? A useful way to begin to answer this question is to look at biographical profiles of women active in the 1950s and 1960s. While any number of black female leaders could be chosen—Ella Baker, Daisy Bates, Rosa Parks, JoAnn Robinson Gibson, Diane Nash, to name only a few,[15] the recent publication of biographical/autobiographical works on Fannie Lou Hamer and Elaine Brown suggest them as appropriate examples.

Indeed, to a substantial extent, Hamer and Brown are nearly perfect icons of the two, often conflicting, sides of the bidirectional road leading out of Selma, Alabama in 1965: the Civil Rights Movement of established and older civil rights groups and the Black Power movement of newer and insurgent militants. Thus, on one side stood Hamer, a symbol of the group of black women allied with the nation's more established civil rights organizations and focused on righting the wrongs (reforming) of the American political system. On the other side stood Brown, a symbol of black (generally younger) women allied with nascent organizations who at least temporarily sought to go well beyond reform of the American political system to transforming its very soul—the capitalist economic structure.

From Hamer's defiant stance at the 1964 Democratic National Convention onward and her visible, vibrant example of self-empowerment, it was clear that a goal of the Civil Rights Movement would be increasing opportunities for not only black men, but also black women, to hold elective office and seek to use political office to determine their own destinies. As Kay Mills's biography of Hamer vividly demonstrates, Hamer challenged the nation to fulfill the promises of constitutional democracy.[16] Thus, not surprisingly, when the Civil Rights Movement finally came to Hamer's small town of Ruleville,

Mississippi in 1962, she was one of the first black citizens to register to vote.

The younger Elaine Brown's eyes were not so much on reforming the system as revolting against it. She took a more openly angry route to influence and power. In 1968, when Shirley Chisholm was becoming the first black woman elected to Congress, Brown left Temple University and joined the Black Panther Party, abandoning the struggle for electoral power for more radical challenges, among them black nationalism.[17]

What the two women had in common, however, was an understanding that the participatory mode was needed in both system-oriented activities and protest politics. To be sure, neither would ever hold a major electoral office. Hamer's radical challenge to President Lyndon Baines Johnson, the Democratic party, and members of Congress to fulfil the promises of democracy practically preordained that neither major party would ever support her in a political candidacy. Far more certain, when in August 1974, Brown assumed control of the Black Panthers, it was clear she had no electoral future (even had she wanted one). *Life* magazine's chilling photograph of seventeen-year-old Jonathan Jackson leading a Marin County judge out of the courtroom with a shotgun to his neck as human collateral for the freedom of the Soledad Brothers was all that many voters needed to seal the fate of most Panthers for political office for decades to come. The Black Panther Party's otherwise successful ventures, such as community programs and encouragement of a new sense of community pride and individual self-esteem, got lost in the public's focus on the party's advocacy of the use of violence in self-defense.

Yet ultimately both Hamer and Brown played key roles in the development of the new post–1964 electoral-representative institutions. When Lyndon Johnson initiated the Great Society and the War on Poverty, both Hamer and Brown found themselves on the crest of an approach that sought to use system-oriented activities and federal money to assist African American communities in solving their own problems. Armed with federal dollars, Hamer implemented a successful Head Start program, attacked the Delta's hunger problem by lobbying for increased assistance from federal sources and wealthy liberals, and started community co-ops and a Freedom Farm. Brown not only used federal aid to further the Panthers' free food programs, medical clinics, and community schools, but proved influential in

Oakland's election of its first black mayor and in initiating changes in long-term Bay area investment plans making them more beneficial to the surrounding, poor black neighborhoods.

In sum, despite the internecine strife that came to characterize the Movement in the post–1965 period, the work of both Hamer and Brown demonstrates how the groundwork for black gains in the electoral sphere were laid even as the seeds for the dominant critique of the limits of those gains were sowed. Like Margaret Archie-Hudson, the current black state legislator quoted at the start of this chapter, Hamer and Brown clearly understood both the potential and the limits of the electoral route to racial equality.

In essence, as poor "underprivileged" black women, both Hamer and Brown had to fight against racism, sexism, and class exploitation. These two women serve as examples of the power of moral energy, and their efforts eclipse cynicism and defeatism. As much as anyone from that era, they understood that in a genuine democracy, people are politically active not to achieve celebrity or money, but to change the lives of oppressed people. Together their voices and their examples of using system-oriented and protest modes of participation created a rare alchemy that produced a basis of coherent thought and practice around freedom, justice, and equality that would encourage black women into political action for decades to come.

What, then, are the legacies from the leadership of women like Hamer and Brown in the Civil Rights–Black Power Movement? The first legacy was the message of civic responsibility and the absolute necessity to be active. In the Civil Rights Era, it was a message widely endorsed. Concomitantly, the 1950s and the 1960s marked an unusually high point of black political activism (and American civic participation more generally). Thus, research conducted during this period showed that when controlling for education and other indicators of social class, blacks engaged more in social and political participation than whites.[18] Moreover, as activist Ella Baker and sociologist Charles Payne have concluded, African American women were more likely than men to participate in the Civil Rights–Black Power Movement.[19] In the words of Baker, "The movement of the fifties and sixties was carried largely by women, since it came out of the church. . . . The number of women who carried the movement was much larger than that of men."[20] If this is correct, then the higher activism of black women during the Civil Rights Era had the potential not only to

heighten female political ambition and explain the higher proportions of black women who vote compared to their male cohorts, but
also to enable black women to gain skills from canvassing, getting out
the vote, organizing and participating in meetings, and so forth that
were directly transferable to the electoral sphere.[21]

A second legacy of Hamer and Brown's leadership is the necessity
to mix multiple modes of political participation. "Politics by any
means necessary," the slogan went, and, like Hamer and Brown, the
African American masses used a wide range of participatory modes.
Although political scientists who study participation usually consider system-oriented activities (such as voting, lobbying, and working in a campaign) and protest activities (such as sit-ins, marches, and
boycotts) as separate and distinct participatory spheres, the participatory norms of African Americans have historically mixed these activities.[22] Survey data measuring political participation in the 1960s is instructive. For example, a 1966 Harris-Newsweek Survey on Race Relations examined the frequency of black participation in eleven
modes of political action: (1) asked people to register to vote; (2) gone
to a political meeting; (3) stopped buying at a store; (4) asked people
to vote for a candidate; (5) marched in a demonstration; (6) written or
spoken to a congressman; (7) worked for a candidate; (8) given
money to a candidate; (9) taken part in a sit-in; (10) picketed a store;
and (11) gone to jail.

What distinguished the modes of participation among blacks in
the mid-1960s was not a difference between protest and system-oriented activities, but rather those activities that required high levels of
individual initiative and resources compared to those activities that
did not. Thus, for example, about an equal number of blacks reported
marching in demonstrations (22 percent), writing or speaking to their
congressional representative (20 percent), and working in a political
campaign (19 percent). Similarly, almost the same proportions reported engaging in conventional forms of political participation such
as asking people to vote for a candidate (30 percent) and unconventional forms such as participating in a consumer boycott (31 percent).[23] Finally, those modes of participation that required heavy individual investments or greater personal costs whether conventional
(such as giving money to a candidate—17 percent) or unconventional
(taking part in a sit-in—14 percent, or going to jail—7 percent) were
the least likely to occur.

The same survey, however, found that whites were almost exclusively likely to engage in conventional forms of participation. While more than 40 percent of whites responded they had asked people to register to vote, gone to a political meeting, and contacted an elected official, for instance, fewer than 2 percent reported boycotting a store, marching in a demonstration, or taking part in a sit-in.

Thus, like Hamer and Brown, the participatory norms of African Americans in the Civil Rights Era embraced what Aldon Morris, Shirley Hatchett, and Ronald Brown describe as the "orderly and disorderly" side of the political process.[24] By orderly and disorderly, they mean that blacks, more directly and for a longer time than whites, have been socialized into employing political tactics that lie both within and outside of conventional political processes. Both system-oriented and protest strategies were used during the Civil Rights Era.

Of course, neither Hamer and Brown, nor the modern Civil Rights Movement in general, hardly innovated this mixing of forms of participation. The key to understanding these different patterns of participation is found in the long exclusion of African Americans from conventional means of participation, beginning in slavery and picking back up with the collapse of Reconstruction and the cementing of Jim Crow. In response to drastically limited options for political mobilization, African Americans developed what Michael Dawson has referred to as a "black counterpublic."[25] This counterpublic, which included black religious institutions, civil rights organizations, social clubs, Masonic groups, the black press, and so forth, encouraged a variety of unconventional political tactics and strategies that encouraged and later nurtured the development of social movements to challenge white supremacist discourse and practices.

African American women played a key role in organizing the black counterpublic and forging an oppositionist culture.[26] In fact, as historiography moves away from standard great man, great event, chronological narratives to a more nuanced study of community- and statewide efforts directed by a variety of formerly faceless individuals and groups, the role of African American women and their organizations in the Civil Rights–Black Power Movement are highlighted.[27] In particular, the women's missionary societies and conventions of black churches provided the early leadership and networks for the secular-based black women's club movement. Concomitantly, the associational life begun by women through the women's club movement and the

National Association of Colored Women's (NACW) "racial uplift" and antilynching campaigns at the turn of the twentieth century provided space for political activism.[28] Middle-class black organizations, such as the college sororities Alpha Kappa Alpha and Delta Sigma Theta, mobilized on behalf of not only black, but women's, suffrage. Along with black men's organizations, such as the Alpha Phi Alpha fraternity, black women's organizations helped develop citizenship schools in the urban South. With the slogan "A Voteless People Is a Hopeless People," these groups registered hundreds of blacks during the 1930s, decades before the Southern Christian Leadership Conference (SCLC) and the Student Nonviolent Coordinating Committee (SNCC) launched the citizenship schools in the 1960s.[29]

What is important to note is that throughout this history, the unconventional and conventional sides of political participation were never viewed by blacks as separate spheres. Black participatory norms involved using tools of the disorderly side to further their aims to gain the means to use the orderly side of politics. Thus, the trajectories of Hamer and Brown reveal the efficacy of historic black participatory norms.

A third legacy of Hamer and Brown's leadership was their understanding of the importance of building a force, an organization, that has the capability over time for mobilizing active grassroots support for initiatives or programs that are directly political—political in the usual sense of expressly seeking to alter the patterns or substance of governance, policy, and economic relations. Thus, neither were satisfied to stop at what Robin D. G. Kelley has labeled "infrapolitics," the region of "daily confrontations, evasive actions, and stifled thoughts."[30] Hamer and Brown understood that infrapolitics are to political movements what carbon, water, and oxygen are to life—the raw materials within which movements for political change emerge, but not the sufficient conditions.[31] Both women understood the need to anchor political action in popular membership organizations, that is, entities with concrete and clearly identified constituencies that are at least in principle empowered to pass and execute judgment on leaders' actions. They sought a politics based on genuinely mass-based, deliberative processes; and concrete, interest-based organizing that connected with people's daily lives and concerns, rather than an undifferentiated, mute mass, the repository of the interpretations of others who presume to speak on its behalf.

Such a mass-based politics helped to define the object of Hamer and Brown's activism. As a result, theirs was a politics that involved far more than combining a laundry list of discrete symbolic issues too remote from people's everyday life to generate either intense support over time or ongoing dialogue, such as affirmative action, majority-minority redistricting, and even police corruption. As important as these issues are, they were not the types of concerns that became the focal point of Brown and Hamer's work. Rather, their concentration was on objects of policy that could directly address the problems of the poor: hunger, jobs, health care, early education, and more general investments in poor communities. Thus, a fourth legacy of their work was a focus on policy not only about freedom (civil rights), but also about redistribution. The next section focuses on the extent to which black female elected officials are fulfilling the civil rights legacy of leaders like Hamer and Brown.

Legacies and Legislative Behaviors

Coming out of the Civil Rights–Black Power Movement, anecdotal evidence suggests that black female elected officials focused their energies directly on the movements' priorities. For example, in 1968 when Congresswoman Shirley Chisholm was placed on the Agricultural Committee, she successfully battled for a committee position more relevant to serving the urban poor.[32] Indeed, the first few black women in Congress (Chisholm, Barbara Jordan, Yvonne Burke, and Cardiss Collins) left Congress with biographies detailing their achievements in the spheres of civil rights and urban and social policy.[33] The first black female U.S. Representatives became nationally known for activities such as holding hearings investigating racism (for example, Chisholm's racism in the army hearings) and expanding civil rights (for example, Jordan's leadership in the expansion of the Voting Rights Act to include language minorities and thereby the state of Texas as well as some non-Southern states such as California and New York).

But what of black female elected officials today? Do they still reflect the policy legacies of the Civil Rights–Black Power Era? Anecdotal evidence on women currently serving in Congress is less clear that black female Representatives remain as concerned about the needs of blacks, particularly poor ones. For example, while Chisholm battled to serve on committees dealing with redistribution, civil rights, and the cities, black female members of Congress now fight to be members of powerhouse committees such as Rules and Ways and Means or committees that allow them to develop highly specialized expertise such as Science and Technology. Similarly, in at least one recent analysis of the Congressional Black Caucus, black female members were found to be more conservative than black men in their voting on issues such as crime and trade policy. Black female members of Congress were also more likely than black male members to define themselves as only "slightly liberal," more likely to say that "racial issues were less critical than economic and health care policy issues."[34] According to Clarence Lusane, the author of this study, the slightly more conservative bent of black female congressional representatives may be a reflection of the fact that black women in Congress are disproportionately likely to represent southern districts, more likely than earlier black women and current black men in Congress to serve rural districts, more likely to have served in hostile southern state legislatures before coming to Congress, and less likely to have flexibility because of their lower seniority.

To further investigate the impact of the Civil Rights–Black Power Movement on the politics of current black women elected officials while reducing the project to manageable proportions, the 179 black women serving in state legislatures as of January 1996 were surveyed in the Spring of 1997.[35] Two hypotheses were tested in the analysis:

1. Women of the New Deal (defined as those 65 years old or older) and civil rights generations (defined as those 40–64 years old) would be more likely to serve on committees overseeing civil rights and redistributive policies and more likely to list these issues among their legislative priorities than women of the post–civil rights era (defined as those under 40 years old); and
2. Women with higher levels of race consciousness would be more likely to serve on committees overseeing civil rights and redistributive policies and more likely to list these issues among their legislative priorities than women with lower levels of race consciousness.

In sum, the research tested the thesis that the further we move from the Civil Rights–Black Power Era, the less important the long-term dual agenda of African Americans (ending racial discrimination and oppression *and* supporting social and economic justice for all Americans) would be centrally important to black female elected officials.[36]

To test this thesis, there were two main dependent variables: committee assignments and legislative priorities. To measure the first, respondents were asked to list their committee assignments. Assignments on civil rights committees were identified as all committees likely to handle constitutional and civil rights issues and oversight of state equal opportunity agencies. Assignments on redistributive committees were identified as service on committees handling children and family services, health, human resources, education, and elderly affairs.[37]

To measure legislative priorities, respondents were provided an open-ended question that asked them to list their legislative priorities for the current session. From the total list of priorities offered, civil rights and redistributive issues were identified as those dealing with equal opportunity, affirmative action, children and family issues, education, health, housing, and so-called "women's issues" such as spousal abuse, abortion, sexual harassment, and so forth.

The major independent variables in the analyses were age (as described above) and racial consciousness. Adopting a direct approach, racial consciousness was defined by asking respondents a set of questions concerning whether they felt their fates were linked to those of other blacks—that is, whether they saw black interests as a proxy for self-interests.[38] Specifically, respondents were asked: (1) "On the whole, would you say that your own self-interests are very linked to the interests of other blacks; somewhat linked to the interests of other blacks; or not linked at all to the interests of other blacks?" (2) "On the whole, would you say that the economic position of blacks is better than that of whites, about the same as that of whites, or worse than that of whites?" (3) "On the whole, would you say that advancing the goals of the Civil Rights Movement is very important to you, somewhat important to you, or not at all important to you?" The three individual variables had a range from 1 to 3. They were then combined in an additive index that had a range from 3 to 9. Responses were coded so that a higher value on this measure indicated stronger racial consciousness.

In the analysis, differences in committee assignments and legislative priorities were examined in comparison to the age category and

TABLE 5

Mean Legislative and Political Differences Among Civil Rights Generation and Non–Civil Rights Generation Legislators

	Post–Civil Rights Generation	Civil Rights Generation	New Deal Generation
Legislative committee assignments	0.27	0.28	0.24
Legislative priorities	0.44	0.51	0.27
N	19	64	27

* Significant at <.01 level
SOURCE: Author's survey

racial consciousness; these differences were then explored after controlling for a series of political and personal factors that might have had an effect on the dependent variable. These control variables included education, years of service in the legislature, level of professionalization of the legislature (for example, whether legislators are full- versus part-time, have substantial office staffs, secure committee assignments through processes, such as seniority, and so forth) ideology (the relative strength in state legislatures of legislators who score high on a liberalism scale versus those who score high on conservatism), marital status, region, and number of children.

As already indicated, the first step in the analysis was to establish whether or not there are significant bivariate differences on the dependent variables between black female state legislators who came to maturity during the Civil Rights Era and those who did not.[39] Table 5 presents the differences by age cohort. This table shows that in examining assignments to committees that handle legislation on civil rights and redistributive issues, the civil rights generation respondents were no more likely to serve on these committees than non–civil rights generation respondents. Of the committees on which those of the civil rights generation served, 28 percent are those classified as civil rights and redistributive committees. For New Deal generation respondents, the figure is 27 percent, and for post–civil rights generation respondents, the figure is 24 percent. In other words, civil rights generation legislators are no more likely than non–civil rights generation ones to serve on committees that would allow them to have an influence related to civil rights and redistributive issues.

However, the data support the hypothesis that civil rights (and New Deal) generation legislators are more likely than their post–civil rights counterparts to report that civil rights and redistributive issues are their legislative priorities. Indeed, civil rights and New Deal legislators are substantially more likely than post–civil rights generation legislators to list more issues concerning civil rights, human resources, children and family, and so forth. In the sample, these legislative priorities made up 44 percent of the priorities listed by New Deal generation respondents and 51 percent of the priorities listed by civil rights generation respondents, but only 27 percent of the priorities of post–civil rights generation respondents.[40] This finding supports the hypothesis that civil rights and New Deal generation legislators rank civil rights and redistributive issues more highly than post–civil rights era legislators.

Analysis of the second hypothesis—the impact of racial consciousness on committee assignments and legislative priorities—produces similar results. While levels of racial consciousness have no impact on committee assignments, those with strong levels of racial consciousness are significantly more likely to report that redistributive and civil rights issues are legislative priorities. The value on this measure is 8.7 percent for those with strong levels of racial consciousness, 7.4 percent for those with moderate levels of racial consciousness, and only 4.1 percent for those with weak or no racial consciousness.

Next, multivariate analysis was used to control for the effects of several important political and personal variables (as identified above) that might have been related to the dependent variables.[41] Even after controlling for other possible influential factors, the multivariate analysis confirms that a black female state legislator who came to political maturity during the New Deal or Civil Rights–Black Power Eras is more likely to report strong commitment to redistributive and civil rights issues. By contrast, a black female legislator who came to political maturity during the conservative post–Civil Rights Era is less likely to be committed to redistributive and civil rights issues.

In short, each hypothesis except for those related to service on committees is demonstrated. At first glance, the lack of a significant relationship between generation and racial consciousness and service on committees focusing on redistributive and civil rights issues may be striking. The results may indicate that these committees are less preferred by black women legislators as they gain seniority within the legislature. One possible alternative explanation, however, is that black women state legislators are not abandoning the issues dealt with by these committees, but pursuing them in a different arena, such as the more powerful committees handling legislation on appropriations, rules, and finance. This explanation gains support from further analysis indicating a significant positive relationship between service on appropriations, finance, and banking committees and strong levels of racial consciousness.[42]

Conclusions

Clearly, more black women serve in public office in the United States than ever before. Their election to office is just as clearly an important legacy of the Civil Rights–Black Power Movement. The success of these black women in winning public office demonstrates that the double disadvantage of race and gender (and for some, class) can be overcome by superior levels of education and background preparation while taking advantage of the policies instituted as a result of the Civil Rights Movement, particularly the majority-minority redistricting included in the Voting Rights Act.

However, black women elected officials are far from reaching descriptive representation in any state. Instead, they remain substantially under-represented compared to their proportion of the population. Recall that in total, black women elected officials still compose slightly less than one out of every three black elected officials, and black elected officials of both genders still compose less than 2 percent of the nation's elected officials. Even within the cohort of black elected officials only, the sphere of black female influence is highly circumscribed. For example, among the 35 black mayors of cities with populations of 50,000 or more in 1997, only three (8 percent) were women. All thirteen of the black women currently serving in Congress were elected in 1990 or later. Thus, in Congress—in large part due to seniority differences—black women exercise even less influence than black men. And there is little use denying that the future looks at least a bit bleak. Given the Supreme Court's decision in *Shaw* and its progenies, limitations on drawing majority-minority redistricting appear to be the order of the day. If this happens, the numbers of black female elected officials may grow much slower in the immediate future and maybe even decline.

This analysis of the voting record of the post–civil rights generation of black female state legislators suggests that future representatives will not consider the redistributive and civil rights issues as a priority as did black female leaders, such as Hamer and Brown, during the Civil Rights–Black Power Era. Meanwhile, global economic change, a technological revolution already eliminating millions of good jobs paying livable wages and providing safe work conditions, and the conservative climate of the 1980s and 1990s have already produced vast retrenchment in the policy agenda and electoral-representative institutions. These conditions have already turned back many of the political gains that the actions of women like Hamer and Brown helped produce.

We must revisit the history of the mixed modes of black political participation and rebuild a politics that not only depends upon the influence that can be garnered through electoral-representative institutions, but engages the disorderly side of politics. Such a politics will not be built solely on the million man or woman marches, racial outrages, symbolic issues, or corporatist myths about an organic black community. What is needed is a politics in the image of Hamer and Brown based on genuinely popular, deliberative processes and concrete, interest-based organizing that connects with people's daily lives and concerns.

NOTES

1. Margaret Archie-Hudson, "Panel IV: Does It Make a Difference? The Impact of Women of Color Elected Officials on Policy and Community," in Paule Cruz Takash, ed., *Critica: A Politics of Difference—Women of Color in Electoral Politics* (San Diego: University of California Press, 1995), 65.

2. For a more extensive discussion of the growth of black elected officials, see Theresa Chambliss, "The Growth and Significance of African American Elected Officials," in Ralph C. Gomes and Linda Faye Williams, eds., *From Exclusion to Inclusion: The Long Struggle for African American Political Power* (Westport, CT: Greenwood Press, 1992), 53–70.

3. All data cited on black elected officials prior to 1990 are from Chambliss, "The Growth and Significance of African American Elected Officials." All post–1989 data on the number of black elected officials (male and female) cited in this chapter were extrapolated from unpublished statistics supplied by Alfred Baltimore, Roster Clerk, Joint Center for Political and Economic Studies (JCPES), Washington, DC, October 14, 1997. It should be noted that JCPES remains the best source for updating the number of black elected officials. The

328 LINDA FAYE WILLIAMS

Washington-based think tank's annual statistics on black elected officials are widely quoted in official sources, including in publications of the U.S. Bureau of the Census.

4. Ibid.

5. Ibid.

6. Ibid.

7. Quoted in Laura Randolph, "Sisters in the Struggle," *Ebony* (August 1994): 18.

8. For a fuller discussion of black women's struggle for suffrage and their exercise of the franchise, see Marianne Githens and Jewel L. Prestage, *A Portrait of Marginality: The Political Behavior of the American Woman* (New York: Longman, 1977), 211–347; Gomes and Williams, eds., *From Exclusion to Inclusion,* 15–52; and Ann D. Gordon, Bettye Collier-Thomas, et al., eds., *African-American Women and the Vote, 1837–1965* (Amherst: University of Massachusetts Press, 1997).

9. Githens and Prestage, *A Portrait of Marginality,* 214.

10. U.S. Bureau of the Census, *Current Population Reports,* "Voting and Registration," Series P-20, 1964–1994.

11. Michael Dawson, *Behind the Mule: Race and Class in African American Politics* (Princeton, NJ: Princeton University Press, 1994), 177.

12. Linda Faye Williams, "The 1992 November Elections: Interpreting Gains Made by African American and Other Women of Color," in Takash, ed., *Critica,* 17–30.

13. For example, *Quiet Revolution in the South,* the data-packed work edited by Chandler Davidson and Bernard Grofman, demonstrates that around 1 percent of majority-white election districts in the South elect black candidates, despite an average black population of 25 percent in that region. See *Quiet Revolution in the South: The Impact of the Voting Rights Act, 1965–1990* (Princeton, NJ: Princeton University Press, 1994), 147.

14. Jewel Prestage, "Black Women State Legislators: A Profile," in Githens and Prestage, *A Portrait of Marginality,* 197; Robert Darcy and Charles Hadley, "Black Women in Politics: The Puzzle of Success," *Social Science Quarterly* 69 (1988): 629–45; and Gary Moncrief, Joel Thompson, and Robert Schulmann, "The Double Disadvantage Hypothesis: A Research Note," *Social Science Journal* 28: (1991): 481–88.

15. For brief discussions of these and other women leaders of the modern Civil Rights Movement, see Vicki L. Crawford, Jacqueline Rouse, and Barbara Woods, eds., *Women in the Civil Rights Movement: Trailblazers and Torchbearers, 1941–1965* (Brooklyn, NY: Carlson Publishing, 1990); and chapters in this volume.

16. Kay Mills, *This Little Light of Mine: The Life of Fannie Lou Hamer* (New York: Dutton, 1993). See also Martha Prescod Norman, "Shining in the Dark:

Black Women and the Struggle for the Vote, 1955–1965," in Gordon and Collier-Thomas, et al., eds., *African American Women and the Vote*, 172–99.

17. Elaine Brown, *A Taste of Power: A Black Woman's Story* (New York: Pantheon, 1992).

18. For discussion, see Richard Shingles, "Black Consciousness and Political Participation: The Missing Link," *American Political Science Review* 75 (1981): 76–91; and Lawrence Bobo and Franklin Gilliam, "Race, Socio-Political Participation, and Black Empowerment," *American Political Science Review* 84 (1990): 377–93.

19. Charles Payne, "Men Led, But Women Organized: Movement Participation of Women in the Mississippi Delta," in Crawford, Rouse, and Woods, *Women in the Civil Rights Movement*, 65–72.

20. Quoted in Teresa Nance, "Hearing the Missing Voice," *Journal of Black Studies* 26 (May 1996): 547.

21. Aldon D. Morris, Shirley J. Hatchett, and Ronald E. Brown, "The Civil Rights Movement and Black Political Socialization," in Roberta S. Siegel, ed., *Political Learning in Adulthood* (Chicago: University of Chicago Press, 1989), 75–91.

22. Frederick Harris, *Will the Circle Be Unbroken? The Erosion and Transformation of African American Civic Life*, Working Paper #9 (College Park: The National Commission on Civic Renewal, University of Maryland, Institute for Philosophy and Public Policy, 1997), 16–30.

23. Ibid., 17–19.

24. Morris, Hatchett, and Brown, "The Civil Rights Movement and Black Political Socialization," 77.

25. Michael Dawson, "A Black Counterpublic? Economic Earthquakes, Racial Agenda(s) and Black Politics," *Public Culture* 7 (1994): 195–223.

26. Evelyn Higginbotham, *Righteous Discontent: The Women's Movement in the Black Baptist Church*, 1880–1920 (Cambridge: Harvard University Press, 1993).

27. See, for example, Crawford, Rouse, and Woods, eds., *Women in the Civil Rights Movement*; John White, *Black Leadership in America: From Booker T. Washington to Jesse Jackson* (New York: Longman, 1990); and Clayborne Carson, *In Struggle: SNCC and the Black Awakening of the 1960s* (Cambridge: Harvard University Press, 1981).

28. For a brief account, see Dorothy Salem, "National Association of Colored Women," in Darlene Clark Hine, Elsa Barkley Brown, and Rosalyn Terborg–Penn, eds., *Black Women in America: An Historical Encyclopedia*, vol. 2 (Brooklyn, NY: Carlson Publishing, 1993): 842–51. See also Dianne Pinder-hughes, "The Role of African American Political Organizations in the Mobilization of Voters," in Gomes and Williams, eds., *From Exclusion to Inclusion*,

39–41; and Evelyn Higginbotham, "Clubwomen and Electoral Politics in the 1920s," in Gordon and Collier-Thomas, et al., eds., *African-American Women and the Vote*, 124–55.

29. For discussion of the roles of black sororities in antilynching and suffrage campaigns as well as voter registration drives, see Earnestine Green McNealey, "Alpha Kappa Alpha," in Hine, Brown, and Terborg-Penn, eds., *Black Women in America*, vol. 1, 24; Paula Giddings, "Delta Sigma Theta Sorority," in Hine, Brown, and Terborg-Penn, eds., *Black Women in America*, Vol. I, 319; Ida B. Wells Barnett, *Crusade for Justice: The Autobiography of Ida B. Wells*, Alfreda M. Duster, ed. (Chicago: University of Chicago Press, 1970); and Harris, "Will the Circle Be Unbroken?" 12–14.

30. Robin D. G. Kelley, "'We Are Not What We Seem': Rethinking Block Working Class Opposition in the Jim Crow South," *Journal of American History* 80 (June 1993) 75–112.

31. Adolph Reed, "Why There Is No Black Political Movement," *Village Voice*, September 1997, 28.

32. Susan Brownmiller, *Shirley Chisholm: A Biography* (Garden City, NY: Doubleday, 1970), 139.

33. Shirley Chisholm, *The Good Fight* (New York: Harper & Row, 1973); Shirley Chisholm, *Unbought and Unbossed* (Boston: Houghton Mifflin, 1970); Brownmiller, *Shirley Chisholm*, 121ff; Barbara Jordan and Shelby Hearon, *Barbara Jordan: A Self-Portrait* (Garden City, NY: Doubleday, 1979); James Haskins, *Barbara Jordan* (New York: Dial Press, 1977); Corrine J. Naden, *Barbara Jordan: Politician* (New York: Chelsea House, 1991); Joan E. Cashin, "Burke, Yvonne Braithwaite," in Hine, Brown, and Terborg-Penn, eds., *Black Women in America*, Vol. I, 195; Kathleen Thompson, "Collins, Cardiss Robertson," in Hine, Brown, and Terborg-Penn, eds., *Black Women in America*, 264–65; and "Cardiss Collins," *Current Biography*, vol. 58, no. 2 (February 1997): Vol. 1, 18–22.

34. Clarence Lusane, "The Interaction and Collaboration Between Black Interest Groups and Black Congressmembers in the 103rd Congress: A Study in Race-Conscious Policy Innovation" (Ph.D. diss., Howard University, 1997), 248.

35. A two-wave mailing procedure was used to conduct the survey; a reminder postcard was sent between survey mailings; and as the response deadline neared, telephone calls were made to tardy legislators offices reminding them to return the survey. There were 110 surveys returned, for a response rate of 61.5 percent. Seventy-seven percent of the respondents served in their states' lower house and 23 percent served in upper houses.

36. For a detailed and eloquent analysis of efforts of civil rights leaders to promote the agenda of civil rights and social welfare since the New Deal through the Civil Rights Era, see Dona Hamilton and Charles Hamilton, *Dual Agenda: Race and Social Welfare Policies of Civil Rights Organizations* (New York: Columbia University Press, 1997). Hamilton and Hamilton thoroughly dem-

onstrate that both equal rights for blacks and social and economic justice for all have been the two main objects of the black liberation movement for more than sixty years.

37. To control for variations in the number of committee assignments across state legislatures, analysis on a variable that measured the number of civil rights and redistributive committees on which a respondent sat was divided by the total number of committee assignments she held.

38. The linked fates thesis is Michael Dawson's sociopsychological theory concerning the importance of race consciousness. See Dawson, *Behind the Mule*.

39. For this purpose, an analysis of variance (ANOVA) of the difference of means for the three age groups was employed. Table 5 presents the means of each variable by age category, as well as the F statistic from the ANOVA.

40. These differences are significant at below the .01 level.

41. Although regression analysis (ordinary least squares estimates) confirms that neither generation nor racial consciousness is related to committee assignment and weakens the influence of generation and racial consciousness on legislative priorities, the original differences remain significant.

42. The coefficient for strong levels of racial consciousness was positive ($b = 0.024$) and significant at the .05 level ($t = 1.74$).

Selected Bibliography

Adams, Julyette Tamy. "Keepers of the Oral Traditions: An Afrocentric Analysis of Representative Plays by African-American Females, 1970–1984." Ph.D. diss., Bowling Green State University, 1995.

Ayers, William. "'We Who Believe in Freedom Cannot Rest Until It's Done': Two Dauntless Women of the Civil Rights Movement and the Education of a People." *Harvard Educational Review* 59 (4, 1989): 520–28.

Barnett, Bernice McNair. "Invisible Southern Black Women Leaders in the Civil Rights Movement: The Triple Constraints of Gender, Race, and Class." *Gender and Society* 7 (June 1993): 162–82.

Blackwelder, Julia Kirk. "Ladies, Belles, Working Women, and Civil Rights." In *The South for New Southerners*, ed. Paul D. Escott and David R. Goldfield, 94–113. Chapel Hill: University of North Carolina Press, 1991.

Blee, Kathleen M., ed. *No Middle Ground: Women and Radical Protest*. New York: New York University Press, 1998.

Bloom, Jack. *Class, Race, and the Civil Rights Movement: The Political Economy of Southern Racism*. Bloomington: Indiana University Press, 1987.

Blumberg, Rhoda Lois. "Careers of Women Civil Rights Activists." *Journal of Sociology and Social Welfare* 7 (1980): 708–29.

———. "White Mothers in the American Civil Rights Movement." In *Research in the Interweave of Social Roles: Women and Men*, ed. Helena A. Lopata, vol. 1, 33–50. Greenwich, CT: JAI Press, 1980.

———. "Women in the Civil Rights Movement: Reform or Revolution." *Dialectical Anthropology* 15 (1990): 133–39.

———. "Rediscovering Women Leaders of the Civil Rights Movement." In *Dream and Reality: The Modern Black Struggle for Freedom and Equality*, ed. Jeannie Swift, 19–28. Westport, CT: Greenwood Press, 1991.

Bramlet-Solomon, Sharon. "Civil Rights Vanguard in the Deep South: Newspaper Portrayal of Fannie Lou Hamer, 1964–1977." *Journalism Quarterly* 68 (Autumn 1991): 515–21.

Branch, Taylor. *Parting the Waters: America During the King Years, 1954–63*. New York: Simon and Schuster, 1988.

———. *Pillar of Fire: America in the King Years 1963–65*. New York: Simon and Schuster, 1998.

Braukman, Stacy. "Women and the Civil Rights Movement in Tampa: An Interview with Ellen H. Green." *Tampa Bay History* 14 (Fall/Winter 1992): 62–69.

Brisbane, Robert. *Black Activism: Racial Revolution in the United States, 1954–1970.* Valley Forge, PA: Judson Press, 1971.

Brown, Cynthia Stokes. *Ready From Within: Septima Clark and the Civil Rights Movement.* New Jersey: Africa World Press, 1990.

Brown, Elaine. *A Taste of Power: A Black Woman's Story.* New York: Pantheon Books, 1992.

Browning, Joan C. "Invisible Revolutionaries: White Women in Civil Rights Historiography." *Journal of Women's History* 8 (Fall 1996): 186–204.

Bryan, Dianetta Gail. "Her Story Unsilenced: Black Female Activists in the Civil Rights Movement." *Sage: A Scholarly Journal on Black Women* 2 (Fall 1988): 60–64.

Bryan, Louis C. "Modjeska A. Simkins: Profile of a Legend." *Sage: A Scholarly Journal on Black Women* 3 (Spring 1986): 56–57.

Bryant, Flora Renda. "An Examination of the Social Activism of Pauli Murray." Ph.D. diss., University of South Carolina, 1991.

Byrd, Richard W. "Interracial Cooperation in a Decade of Conflict: The Denton Christian Women's Inter-Racial Fellowship." *Oral History Review* 19 (1–2 1991): 31–53.

Calloway-Thomas, Carolyn and Thurmon Garner. "Daisy Bates and the Little Rock School Crisis: Forging the Way." *Journal of Black Studies* (May 1996): 616–28.

Campbell, Lucenia Williams. *Black Women Community Leaders in the Rural South: A Study of Power and Influence.* Ed.D. diss., University of Pittsburgh, 1983.

Cantarow, Ellen, Susan Gushee O'Malley, and Sharon Hartman Strom. *Moving the Mountain: Women Working for Social Change.* Old Westbury, NY: Feminist Press, 1980.

Caraway, Nancie. *Segregated Sisterhood: Racism and the Politics of American Feminism.* Knoxville: University of Tennessee Press, 1991.

Carson, Clayborne. *In Struggle: SNCC and the Black Awakening of the 1960s.* Cambridge: Harvard University Press, 1981.

———. *The Student Voice, 1960–1965: Periodical of the Student Nonviolent Coordinating Committee.* Westport, CT: Meckler Corporation, 1990.

Cash, Gail Ellayne. "Women at Hampton, 1930–1959." Ph.D. diss., Marquette University, 1994.

Chateauvert, M. Melinda. *Marching Together: Women of the Brotherhood of Sleepingcar Porters, 1925–1957.* Urbana: University of Illinois Press, 1998.

Clark, Septima P. *Echo in My Soul.* New York: E. P. Dutton, 1962.

Cluster, Dick. "The Borning Struggle: An Interview with Bernice Johnson Reagon." *Radical America* 12 (November/December 1978): 8–25.

Collier-Thomas, Bettye. *Daughters of Thunder: Black Women Preachers and Their Sermons, 1850–1979*. San Francisco: Jossey-Bass Publishers, 1998.

Collier-Thomas, Bettye and V. P. Franklin. *My Soul Is a Witness: A Chronology of the Civil Rights Era, 1954–1965*. New York: Henry Holt, 2000.

Collins, Patricia Hill. *Black Feminist Thought: Knowledge, Consciousness and the Politics of Empowerment*. New York: Routledge, 1991.

Conzett, Karen Sue. "Female College Students' Perceptions of their Role in the Civil Rights and Antiwar Movements of the 1960s." Ph.D. diss., University of Iowa, 1994.

Cook, Melanie B. "Gloria Richardson: Her Life and Work in SNCC." *Sage: A Scholarly Journal on Black Women* (Student Supplement 1988): 51–53.

Craig, Maxine B. "Black Is Beautiful: Personal Transformation and Political Change." Ph.D. diss., University of California, Berkeley, 1995.

Crawford, Vicki L. "We Shall Not Be Moved: Black Female Activists in the Mississippi Civil Rights Movement." Ph.D. diss., Emory University, 1987.

———. "Grassroots Activists in the Civil Rights Movement." *Sage: A Scholarly Journal on Black Women* 2 (Fall 1988): 24–29.

———. "Race, Class, Gender, and Culture: Black Women's Activism in the Mississippi Civil Rights Movement." *Journal of Mississippi History* 58 (Spring 1996): 1–21.

Crawford, Vicki L., Jacqueline A. Rouse, and Barbara Woods, eds. *Women in the Civil Rights Movement: Trailblazers and Torchbearers*. Brooklyn, NY: Carlson Publishing, 1990.

Curry, Constance. *Silver Rights*. Chapel Hill: Algonquin Books, 1995.

Darcy, R. and Charles D Hadley. "Black Women in Politics: The Puzzle of Success." *Social Science Quarterly* 69 (3, 1988): 629–45.

Davis, Beverly. "To Seize the Moment: A Retrospective on the National Black Feminist Organization." *Sage: A Scholarly Journal on Black Women* 5 (Fall 1988): 43–47.

Davis, Ella Joan. "African-American Women Writers of Detroit." Ph.D. diss., University of Michigan, 1990.

Deirenfield, Kathleen Murphy. "One 'Desegregated Heart': Sarah Patton Boyle and the Crusade for Civil Rights in Virginia." *Virginia Magazine of History and Biography* 104 (Spring 1996): 251–84.

Demuth, Jerry. "Tired of Being Sick and Tired." *The Nation* 198, no. 23 (June 1, 1964): 548–51.

Diamond, Arlyn. "Choosing Sides, Choosing Lives: Women's Autobiographies of the Civil Rights Movement." In *American Women's Autobiographies: Fea(s)ts of Memory*, ed. Margo Cully, 218–31. Madison: University of Wisconsin Press, 1992.

Dittmer, John. *Local People: The Struggle for Civil Rights in Mississippi*. Urbana: University of Illinois, 1994.

Dudziak, Mary L. "Josephine Baker, Racial Protest, and the Cold War." *Journal of American History* 81 (September 1994): 543–70.

Egerton, John. *A Mind to Stay Here: Profiles from the South.* New York: Macmillan, 1970.

Elbaz, Robert. *The Changing Nature of the Self.* Iowa City: University of Iowa Press, 1987.

Elliot, Aprele. "Ella Baker: Free Agent in the Civil Rights Movement." *Journal of Black Studies* 26 (May 1996): 593–603.

Elliot, Joan C. "Ella Jo Baker: A Civil Rights Warrior." *Griot* 11 (Spring 1992): 18–28.

Evans, Sara. "Women's Consciousness and the Southern Black Movement." *Southern Exposure* 4, no. 4 (1977): 10–18.

————. *Personal Politics: The Roots of Women's Liberation in the Civil Rights Movement and the New Left.* New York: Alfred A. Knopf, 1979.

Fairclough, Adam. *"To Redeem the Soul of America": The Southern Christian Leadership Conference and Martin Luther King, Jr.* Athens: University of Georgia Press, 1987.

Fleming, Cynthia G. "Black Women Activists and the Student Nonviolent Coordinating Committee: The Case of Ruby Doris Smith Robinson." *Journal of Women's History* 4 (Winter 1993): 64–82.

————. "'More Than Just a Lady': Ruby Doris Smith and Black Women's Leadership in the Student Nonviolent Coordinating Committee." In *Hidden Histories of Women in the New South,* ed. Virginia Bernhard, Betty Brandon, et al., 204–23. Columbia: University of Missouri Press, 1994.

————. *Soon We Will Not Cry: The Liberation of Ruby Doris Smith Robinson.* New York: Rowman and Littlefield, 1998.

Foeman, Anita K. "Gloria Richardson: Breaking the Mold." *Journal of Black Studies* 26 (May 1996): 604–15.

Fosu, Augustin Kwasi. "Occupational Mobility of Black Women, 1958–1981: The Impact of Post–1964 Antidiscrimination Measures." *Industrial and Labor Relations Review* 45, no. 2 (1992): 281–94.

Franklin, V. P. *Black Self Determination: A Cultural History of African-American Resistance.* Brooklyn: Lawrence Hill Books, 1992.

————. "Bates, Daisy Lee Gatson (1920–[1999])." In *Black Women in America: An Historical Encyclopedia,* ed., Darlene Clark Hine, Rosalyn Terborg-Penn, Elsa Barkley Brown, Vol. I, 94–96. New York: Carlson Publishing, 1993.

————. *Living Our Stories, Telling Our Truths: Autobiography and the Making of the African American Intellectual Tradition.* New York: Oxford University Press, 1996.

Garland, Phyll. "Builders of a New South." *Ebony* 21 (August 1966): 27–37.

Gates, Lorraine. "Power from the Pedestal: The Women's Emergency Committee and the Little Rock School Crisis." *Arkansas Historical Quarterly* 55 (Spring 1996): 26–57.

Giddings, Paula. *When and Where I Enter: The Impact of Black Women on Race and Sex in America.* New York: William Morrow, 1984.

Gilkes, Cheryl Townsend. "Building in Many Places: Multiple Commitments and the Ideologies in Black Women's Community Work." In *Women and the Politics of Empowerment,* ed. A. Bookman and S. Morgan, 53–76. Philadelphia: Temple University Press, 1988.

Gilliam, Nancy T. "A Professional Pioneer: Myra Bradwell's Fight to Practice Law." *Law and History Review* 5 (1, 1987): 105–33.

Goodman, Diane J. "African-American Women's Voices: Expanding Theories of Women's Development." *Sage: A Scholarly Journal on Black Women* 7 (Fall 1990): 3–14.

Gordon, Ann, Bettye Collier-Thomas, et al., eds. *African American Women and the Vote, 1837–1965.* Amherst, MA: University of Massachusetts Press, 1997

Gordon, Linda. "Black and White Visions of Welfare: Women's Welfare Activism, 1890–1945." *Journal of American History* 78 (Spring 1991): 559–89.

———. *Pitied But Not Entitled: Single Mothers and the History of Welfare, 1890–1935.* Cambridge: Harvard University Press, 1994.

Grant, Joanne. *Ella Baker: Freedom Bound.* New York: John Wiley and Sons, 1999.

Green, Judith Mary and Blanche Radford Curry. "Recognizing Each Other Amidst Diversity: Beyond Essentialism in Collaborative Multi-Cultural Feminist Theory." *Sage: A Scholarly Journal on Black Women* 8 (Summer 1991): 39–49.

Greene, Christian. "'We'll Take Our Stand': Race, Class, and Gender in the Southern Student Organizing Committee, 1964–1969." In *Hidden Histories of Women in the New South,* ed. Virginia Bernhard, Betty Brandon, et al., 173–203. Columbia: University of Missouri Press, 1994.

Gyant, LaVern. "African American Women's Contributions to Nonformal Education during the Civil Rights Movement, 1954–1964." Ed.D. diss., Pennsylvania State University, 1990.

———. "Passing the Torch: African American Women in the Civil Rights Movement." *Journal of Black Studies* (May 1996): 629–47.

Gyant, LaVern and Deborah Atwater. "Septima Clark's Rhetorical and Ethnic Legacy: Her Message of Citizenship in the Civil Rights Movement." *Journal of Black Studies* 26 (May 1996): 577–92.

Hall, Jacquelyn Dowd. "'The Mind That Burns in Each Body': Women, Rape, and Racial Violence." *In Powers of Desire: The Politics of Sexuality,* ed. Ann Snitow, Christine Stansell, and Sharon Thompson, 328–49. New York: Monthly Review Press, 1983.

Hamer, Fannie Lou. "Fannie Lou Hamer Speaks Out." *Essence* 1, no. 6 (October 1971): 53–75.

Hamer, Fannie Lou. *To Praise Our Bridges*. Jackson, MS: KIPCO, 1967.

Hamlet, Janice D. "Fannie Lou Hamer: The Unquenchable Spirit of the Civil Rights Movement." *Journal of Black Studies* 26 (May 1996): 560–76.

Hase, Michiko. "W. Gertrude Brown's Struggle for Racial Justice: Female Leadership and Community in Black Minneapolis, 1920–1940." Ph.D. diss., University of Minnesota, 1994.

Hawkes, Joanne V. "A Challenge to Racism and Sexism: Black Women Who Served in Southern Legislatures, 1965–1986." *Sage: A Scholarly Journal on Black Women* 5 (Fall 1988), 20–23.

Heacock, Maureen Catherine. "Sounding a Challenge: African American Women's Poetry and the Black Arts Movement." Ph.D. diss., University of Minnesota, 1995.

Hendrickson, Roberta Makashay. "The Civil Rights Movement in American Fiction: A Feminist Reading." Ph.D. diss., Brandeis University, 1990.

Hill, Ruth Edmonds, ed. *The Black Women Oral History Project*. 10 vols. Westport, CT: Meckler Publishing, 1991.

Hudson-Weems, Clenora. "From Malcolm Little to El Hajj Malik El Shabazz: Malcolm's Evolving Attitudes Toward the Africana Woman." *Western Journal of Black Studies* 17 (Spring 1993): 26–31.

Hunter Gault, Charlayne. *In My Place*. New York: Vintage Books, 1993.

James, Joy. *Shadowboxing: Representations of Black Feminist Politics*. New York: Broadway Books, 1998.

Jennings, Regina. "Why I Joined the Party: An Africana Womanist Reflection." In *The Black Panther Party [Reconsidered]*, ed. Charles Jones, 257–65. Baltimore: Black Classics Press, 1998.

Johnson, Joni L. "Ella Baker: An Unknown Soldier." *Sage: A Scholarly Journal on Black Women* 4 (Student Supplement 1988): 48–49.

Jones, Jacqueline. *Labor of Love, Labor of Sorrow: Black Women, Work, and the Family from Slavery to the Present*. New York: Basic Books, 1985.

Jordan, June. *Fannie Lou Hamer*. New York: Crowell, 1972.

Katz, Milton S. and Susan B. Tucker. "A Pioneer in Civil Rights: Esther Brown and the South Park Desegregation Case of 1948." *Kansas History* 18 (Winter 1995–1996): 234–47.

Kaufman, Peggy Welts. "Building a Constituency for School Desegregation: African-American Women in Boston, 1962–1972." *Teachers College Record* 92 (Summer 1991): 619–31.

King, Mary Carolyn. "Occupational Mobility: Changing Boundaries for Black Women, 1940 to the Present." Ph.D. diss., University of California, Berkeley, 1991.

Kling, Susan. "Fannie Lou Hamer: Baptism by Fire." In *Reweaving the Web of Life*, ed. Pam McAllister, 106–11. Philadelphia: New Society Publishers, 1982.

————. *Fannie Lou Hamer: A Biography*. Chicago: Women for Racial and Economic Equality, 1979.

Knotts, Alice G. "Bound By the Spirit Found on the Journey: The Methodist Women's Campaign for Southern Civil Rights, 1940–1968." Ph.D. diss., Illif School of Theology, 1989.

Krueger, Thomas. *And Promises to Keep: The Southern Conference for Human Welfare, 1938–1948*. Nashville: Vanderbilt University Press, 1967.

Lawson, Steven F. *Black Ballots: Voting Rights in the South*. New York: Columbia University Press, 1976.

LeBlanc-Ernest, Angela. "'The Most Qualified Person to Handle the Job': Black Panther Party Women, 1966–1982." In *The Black Panther Party [Reconsidered]*, ed. Charles Jones, 305–34. Baltimore: Black Classics Press, 1998.

Lee, Chana Kai. "A Passionate Pursuit of Justice: The Life and Leadership of Fannie Lou Hamer, 1917–1967." Ph.D. diss., University of California, Los Angeles, 1993.

————. *For Freedom's Sake: The Life of Fannie Lou Hamer*. Urbana: University of Illinois Press, 1999.

Leone, Janice. "Integrating the American Association of University Women, 1946–1949." *Historian* 51 (3, 1989): 423–45.

Lindsay, Beverly. "The Role of African-American Women in the Civil Rights and Women's Rights Movements in Hinds County and Sunflower County, Mississippi." *Journal of Mississippi History* 53 (August 1991): 229–39.

————. "African American Women and *Brown*: A Lingering Twilight or Emerging Dawn?" *Journal of Negro Education* 63 (Summer 1994): 430–42.

Ling, Peter and Sharon Monteith, eds. *Gender and the Civil Rights Movement*. New York: Garland Publishing, 1999.

Marable, Manning. *Race, Reform and Rebellion: The Second Reconstruction in Black America, 1945–1982*. 2d ed. Jackson: University Press of Mississippi, 1991.

Matthews, Tracye. "'No One Ever Asks What a Man's Place in the Revolution Is': Gender and Sexual Politics in the Black Panther Party, 1966–1971." Ph.D. diss., University of Michigan, 1998.

McAdam, Doug. *Freedom Summer*. New York: Oxford University Press, 1988.

McDonough, Julia Anne. "Men and Women of Good Will: A History of the Commission on Interracial Cooperation and the Southern Regional Council, 1919–1954." Ph.D. diss., University of Virginia, 1994.

McNeil, Maurice Morrison. "Ordinary Women/Extraordinary Efforts: African American Churchwomen in Chicago as Leaders and Adult Educators, 1920–1940." Ph.D. diss., Northern Illinois University, 1994.

Mills, Kay. *This Little Light of Mine: The Life of Fannie Lou Hamer*. New York: Dutton, 1993.

Minkoff, Debra Carol. "Organized Social Action: American Women's and

Minority Group Organizational Responses to Inequality, 1955–1985." Ph.D. diss., Harvard University, 1991.

Moody, Anne. *Coming of Age in Mississippi.* New York: Dial Press, 1968.

Murray, Pauli. *Song in a Weary Throat: The Autobiography of a Black Activist, Feminist, Lawyer, Priest and Poet.* Knoxville: University of Tennessee Press, 1989.

Nance, Theresa A. "Hearing the Missing Voice." *Journal of Black Studies* 26 (May 1996): 543–59.

Nasstrom, Kathyryn L. "Women, the Civil Rights Movement, and the Politics of Historical Memory in Atlanta, 1946–1973." Ph.D. diss., University of North Carolina at Chapel Hill, 1993.

Parks, Rosa and James Haskins. *Rosa Parks: My Story.* New York: Dial Books, 1992.

Payne, Charles. "Ella Baker and Models of Social Change." *Signs* 14 (1989): 885–99.

———. *I've Got the Light of Freedom: The Organizing Tradition and the Mississippi Freedom Struggle.* Berkeley: University of California Press, 1995.

Perkins, Margo Valencia. "Writing Resistance: Gender, Political Struggle, and Pedagogy in the Autobiographies of Angela Davis, Assata Shakur, and Elaine Brown." Ph.D. diss., Cornell University, 1996.

Pruitt, Mary Christine. "'Women Unite!' The Modern Women's Movement in Minnesota." Ph.D. diss., University of Minnesota, 1988.

Raines, Howell. *My Soul Is Rested.* New York: Penguin Books, 1977.

Ransby, Barbara. "Ella J. Baker and the Black Radical Tradition." Ph.D. diss., University of Michigan, 1996.

Reed, Linda. *Simple Decency and Common Sense: The Southern Conference Movement,* 1938–1963. Bloomington: Indiana University Press, 1991.

Robnett, Belinda. *How Long? How Long? African American Women in the Struggle for Civil Rights.* New York: Oxford University Press, 1997.

———. "African-American Women in the Civil Rights Movement, 1954–1965: Gender, Leadership, and Micromobilization." *American Journal of Sociology* 101 (May 1996): 1661–93.

Ross, Rosetta E. "The Life and Work of Victoria Way DeLee: A Study of Transformative Ethical Practice." Ph.D. diss., Emory University, 1995.

Rothschild, Mary Aickin. *A Case of Black and White: Northern Volunteers and the Southern Freedom Summers, 1964–65.* Westport, CT: Greenwood Press, 1982.

———. "White Women Volunteers in the Freedom Summers: Their Life and Work in a Movement for Social Change." *Feminist Studies* 5, no. 3 (1979): 466–95.

Rubel, David. *Fannie Lou Hamer: From Sharecropping to Politics.* Englewood Cliffs, NJ: Silver Burdett Press, 1990.

Sewell, George. "Fannie Lou Hamer's Light Still Shines." *Encore American and Worldwide News* (July 18, 1977): 3.

Smith, Jesse Carney, ed. *Notable Black American Women*. 2 vols. Detroit: Gale Research Inc., 1992, 1996.

Smith, Susan L. *"Sick and Tired of Being Sick and Tired": Black Women's Health Activism in America, 1890–1950*. Philadelphia: University of Pennsylvania Press, 1995.

Sosna, Morton. "Race and Gender in the South: The Case of Georgia's Lillian Smith." *Georgia Historical Quarterly* 71 (3, 1987): 427–37.

Sugarman, Tracy. *Stranger at the Gates: A Summer in Mississippi*. New York: Hill and Wang, 1966.

Valk, Anne Marie. "Separatism and Sisterhood: Race, Sex, and Women's Activism in Washington, D.C., 1963–1980." Ph.D. diss., Duke University, 1996.

Walker, Melissa. *Down from the Mountaintop: African-American Women's Novels in the Wake of the Civil Rights Movement*. New Haven: Yale University Press, 1991.

Waters, Roderick, Dion. "Sister Sawyer: The Life and Times of Gwendolyn Sawyer Cherry." Ph.D. diss., Florida State University, 1995.

Watters, Pat and Reese Cleghorn. *Climbing Jacob's Ladder, The Arrival of Negroes in Southern Politics*. New York: Harcourt, Brace and World, 1967.

Weisbrot, Robert. *Freedom Bound: A History of America's Civil Rights Movement*. New York: Norton, 1990.

West, Cynthia S'thembile. "Nation Builders: Female Activism in the Nation of Islam, 1960–1970." Ph.D. diss., Temple University, 1994.

———. "Ruth Williams and Company: Four Generations of Dance in Harlem." *Sage: A Scholarly Journal on Black Women* 8 (Fall 1994): 46–48.

White, Deborah Gray. *Too Heavy a Load: Black Women in Defense of Themselves, 1894–1994*. New York: Norton, 1999.

White-Dixon, Melanye. "Marion Cuyjet: Visionary of Dance Education in Black Philadelphia." Ph.D. diss., Temple University, 1987.

———. "Marion Cuyjet: Dance Educator." Sage: A Scholarly Journal on Black Women 5 (Fall 1988): 65–68.

Wigginton, Elliot, ed. *Refuse to Stand Silently By, An Oral History of Grass Roots Social Activism in America, 1921–1964*. New York: Doubleday, 1992.

Williams, Juan. *Eyes on the Prize: America's Civil Rights Years, 1954–1965*. New York: Viking Press, 1987.

Woods, Barbara A. "Black Women Activists in Twentieth Century South Carolina: Modjeska Monteith Simpkins." Ph.D. diss., Emory University, 1978.

Young, Jaqueline Ann. "A Study of the Educational Philosophies of Three Pioneer Black Women and Their Contributions to American Education." Ed.D. diss., Rutgers, State University of New Jersey, New Brunswick, 1987.

Zinn, Howard. *SNCC: New Abolitionists*. Boston: Beacon Press, Press, 1964.

Permissions

We are grateful to the following for permission to use photographs and previously published material in this work.

Photographs

African American Museum in Philadelphia
Bethune Council House National Historic Site, National Park Service
Black Star Publishers
Highlander Research and Education Center
Moorland-Spingarn Research Center, Howard University
Schomburg Center for Research in Black Culture, The New York Public Library, Astor, Lenox, and Tilden Foundation

Documents and Published Materials

"Closed Doors," by Mary McLeod Bethune. Reprint by permission of Bethune Cookman College, Daytona Beach Florida.

Excerpt from "The Second Sermon on the Warpland," by Gwendolyn Brooks. Reprint by permission of Gwendolyn Brooks.

Excerpt from "Joanne Is You and Joanne Is Me," lyrics composed by Bernice Johnson Reagon, Songtalk Publishing Co., copyright 1975. Reprint by permission of Bernice Johnson Reagon.

"'Tired of Giving In': The Launching of the Montgomery Bus Boycott," excerpt from *Rosa Parks: My Story,* by Rosa Parks with James Haskins, copyright 1992 by Rosa Parks. Reprint by permission of Dial Books for Young Readers, a division of Penguin Putnam.

Contributors

Bettye Collier-Thomas is Professor of History and Director of the Center for African American History and Culture at Temple University. She is the author of *Daughters of Thunder: Black Women Preachers and Their Sermons, 1850–1979* (1998); co-author of *My Soul Is a Witness: A Chronology of the Civil Rights Era, 1954–1965* (2000); and the compiler and editor of *A Treasury of African American Christmas Stories*, Vols. I and II (1997, 1999). Collier-Thomas is a co-editor of the award winning *African American Women and the Vote* (1997). She is currently working on a comprehensive history of "African American Women and Religion, 1780–2000."

Vicki Crawford is Associate Professor of History at Clark-Atlanta University. She is a co-editor of *Women in the Civil Rights Movement: Trailblazers and Torchbearers* (1990). She has published numerous articles on African American women in the black freedom struggle, including "Race, Class, Gender and Culture: Black Women's Activism in the Mississippi Civil Rights Movement." Crawford is currently working on an oral history entitled "Harmony: The Life and Times of Winson Hudson, A Black Woman Activist in the South."

Cynthia Griggs Fleming is Associate Professor of History and African-American Studies at the University of Tennessee, Knoxville. She is the author of *Soon We Will Not Cry: The Liberation of Ruby Doris Smith Robinson* (1998), and the co-author of *The Chicago Handbook for Teachers: A Practical Guide to the College Classroom* (1999). Fleming is currently working on a study of the Civil Rights Movement in Wilcox County, Alabama.

V. P. Franklin is Professor of History and Education at Teachers College, Columbia University; and Rosa and Charles Keller Professor of Arts and Humanities, Xavier University of Louisiana. He is the author of several books, including *Martin Luther King, Jr.: A Biography* (1998);

Living Our Stories, Telling Our Truths: Autobiography and the Making of the African-American Intellectual Tradition (1996); *Black Self-Determination: A Cultural History of African-American Resistance* (1993); and co-author of *My Soul Is a Witness: A Chronology of the Civil Rights Era, 1954–1965* (2000). Franklin is an editor of *African Americans and Jews in the Twentieth Century: Studies in Conflict and Convergence* (1998).

Charlayne Hunter Gault is the author of *In My Place* (1993), a memoir which traces her life from birth to her historic role in desegregating the University of Georgia. Following her graduation in 1963, Hunter pursued a career in journalism working for the *New Yorker, Trans-Action* magazine, and the *New York Times*. Hunter Gault joined *The MacNeil/Lehrer Report* on PBS in 1978, and was named national correspondent in 1983 when the show was expanded to *The MacNeil/Lehrer NewsHour*.

Farah Jasmine Griffin is Professor of English at the University of Pennsylvania. She is the author of *"Who Set You Flowin": The African-American Migration Narrative* (1995); editor of *Beloved Sisters and Loving Friends: Letters from Rebecca Primus of Royal Oak, Maryland, and Addie Brown of Hartford, Connecticut, 1854–1868* (1999); and the co-editor of *A Stranger in the Village: Two Centuries of African-American Travel Writing* (1998). Griffin is currently completing a book-length manuscript on "The Myths and Meanings of Billie Holiday."

Duchess Harris is Assistant Professor of Political Science at Macalester College. She is the author of several articles, and the co-author of *Race and Poverty: Wrongs and Policies* (forthcoming, Temple University Press, 2002).

Sharon Harley is Associate Professor in the Afro-American Studies Program at the University of Maryland, College Park. She is the co-editor of *Afro-American Women: Struggles and Images* (1978, 1998); and a co-editor of *Women in Africa and the African Diaspora* (1987). Harley is the author of a number of articles, including "For the Good of Family and Race: Gender, Work, and Domestic Roles in the Black Community" (1990), "When Your Work Is Not Who You Are: The Development of a Working-Class Consciousness Among Afro-American Women" (1991), "Reclaiming Public Voice and the Study of Black Women's Work" (1994), and "Speaking Up: The Politics of Black Women's Labor History" (1997).

Dorothy I. Height served as President of the National Council of Negro Women from 1957 to 1998. She spent most of her professional life as a staff member of the Young Women's Christian Association (YWCA). Beginning in 1938 as the assistant director of the Emma Ransom House, the Harlem, New York YWCA for black women, by 1944 Height had advanced to the national board YWCA, where she developed training programs for volunteers and YWCA staff members. Height played a key role in planning the YWCA's 1946 landmark convention, where the membership voted to support an interracial charter to mandate integration of public accommodations. From 1946 to 1963, Height served as the YWCA's interracial education secretary. In 1963, she was appointed secretary of the YWCA's Department of Racial Justice.

Chana Kai Lee is Associate Professor of History and Women's Studies at the University of Georgia in Athens, and the author of *For Freedom's Sake: The Life of Fannie Lou Hamer* (1999).

Tracye A. Matthews received her Ph.D. in History from the University of Michigan and is currently an Assistant Professor in the Africana Studies Department at the University of Massachusetts in Boston. Previously, she spent five years at the Chicago Historical Society as a public historian working on community-based historical exhibitions, multimedia educational products, and public programs. She continues to be involved in political organizing efforts both on campus and in the larger community.

Genna Rae McNeil is Professor of History at the University of North Carolina, Chapel Hill. She is the author of *Groundwork: Charles Hamilton Houston and the Struggle for Civil Rights* (1985). She has co-edited several anthologies, including *Historical Judgments Reconsidered: Selected Howard University Lectures in Honor of Rayford W. Logan* (1988); *African Americans and the Living Constitution* (1995); and *African Americans and Jews in the Twentieth Century: Studies in Conflict and Convergence* (1998).

Rosa Parks, the recipient of the Congressional Medal of Freedom in 1999, is frequently referred to as the mother of the modern Civil Rights Movement. Well known for her work with the NAACP Youth Council in Montgomery, Alabama, Parks's refusal to give up her seat on a bus in Montgomery, Alabama helped to launch the

1955 Montgomery bus boycott, which ignited a mass movement of nonviolent resistance that lasted for over a decade. Following her departure from Alabama in 1957, she settled in Detroit, Michigan, where she was employed by Congressman John Conyers as a staff assistant.

Barbara Ransby is Assistant Professor of History and African-American Studies at the University of Illinois, Chicago. She is the author of several essays on African American women's history and *Ella Jo Baker: A Biography* (forthcoming, University of North Carolina Press).

Jacqueline A. Rouse is Associate Professor of African American History at Georgia State University. She is the author of *Lugenia Burns Hope: Black Southern Reformer* (1989); and a co-editor of *Women in the Civil Rights Movement: Trailblazers and Torchbearers, 1941–1965* (1990). Rouse is currently working on a biography of Septima Poinsette Clark.

Elaine M. Smith teaches history at Alabama State University. She has published extensively on Mary McLeod Bethune and her times. She is co-editor of *Mary McLeod Bethune: Building a Better World* (1999), the first scholarly book on the subject. She is the editorial advisor for the University Publications of America's microform edition of Mary McLeod Bethune's papers and serves as consultant to the Mary McLeod Bethune College Archives and Foundation at Bethune Cookman College.

Linda Faye Williams is Associate Professor of Government and Politics at the University of Maryland, College Park. Formerly the Director of the Congressional Black Caucus Foundation's Institute for Policy Research and Education, Williams is the co-editor of *From Exclusion to Inclusion: The Long Struggle for Black Political Empowerment* (1992), and the author of numerous essays on race and gender politics and social policy.

Index

Abernathy, Ralph David, 66, 69, 70, 74
ABWH. *See* Association of Black Women Historians
ACCA. *See* Atlanta Committee for Cooperative Action
Adams, Malika, 245
AFDC. *See* Aid to Families with Dependent Children
African Americans: attitudes toward women in politics, 311–12; and philanthropy, 83; and political participation, multiple models of, 318–19; poverty among, 185
African American women: activists, marginalization of, 121, 188–89; and black counterpublic, 319; black nationalism and, 293, 316; in Black Panther Party, 234, 243–47, 248–49, 316; in Black Power Movement, 171–73, 207; and Black Power Movement, frustration with, 288; blame on, 250; in Civil Rights Movement, 9–10, 60, 211; color hierarchy and, 220–21; electoral success of, reasons for, 310–15; faith connection of, 129–30, 136; feminist consciousness of, 60; and feminist organizing, 237–38, 280–301; and grassroots leadership, 96–97, 112, 115–16; in Kennedy Commission, 281, 285–86; in leadership positions, 93, 175, 188; and Malcolm X, appeal of, 214–15, 223–24; in military, 30–31; in MFDP, 125–33, 135–36; in NOW, 286–87; and patriarchy, 216; political ambitions of, 313; and protection, promise of, 215–19; in public service, 12, 32, 258, 306–27; in quest for equality, 89; sisterhood among, development of, 257, 267–68; in SNCC, 204–5; subjectivity of, 139; violence against, 153–54, 298–99; vs. white

women, as percentage of elected officials, 309–10; and womanhood, exclusion from, 244. *See also specific women*
African women, experiences in New World, 1–2
Aid to Families with Dependent Children (AFDC), 285
AKA. *See* Alpha Kappa Alpha
Alabama: Montgomery Bus Boycott, 43, 59, 61–74; NAACP in, 69
Alexander, Margaret Walker, 224
Alexander, Sadie T. M., 34, 73
ALFA. *See* Alliance of Lesbian Feminists of Atlanta
Allen, Elizabeth, 160
Allen, Louis, 160
Alliance of Lesbian Feminists of Atlanta (ALFA), 273
Alligood, Clarence, 259–60, 264
Alpha Kappa Alpha (AKA), 28, 320; and civil rights activism, 28–29, 37, 38; and Mississippi Health Project, 28; Non-Partisan Council on Public Affairs, 28, 31, 32; "Recommendations for Peace," 31–32; and Summer School for Rural Negro Teachers, 28; during World War II, 29–31
Alpha Phi Alpha, 320
American Council on Human Rights, 32, 37
Angelou, Maya, 310
anger: Fannie Lou Hamer and, 142, 161; as personal power, 140
antilynching campaign, 34; Gavagan-Wagner-Van Nuys bill, 22; New Jersey State Federation of Colored Women's Clubs and, 23–24
Archie-Hudson, Margaret, 306, 317
armed services. *See* military

Equal Rights Amendment (ERA), 266;
NBFO and, 290
Evers, Medgar, assassination of: black organizations' response to, 84; and national civil rights crisis, 85
eyewitness accounts, 4

Fair Employment Practices Commission
(FEPC), 29, 33; campaigns for establishment of, 33
faith connection, of black female leaders,
129–30, 136
family: black, matriarchy in, 240–41, 285;
nuclear, Panthers' challenge to, 241
Fanon, Frantz, 235
Farmer, James, 83; and Freedom Rides,
201; and MFDP, 131; and women's participation in March on Washington, 87
Fauset, Crystal Bird, 308
Federal Bureau of Investigation (FBI), activities against Black Panthers, 246–47
Federal Council on Negro Affairs ("Black
Cabinet"), 12
federal government: African American
women in, 32, 308; discrimination in
employment in, campaign against, 33;
special attention to black women, 285
feminism: across historical periods, 233;
black, evolution of, 282–83, 293–95, 296;
black, legacy of, 301; black nationalism
and, 219, 289, 292; Black Panthers and,
237–39; black women and, 237–38,
280–301; Free Joan Little Movement
and, 273; second wave of, 291–92;
SNCC and, 283. *See also* Women's Liberation Movement
feminist consciousness, of African American women, 60
FEPC. *See* Fair Employment Practices
Commission
Foeman, Anita K., 175, 176
Ford Foundation, 113
Forman, James, 42, 83, 202, 206
Frances, Mary, 68
Franklin, C. L., 190
fraternities, and civil rights activism, 320
Frazier, Demita, 294, 295
Frazier, E. Franklin, 240
Frazier, George, 186
free breakfast program, BPP, 246

freedom elections, 123
Freedom Farm Corporation, 164
Freedom Rides, 199–201
Freedom Singers, 203
Freedom Summer Project, 123–24, 157–60;
goals of, 124; idea for, 123; white female
volunteers in, 157–59
*Freedom's Daughters: The Unsung Heroines
of the Civil Rights Movement from 1830 to
1970* (Olson), 3
Free Joan Little Movement, 257, 259–75;
and feminism, 273; and sisterhood, de-
velopment of, 266–67
Freeman, Goldie, 179–80
Freire, Paulo, 108
Friedan, Betty, 281, 284, 287
Frinks, Golden, 262

Galamison, Milton, 190
Galloway, Karen Bethea, 260, 267–68,
269–70
Garvey, Marcus, on black beauty, 220
Gates, Henry Louis, 220
Gault, Charlayne Hunter, 59; personal testimony of, 75–82; role models of, 76;
values of, 80–81
Gavagan-Wagner-Van Nuys antilynching
bill, 22
Gelston, George C., 187–88
gender: daily struggles over, Black Panthers and, 242–43; diversity, within
Black Panther Party, 233–34; focus on,
evolution of, 282; interacting factors affecting, 232–33; power struggles over,
232; roles, complementary theory of,
235–36; *See also* gender issues; gender
politics; gender relations, as power
relations
Gender in the Civil Rights Movement (Ling
and Monteith), 4
gender issues: Ella Baker and, 51; March
on Washington (1963) and, 91; vs. race
issue, 86, 88, 232, 286; vs. race loyalty,
206–7; Student Nonviolent Coordinating Committee and, 237
gender politics: of Black Panther Party,
231, 232, 234, 236–37, 242, 248; of cultural nationalism, 208–9, 235–36; of Million Man March, 250; of US organization, 235, 236

tivist career of, beginning of, 199; administrative style of, 202–4; and Black Power, 198, 205–6, 209–10; death of, 210; *Ebony* magazine interview with, 206; and Freedom Rides, 199, 200, 201; in Grady Hospital demonstration, 201
Robinson, William P., 28
Robnett, Belinda: on bridge leaders, 96, 135, 149, 176, 211; *How Long? How Long? African-American Women in the Struggle for Civil Rights*, 3, 96–97, 211; on Gloria Richardson, 176–77
Rock Hill, South Carolina, SNCC action in, 199
Roosevelt, Eleanor, 284
Roosevelt, Franklin D.: and Mary McLeod Bethune, 13, 14, 19; Executive Order 8802, 33
Rouse, Jacqueline A., 3
Rowen, William A., 30
Ruffin, Josephine St. Pierre, 21
Rustin, Bayard, 86, 88

Sacks, Karen, 149
Sanchez, Sonia, 223, 224
Sayer, Michael, 204
schooling. *See* education
schools: citizenship. *See* Citizenship Schools; integration, school
Schuyler, George, 48
SCLC. *See* Southern Christian Leadership Conference
SDS. *See* Students for a Democratic Society
Seale, Bobby, 230, 242
segregation: Mary McLeod Bethune on, 14–20; campaign against, Bethune and, 13; laws, changing, 68; in Maryland's Eastern Shore, 179, 181; on Montgomery buses, Supreme Court on, 73; persistence of, 123; Gloria Richardson's experience of, 180–81; and schooling, 15, 17; and travel, 14–15, 17–18, 61–62. *See also* integration
Sellers, Cleveland, 177
separate but equal doctrine, 76
sexism: Black Panther Party and, 236, 243; Black Power and, 207–8, 207–9, 257; cultural nationalism and, 208–9, 235–36; Malcolm X and, 223; male leadership

and, 87, 88, 89; opposition to, African American women and, 60; and racism, link between, 236, 287
sexuality, power struggles over, 232
sexualized violence, 153–54
sexual orientation, vs. gender and racial identity, 282
sexual relations, in Black Panther Party, 247
Shabazz, Betty, 219, 222
Shakur, Afeni, 244
Shakur, Assata, 243, 248
Shaw v. Reno, 313, 326
Sherrod, Charles, 199
Simkins, Modjeska, 101, 115–16
Simmons, J. Andrew, 101
Simmons, Michael, 205
Simone, Nina, 221
Simpson, Euvester, 152
sisterhood: development of, 257, 267–68; Free Joan Little movement and, 266–75
Sloan, Margaret, 288
Sloan-Hunter, Margaret, 280–81
Smiley, Glen, 74
Smith, Barbara, 293, 294, 295, 296, 297, 299; on identity politics, 300
Smith, Jean Wheeler, 204
Smith, Ruby Doris. *See* Robinson, Ruby Doris Smith
SNCC. *See* Student Nonviolent Coordinating Committee
Social Security Act, NCNW on, 35
socialism, CRC and, 294
sociopolitical analyses, 4–5
Sojourner: The Women's Forum (newsletter), 296
songs. *See* music
sororities, black: and civil rights activism, 37, 38, 320; first, 28
Southern Christian Leadership Conference (SCLC): Ella Baker in, 43–44; and Citizenship School program, 93; Septima Clark in, 111–17; Crusade for Citizenship, 111; founding of, 111; male-dominated leadership of, 188; women in, 116
spirituality, of black female leaders, 129–30, 136
Staples, Roberta, 296
Starr, Brenda, 76

Voting Rights Act of 1965, 306, 326; expansion of, 321; support for, MFDP and, 134

WACS. *See* Women's Army Corps
Waiters, Viola Lewis, 47
Walker, Alice, 223, 224, 226, 288
Walker, Jenny, 176, 189
Walker, Wyatt T., 113
Wallace, George, 187
Wallace, Michele, 292
Ward, Horace, 78
Waring, J. Waties, 101–2
Washington Committee for the Negro Woman in the National Defense, 35
Watkins, Hollis, 127, 128
Wells Barnett, Ida, 38, 174
West, C. S'thembile, 284
When and Where I Enter (Giddings), 281
White, Deborah Gray, 22, 292
White, E. Frances, 219, 234, 236, 241
White, Kevin, 298
White, Walter, 220
white women: Black Freedom Movement and, 237; vs. black women, as percentage of elected officials, 309–10; in Mississippi Freedom Summer, 157–59
Wilkins, Roy, 83, 84, 131
Williams, Arthur, 263
Williams, Aubrey, 12–13
Williams, Hosea, 114
Williams, Jessie, 272
Williams, Willis, 263
Wilson, Emma J., 11
Wine, Annie, 105–6
Wise, Stanley, 202, 210
Wolfe, Deborah Partridge, 86
womanhood, construction of, black women excluded from, 244

womanism: groups espousing, 13; Malcolm X and, 223–27
Woman's Convention , auxiliary to the National Baptist Convention, 25
women: in politics, attitudes toward, 311–12; *See also* African American women; white women
Women in the Civil Rights Movement: Trailblazers and Torchbearers (Crawford, Rouse, and Woods), 3
Women's Army Corps (WACS), 30
Women's Liberation Movement (WLM): black feminism and, 282; and Black Panther Party, 238, 239; emergence of, 267; Joan Little and, 266; NOW and, 287
Woodhouse, Chase Going, 29
Woods, Barbara, 3
working class, Gloria Richardson's identification with, 182
Works Progress Administration (WPA), Worker's Education Project of, 46–47
World War I, New Jersey State Federation of Colored Women's Clubs during, 24
World War II: Alpha Kappa Alpha (AKA) during, 29–31; New Jersey State Federation of Colored Women's Clubs during, 26
WPA. *See* Works Progress Administration
Wright, Richard, black feminist critique of, 214

Young, Andrew, 85, 96, 113
Young, Whitney M., Jr., 78, 83, 84–85, 87
Young Negroes Cooperative League, 43, 48
Young Women's Christian Association (YWCA): Charleston branch of, 100, 102; Harlem branch of, 47